# Rufus Woods,
## THE COLUMBIA RIVER,
## & THE BUILDING OF
## MODERN WASHINGTON

# RUFUS WOODS,
## THE COLUMBIA RIVER,
## & THE BUILDING OF
## MODERN WASHINGTON

## ROBERT E. FICKEN

Washington State University Press
Pullman, WA 99164-5910

Washington State University Press, Pullman, Washington, 99164-5910
First printing 1995

*Library of Congress Cataloging-in-Publication Data*
Ficken, Robert E.
   Rufus Woods, the Columbia River, and the building of modern Washington / Robert E. Ficken.
      p.   c.m.
   Includes bibliographical references and index.
   ISBN 0-87422-121-8 (alk. paper).—ISBN 0-87422-122-6 (pbk.  :  alk. paper)
   1. Woods, Rufus, 1878-1950.   2. Newspaper editors—Washington (State)—Biography.   3. Publishers and publishing—Washington (State)—Biography.   4. Grand Coulee Dam (Wash.)—History.   5. Water resources development—Columbia River Watershed—History—20th century.   I. Title.
PN4874.W6934F53   1995
070.4'1'092—dc20
[B]                                                             95-31787
                                                                    CIP

Washington State University Press
Pullman, Washington 99164-5910
Phone: 800-354-7360
Fax: 509-335-8568

*For*
*Wilfred Woods*
*and*
*Bruce Mitchell*

# Contents

# Introduction

THE ROTARY CLUB in the sweet-smelling apple town of Cashmere, Washington, spent a pleasant May evening in 1946 honoring Rufus Woods as the "High Priest and Prophet of the Columbia." Dressing the veteran newspaper publisher in mock priestly garb, the Rotarians pledged fealty to the premier "shouter" of the Pacific Northwest, to the man who for decades had been unable to silence himself on the subject of the region's water resources. Woods happily pled guilty to the charge of being "crazy" about the Columbia River. His *Wenatchee Daily World* was, after all, produced, according to its venerable masthead slogan, "in the very BUCKLE OF THE POWER BELT OF AMERICA!" The vast potential of the Columbia for energy production and irrigation was certainly "something to be crazy over." The generation of electricity and the reclamation of arid lands meant sustained economic growth and, quite literally, regional independence. The residents of the four counties—Chelan, Okanogan, Douglas, and Grant—bordering upon the great looping Big Bend of the Columbia in North Central Washington had a particular responsibility and a unique opportunity. "Here we will live for the rest of our days," wrote Rufus. "And here the children of the coming generation will spend their lives."[1]

Rufus Woods was honored on a regular basis for his efforts on behalf of Columbia River development, especially for construction of the mammoth Grand Coulee Dam, the supposed "Eighth Wonder of the World." Admirers at home and abroad singled him out for praise as "the individual most responsible for the start and for the completion of the Coulee Dam." He was, and was so acknowledged, one of several essential members of the Dam University, the band of enthusiasts formed to promote utilization of the river, no matter what the political and economic odds. The campaign for Grand Coulee was the defining highlight in the life of Rufus Woods. Belittling the outsized Pacific Northwest folk hero, Woods saw no purpose in "all this Paul Bunyan stuff." Washington, and Oregon too, had surging rivers, soaring mountains, tall trees, and gigantic engineering projects. "The truth," unadorned by myth, was "good enough" and there was no need for "Paul Bunyan and his Blue Ox up at Grand Coulee Dam."[2]

Born on the golden prairies of Nebraska, a veteran of the Alaska gold rush, and trained as a lawyer, Woods arrived in Wenatchee in 1904 and took up a career in journalism. The town was planted in a superficially depressing "country of sage-brush, sand, dust, flies, poor water, shacks and few bath tubs." Yet the place had definite prospects and the inhabitants were confident of the future. The Great Northern Railway mainline ran through town on the way to Puget Sound. Wenatchee's location close to the point where the railroad crossed the Columbia was enhanced by the infant community's status as terminus for steamboats running upriver to the Okanogan country. Nurtured by irrigation water, the valley's first orchards had just entered bearing stage. The Wenatchee apple—dark, firm and delicious—soon became a dominant force in the American fruit trade. Blessed by apples and by the commercial advantages of the river-to-the-rails linkage, Rufus's new home was the metropolis of North Central Washington, the "last and best part of Uncle Sam's West."[3]

After working on Wenatchee's weekly newspapers, Woods took over the *Daily World* in 1907. Founded by local conservative Republicans, the *World* had few readers, no style, and little prospect of survival. Rufus transformed it into one of the better dailies of the Pacific Northwest, with an influence extending far beyond the confines of the Wenatchee Valley. The makeover reflected the new owner's basic philosophy that "the providence of the newspaper is much broader than just a concern from which to make money." A paper "should stand for something" beyond narrow political partisanship, should "promote discussion" and "unite the CONSTRUCTIVE FORCES of the community it endeavors to serve." The responsible newspaper provided information, but also entertained in the sense of being fun to produce and enjoyable to read. Stories, Woods constantly lectured his staff, "should have splash, color, [and] action."[4]

There were, by design, no "distant" editorials in the *Wenatchee Daily World*. "The folks know who is writing the column anyway," Rufus explained, "so I feel that I might just as well use the pronoun 'I' which I do." In content and in style, the newspaper reflected the personality and varied interests of its publisher. Woods usually commenced work on a personal commentary while sitting calmly at his desk. As he became absorbed in the topic, he rose and paced back-and-forth, dictating at a rapid pace. Drafted in this fashion, published editorials expanded from staid reflection to emotional bombast, first with individual words, then sentences and, on especially exciting issues, entire paragraphs in capital letters. His duty, asserted Rufus, was to publish the facts, to never be afraid "to rise, speak and be counted," regardless of the impact on powerful corporations or political parties.[5]

Woods never lost a childlike faith that life, including the conduct of business, ought to be fun. He dressed in funny clothes when the opportunity offered, ran off in middle age with the circus, and regularly offered wild suggestions, like the 1949 proposal that Lake Roosevelt, the reservoir behind Grand Coulee Dam, be stocked with whales. Rufus was also a serious individual, with a mature agenda to promote. He might be the "high priest and prophet of the Columbia" to the Cashmere Rotarians, but to other contemporaries he was "the William Allen White of Washington." Like the famous Kansan, he was an atypical small town publisher whose wit, energy, and political connections made possible an influential role in matters of regional and national importance. Woods fought, from the early twentieth century on, for a reformist goal, the freeing of the Pacific Northwest from domination by outside corporate and governmental forces. "All too long," he insisted, "have we been a colony of the East."[6] This consistent point-of-view made him, in the first years with the *World*, a leader of Washington's progressive movement. The newspaper and its owner fought the railroads, supported the initiative and the referendum, promoted the state's leading reformer, Miles Poindexter, and trekked along behind Theodore Roosevelt on the dramatic Bull Moose trail of 1912.

Woods later utilized the methods perfected in these progressive campaigns in the fight for Grand Coulee Dam. Through years of energetic travel, Woods knew "many thousands of people," providing him with well-placed contacts from Olympia to Washington, D.C. The press, moreover, was the major source of news and opinion for Americans and the *World* was read throughout the four-county North Central Washington area. "I find it," wrote one business executive, "on trains and in hotels, stores [and] farmhouses and in fact everywhere & in all sorts of out of the way places." Many of the 200 weeklies in the state, including the dozen published in the Wenatchee district, reprinted columns and editorials from the *World*, forming an additional outlet of influence. Rufus also realized, from his earliest experiences in Wenatchee, the value of assembling like-minded individuals to develop goals, plan strategies, and raise money. "It takes two things to build communities," Woods maintained, "resources and men." When these necessary factors were combined with "imagination and vision," a potent lobbying effort—based upon a network of small towns—might be ventured on behalf of programs in the public interest.[7]

As progressivism waned during the tempestuous homefront years of the First World War, Rufus concentrated his energy and organizational talent on the subject of Grand Coulee. The suggestion that the Columbia ought to be dammed at Grand Coulee had first been made in the 1890s. Engineers had briefly studied the proposition, to no avail and with little public notice. "If there was a survey made," Woods recalled, "it was submerged in such a way that none of us knew anything about it." For Rufus, the origin of Grand Coulee was "another case like Christopher Columbus and the Norsemen." The Vikings "may have been here" centuries in advance of 1492, "but nothing came of their discovery." So too with Grand Coulee and Columbia River development. It was given birth, as far as the local boosters were concerned, by the 1918 publication in the *Wenatchee World* of Ephrata attorney Billy Clapp's audacious high dam proposal.[8]

Grand Coulee served the same purpose as the progressive reforms championed by Woods earlier in his newspaper career. The Columbia stood, in his view, "in a class by itself with water in abundance." Local interests need only realize and act upon the fact that the river "IS OUR HERITAGE AND THAT OF OUR CHILDREN AND OUR CHILDREN'S CHILDREN." Properly utilized, the stream, once "the wildest . . . in all the civilized world," provided the liquid stimulus for the opening of thousands of prosperous farms in the previously barren Columbia Basin. Industry, moreover, went "side by side with agriculture," as manufacturers would locate in Wenatchee and the other towns of the region to take advantage of cheap electricity. Development of the Columbia was the latest, and potentially the most effective, manifestation of the long struggle for "western autonomy and western control . . . of the resources of the West."[9]

The dam was secured because of the willingness of local groups to buck corporate wishes and federal indifference. The Dam University, with Rufus Woods and the seldom-paid fanatical lobbyist James O'Sullivan the most active members, kept the project alive against long odds from 1918 onward. The state of Washington endorsed a rival plan for irrigation of the Columbia Basin, a plan drawn specifically by the representatives of capital to preclude the generation of electricity. The Bureau of Reclamation, meanwhile, steadfastly opposed any involvement by the government of the United States. An adroit maneuver by Washington Senator Wesley Jones at the outset of the Herbert Hoover administration secured from the Army Corps of Engineers its "308 Report," endorsing Grand Coulee and presenting a plan for full-scale development of the Columbia. President Hoover, however, rejected the Corps' findings, thereby losing the opportunity, as Woods later regretted, of entering the history books as the progenitor of federal dam construction in the Pacific Northwest.[10]

New Deal Democrats, entering office at the national and state levels in 1933, took prompt advantage of the Hoover fumble. Franklin D. Roosevelt, who in the 1932 campaign had called for the building of at least one government dam on the Columbia, personally worked out the financial details and general engineering dimensions of Grand Coulee in a series of meetings with Senator Clarence Dill. At home, Rufus Woods, the most outspoken member of Washington's Columbia Basin Commission, hoped to use the proffered funds to construct a locally owned and controlled project. Unfortunately, Secretary of the Interior Harold Ickes, the official in charge of federal public works spending, demanded that Woods and the other commissioners agree to a contract under which Grand Coulee became the property of the United States.

Two developments prevented Woods and the Dam University from regaining at least some of the local control lost to Ickes in 1933. Created in 1937 to handle sales of Columbia River energy, the Bonneville Power Administration established a decision-making apparatus in distant Portland and promulgated an electricity rate structure bound to discourage the building of industry anywhere close to Grand Coulee. The Second World War, meanwhile, literally sent the dam's power downriver, on a permanent basis, to run aluminum plants, shipyards, and the mysterious Hanford atomic works project. Reading the self-described "massive pile of old correspondence" generated by Rufus Woods during the 1940s, one readily detects an element of tragedy. Grand Coulee had been built, but most of the benefits had been lost to faraway urban areas and industry. Decisions were made, not by local people, but by the Bureau of Reclamation and by the Bonneville Power Administration.[11]

Although disappointed, Woods was by no means embittered by the frustration of his dreams. The fight for Grand Coulee had been "a real drama" and construction of the dam a "miracle." With his friends, Rufus had produced, for all its imperfection, "something grand, noble, heroic, [and] imposing." Unwilling to give up, he continued to rush "hither, thither and yon" on behalf of new development proposals. Singly or in concert, additional Columbia River dams and activation of the Columbia Basin Irrigation Project might still bring local autonomy to Wenatchee. North Central Washington, after all, was "a pioneer country," well-outfitted by nature with ample opportunity for enterprising men and women. All that was necessary was to continue working upon the basis of a fundamental proposition. "Let us never forget," urged Rufus Woods, "the importance of water water water."[12]

# Prologue

D IRTY, THIRSTY, AND DESPAIRING, the Canadian artist Paul Kane and his hired helper Donny wandered for days in the sandy wasteland of the Columbia Basin's Big Bend. Touring the Pacific Northwest in 1847 under the sponsorship of the Hudson's Bay Company, Kane had decided to ride from Fort Walla Walla to Kettle Falls, deviating from the normal route of overland travel to explore the mysterious Grand Coulee, said by local Indians to be "the abode of evil spirits and other strange things." Sighting a line of cliffs on August 3, the artist feared for a moment that he had somehow bypassed the coulee and was once again upon the bank of the Columbia. Peering over the edge of the chasm, Kane saw instead that the floor of "this wonderful gully," hundreds of feet below, was dry and over-grown in grass.[1]

Running on a southwesterly axis from the Columbia for fifty miles, the Grand Coulee was the creation of epic prehistoric floods. Ice flows thousands of feet thick had repeatedly dammed the Clark Fork drainage near Pend Oreille Lake in the Idaho panhandle, forming giant Glacial Lake Missoula. Upon the retreat of each cycle of glaciation, the collapse of the ice blockage sent a massive surge of water across the Columbia Plateau, submerging stream channels and excavating coulees large and small. The Grand Coulee was far and away the most spectacular product of this exercise in natural hydraulic engineering.[2]

Kane stumbled upon the coulee at a point where a break in the rim provided a rocky trail for the descent to the valley floor. The coulee, four miles wide, had cliff faces three to four hundred feet high. "Enormous rocky islands" rose here and there from a sea of grass, the only vegetation. Turning in the direction of the Columbia, Kane and Donny rode north for three days. Even though maggots infested their supply of dried salmon, the travelers considered extending the visit "at the risk of starvation." They lay awake at night, transfixed by the booming reverberations of thunderstorms off the canyon battlements. "In the whole course of my life," Kane recorded in his journal, "I never heard anything so awfully sublime."[3]

Near dusk on August 5, the hungry explorers arrived at the mouth of the coulee, five hundred feet above the Columbia. The great river at this point was eight hundred miles from its obscure headwaters and six hundred miles from the sea. Working their way down the cliffside, Kane and Donny camped beside the rushing stream. Looking upward, they discovered that, when viewed from the riverbank, the "wonderful gully" disappeared into the gray background of the looming palisade. Except for the experienced and the observant, travelers on the Columbia River usually failed to see the Grand Coulee, stranded high above the torrent. Lost in the fearsome aridity of the interior Pacific Northwest, it was apparently forever beyond the designs of humanity.[4]

# Chapter One
# The Westward Urge

Just as the magnetic needle has something within it which pointed to
the Magnetic Pole in the North, if you will analyze fine enough a drop
of blood of the average person living in the West, you will find some
kind of an urge which points Westward. It is the will to new life, new
adventure, new experiences.

Rufus Woods[1]

NEBRASKA WAS A road and a political issue before becoming a center of
white American settlement. Beginning in 1842, families bound for
Oregon and adventurers on the way to California rode or walked up the
valley of the Platte River. In 1854, Congress passed the Kansas-Nebraska
Act, authorizing the residents of the territories bearing those names to decide for themselves whether to accept or reject slavery. The Missouri Compromise was repealed, sectional debate over expansion of the peculiar
institution was rekindled, and the nation took a long step forward in the
direction of civil war. Nebraska itself remained a sparsely populated jump-
ing-off place, with fewer than 30,000 settlers as of 1860, most in farm-
steads and hamlets along the Missouri River.

Brutal frontier fighting during the Civil War removed the Indians as
obstacles to the settlement of Nebraska. The Homestead Act, approved by
Congress in 1862, allowed individuals to claim up to 160 acres of the
public domain for $1.25 an acre. The Union Pacific and the Burlington
and Missouri railroads, owning several million acres in Nebraska, provided
an additional incentive by offering extensive tracts of land for sale to incoming settlers. The railroads recruited heavily in Europe, enjoying particular success among the Scandinavians, Germans, and Bohemians later
portrayed in the novels of Willa Cather. Nebraska's population increased

by a factor of five in the 1860s (statehood came in 1867) and by 400 percent in the 1870s.[2]

In the fall of 1871, Lebbeus and Mary Woods and their children Jacob, Joseph, and Elizabeth joined the Nebraska-bound current. Husband and wife—German in ethnic heritage, Lutheran in religion—were natives of Pennsylvania. Now 29 years of age, Lebbeus had served, with his three brothers, in the Civil War. Wounded at Spotsylvania Courthouse, one of the bloodiest engagements of Ulysses Grant's 1864 Virginia campaign, he was briefly held prisoner by the Confederacy before securing release on parole. Like many Union veterans, Lebbeus headed west after the war in search of a new life. Accompanied by his recent bride, he settled in Illinois in 1867, moving on to Iowa in 1870 before taking up land in Nebraska the following year.[3]

Lebbeus filed a homestead claim in Butler County, south of the Platte River and sixty miles from Lincoln, the state capital. Rich prairie soil and ample rainfall made Butler and its neighboring counties the focal point of Nebraska's burgeoning wheat and corn belt. A few miles from the Woods home place, the village of Surprise, with barely 300 inhabitants, served the needs of the surrounding countryside. Nestled beneath hills on the Big Blue River, Surprise began as a flour mill on the property of Walter Greenslit, the wealthiest settler in the vicinity. Eventually, a general store, a pool hall, and a forlorn Burlington and Missouri depot clustered about the millsite.[4]

Adding to their family, Lebbeus and Mary Woods produced a series of Nebraska offspring. Oscar was born in 1872 and Albert in 1874. Identical twins Ralph and Rufus entered the world on May 17, 1878. Mary gave birth three more times, to Lebbeus in 1881, Mary Ethel in 1883, and Oliva in 1884. Despite the diseases and uncertain medical practices of the late-nineteenth century, all survived to live long lives. Uncommon status as identical twins made Ralph and Rufus the center of attention. Ralph's facial scar, the result of a childhood accident, served as a distinguishing mark for family members, but casual acquaintances and strangers had difficulty telling one from the other. The boys shared many personality traits and were inseparable companions.

Ralph, Rufus, and their siblings walked or rode on horseback several miles across the prairie each day to attend a one-room school. Trips to Lincoln were special events, "preceded," as Rufus remembered, "by weeks of preparation and anticipation." At home, the lack of indoor plumbing limited bathing to a once-a-week luxury, family members taking turns in a washtub filled with water heated on the kitchen wood stove. The children learned the importance of books, education, and moral standards. Tobacco, alcohol, cards, dancing, swearing, and traveling salesmen were strictly prohibited in the Woods house.[5]

The twins in particular grew up strait-laced and semi-bookish in nature. They also developed a countervailing trait for pranksterism. A favorite trick involved one of the twins challenging an unsuspecting boy to a long distance foot race. Jumping from a hiding place, the other brother took over midway through the contest, sprinting to unwinded victory over his exhausted and confused opponent. When they were eight, the boys attended a performance by a traveling circus, sneaking under the tent wall. Returning home, the excited brothers transformed the farmyard into a makeshift big top, swinging from a trapeze and turning handstands. After several days of playacting, they decided to leap from the hayloft in an exercise of daredevil acrobatics. Jumping first, Ralph landed on his head and lay unconscious for several minutes. Parental edict promptly disbanded the Woods brothers' act, but Rufus vowed to someday run away with a real circus.[6]

Personal experience made the boys curious about the larger world beyond Surprise and Butler County. They watched covered wagons carrying expectant dryland farmers pass on the way to the plains of western Nebraska. Nearby, an abandoned feeder line of the storied Oregon Trail led toward the Platte River. "Across the prairie ran a great number of parallel tracks cut deep into the terrain," recalled Rufus. The twins talked at length of the westward movement undertaken by their own parents. In an early gesture of independent adventurism, they visited, unescorted, the 1893 Chicago World's Fair.[7]

Ambitious and intelligent young Nebraskans of the time sooner or later turned their backs on the homesteads. Compounding the normal physical and emotional strains of farm life, wheat and corn prices collapsed in the late 1880s. A prolonged drought accompanied the national economic depression brought on by the Panic of 1893. "Conditions were hopeless," remembered Rufus, "and some said they would never come back." Each year, the top high school graduates headed for the cities or for the Pacific coast. Later in life, Woods divided natives of Nebraska into two classes. Those who left more often than not found personal and professional success. Those who remained—"the easy-goers, [and] the loafers"— endured "toil and disappointment."[8]

Preparing for great adventures beyond Nebraska, Ralph and Rufus completed their country education. The brothers graduated with the eleven-member Ulysses High School Class of 1898. As valedictorian, Rufus delivered a florid address on the subject of tyranny, the current war between American democracy and Spain's decrepit monarchy serving as his prime talking point. Woods had already perfected his oratorical style, featuring arm-waving and platform-stalking. Rufus devoted fifteen minutes to "plenty of aspiration and especially perspiration," then sat down, to universal relief, half expecting his diploma to be withheld. After the ceremony, the graduates celebrated by riding about the countryside in a wagon decorated with American flags and banners glorifying the nation's one-sided victories in Cuba and at Manila Bay.[9]

For his first adult employment, Rufus secured appointment as teacher at a country school near Brainard, Nebraska. He earned $35 a month for the 1898-1899 academic year, while boarding with a bizarre family of spiritualists. The class numbered forty-five pupils, ranging in age from five to twenty, and was taught in three simultaneous sections: one group reading, the second reciting, and the third practicing penmanship at the blackboard. Adding to the confusion, some of the students, from a nearby Bohemian colony, were unable to speak or write English. The experience at least taught young Woods that teaching was, for him, an unsuitable profession. In addition to low pay and disciplinary problems, the rote methodology favored by American educators was destructive to intelligence and individualism. Schools, he maintained, ought to foster creativity by encouraging children to think for themselves.[10]

Government service and the law appeared to offer appealing career alternatives. Rufus and Ralph grew up in a period of political turmoil. During the 1880s, Nebraska politics had focused on divisive social issues, prohibition in particular. The self-styled "better elements," mainly native-born Americans and Protestant immigrants, formed the basis of a Republican dry majority. Catholic newcomers gravitated toward the wet Democratic platform. Drought, depressed farm prices, and the Panic of 1893 transformed state politics. Economic questions came to the fore, especially the matter of regulating railroads and other Eastern corporations accused of sacrificing rural and small-town America to the interests of Wall Street. Democrats and the new Populist Party made common cause against capital, and the Republicans split into pro- and anti-regulation factions.[11]

Alcohol and the relationship between government and business remained lifelong preoccupations of the Woods twins. Rufus, in particular, always regarded political affairs in terms of good versus evil, of the public welfare on one side and private greed on the other. Although a Republican, Woods had no qualms about working with Democrats. His first hero— "the most lovable character that I have ever known in public life"—was Nebraska's leading citizen, William Jennings Bryan, three times the Democratic presidential candidate. On one occasion, young Rufus visited Bryan's Lincoln home, there to listen with rapt attention as the Great Commoner expounded upon the importance of morality in human affairs.[12]

Reunited at the end of Rufus's year of school teaching, the twins enrolled in a business course at Grand Island College. They then laid aside prospective careers in law and politics to travel. Uncle Isaac Woods had migrated to the Pacific Northwest in 1889, eventually settling on the Olympic Peninsula. For years, Ralph and Rufus pored over letters from Isaac, reading of such places as the eastern Washington town whose name they pronounced as "Ya-ky-ma." The Washington state exhibit at the Chicago World's Fair, a giant log cabin, also drew their attention to the land of the towering forest. The death of Mary Woods in 1896 removed the only compelling reason for staying at home. Stories of gold discoveries in the frozen Yukon made the prospect of leaving Nebraska impossible to resist. Taking advantage of a railroad fare war in early 1900, Rufus and Ralph borrowed $25 and set out for Puget Sound on the definitive journey of their lives.[13]

After a reunion with Uncle Isaac, Rufus secured employment on the Skokomish Valley railroad operated by the Simpson Logging Company. He became acquainted with the firm's general manager, Mark Reed, and also made friends with Grant Angle, publisher of the weekly *Mason County Journal* and a member of the state legislature. "Politics and newspaper work," Woods recalled, ". . . seemed to me like a thrilling combination." Sleeping in a box car with two dozen fellow laborers, Rufus experienced at first hand the various aspects—some humorous and some tragic—of life in the timber. The pay was $2.10 a day, with $5 deducted weekly for room and board. All but two members of the crew wasted their net earnings on drinking and other forms of debauchery. The ever-present prospect of accidental maiming and death was made explicit when Rufus hauled two "mangled bodies" down the rail line to town.[14]

In the early summer of 1900, the Woods brothers set out for their original destination, Alaska. Rufus and Ralph worked for their passage north on a steamer bound for Skagway via the uncharted hazards of the Inside Passage. They crossed the desolate hundred miles of Chilkoot Pass to the Yukon River, then pushed on to Dawson, headquarters of the Klondike boom. When promised employment with a surveying crew fell through, the twins secured jobs on a riverboat. Working as stewards, they earned $100 a month, plus room, board, and gratuities. Baseball—Rufus posed as a Canadian to play for White Horse against an American team from Skagway—was their principal outside avocation.[15]

Beginning with this trip, Rufus and Ralph spent four summers in the far north. Alaska taught harsh lessons about greed and human frailty. Mining and transportation firms deliberately recruited an excess supply of workers from the states, driving down wages and causing great suffering among the stranded and the unemployed. (The brothers secured their jobs by bribing employment office personnel.) The impact of alcohol on a totally materialistic society, meanwhile, was shocking. Rufus and Ralph saw friends and associates lose wages in saloons and gambling halls. Momentarily wealthy prospectors were, as Rufus recalled, "easy marks" for confidence artists, card sharps, and purveyors of sin. Offering adventure, the Yukon also provided graphic daily evidence of social and material waste.[16]

The brothers returned to the states each fall, exchanging the adventurous life for serious career-oriented activity. They spent the 1901 school year at Vashon College, a little-known and long-forgotten Puget Sound academy, completing the intellectually suspect "undergraduate" training begun at Grand Island. Despite questionable academic credentials, Rufus and Ralph secured admission to the University of Nebraska law school, attending that institution the next two winters. The weather-oriented Alaskan work schedule dictated late arrivals and early departures from Lincoln. "As we would come back about Thanksgiving," remembered Rufus, "old Dean Reese would announce: 'Well, I see the "byes" are back from the Frigid Fields.'" Gumption, not to mention a lenient faculty, rather than sustained attention to class work won out and the twins received law degrees in the spring of 1903.[17]

Newly minted attorneys, Rufus and Ralph went to Alaska a final time that summer. Intending to practice law, they viewed the northland as a fun-filled way station rather than a final destination. Despite its many attractions, Alaska was a dangerous place for moralistic Nebraska farmboys. The mining camps and the riverboats offered too debauched a display of human depravity. Alaska was wild in the extreme, but Washington, a state for only fourteen years in 1903, was a sedate frontier, with both opportunity and respectability. The forests were vast, the mountains awesome, and the rivers powerful, while urban comforts were available in Seattle, Tacoma, Spokane, and dozens of smaller communities. The "marvelous climate" and the breathtaking scenery appealed to newcomers fleeing the frozen winters, blasted summers, and flat expanses of the Great Plains. For the politically inclined, the issues of the day—prohibition and capitalistic exploitation—linked the Pacific Northwest and the Middle West in common cause against the social and economic ills of modern times.[18]

Thanks to an ill-advised investment in a friend's unsuccessful venture, Rufus and Ralph returned to Puget Sound virtually penniless in the fall of 1903. Ralph secured a position in Tacoma, launching a long and prosperous legal career. Rufus went to work for the Seattle firm of Brady and Gay, where clients were nonexistent and prospects unflattering. Sitting behind a desk waiting for business to turn up was a depressing experience for a hyperactive individual. Day-to-day exposure to the profession, moreover, swept away youthful illusions. Instead of justice, lawyers dealt in paperwork routine and sought courtroom victory at all costs. Realizing that he was entirely unsuited to the practice of law, Rufus retired from the bar in December without trying a case or earning a fee.[19]

With twenty borrowed dollars in his pocket, Woods boarded the eastbound Great Northern passenger train on the evening of January 2, 1904. His destination, the Columbia River town of Wenatchee, was determined by considerations more substantial than the maximum affordable ticket price. Wenatchee was the commercial center of North Central Washington, of Chelan, Okanogan, Douglas, and Grant counties. Three Nebraska law school classmates resided in the vicinity. Stopping for a visit on their way to the coast in 1903, Rufus and Ralph had learned of the region's potential for growth. The nearby mountains and the riverfront setting, moreover, reminded Rufus of his favorite Yukon community. Wenatchee, he asserted of the place that would be his home for the next forty-six years, was "the American Dawson."[20]

A thousand miles and more separated Chelan County, Washington, from Butler County, Nebraska. Differences of climate, topography, and economic endeavor distinguished one from the other. Key aspects of his Nebraskan upbringing nonetheless influenced the long career of Rufus Woods in the Pacific Northwest. He grew up in a rural society of hardworking native

American and north European families. Through reclamation, Woods promoted the settlement east of the Cascades of industrious and family oriented water pioneers, aiming to recreate nineteenth century Nebraska in the twentieth century Columbia Basin. He carried to Wenatchee his youthful conviction that Nebraska was at the mercy of outside forces, that the state prospered or suffered according to the whims of bankers and railroad magnates. For a half century, Rufus Woods fought to protect his adopted home from the designs of governments and corporations, defending it against Seattle and Spokane, against New York and Washington, D.C.

# Chapter Two
## Home of the Big Red Apple

The ranks of mediocrity—of the half-successful—are crowded with people of fine natural abilities, who never rise above inferior stations because they never act independently. They are afraid to take the initiative in anything—to depend upon their own judgment and resources—and so let opportunity after opportunity pass them by.

*Wenatchee Daily World* [1]

RUFUS WOODS arrived, unmet and unnoticed, in Wenatchee on Sunday morning, January 3, 1904. East of the Great Northern depot, the Columbia River flowed in gray winter dignity, before disappearing around a bend and entering, to quote official government surveys, the "great masses of reef, rocks, and high projecting islands" of Rock Island Rapids.[2] Above the left bank of the stream, bare terraces climbed toward the black escarpment of the Columbia Plateau. To the south and north, ridgelines came down from the Cascades to the river's edge. A series of hills, some round-shouldered and some finely sculpted, rose above the town in the west. Here and there, stunted pines straggled up the slopes in the manner of dispirited soldiers in a defeated army.

If the scenery was striking, Wenatchee itself was uninviting. The community, Woods remembered, was "rag-tag and bobtailed" and "about the worst layout on the entire railroad." West of the tracks and running parallel to the Columbia, several blocks of wooden shanties made up, with the occasional brick building, the business district. Sidewalks were nonexistent, wagons churned the streets into mud, and traffic detoured around giant boulders. Beyond the town center, rectangular patches of skeletal trees testified to the early impact of irrigation. Unwatered tracts, in contrast, were rock-strewn and sage-covered.[3]

Historical deficiencies in transportation made Wenatchee a late-blooming community. In its natural state, the Columbia River hampered rather than encouraged settlement. Above the Columbia's confluence with the Snake River, towering cliffs broke away only in a few places to accommodate town building, and dangerous rapids prohibited navigation. Railroad construction gradually overcame these obstacles. In 1883 the Northern Pacific built up the Yakima Valley and crossed the Cascades to Tacoma. Until its bankruptcy in 1890, the Seattle, Lake Shore and Eastern worked to link Puget Sound with Spokane. Homesteaders, encouraged by construction in the direction of the Grand Coulee, filed claims in the countryside about Waterville. Forced to ship wheat to Seattle and Tacoma by way of Spokane, the settlers demanded the opening of the upper Columbia to navigation. The steamer *City of Ellensburgh* was carefully worked upstream through Priest Rapids and Rock Island Rapids in 1888 to a landing near the mouth of the Wenatchee River. Attempts by the federal government to make the Columbia safe for commercial traffic failed, however, and the vessel remained tied to the riverbank.[4]

Railroad-related developments produced the beginnings of a town at the mouth of the Wenatchee. Judge Thomas Burke and other investors in the Seattle, Lake Shore and Eastern, expecting their line to cross the Columbia at that point, laid out Wenatchee, on a site approximately a mile north of the modern city center, in 1888. The failure of the Seattle, Lake Shore and Eastern brought railroad work to a halt at the Grand Coulee, but proved to be only a temporary setback for town builders. In 1890, James J. Hill proclaimed the birth of the Great Northern Railway, a new transcontinental road expected to reach Puget Sound by way of Stevens Pass at the head of the Wenatchee Valley. Judge Burke—Hill's attorney in Washington state—and his colleagues moved quickly to take advantage of this opportunity. The Great Northern received a quarter interest in the Wenatchee Development Company and the town was relocated to accommodate Hill's construction plans.[5]

Built through town in 1892, the Great Northern made Wenatchee the place where the river met the rails. Running west across the Cascades and east to the far side of the Rocky Mountains, the tracks opened markets for the agricultural and mineral output of the Big Bend. The Columbia was navigable above Wenatchee, provided care was taken, as far as the mouth of the Okanogan River. By the end of the decade, the Columbia and Okanogan Steamboat Company had a half dozen vessels in service. Boats churned slowly upstream against the current, belching clouds of smoke. Laden with wheat on the return trip, the steamers raced through Methow, Chelan, Entiat, and Rocky Reach rapids, relying for survival upon shallow draft, skillful maneuver, and blind luck.[6]

Wenatchee profited from the transshipment of wheat and other goods, but only to a certain point. The town had 461 residents in 1900, a tally regarded as one of several indicators of stagnation. Homes and business establishments remained unpainted while oil lamps provided the only artificial light. The flies, according to John Gellatly, the community's leading citizen, outnumbered the trees. If Wenatchee was to grow beyond its original river-to-rails base, some form of locally generated economic activity must be found. Agricultural opportunities, unfortunately, were strictly limited by factors of topography and climate. Flowing out of the Tumwater Canyon near Leavenworth, the Wenatchee River was confined between crouching brown hills, leaving only narrow tracts available for would-be farmers. Annual rainfall ranged from twenty inches in the upper valley to ten in the lower. Most of the precipitation fell in the winter, however, and the dry months coincided with the natural growing season.[7]

Irrigation was the obvious solution to this problem. "Every body who has any interest here," one of Judge Burke's local agents reported in September 1894, ". . . is anxious to see this valley watered." Settlers and pioneer entrepreneurs opened a number of ditches. In 1896, Arthur Gunn purchased, with backing from the Great Northern, the largest of these projects, a ditch originally developed by Jacob Shotwell. Railroad-supported irrigation, however, benefitted only those tracts owned by the Wenatchee Development Company. Aided by that firm, William T. Clark completed a sixteen-mile-long high-line canal in 1903. The flume ran along the hillsides from near the mid-valley town of Dryden to just above the mouth of the Wenatchee, where a pipeline crossed the river, reclaiming 9,000 acres of land.[8]

Together, the irrigation ditches and the high-line canal made commercial agriculture possible. However, the cost of reclaimed land forced settlers to concentrate on high-value crops and, with prevailing labor shortages, limited the size of viable homesteads. With a normal last-frost in April and first-frost in October, the Wenatchee Valley was ideally suited to fruit cultivation. Although tinged with boosterism, the local slogan "Home of the Big Red Apple" conveyed a signal truth about Wenatchee. Over 100,000 trees, mostly Winesaps and Jonathans, were planted in the decade prior to 1907. As these trees came into bearing five to seven years after planting, production expanded at a rapid rate. The original 1902 shipment of apples for market filled two Great Northern freight cars. Exports thereafter mounted from 116 carloads in 1903 to 2,197 in 1910 and 6,893 in 1914. By the latter year, the Wenatchee district grew one-eighth of the apples sold in the United States.[9]

Evidence of the apple boom was everywhere to be seen by the time Rufus Woods arrived in Wenatchee. The town's population had reached 2,000, a four-fold increase in three years. The assessed valuation of local property had mounted by 300 percent in the same period, reflecting the impact of irrigation on land prices. Wenatchee had been electrified via a water-powered plant installed on the nearby Squilchuck Creek in 1901, a system currently in the process of enlargement. The so-called "Barbary Coast" shared in the rough-and-ready prosperity, with a half dozen bawdy houses in operation along Columbia Street. These dens of iniquity, noted an observer, "were as widely known as . . . [the] best hotels, and the brazen madams were known by name to as many as knew the names of [the] hotel clerks."[10]

Two weekly newspapers served Wenatchee. The *Advance* had been founded in 1891 with the assistance of the Wenatchee Development Company, which provided a free lot in return for favorable newspaper coverage. The first owners, Frank and Belle Reeves, hauled a wagon load of type over the mountains from Ellensburg and acquired the printing press of a defunct Waterville paper. Commencing business in 1898, the rival *Republic* went through several proprietors before becoming one of the local investments of William T. Clark, the builder of the high-line canal. "Bent on newspaper work," as he later recalled, Rufus Woods toiled as a carpenter's assistant while waiting for a job to open at one of the weeklies. On January 25, 1904, according to a career-opening diary entry, he "went to work with [the] Republic."[11]

At the *Republic*, Woods came under the spell of Leonard Fowler, a flamboyant and unbusinesslike newspaperman who used high-quality book stock in place of newsprint and favored garish headlines. Impressed by the new employee's law degree, Fowler promptly made Rufus the paper's editor. Small-town journalism required a variety of talents, and Woods also handled advertising and promotions. Among other assignments, he sold Big Red Apple envelopes and organized Chelan County's first automobile rally, featuring all five locally owned horseless carriages. When printers vanished on drinking sprees, he learned, by trial-and-error, the skills utilized in the mechanical department.[12]

Fowler was often out of town, leaving Woods in charge of the editorial page. His contributions in this role dealt with the virtues of Wenatchee and the deficiencies of rival papers and communities. He made fun of the bedraggled settlement on the east bank of the river, known to bemused local residents as "the flat across the Columbia." Announcing a name-the-town contest, Rufus favored "Poverty Flat" and "Sand Toad Flat" as appropriate designations for what eventually became East Wenatchee. Other signed editorials, however, revealed a serious progressive-in-the-making. Woods called for institution of the direct primary in Washington state, demanded federal regulation of railroad rates, and supported construction of reclamation projects east of the Cascades under the terms of the federal Newlands Act. In a foretaste of the approach later followed in the campaign for Grand Coulee Dam, he urged the inhabitants of North Central Washington to cooperate on behalf of common interests. "It is an axiomatic fact," Rufus pointed out in early 1905, "that . . . people working in unison can have most anything they want."[13]

Always a booster of Wenatchee first, regardless of partisan considerations, Woods got into trouble in March 1905 by throwing the paper's support, in Fowler's absence, behind Arthur Gunn in a special election for the state senate. Gunn, a major economic force in the town, was a Democrat, causing John Gellatly and other Republican leaders to favor their party's standard-bearer, a resident of Ellensburg in neighboring Kittitas County. The alternatives, proclaimed Rufus in criticizing the Wenatchee political establishment, were to vote for "the business interests of this section" or for those of Ellensburg. In street-corner debates, he urged the importance of local patriotism upon friends, acquaintances, and complete strangers. Although Republicans outnumbered Democrats two-to-one in Chelan County, Gunn won by a margin of 42 votes. "The Republican organization," Woods later wrote, "never quite forgave me and for years regarded me as a non-conformist."[14]

Unhappy with the independent tendencies of the *Republic*, especially when Rufus Woods wrote the editorials, John Gellatly established a new paper in July 1905. Investing $100 apiece, conservative Republicans imported brothers-in-law C.A. Briggs and Nat Ament from Seattle to run their venture, named the *Daily World*. Expressly dedicated to "the principles of the Republican party"—in other words to those principles favored by Gellatly—Wenatchee's first daily was produced in cramped quarters on the second floor of the Columbia Valley Bank. Employees of the weeklies scoffed at the upstart journal's four-page layout and "precarious" fiscal status. How, they wondered, could Wenatchee and the surrounding territory, with a total population, children included, of 4,000 persons, possibly support three newspapers?[15]

Meanwhile, Woods was offered the editorship of the *Advance*, then the Democratic paper in Chelan County. Although willing to work with Democrats on specific issues, Rufus was incapable of abandoning the Republican Party and therefore rejected the opportunity. In the fall of 1905, however, he purchased the *Advance*, in partnership with Charles Graham, transforming the weekly into a vigorous defender of Republicanism. Graham provided the financing and looked after the business details, while Woods ran the news department. Despite an increase in circulation, the arrangement lasted only three months. Returning from a visit to Nebraska in January 1906, Rufus discovered that Graham had, in his absence, sold the *Advance* to the *Daily World*. At the age of twenty-six, his newspaper career was apparently at an end, at least as far as Wenatchee was concerned.[16]

By then, Woods was one of Wenatchee's most familiar figures. Wearing a bowler tipped low over his forehead, indoors and out, he exuded self-confidence, even cockiness. Watching Rufus stride about in distinctive "scissor-kicking" fashion, onlookers wondered "if he hasn't almost . . . sheared away all external evidence of his sex."[17] Five feet, nine inches tall and still youthfully slender, he played on the town baseball team and volunteered at the fire department. Political unreliability of the sort demonstrated in the Arthur Gunn affair, however, made him an outsider, a suspect figure never invited to join any of Wenatchee's several fraternal organizations. Himself an optimist and something of an innocent, Rufus was oblivious to personal slight. He was a friend to all men and women and believed, despite occasional evidence to the contrary, that all men and women reciprocated the feeling.

Fortunately for his future prospects in Wenatchee, Rufus was in complete agreement with conservative Republicans on the principal issue of the day, alcohol. On the *Republic* and then as co-proprietor of the *Advance*, he had supported the successful campaign for local enforcement of

Washington's Sunday closure law. This alliance with the anti-saloon forces helped Woods recover in the aftermath of the unexpected *Advance* sale. In February 1906 he became paid secretary of the local chamber of commerce, the Wenatchee Commercial Club. The organization promoted regional settlement, encouraged specific development projects, and maintained a thoroughly middle-class point of view on every issue of significance to the community.[18]

As secretary of the Commercial Club, Woods supervised the campaign for construction of the first automobile bridge across the Columbia River. The necessary funds were raised and the structure, built by William T. Clark, opened to public use in January 1908. By inviting representatives of outlying North Central Washington towns to its meetings, the club also provided Rufus with region-wide contacts. The weekly luncheons, he recalled, "were the meeting point for every person who was willing to be helpful in building a community." Saturday evening open forums, meanwhile, featured speeches and debate on the principal questions facing the region. As a result, a potent lobbying force for the advancement of business interests was mobilized.[19]

Commercial Club duties took only a portion of the week, leaving Rufus with time to engage in his favorite avocation of these years, land speculation. Wenatchee's population was expected to triple by 1910 and he intended to "make a barrel of money" out of urban growth. The resources of Wenatchee's two financial institutions, the Columbia Valley Bank and W.T. Clark's First National, were usually tied up in loans to apple growers, so Woods relied on money from brother Ralph and family members and friends east of the Rockies. Seeking the "quick clean-up," he bought and sold town lots, orchards along the Columbia, and timber on the slopes above the valley. "I have never missed it on a real estate deal yet," Rufus boasted in letters to prospective backers.[20]

His biggest shot at wealth, though, resulted in a definite miss. The vast Quincy Flats region, south of the Grand Coulee, rested above the Columbia like an upside-down frying pan. In the first years of the century, abnormally heavy rainfall and overly optimistic crop reports produced a sudden burst of settlement. "Every team in the country," according to one account, "was pressed into service," hauling the household goods of incoming landseekers. Ephrata, Quincy, and other towns aspired to the title of "metropolis of Central Washington." Making use of the knowledge gained on extensive tours of the countryside, Rufus Woods expected to take full advantage of the boom.[21]

Through the assistance of Ralph, Rufus became the agent for a syndicate of Tacoma attorneys and physicians. The investors had purchased 17,000 acres near Quincy in early 1906 for $7 an acre. Agreeing to locate a buyer for the entire tract, in return for an $8,500 commission, Woods secured an offer of $8.50 an acre from a Minnesota speculator. The syndicate, unfortunately, held out for $10, a monumental miscalculation in light of new developments in the Columbia Basin. Precipitation returned to normal levels, the boom collapsed, and the value of the land fell to $2 per acre. His fee lost, Woods at least learned that irrigation was an absolute necessity on the Quincy Flats, a region destined to become the focal point of the Columbia Basin Project.[22]

In the aftermath of his Quincy Flats failure, Rufus was presented with an opportunity to return to the newspaper life. C.A. Briggs and Nat Ament had struggled in vain to keep the *Daily World* afloat. They obtained close to 500 subscriptions in the first year of operation, but thereafter circulation failed to increase. Chelan County Democrats, supported by the liquor interests, expressed outrage over the paper's militant anti-saloon stance. Wenatchee's outgoing mayor, H.C. Littlefield, threatened the lives of Briggs and Ament in December 1906 and vowed to drive the *World* out of business. Attempting to follow through on these threats, Littlefield's son and Percy Schneble, the son of the Democratic mayor-elect, cornered Ament in the post office and beat him senseless.[23]

As veteran newspapermen, Briggs and Ament were used to criticism. Physical assault was another matter, however, and the brothers-in-law fled town. John Gellatly and the other investors suddenly faced the complete loss of the funds advanced to the *World*. Fortunately, Rufus Woods offered to assume the management. Although memories of the Gunn campaign aroused concern on the matter of political reliability, Rufus was the only alternative to bankruptcy. On February 27, 1907, Rufus and Ralph Woods leased the *Daily World* for one year, with an option to buy at the end of that period. A front-page advertisement in their debut issue testified to the shoestring nature of the arrangement. "I Need the Money," proclaimed Rufus in offering for sale a seven-room house "in one of the sightliest locations in the city."[24]

Signed and boxed, the same issue's feature editorial broadcast the goals of the new publisher. "In the newspaper field," wrote Rufus, "there is lots of fun, lots of work and lots of money so it is hoped." He confessed to doubt only the third, absolutely vital, aim: "we will pray to the gods who guard the exchequer that they may open the treasury bags as they go by and drop a few nuggets our way." The *World*'s weaknesses were certainly evident to any observant person. The circulation was small, the mechanical equipment ancient, and the staff overworked and underpaid. The paper's single reporter received six dollars a week and had to moonlight as a stringer for several Puget Sound dailies in order to pay his room and board. The *Daily World*, Woods privately admitted, was "a business which was no business."[25]

Undeterred by the lack of prospects, Woods expected energy and efficiency to overcome long odds. With Ralph as a silent partner, Rufus named himself manager of the Wenatchee World Advance Publishing Company and publisher of the *Daily World*. Frank M. Dallam, Jr., the son of a veteran eastern Washington newspaperman, signed on with the new regime as editor. When Dallam left in July to become private secretary to Governor Albert Mead, William S. Trimble inherited his role of confidante to Woods and supervisor of day-to-day operations. Fred Simpich, in later years a state department consular agent and *National Geographic* writer, employed a style so vigorous as chief reporter that "there were fifteen or twenty in town who wanted to shoot him." These individuals brought enthusiasm to the *World* and made the paper for the first time worth reading.[26]

Rufus quickly expanded circulation by giving away sets of dishes to the first 500 new subscribers. The initial recipient was Percy Schneble, one of the men who had assaulted Nat Ament and made possible the Woods takeover of the paper. A similar promotional campaign followed, featuring free knives. The *World* mounted its delivery boys on horseback, increasing the timeliness of the service and providing, in the case of an animal painted in zebra stripes, new opportunities for publicity. Helped along by premiums and stunts, circulation reached 2,700 by 1910, a 600 percent increase over March 1907.[27]

Circulation growth created the need for improvements in the mechanical department. Woods inherited from Briggs and Ament a battered flatbed press valued at $350. A recently purchased Linotype (resembling a giant typewriter, the device allowed its operator to set type at a rapid pace) was the only piece of equipment worth saving from the junkyard. Revenue from new subscriptions allowed Rufus to acquire a two-resolution Optimus press, capable of printing and folding 1,900 copies per hour. Job work—

the printing of legal forms and circulars—increased in volume, contributing to the overall performance level of the company. Telegraph service, through the United Press and then via membership in the Associated Press, provided breaking national and international news for readers. The *World* was soon made over from a four-page into an eight-page, six-column paper.[28]

New equipment and wire service membership, with other expenses, required infusions of capital. Taking over full ownership of the *World* upon the expiration of their lease in 1908, Rufus and Ralph thought of selling out in return for a quick and substantial profit. Negotiations began with a prospective Seattle purchaser on the basis of a $10,000 transaction. The genuine pleasure he derived from the business caused Rufus to decide, however, in favor of the alternative of taking on minority investors. Frank Dallam, though remaining on political duty in Olympia, put $2,400 into the *World*. Cousin Warren Woods, a Nebraska high school teacher, contributed $2,000 and came west in 1909 to work at the newspaper.[29]

Machinery and money were complemented by honest reporting and a reasoned editorial viewpoint. America's premier newspapers, according to Woods, were "willing to wear a party name but not a party yoke." Excessive partisanship was ruinous to a paper's reputation, a truism affirmed by the contemporary state of the Seattle media. The *Seattle Times* reflected the whims of its mercurial owner, Alden Blethen, and was, said Woods, "a journalistic prostitute." The *Post-Intelligencer* was governed by the political ambitions of publisher John L. Wilson, a former United States senator in permanent quest of a return to office. Rufus also realized that a newspaper was first and foremost "a business proposition." With profit a "determining" consideration, the responsible proprietor paid close attention to public opinion and avoided boring subscribers with lengthy treatises on dull subjects. Coverage must always be balanced between what readers needed to know and what readers wanted to know. The properly managed daily therefore entertained as well as informed, enlivening the presentation of facts with "splash, color, [and] action."[30]

Governed according to these strictures, the *World* was an independent Republican paper, supporting the party's candidates and platform except when the welfare of Wenatchee dictated otherwise. As a "mouthpiece of the people," the *World* identified with the aspirations and philosophy of the Commercial Club. "It stands," asserted an early Woods editorial, "for a Greater Wenatchee, for a moral and intelligent citizenship, for an ideal place in which to live." Business interests and values, in particular, must be accorded priority. "Men who have demonstrated their ability to conduct a private business successfully," reasoned the *World*, ". . . manage the city's affairs in the same way." Unhampered by impractical theories or by partisan loyalties, such individuals invariably sought efficient services, low taxes, and honest municipal life.[31]

Moral questions continued to dominate local politics, keeping intact a coalition that might otherwise have broken apart over economic issues. Responsible business people, backed by the churches and the Republican Party, worried, for instance, that "houses of public putridity" conflicted with Wenatchee's wholesome Big Red Apple image, retarding long-term economic growth. In March 1908, Mayor John Gellatly ordered all prostitutes to leave the city "within ten days or reform." Practitioners of the ancient trade, of course, merely concealed themselves behind discretely closed doors, but the end of the bawdy house era was considered a major urban advance. "The class of people who infest a wide open town are not producers of wealth," the *World* pointed out in agreement with Gellatly. "Rather they are leeches upon the body politic, draining the country of its wealth and leaving nothing of value."[32]

Briefly diverted by the war on prostitution, Wenatchee residents soon returned to their principal concern, the liquor question. In 1909 the state legislature approved a local option law, allowing communities to prohibit the sale or distribution of alcohol within their limits. Voting under the statute, Wenatchee went dry that August, by a margin of 400 to 293. "It is the duty of the minority," the *World* advised afterward, "to accept in good spirit the mandate of the majority." Ignoring this helpful suggestion, displaced saloon owners and their thirsty former customers mounted petition drives for new elections. On behalf of the prohibition forces, the *World* enumerated the beneficial consequences of the ban. Women and children walked the streets "without having to listen to ribald talk," and the arrest rate had fallen by 80 percent. The individual who endorsed the saloon, asserted Rufus Woods, "possesses an intelligence little above that of a Simian ape." By increasing majorities, the wets lost again in 1910 and 1912. The disappearance of the long mahogany bar, like the dimming of the red light, reflected the end of frontier Wenatchee, now a sober apple-producing domain.[33]

Closure of the saloons exhausted the ambitions of most reformers, but Woods conceived of the clean-up Wenatchee effort in broader and even literal terms. Homeowners, he insisted, must remove the "mounds of ill-smelling refuse" deposited in their yards. In addition to being unsightly, garbage attracted the swarms of flies infesting the town each summer. "Putrid

Premises are the provinces of Pig Styes and Slaughter Houses," Rufus reminded his readers; "they have no place in a well regulated community."
Stables must be removed from residential neighborhoods and horses prevented from wandering about, feasting upon lawns and shrubbery. The
*World* also called upon residents to plant trees, abandon the carrying of
firearms, and avoid the disgusting practice of spitting in public.[34]

Individual efforts, according to the Woods prescription, must be
supplemented by the municipality and by business. Wenatchee's water,
which came from Squilchuck Creek and had to be "chewed like a mouth-
ful of Christmas pudding," was clearly unsuited to present needs, to say
nothing of future requirements. The *World* therefore supported construction of a pumping plant on the Columbia River, arguing that the stream's
"cool mountain fed waters" represented a major improvement "from a sani-
tary point of view." The Wenatchee Electric Company's Squilchuck plant
also failed to keep pace with the rate of urbanization. Frequent power out-
ages aggravated commercial and domestic consumers alike. Woods considered the development of a new power site up the Wenatchee Valley in
1908 the initial step in the dependable electrification of the community.
Rufus also regarded the installation of Wenatchee's first sewer system in
1909 as a significant advance in terms of public health. Previously, noted a
*World* editorial, "filth unavoidably accumulate[d] in back yards and al-
leys," assailing the senses with malodorous "putrefaction."[35]

The regrading of Wenatchee Avenue, then undulating, dusty, and
boulder-strewn, was another essential component of the Woods program.
Rufus believed the town's principal thoroughfare was "a reproach to the
municipality" and "the worst road in the whole country." Prospective investors supposedly fled Wenatchee in horror after a single "look at that
disgraceful street." Financed by the city, regrade work commenced in 1909.
The avenue was levelled off, oiled, and provided with electric lights. Ce-
ment sidewalks replaced the old system of intermittent plank walkways.
Business owners, out of necessity, raised or lowered their premises to match
the level of the street.[36]

Road improvements inspired the construction of modern brick and
stone buildings. On July 6, 1909, windblown flames destroyed shacks and
other wooden structures, including the fire station, opening valuable lots
to development. Within six months, Wenatchee deserved recognition as
an up-to-date metropolis. The Commercial Club and the Columbia Valley Bank occupied fireproof quarters and the Olympia Hotel, a first-class

hostelry, opened its doors. Town residents boasted of their new high school and city hall and of the public library, under construction thanks to a grant from Andrew Carnegie. "Disorder," proclaimed the *World* in assessing the urban makeover, "has given way to order."[37]

Woods himself actively participated in the building boom, an involvement necessitated by the *World*'s need for additional space. In March 1909, Rufus and T.F. Lewis, an investor from Wyoming, purchased a lot at the corner of Mission and Palouse streets. Although their agreement described the transaction as "for the purposes of speculation," the partners intended to develop the property themselves. They originally planned a four-story building, accommodating the newspaper offices and press, with ample room left over for income-generating rentals. Woods also expected to secure a political appointment as postmaster of Wenatchee upon expiration of the incumbent's term in May 1910. "We can probably plan to locate the [post] office in our building," he informed Lewis. The structure would, as a result, become "the center of town" and, as such, produce a monthly income of at least $400.[38]

Several unexpected developments forced significant alteration of the scheme. Due to the demands of competing projects and apple growers on local banks, Woods and Lewis experienced difficulty securing financing. The 1909 fire destroyed the existing structures on their lot, prematurely cutting off rental income. The crucial postmastership became embroiled in a political dispute and was eventually lost to a rival aspirant. Completed in February 1910 at a cost of $20,000, the Daily World Building had only two stories. The paper's office and composing room opened off the main floor lobby and the press was installed in the basement. The El Mundo Hotel occupied the second floor. On the roof, an electric sign spelled out "World" in vertical letters.[39]

The new building was the first of several steps forward by the *World*. After making the final payment due on the paper, Woods incorporated the business. The World Publishing Company, capitalized at $25,000, was formally organized in August 1910, with Rufus as president, Frank Dallam as vice-president and Warren Woods as secretary-treasurer. In November, the paper purchased a Goss perfecting press from the *Tacoma Tribune*. The machine printed from a single roll of paper, turned out up to 12,000 folded copies an hour, and signalled the emergence of the *Daily World* as one of the leading small city newspapers in the state of Washington.[40]

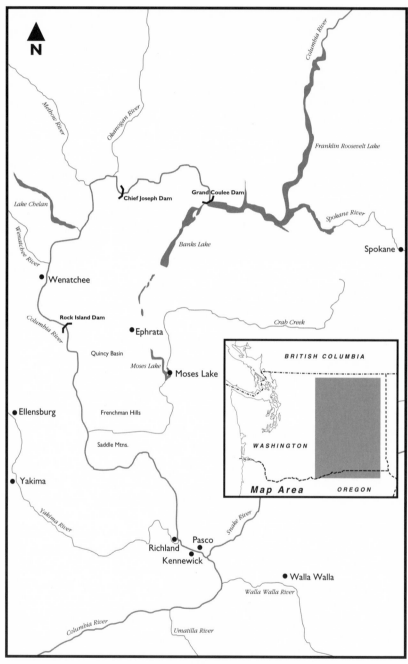

Big Bend Map

From the beginning of the Rufus Woods era, the *World* promoted the needs of a region, not just the interests of Wenatchee. The Big Bend of the Columbia River bound Chelan, Okanogan, Douglas, and Grant counties into a cohesive geographical unit. Fighting to protect the Pacific Northwest from domination by outside financiers and politicians, Woods sought at the same time to build a stable four-county hinterland for Wenatchee. The term North Central Washington was a conscious promotional device, defining and maintaining a separate identity from east-of-the-Cascades sections dominated by Spokane and Yakima. Encouraging the linkage between Wenatchee and the outlying districts, the *Daily World* organized an NCW Development League and sponsored all legitimate development projects.[41]

The paramount demand of North Central Washington was for improved transportation, especially the opening of the Columbia River to hazard-free steamboat traffic. Unhampered navigation, enthused the *World*, meant an end to "railroad oppression" and the "excessive . . . rates" charged by the monopolistic Great Northern. Reduced freight and passenger charges would, in turn, stimulate the settlement and industrialization of Wenatchee. The open river campaign, unfortunately, ended in complete disappointment. Expensive dams and locks would be required at Rock Island and at Priest Rapids, the Army Corps of Engineers concluded, in order for steamers to safely pass downstream. Under a project approved by Congress in 1910, the Army removed rocks and installed wing dams at hazardous places between Wenatchee and Kettle Falls, 40 miles from the Canadian border. The first spring runoff, however, washed away the work, eliminating any benefit to commerce.[42]

Frustrated by the failures of the Corps of Engineers, local development advocates also struggled on the land. Travelers on the 141 miles of supposed "improved" roads in Washington state endured excessive dust in summer and mud in winter. Allying itself with the statewide Good Roads Association, the *World* called for construction of modern hardtop roadways, including completion of the Sunset Highway, linking Seattle with Spokane via Wenatchee. To dramatize the need for transportation improvements, the paper organized an automobile caravan to Okanogan County in 1910. Fifty-four motorists, equipped with towlines and water cans, set out from Wenatchee in single-file convoy. Frequent stops were necessary to cool overheated engines, and the vehicle carrying Rufus Woods broke down entirely. Altogether, the journey took five days to complete, ample evidence of the sorry state of North Central Washington roads.[43]

Woods expected road construction to encourage the diversification of agriculture and the development of industry. Transfixed by apples, local residents devoted virtually all of their resources to the cultivation of orchards, leaving the region dangerously dependent upon a single crop. The *World* advocated the building of canneries to handle surplus production and of by-products facilities for the utilization of cull apples. Mines, lumber mills, and other large enterprises were also on the agenda, to be developed in conjunction with expanding electricity generation. Looking to future growth, Woods saw early-on the necessity of dams in the canyon of the Chelan River and on the Columbia itself at Rock Island. Hydroelectricity, he believed, guaranteed industrialization, and industry, in turn, guaranteed urban growth, the expansion of markets, and the development of a prosperous and self-sufficient region.[44]

Obstacles of nature and cost, unfortunately, retarded utilization of the Columbia River and its tributaries, preventing the expansion of agriculture and the introduction of industry. Farmers and small business interests lacked the capital and the technical expertise to build dams on the swift-flowing streams of the region. The Reclamation Act of 1902, however, authorized government water projects, financed by the sale of public land and by settler repayment of the construction costs. Through tireless promotion and adroit lobbying of the U.S. Reclamation Service, Representative Wesley Jones of eastern Washington secured vast federal irrigation works for the Yakima Valley. In Wenatchee, Rufus Woods read the tracts of reclamation enthusiasts William Ellsworth Smythe and Elwood Mead, contemplated the success of Jones in Yakima, and planned a similar massive undertaking for the Big Bend.[45]

Annual rainfall had declined to less than seven inches in the Quincy Flats, leaving the once-enthusiastic settlers, according to reports from the scene, "disillusioned" and "practically bankrupt." In late 1906, Rufus Woods and David McGinnis, an owner of extensive tracts in the Big Bend, developed a plan for irrigating a half million acres via a canal from Lake Wenatchee on the eastern slope of the Cascades. Woods and McGinnis assembled the necessary topographical data and investigated such vital technical matters as the expenditure involved in excavating a tunnel under the Columbia River. Concluding that the project, at an estimated cost of $12 million, was too expensive for them to undertake, the two enthusiasts made their proposal available to the interested public.[46]

Organized in 1909 and cheered on by the *Daily World*, the Quincy Valley Water Users Association took up the Woods-McGinnis scheme.

Financing the work with a two-cents-an-acre assessment upon the membership, the organization employed engineer Joseph Jacobs to investigate the available sources of water. In a March 1910 report, Jacobs concluded that construction of a gravity canal from the Pend Oreille River northeast of Spokane, a project already studied by the Reclamation Service, required too much money. Another possibility, taking water directly from the Columbia, was also fiscally unsound, since it would require a dam to supply electricity for the pumps. Lake Wenatchee, however, was a feasible source, even though the canals and the Columbia River tunnel would cost $28 million, far in excess of the figure posited by Woods and McGinnis. With the Jacobs report in hand, the Water Users Association secured from the Department of the Interior the reservation of Lake Wenatchee for purposes of irrigation.[47]

Rather than wait for the supposedly dilatory Reclamation Service to take action, the impatient Water Users Association sought private financing to construct the project. Capital was available, however, only if the state of Washington guaranteed repayment of the bonds. The legislature approved the guarantee, but the voters, in a statewide referendum, rejected the measure in 1914 by a two-to-one margin. In a last desperate gesture, the Quincy Flats landowners turned, after all, to the Reclamation Service. The politically controversial nature of the initial federal water projects, plus the outbreak of the First World War, precluded any chance of securing funds in the nation's capital. All that remained from the first serious attempt to reclaim the Columbia Basin were survey reports and booster groups eventually of use in the campaign for Grand Coulee Dam.[48]

Fighting for the Quincy Project and for the growth of North Central Washington, the *World* followed the Rufus Woods dictum that "the spirit of optimism" was the key to community well-being. "The Daily World," Rufus pronounced in an early issue, "is not a Knocker." Regional prosperity was possible only if the "croaker" element remained small in number and influence. Woods occasionally reprinted William Allen White's famous essay "What's the Matter with Kansas?" as a prelude to asking a similar question about the local state of affairs. "'What's Wrong With Wenatchee?'" he queried. "Nothing. What's needed in Wenatchee, [is] a hopeful, optimistic view, an appreciation of the things that have been accomplished by public spirit."[49]

Certainly, or so local people contended, the application of positive thinking and honest sweat to the cultivation of orchards had created a regional society worth defending against any and all threats. The never-ending toil and mental calculation required in the growing, harvesting, and marketing of apples supposedly stimulated intelligence, improved character, and fostered "an independent and self-reliant spirit." The hands-on management style typical of the Wenatchee Valley erased class distinctions and promoted social equality. "The rich are here," observed the *World*, "but you can't tell the rich man from the other fellow—for he works right along side the day laborer who is working for him." No matter what the source of danger, Woods asserted, this vision of democracy on the Columbia River must be protected.[50]

Establishing himself as the prophet of regional development, Rufus Woods, at the age of 31, had attained the secure stature and future prospects necessary for the mature contemplation of marriage. On May 1, 1909 he married long-time Nebraska friend and neighbor Mary Marcia Greenslit. The bride, described by Rufus as "accomplished, [and] attractive," was twenty-six and a member of Surprise's founding and wealthiest family. After growing up in a hilltop home above the village, she taught in local schools before becoming an instructor at the Nebraska Wesleyan Teachers College in Lincoln. The Greenslits traced their lineage back to Puritan New England—a Salem ancestor, they boasted, was condemned as a witch—and at first objected to Rufus as an irresponsible upstart. The success of the *World*, however, suggested that Woods must have grown up since leaving Surprise for the Pacific Northwest.[51]

Following a brief honeymoon, the newlyweds rented John Gellatly's temporarily vacant Wenatchee house for the summer. Mary and Rufus built their own home in 1911, on a lot west of Mission Street. A woman of considerable cultural accomplishment, Mary devoted herself to household management, volunteer work in the Wenatchee schools, and the sometimes vexing task of entertaining her husband's many friends and acquaintances. On any given evening, Rufus might return from the newspaper with a visiting politician, vaudeville performer, or Indian leader, invited at the last minute for dinner. The birth of a daughter, Wilma Cecilia, in 1910 and of a son, Walter, in 1912 added the responsibilities of motherhood to domestic chores.[52]

"Running a daily in a town of this size," Rufus remarked early in his career with the *World*, "is not exactly like going on a honeymoon."[53] By 1910, this statement appeared badly out-of-date. Circulation had increased by a factor of six and the paper now occupied modern quarters. Read throughout the region, North Central Washington's only daily newspaper was relied upon for untainted news and public-spirited commentary. The campaign to clean up Wenatchee placed Woods in the front ranks of community leaders. Marriage and impending fatherhood added to a well-earned sense of personal satisfaction. Daily life in Wenatchee might, after all, be equated to a honeymooning experience. A sudden and entirely unexpected political upheaval, however, nearly destroyed the *World* and the fortunes of Rufus Woods.

# Chapter Three
# Healthful Innovations

Nations are always in more danger of perishing from dry rot than they are from healthful innovations.

*Wenatchee Daily World* [1]

FOR RUFUS WOODS, the newspaper and the political party were front office and backroom components of the same mission: the mobilization of opinion for the betterment of the community, regardless of partisan connection. Despite operating a Republican paper, Woods remained under the spell of his Nebraska hero, William Jennings Bryan. He was a proud host when the Great Commoner visited Wenatchee on a lecture tour and regularly praised the perennial Democratic standard-bearer's "high moral character" and "earnestness and sincerity." In his view, the ideal, if improbable, national ticket would combine Bryan for vice-president and Theodore Roosevelt for president. The two men "stood at the front of American thought today," linking the rural populism of the 1890s with the urban-oriented progressivism of the twentieth century.[2]

Ascending to the presidency upon the assassination of William McKinley in 1901 and elected in his own right in 1904, Roosevelt exceeded even Bryan as the ideal politician. The vigorous President, claimed Rufus, was the "foremost citizen of the world." Flaunting tradition, T.R. recognized that the United States needed a government outfitted with the power to protect individuals against corporate greed and political bossism. His Square Deal program aimed at the reestablishment of social justice in a nation torn from its agricultural roots. "Special privilege to none, equal opportunity to all," enthused Woods, was "the ideal toward which the efforts of Roosevelt have been steadily directed."[3]

Hero worship was by no means the only factor making Rufus Woods a reformer. Something, in his view, had gone seriously wrong with America. The modern industrial corporation was able, through the concentration of economic power, to ignore the welfare of society. The necessary response, according to Woods, was progressivism, which erected a "barrier between public interest and monopolistic greed" in the form of a federal government strong enough to check big business. Legal and social precepts surviving from an era when America was a land of small property-owning farmers must be altered, or even abandoned, to meet new problems. "To permit the control of this nation," argued the *World*, "to pass into the hands of a few men by reason of archaic and unjust laws which permit the accumulation of boundless wealth is unworthy [of] a free and intelligent people."[4]

Years before the liberal journalist Bernard DeVoto bemoaned the fate of the West as a "plundered province," Rufus Woods wrote in the same vein of the region's colonial status. Through fortunate circumstance and sharp manipulation of the law, he believed, eastern capitalists had seized control of forests, mines, and waterpower sites. Locally, the Great Northern Railway demonstrated the consequences of corporate domination. Although Wenatchee was, for all practical purposes, a company town dependent upon the James J. Hill line, the *Daily World* subjected "the poorest excuse for a railroad in the country" to relentless attack. Excessive freight rates and indifferent service, the newspaper charged, were the norm on the Great Northern. The *World* reported upon the "profound sensation" created when trains arrived on time. Rotten ties, loose spikes, and indifferent maintenance accounted for the high rate of accidents on the hard pull over Stevens Pass. The Great Northern's Wenatchee depot, moreover, was a disgrace, with a tiny unventilated waiting room and no toilets.[5]

Wenatchee also suffered from home-grown corruption and incompetence. The *Daily World* pursued a steady campaign against Seattle. In the early years of the apple boom, orchardists sent much of their crop west to the Puget Sound metropolis, only to be cheated, as they alleged, by dishonest warehouse owners and wholesalers. Political radicalism and unwholesome tolerance for eccentricity made Seattle "the dumping ground for the riffraff of the western . . . United States" and explained the mayoral election of Hiram Gill, a spoilsman from "the sewers of vice and pollution." Seattle also had no qualms about frustrating the aspirations of other sections of the state. Exercising its political muscle in Olympia, the city arranged for most of the highway funding to go to its favored Snoqualmie Pass

route. In contrast, the Stevens Pass road, passing through Wenatchee, secured only limited financial support.[6]

To the detriment of good government, partisanship drove the political process in Washington state. Until 1907, party nominees were selected
in conventions, forcing voters to choose between two machine candidates
at the November general election. In Chelan County, "some half dozen
men," according to the *World*, "dictated the patronage of this locality."
Prior to ratification of the Seventeenth Amendment in 1913, moreover,
United States senators were elected by the legislature, a process open to
various ingenious forms of manipulation. The arrangement under which
Samuel Piles was sent to the Senate in 1905, in return for promising to
support the reelection of Senator Levi Ankeny in 1909, made the state, in
the view of Rufus Woods, "the laughing stock" of the nation.[7]

Government must reflect the popular will, maintained Woods and
other advocates of reform, rather than the shabby ambitions of political
parties. In 1907 the legislature replaced the convention method of nominating candidates with county and state primaries. The measure also provided for an advisory U.S. Senate primary. Sponsors of the latter provision
expected that legislators, held to account by a vigilant press, would have no
choice but to endorse the preference of the electorate. Further experiments
in direct democracy followed upon these initial victories of progressivism.
Approved by the voters in 1912, amendments to the state constitution
authorized the initiative and the referendum as potentially powerful counters
to governmental inattention and irresponsibility. "The fact," stated Woods,
"that the people possess the machinery to make their will effective is the
best expedient yet devised to check corruption."[8]

As a complement to direct democracy, Woods expected conservation
to overcome Washington's colonial dependence upon outside capital. "Sordid commercialism," in his view, had resulted in the wasteful destruction
of the "nation's bounties." In the Pacific Northwest, careless corporate
managers engaged in heedless overcutting of timber and produced devastating forest fires, consuming trees worth millions of dollars. The supreme
contribution of the Roosevelt administration was its "underlying principle
of conservation," the "application of common sense to common problems
for the common good." Major additions to the national forests, the withdrawal of waterpower sites from private entry, and the development of
forestry doctrine accounted in large measure for the heroic status accorded
T.R. and Forest Service chief Gifford Pinchot by the *Wenatchee Daily World*.[9]

Uppermost in Woods's mind was the fact that progressive conservation encouraged the intelligent utilization of natural resources on behalf of genuine economic development. Pre-Roosevelt land policies had allowed "big eastern capitalists" to gain title to forests, minerals, and water, placing the West "under the control of great centralized agencies . . . to exploit for their own advantage solely." Outside investors supposedly intended to postpone exploitation of their ill-gotten holdings until some uncertain future date—"be it ten years or a century from now"—when resource depletion elsewhere would enable them to "charge the public what the traffic will bear." The conservationist ethos, in contrast, made the public welfare superior to private greed, allowing genuine local interests to beat down the doors to the monopoly-controlled storehouse. Like the primary, the initiative, and the referendum, conservation entailed the restoration of old community-oriented values in a society bedeviled by industrialization and urbanization.[10]

Born in Nebraska and refined in Wenatchee, the Woods political philosophy emerged in full intensity only in the final months of 1909. Until then, Rufus avoided a break with the conservative Republicans who had founded the *World*. Editorial content emphasized social issues and boosterism, the matters upon which party members found common cause. The attacks on the Great Northern, though irksome to individuals beholden to James J. Hill, reflected the general tenor of local public opinion. Despite the presence, for the third and final time, of William Jennings Bryan at the head of the Democratic ticket in 1908, Woods remained a loyal Republican, endorsing William Howard Taft, Roosevelt's anointed successor.[11]

Certain actions revealed, at least in hindsight, that a genuine long-term alliance between Woods and Republican conservatives would be impossible. In 1908, Rufus backed the successful effort of Representative Wesley Jones to unseat "that fossilized gentleman," the incumbent Republican Senator Levi Ankeny. To succeed Jones in the House, Woods endorsed Republican Judge Miles Poindexter of Spokane, a vigorous proponent of good government and a close associate of the city's influential publisher, William H. Cowles of the *Spokesman-Review*. John Gellatly and other Chelan County Republican leaders demanded a retraction of the endorsement in favor of their preferred Old Guard candidate. Woods instead took an active role in the Poindexter campaign, organizing support among the weekly papers of North Central Washington and sharing the credit for the Judge's victory.[12]

During the tumultuous congressional session of 1909, Woods supported the rebellion of Washington's outspoken freshman congressman. At the outset of the Taft Administration, Congress convened to redeem a GOP campaign pledge to lower tariff duties. The controversial result, thanks to the machinations of pro-corporation party leaders, was the highly protectionist Payne-Aldrich Tariff. Poindexter and other "Insurgents" immediately launched a challenge to the autocratic powers of House Speaker Joseph Cannon. Later in the year, a dispute between Secretary of the Interior Richard Ballinger and Gifford Pinchot over management of federal lands in Alaska ended in the dismissal of the Forest Service chief, producing new outrage among progressives.[13]

Although the *World* stood with the Insurgency as a matter of principle, the final split with the Old Guard, as far as Rufus Woods was concerned, resulted from considerations of patronage. Rufus had based his plans for the *Daily World* Building on the expectation of becoming postmaster of Wenatchee. If traditional practice was followed, the position would be filled according to the recommendation of Representative Poindexter. Political developments in the fall of 1909 appeared to make the appointment of Poindexter's local champion a virtual certainty. In October, Woods, William H. Cowles, and other eastern Washington publishers formed the Progressive Republican League, with Rufus as president. When Poindexter declared his intention of running for the Senate in 1910, the league became the organizational basis of the campaign.[14]

Unfortunately for Rufus, Judge Thomas Burke of Seattle decided to cap his long and discrete career in Washington politics by winning election to the United States Senate. As the "Father of Wenatchee" and a substantial property owner in the community, Burke expected the support of Chelan County in his quest for the Republican nomination. Local conservatives, outraged by Poindexter's Insurgent stance, fell in line behind Burke's candidacy. Senator Wesley Jones, meanwhile, worried that opposition west of the Cascades to retention of both senatorial seats by eastern Washingtonians would hurt his chances for reelection in 1914. The senator therefore became active behind the scenes in the campaign against Poindexter. Burke, Jones, and the Wenatchee Old Guard expected to undermine the progressive favorite by depriving Rufus Woods of the postmastership.[15]

As a native of Nebraska and a friend of the Great Commoner, Woods was obviously "a Bryan democrat, at heart." So, at least, claimed John Gellatly in calling upon Senator Jones to "go over brother Poindexter's head in the Post Office matter." For the benefit of Jones, Gellatly detailed the Wenatchee publisher's suspect political record—dating back to the Arthur Gunn campaign—an obviously heretical background that left Rufus "in no wise entitled to a republican plum." Millard Hartson, the senator's principal confidante in the state, reported, with an eye on 1914, that Poindexter intended to replace "Postmasters with good records"—in other words, fealty to Jones—with "such people as Rufus Woods," a move that must be countered on behalf of sound Republicanism and personal interest.[16]

Emerging from a period of bankruptcy, the *Wenatchee Republic* entered the postmaster fight, fortified by infusions of cash from William T. Clark and the supporters of Judge Burke. In news and opinion columns alike, editor David Tewkesbury contended that the Woods appointment "has the opposition, not only of the rank and file of the Republican party, but of almost every merchant and citizen, irrespective of politics." Good government and timely delivery of the mail were at stake, he maintained, since the "favored aspirant" was unqualified "on the ground of incompetence." The *Republic's* real target, of course, was Poindexter. Week after week, Tewkesbury accused the congressman of "bribing newspapermen" and of contributing to the "debauchery of a venal press" through the "Pork-Barrel League of Alleged Republican Editors." Poindexter was, in a sampling of *Republic* invective, a "political trickster," a "traitor to the people" and a "deceitful, hypocritical politician."[17]

Ignoring Tewkesbury's advice to "withdraw his candidacy," Rufus remained steadfast in pursuit of the postmastership. He corresponded on a regular basis with the Post Office Department, detailing the modern fixtures and efficient services available in the new *Daily World* Building. In retaliation for the Insurgent attacks upon Speaker Cannon and Secretary Ballinger, President Taft revoked Poindexter's control of congressional district patronage. The congressman's power to make appointments went to Senator Jones, who, looking to his own welfare, immediately placed a pro-Burke postmaster in Wenatchee. By humiliating Woods the Taft administration had dealt "a death blow to Insurgency here," chortled John Gellatly upon learning the news.[18]

Disappointed yet undaunted, Rufus remained active in the Poindexter campaign, proof that the postmastership was a fringe benefit, rather than the principal reason for his adherence to progressivism. The *World* subjected Poindexter's rivals to expert journalistic attack. In contrast to "the disgusting, inane, senseless blarney" of the *Republic*, the newspaper treated

Burke "very kindly," avoiding direct criticism of the Judge. Woods instead used news columns to report that "other papers" had "made great capital out of . . . his connection with corporate interests." The *World* published third-party accusations that Burke was "too old and out of touch with conditions" in the form of supposedly objective reports on the campaign. The last minute withdrawal of John Wilson solidified Old Guard support behind Burke, but failed to stem a statewide progressive victory, with 58 percent of the advisory primary vote going to Poindexter. The legislature officially elected the popular favorite to the Senate in January 1911, placing the state of Washington, as Rufus Woods proclaimed, "in the vanguard of political progress."[19]

Nationally, Old Guard and progressive Republicans blamed one another for the loss of Congress in 1910 and for the prospect of a Democrat being elected president in 1912. Following a conference with Poindexter, Woods wrote that voters from coast to coast had repudiated Taft due to his failure to implement "what is known as the 'Roosevelt policies.'" The President was "able, high minded and conscientious," but had been fatally misled by "designing instruments" in his administration. Taft's belated and ponderous efforts to restore Republican harmony came too late to repair the damage. Joining in the movement to prevent the President's renomination, Washington progressives looked first to Senator Robert LaFollette of Wisconsin as a rallying point. Early in 1912, however, an ad hoc coalition of reform-minded Republicans, Rufus Woods included, "persuaded" a supposedly reluctant Theodore Roosevelt to emerge from retirement and again seek the presidency.[20]

Progressives and conservatives alike sacrificed the prospects of victory in the election of 1912 to the paramount necessity of winning the struggle within the Republican Party. Supporters of the Old Guard in Wenatchee waited until Woods and other Roosevelt backers went to lunch, then pushed an endorsement of Taft through a rump Chelan County GOP convention. Although uncontested delegates to the state convention, meeting in Aberdeen in May, favored T.R. by a large majority, a dozen counties sent rival delegations. Controlling the proceedings, Old Guard officials resolved all disputes in favor of Taft. The outcome was predictable: the President secured Washington's votes at the national convention. The Roosevelt camp was, of course, outraged. The "defenseless acts" of "desperate, reactionary bosses," thundered the *World*, had resulted in creating "two republican parties in this state," one "of the people" and the other "of a few old time political bosses."[21]

Roosevelt was far and away the popular favorite at the Chicago national convention. Taft, though, controlled the party machinery and had the advantage of virtually unanimous support of the federal appointees in attendance as delegates from the solidly Democratic South. "The decision," Woods forecast, ". . . is going to rest with a mere handful of nominal members of the party living in states which never cast an electoral vote for the republican candidate." Contested delegations loyal to Taft were seated and the President emerged from the controversial proceedings with the nomination. The *World*, following the line of the nation's progressive press, reacted in an outraged and even hysterical tone. William Howard Taft, said Woods, was the choice of "political pimps" and "abandoned men who would strike a dagger into the heart of a defenceless maiden and ravish the corpse."[22]

In the aftermath of Chicago, progressives announced their unwillingness to abide by the outcome of the convention. Some endorsed the Democratic nominee, Governor Woodrow Wilson of New Jersey. Rufus Woods thought Wilson a superior alternative to Taft, but joined most Republican reformers in supporting Roosevelt as the candidate of a new Progressive, or Bull Moose, party. Although the GOP split made Wilson's national victory inevitable, Washington Bull Moosers were heartened by the fact that Roosevelt won their state. Governor Marion Hay, burdened by his refusal to break with Taft, lost to Democrat Ernest Lister by a margin of 622 votes. Woods had supported Hay to the end, primarily as a means of saving stockholder Frank Dallam's job in the gubernatorial office. The incumbent's defeat, except for the impact upon Dallam, was no cause for deep regret. Lister appeared to be a sound and reflective individual who would surely preserve and even expand upon the reforms of recent years. Personalities aside, the significance of the election appeared to Woods as a definitive political realignment, produced by the birth of the third party. "A large body of citizens," claimed the *World*, "wants the privilege of voting for a party that stands unequivocally for . . . reforms." Republican reunification was impossible so long as discredited conservatives, forever tarnished by "financial rings . . . reaction and stagnation," remained in control.[23]

Before, during, and especially after the 1912 campaign, the *Wenatchee Republic* subjected Rufus Woods to venomous attack. Shifting to daily publication, the paper sought, as its only reason-for-being, the ruination of the *World*. Editor David Tewkesbury, dropping all pretense of journalistic objectivity, accused "our funny contemporary" of betraying Wenatchee and the Republican Party. Woods, charged Tewkesbury, had conspired to stuff Chelan County ballot boxes with fraudulent Roosevelt votes, thereby establishing himself as "either a rogue or a fool," not to mention "a loathsome wretch." John Gellatly's charge that Rufus had attempted to extort $5,000 from Miles Poindexter received front-page coverage. When the senator angrily denied the allegation, expressing complete confidence in his Wenatchee friend, Chelan County conservatives asserted that Representative William LaFollette of eastern Washington had been the real target of the extortion scheme. The accusation, an outrageous lie without any supporting evidence, presented the *Republic* with new dirty grist for its out-of-control mill.[24]

On April 30, 1913, Tewkesbury devoted two-thirds of his front page to an exposure of "The Sordid Motive of Our Strumpet Contemporary." Detailing again the purported attempt to corrupt LaFollette, the article also accused Woods of demanding payment from individuals and organizations accorded favorable coverage in the *World*. Rufus, concluded a horrified Tewkesbury, was a "brazen blackmailer" who had transformed a once-honorable newspaper into "a perverted thing," a "diseased publication" and a "chronicle of deliberate falsehood."[25]

Under continuous attack from the *Republic*, the *World* lost advertisers and subscribers and found itself on the brink of financial collapse. Woods, "hard up," had to resort to the "slow pay" method of handling personal and business debts. Desperate for cash, Rufus sold off his outside investments and procured loans from brother Ralph and mother-in-law Kate Greenslit. William H. Cowles, the publisher of the *Spokesman-Review*, loaned Rufus $5,000, taking 400 shares of *World* stock as collateral. The money, absolutely crucial to the survival of the paper, also placed the *World* under obligation to Cowles, a potentially compromising relationship should the interests of Wenatchee conflict with those of Spokane.[26]

Rather than concede defeat, Rufus fought back with a variety of subtle and effective strokes. The *World* responded only once to David Tewkesbury's allegations. Following publication of the "The Sordid Motive of Our Strumpet Contemporary" diatribe, Warren Woods, acting in the absence of his cousin, published a signed statement on the *World* front page. The charges of extortion made by the *Republic*, he claimed, had "besmirched" the Woods family "honor." Returning to town, Rufus demanded a retraction and joined Warren in threatening to sue the *Republic* for libel. Unfazed, Tewkesbury welcomed a lawsuit as an "opportunity to place on imperishable record in the perpetual archives of . . . Chelan county the character of Rufus Woods."[27]

Agreeing at first that a "war to the knife" was necessary, Ralph Woods prepared the necessary legal papers. Upon reflection, however, Ralph, whose deliberate manner of appraising events contrasted with his brother's impetuosity, was "sorry that the World published any threat." A lawsuit, he warned, would cause conservative Republicans to rally round Tewkesbury. Unless William Clark, the principal investor in the *Republic*, was personally responsible for the "Strumpet Contemporary" article, moreover, meaningful victory, in terms of monetary damages, was unlikely. (Ralph suggested that Rufus "smuggle some one in to the office of the Republic to swipe the original copy . . . to prove hand writing.") The prospect of one newspaper suing another for libel also established a dangerous precedent, potentially as harmful to the victor as to the loser. "If you have been damaged in any way," Ralph advised, ". . . all injury will have faded away within a short time."[28]

Following Ralph's advice to "meet the common enemy" indirectly, Rufus countered the *Republic* by discrediting its financial backer. In addition to irrigation, land, banking, and newspaper ventures, William T. Clark was general manager of the Fruit Growers' Association, an early experiment in the cooperative marketing of Wenatchee Valley apples. For the first time in the brief history of the local industry, orchardists experienced falling prices in 1912 and 1913. Blaming Clark personally for "a stagnation of business which never before has been equalled," the *World* called for his prompt dismissal. The man, after all, knew "little of the fruit business" and possessed "no other qualification to recommend him . . . other than that he is a promoter." Unspecified parties, reported Woods in a backhanded journalistic swipe, had accused Clark of "extravagance, secretiveness and arbitrariness."[29]

Another opportunity to undermine Clark's standing in the community arose from the problems of the high-line canal, Wenatchee's water link to prosperity. As the project developer, Clark failed to provide for maintenance of the canal. Leaks went unrepaired and hillside washouts occurred with increasing frequency. In the spring of 1914, Clark announced that customers of his Wenatchee Canal Company would have to assume the firm's fiscal obligations, currently estimated in excess of $100,000, and take over operating responsibility. Conceding that these measures were unavoidable under prevailing conditions, the *World* nonetheless accused Clark of attempting to "foist . . . unnecessary burdens" upon water users.[30]

While Gellatly, Tewkesbury, and other enemies thought only in terms of Wenatchee, Rufus realized that subscribers and advertisers were to be had outside of town. The *World* had always stood for development of the four North Central Washington counties, advocating such measures as the open Columbia River and the Quincy reclamation project. Challenged by the *Republic* in the metropolis, Woods placed new emphasis upon these and other region-wide concerns. Henceforth, stories about Wenatchee were banned from the front page, so that the space might be devoted to NCW matters.[31]

Instead of waiting for favorable reaction to the *World's* new policy, Rufus went after readers and advertising accounts. Beginning in 1912, he undertook regular tours of the upriver country, often spending weeks at a time away from Wenatchee. Negotiating on the first of these forays the "great line of terrible chuck holes" that passed for the Okanogan River highway, Woods called upon the small towns of that isolated valley: Brewster, Okanogan, Omak, Tonasket, and Oroville. In return for two-year subscriptions, he promised local business owners prominent and favorable coverage. The *World* also printed "special edition" supplements promoting each target community. The paper accorded similar treatment to other parts of North Central Washington, with "special editions" featuring such locales as the Methow Valley, Lake Chelan, and the Columbia River town of Entiat.[32]

The special editions, Rufus calculated of the vital dividends, each brought $800 to $1,000 profit in the form of subscription and advertising revenue. Reviled in Wenatchee, the *World* survived because of its hinterland appeal. By 1915, two-thirds of the circulation was outside town, the Okanogan Valley alone taking one-sixth of the total copies. Rufus improved the efficiency of his travel arrangements by outfitting an automobile with a portable typewriter, a primitive dictating machine, two cameras, and boxes of supplies. Heavily promoted by the *World* as its "Traveling Office," the Woods touring car garnered national publicity for the paper and for the hard-driving publisher.[33]

Despite energy and initiative, the *World* barely kept afloat amidst mounting financial pressure. Unpaid bills and angry creditors made the situation all but untenable. At an early stage of the *Republic* war, the Mergenthaler Company of New York vainly "insist[ed] on . . . immediate remittance" of payment overdue for a new Linotype machine shipped to Wenatchee. A rapidly deteriorating relationship between Woods and the Richmond Paper Company of Seattle, meanwhile, threatened the *World's* supply of newsprint. From 1912 onward, the firm complained of Rufus's "habitually delinquent" account. Future carloads of paper, it threatened, might be withheld or provided only upon a cash-on-delivery basis.[34]

Fully aware of the fact that the *World* would have to cease publication without a continuing supply of newsprint, Woods struggled to delay a final reckoning with his supplier. Throughout 1913, Richmond Company executives lectured him on the subject of commercial ethics. "Business," according to a typical hectoring letter, was "a game of confidence between the buyer and seller." Rufus countered that his promotional tours up the Columbia prevented him from promptly handling bills: "to spend my time raising money just now means that I am liable to sacrifice $2,000 or $3,000 worth of up river business." Richmond management finally demanded that the *World* and the *Republic*, another customer behind on payments, merge. Woods actually agreed to negotiate with William T. Clark, albeit only for the sake of appearances.[35]

Part way through the *Republic* war, tragedy struck the young family of Rufus and Mary Woods. In July 1913 their children, along with several other Wenatchee residents, died after drinking tainted milk from a local dairy. Despite round-the-clock attention from doctors and nurses, Wilma passed away on the 26th and Walter on the 31st. The despairing parents departed for weeks of aimless travel about eastern Washington, burdened by guilt. Mary, in particular, never recovered from the loss. She gave up music—previously a passion in her life—and was, for years, unable to bear any mention of Wilma and Walter. The rebuilding of the family, however, commenced in August 1914 with the birth of daughter Willa Lou.[36]

Despite economic woes, Woods had continued to purchase modern equipment. By nearly spending the *World* into bankruptcy, Rufus finally cast the *Republic* down in defeat. Unable to match him in the acquisition of modern equipment, the *Republic* at last ceased publication in July 1914. Woods sent a copy of David Tewkesbury's final issue, "a swan song that was a long time coming," to William Cowles, along with thanks for "the great personal favor" extended by the Spokane publisher in loaning $5,000. Rufus soon resumed cordial personal relations with William T. Clark, who admitted that he had lost $38,000 in backing the defunct newspaper. According to Clark, the combined losses of the minority investors exceeded $12,000.[37]

Woods survived the newspaper war because he could not afford to lose. With his resources tied up in the *World*, defeat meant personal ruin. Clark, in well-cushioned contrast, lacked the personal stake of his progressive opponent. Thanks to his other business enterprises, he lost *and* survived. The *Republic*, moreover, was a one-dimensional paper, devoted to the destruction of Woods. The *World* stood instead for positive things, reaching out to a region-wide audience with a pro-development message. It embraced new readers, while the Clark-owned daily repelled all who disagreed with editor Tewkesbury's negative creed. The *Republic* "spent considerable money," Rufus recalled in a later reflection upon his strategy. The *World* shrewdly "played its own game, made no mention of its competitor and as a result people . . . apparently did not know that there was another newspaper being published in Wenatchee."[38]

Heated to blistering intensity in 1912, political passions cooled rapidly, contributing to the redundancy of the *Republic*. For a time, the Republican Party appeared to have been permanently sundered. "Personally," observed Rufus Woods, "I can not think of a single Bull Mooser who wants to switch back to the G.O.P." Practical-minded Progressive and Old Guard leaders knew, however, that continued division insured further Democratic victories. The validity of this unhappy truism was confirmed in 1914 by the triumph, in a three-way race, of Spokane Democrat Clarence C. Dill in the new Fifth Congressional District. An accommodation allowing Republicans to reunify on the basis of mutual self-interest was obviously necessary, particularly at the local level.[39]

Because Dill, one of the few public figures Woods genuinely detested, was "a political accident," Rufus considered running for Congress as a Republican in 1916. The other prospective contenders for the nomination all resided in Spokane, suggesting that a North Central Washington candidate might win out over the divided vote in that city. Preparing to enter the race, Woods consulted members of Congress with backgrounds in journalism. Hoping for advice confirming his intention of serving in public office while continuing to personally run the *World*, Rufus learned that he would have to give up an active role with the newspaper. William Cowles, still holding stock in the *World* as collateral for his loan to Woods, raised a telling doubt: "I hope if you do decide to go in, that you will be able to get your newspaper organization so solid that the business will not go to pieces owing to your absence." Conceding that the debts left over from the *Republic* war made separation from day-to-day management unwise, Rufus abandoned his congressional ambitions.[40]

As far as Rufus Woods was concerned, his near-candidacy for Congress was the high point of the 1916 election year. At the national level, Theodore Roosevelt declined to run on a Progressive Party ticket, terminating that organization's brief existence as a serious factor in American politics. The *World* expressed considerable admiration for Woodrow Wilson, the Democratic incumbent. The new Federal Reserve System, plus the administration's policies on the tariff and trusts, appeared to reflect a reduction in the influence of the East over the West. Wilson's proclamation of neutrality in the European war, issued in August 1914, was "one of the noblest appeals of a national leader to his people recorded in history." Rufus Woods, however, could not forthrightly support a Democrat for president. Late in the campaign he endorsed, in the least enthusiastic terms possible, Republican nominee Charles Evans Hughes as "a man having definite principles."[41]

Commenting upon Wilson's narrow victory, Rufus placed a weary editorial finger upon the basic reason for his striking disinterest in the presidential election. The campaign had lacked "pep" and was, altogether, "apathetic." Personality, so dominant in preceding contests, was completely lacking in 1916. Woods mourned the absence of "Teddy, the alert, the expert" and missed the presence of Bryan, "the 'cross of gold' we cannot forget." These heroes of the past might rise again, or so Rufus fervently hoped, for the overall election results appeared to reflect an endorsement of reform. Miles Poindexter won a second Senate term in 1916 and so did Hiram Johnson in California. Looking ahead to 1920, Woods expected Poindexter, assuming that Roosevelt again kept to the sidelines, to secure the Republican nomination for the presidency.[42]

Nineteen sixteen was best regarded, according to Rufus, as an interlude between the colorful politics of the immediate past and the equally dramatic campaigns of the impending future. His own political interest, however, narrowed to a focus on issues of immediate material importance to North Central Washington, specifically to the development of the Columbia River. Dams and irrigation works were progressive measures, harnessing rivers previously flowing unused to the sea. Nature's wasteful habits gave way, under expert management of resources, to the public interest. The reform era came to an end, but the progressive movement persisted in the form of reclamation and power generation.

Sobering developments in his personal life also caused Rufus to concentrate more closely upon essential matters near to home. The deaths of Wilma and Walter delivered a well-hidden blow, covered by an outgoing personality and a tendency to avoid overt rumination about uncomfortable or disturbing private subjects. The children, lost to sudden and terrible illness, were mentioned in only a few letters and in none of the many autobiographical accounts published over the years in the *World*. Woods filed away the tragedy in a psychic pigeonhole, hidden from public view. He remained an extrovert, as prepared for fun as he was for work. Now, however, the broad smile and the glad hand masked a degree of inner emptiness.

Barely survived, the *Republic* war also led to a maturing process, suggesting that vision must be balanced by calculations of dollars and cents. This fundamental realization helped explain the newfound concentration on Columbia River development, a subject of definite regional importance. Emerging with new purpose from the turmoil of progressivism, Woods undertook the task, visionary and hardheaded, of building an empire.

# Chapter Four
## This Old Valley of Dry Bones

WHAT THIS SECTION OF THE STATE NEEDS AT THIS PAR-
TICULAR TIME IS AN EZEKIEL WHO CAN WAKE UP THIS
OLD VALLEY OF DRY BONES. . . . A FEW OF THOSE IN THIS
SECTION ARE TAKING A PASSING INTEREST—BUT AS A
RULE THE PEOPLE OF THIS PART OF THE STATE ARE AS-
SUMING THE ATTITUDE OF LETTING GEORGE DO IT.

Rufus Woods[1]

Rufus Woods-style progressivism hardly required a revolutionary upheaval, nationally or in the state of Washington. The primary, initiative, and referendum, after all, encouraged honest and efficient government. Rooseveltian conservation called for the ordered exploitation (as opposed to supposedly wasteful preservation) of natural resources. "We want to move forward," wrote Rufus on behalf of his reformist colleagues, ". . . but the most of us are not ready for a radical overthrowing of our present system of government." The challenge, posed in appropriately capitalized form, was to locate the "SANE, SENSIBLE, AND SAFE CHANNEL IN WHICH TO STEER THE SHIP OF STATE, WITHOUT LANDING HER EITHER ON THE SCYLLA OF RADICALISM, OR THE CHARYBDIS OF CONSERVATISM." Corporate greed must be fought, without hamstringing legitimate business enterprise. The genuinely downtrodden deserved assistance, but the indolent and irresponsible did not.[2]

Progressives, by the very moderation of their platform, found the return to the Republican fold a relatively painless experience. Woods had come to realize, moreover, that reform had built-in limitations and unanticipated consequences. By focusing too narrowly upon bigness alone as evidence of malfeasance, trust-busters made no distinction between criminal and ethical behavior, an oversight bound to retard economic growth and result in "killing the goose which lays the golden egg." The volatile nature of public opinion made the initiative and the referendum potential instruments of majoritarian tyranny. Through direct democracy, poorly conceived and fiscally burdensome laws might well be forced upon the minority of Washington voters who paid property taxes. Taxation was indeed a growing concern, as the *World* complained of the "surfeit of elections" and the "evil of over-legislation." In particular, Wenatchee Valley apple growers paid a heavy price for their prosperity in good years and suffered mightily from the annual tax levy in bad seasons.[3]

As a close student of the local economic scene—for *World* subscriptions and advertising depended, ultimately, upon the well-being of apple producers—Woods grew increasingly concerned with the need to limit government spending at all levels. The sharp and unexpected drop in prices paid growers during the 1912 season made a compelling argument for the need to reduce the burden on owners of property. Because forty cents of every tax dollar collected in the state went to schools, economizers demanded a cutback in spending on education. Rufus bemoaned the "lavish" rate of expenditures at Washington's institutions of higher learning. The various public colleges were managed in an entirely unbusinesslike manner. There was no sense, in one of many distressing examples cited by the *World*, for both the University of Washington and Washington State College to teach journalism. The normal schools at Cheney, Ellensburg, and Bellingham, moreover, ought to be consolidated at one location in the interest of economy and taxpayer relief.[4]

Unable to secure reductions in state spending, Rufus helped implement the economy-in-government philosophy at home in North Central Washington. Local officials, the *World* charged, had for too long engaged in "extraordinary extravagance." Overly zealous school boards, eager to spend other people's money, had "foist[ed] too high taxes on the taxpayers." Prospective homeseekers supposedly avoided settling in Wenatchee once they learned of the tax burden. Current residents by the score were supposedly ready to move away, needing only to find buyers foolish enough to purchase their homes. Pressed by the *World* and by delegations of irate citizens, the Wenatchee city council instituted a substantial budget reduction in 1915. Subjected to similar appeals, Chelan County cut its expenditures by 25 percent.[5]

Tax reduction, unfortunately, conflicted with another Woods preoccupation, road improvements. Under the existing system, annual revenue paid for all construction and maintenance in the state. Spending, inevitably, lagged far in arrears of the demand for modern highways. Chelan County roads, complained the *World*, were "inches deep with dust, [and] cut up by chuck holes." Apple growers struggled each fall with "heavy loads through the muck and mud" in order to reach the packing houses. The sorry condition of Route 10 between Wenatchee and Lake Chelan impeded settlement up the Columbia. Inadequate financing meant that the planned cross-state highways, one by Snoqualmie and the other by Stevens Pass, were years behind their originally scheduled dates of completion.[6]

Unwilling to sacrifice the good roads campaign in the name of cutting taxes, Rufus advocated a method that would provide both relief and modern highways. Addressing his readers on the subject of "How to Eat the Goose and Still Have It," he proposed that Chelan County issue bonds to finance road construction. Replacing the traditional "pay-as-you go" approach, the plan "allow[ed] future generations" to pay for "the improvements that of necessity have to be made." After years of editorial support in the *World*, local voters finally approved an $830,000 bonding measure in 1919.[7]

Making common cause with one-time conservative antagonists on the issue of spending, Rufus also worked toward a mutually beneficial truce with another longtime enemy. "The interests of the Great Northern and of the Wenatchee Daily *World*," he proclaimed in 1916, "are . . . almost identical." In a series of propitiatory gestures toward Wenatchee, the railroad had begun advertising regional tourist attractions, made a change in freight charges desired by local merchants, and revised its schedule to enable the *World* to provide same-day service to mail subscribers. The Great Northern also began work on its long-delayed branch up the Columbia to the Okanogan Valley. Completed in July 1914, the line had an immediate impact upon economic life in North Central Washington. Unable to compete with the railroad, steamboats went out of service, ending the era of commercial navigation on the upper Columbia. The daily freight and passenger trains out of Wenatchee, meanwhile, produced boom conditions in the formerly isolated towns of the Okanogan.[8]

Boom times in the Okanogan created new promotional opportunities for Rufus Woods. The Wenatchee hinterland was "an undiscovered country," he announced, "still in its infancy of development." The *World* supported the proposed thirty-two-mile-long railway tunnel under the Cascades, the prospective Methow Valley railroad, and the construction of electricity-generating dams at Rock Island Rapids and Chelan Falls. Business calculations justified journalistic efforts on behalf of these development objectives. Already, according to Rufus, most of the adults in North Central Washington read his paper on a regular basis. A substantial increase in circulation therefore depended upon future sustained growth in the region's population.[9]

The Quincy reclamation project was one attempt by Woods to promote the immigration of new settlers and subscribers. Another involved the opening to settlement of the vast Colville Indian Reservation, stretching from the north bank of the Columbia's Big Bend all the way to the Canadian border. Members of the resident tribes began receiving eighty acre allotments of land in 1906. Tracts left over at the conclusion of this process were to be transferred to the public domain, according to a schedule determined by the Bureau of Indian Affairs. Tired of waiting for the BIA to dispose of the surplus lands, Woods decided in 1914 to force the government into action. He placed advertisements in dozens of newspapers, magazines, and farm journals, offering special Colville editions of the *World* to persons sending in twenty-five cents. Rufus supplied the names and addresses of respondents to the Great Northern, which mailed its own promotional literature promising "homesteader rates" to land buyers. Representative Clarence Dill visited the reservation and posed for pictures on horseback. More interested in results than in publicity, Senators Miles Poindexter and Wesley Jones quietly pressed the Wilson Administration to open Colville to settlers. In May 1916 the Interior Department announced plans for a lottery to select the purchasers of lands supposedly unneeded by the Indians.[10]

Wenatchee was one of five communities selected as registration points for the July lottery. The Great Northern placed special trains into service and a traffic signal was installed in Blewett Pass to control the flow of automobiles crossing the Cascades. Every hotel in Wenatchee was filled to, and beyond, capacity and the town's restaurants ran out of food. Frantic persons, somehow convinced that being at the head of the line increased their chances, assembled outside the lottery headquarters. Twenty thousand individuals, in the final tally, signed up in Wenatchee alone for a chance at Colville land.[11]

Out of the 90,000 total registrants from all of eastern Washington, 5,500 apparently lucky persons were chosen for the right to locate homesteads on the acreage removed from the reservation. The Colville affair revealed both Rufus Woods's promotional flair and his tendency to exaggerate facts and ignore negative consequences. The *World* assured lottery entrants that "three-fourths of the land" opened to settlement was suitable for wheat or fruit production. "Vegetables of all kinds" supposedly already grew "in boundless profusion and to great size." In reality, most of the tracts opened to settlers were poorly watered or timber-covered and altogether ill-suited to agriculture. Moreover, his campaign cost the Colville tribes a large part of their reservation, lands that might someday have been of considerable value if retained in Native American ownership.[12]

In yet another conscious effort to promote the region's best interests, the *World* attempted to rationalize the apple industry. Rufus had once speculated in orchard properties, but in the aftermath of the *Republic* war he avoided personal involvement in the production or marketing of fruit. He was therefore in a distinct minority, for a local aphorism maintained that in Wenatchee business was "simply a side-line" for people otherwise engaged in apples. Self-interest nonetheless made Woods the leading booster and constructive critic of the region's vital economic activity. Accused by some readers of incessant "meddling," the *World* responded that "the prosperity of each institution of the valley is dependent almost wholly on the prosperity of the [fruit] rancher."[13]

Wenatchee district output tripled between 1910 and 1914, approaching the 9,000 carload export mark in the latter year. Although the mounting rate of production was initially thought to be a positive development, a number of problems became clearly evident. Varying conditions of soil and rainfall forced growers to constantly search for the best-adapted varieties of trees. Winesaps and Delicious were, by overwhelming majority, the current favorites, while Jonathans and other once-desirable varieties declined in popularity. In comparison to the Yakima Valley, which had diversified into other fruits and vegetables, Wenatchee was dangerously dependent upon a single crop, and only a few varieties of that crop. Expensive chemical sprays only partially curbed infestation by insects. Under the best conditions of weather, picking had to be completed within sixty days, a timetable overstraining the supply of labor. The lack of storage facilities forced orchardists to accept whatever price was offered, rather than hold apples for possible late-season increases. Some growers discarded their inferior and cull apples, but others concealed poor-quality fruit in shipments to unsuspecting customers, compromising the reputation of the entire industry.[14]

The growers' accurate forecast of a large crop of apples in 1912 nonetheless failed entirely to anticipate the dimensions of the disaster experienced by growers. Local production doubled in the same year that national orchard yields attained a level unmatched in a quarter century. Supplies mounted amidst a continuing long-term decline in the consumption of apples by the American people. The Wenatchee Valley Fruit Growers' Association failed to withstand the falling prices. The Yakima Valley, where producers were entirely unorganized, dumped fruit on an Eastern market already in the throes of collapse. Wenatchee orchardists, who had borrowed money and based other business decisions upon the expectation that prices would average between $1.25 and $1.50 a box, now faced the frightful prospect of actual per-box earnings of twenty-four cents.[15]

When not blaming the disaster on Association manager William T. Clark, the *World* devoted considerable space to serious analysis of the industry's underlying weaknesses. "Producing big, red . . . apples," Woods reminded forgetful readers, "is a business." The typical grower, however, acted the part of "the spoiled child" by relying upon and then blaming outside forces: "He simply ships his stuff to the middleman and then proceeds to curse said middleman because he does not compel the capricious public to take said apple and pay a fancy price." The genuine business person/ orchardist, in contrast, thinned and pruned trees to increase the proportion of high-quality fruit and joined other producers in setting standards and intelligently marketing the crop. The up-to-date grower also advertised, convincing consumers that sparkling apples from the Pacific Northwest, packed in colorfully labeled boxes, were a better buy than Atlantic coast varieties that were low-priced but bruised and sold out of barrels.[16]

Exercising his "persuasive powers and promises" to the fullest, William Clark retained control of the failing Growers' Association. A new organization, Pacific Fruit Distributors, attempted in the meantime to sign up 60 percent of the Northwest crop. The decentralized nature of the industry, however, obstructed formation of this joint sales agency. Only a sharp downturn in production kept the 1913 season from experiencing a repeat of the disaster of the previous year. The long-term prognosis appeared grim at best and suicidal at worst, especially with recently planted orchards reaching bearing stage. "The law of the survival of the fittest," advised the *World*, "will soon be invoked to settle the question of over production." The paper warned against the planting of more fruit trees in the Wenatchee Valley unless a sudden and near-universal conversion to the spirit of cooperation developed.[17]

The outbreak of war in Europe in August 1914 had a direct and initially negative impact on Wenatchee. The financial dislocations from the overseas conflict worsened an already-depressed apple season that year. Good times returned in 1915, however, as Allied demand for food, munitions, and loans stimulated the American economy and greatly improved market conditions for fruit. Chastened by their recent experiences, growers made a notable advance in what Woods termed the "Napoleonizing [of] the Northwest apple." Cheered on by the *World*, orchardists instituted a system of crop inspection and grading to limit the shipment of culls and low-quality fruit. Special assessments funded advertising campaigns in the major cities of the East. The Northwestern Fruit Exchange developed the Skookum brand name and acted as supplier and sales agent for farmers in the surrounding countryside.[18]

With his interests expanding beyond the parochial concerns of eastern Washington, Rufus Woods devoted considerable time to studying the war and America's relations with the belligerent powers. In the first weeks of the conflict, he applauded President Wilson's call for neutrality. The only foreign nations worthy of his admiration—Germany and England—were on opposite sides of the trenches. Still, Woods unhesitatingly blamed the outbreak of war on "the German Emperor and the imperialistic class . . . who support him." As a genuinely democratic society, Britain deserved the sympathy of the United States. Although pro-Allied, Rufus hoped to avoid active involvement in the fighting. "It is scarcely conceivable," asserted the *World* on August 14, 1914, "that any occasion might arise which would force this country into the general war in Europe." When peace came, America must be able to sit at the conference table as "an arbiter, without bias," placing its "firm will, broad views, justice and . . . large amount of common sense" in the service of international comity.[19]

Wilsonian in style and content, Woods abandoned these views upon the German declaration of submarine warfare against Allied merchant shipping in February 1915. One hundred and twenty-eight Americans died in the sinking of the *Lusitania* in May and U.S. citizens also perished in other U-boat attacks. Outraged, Woods demanded that the Wilson Administration prepare for war. Although Congress appropriated $685 million for defense in 1916, a sum greater than the entire federal budget for any year prior to 1911, Woods wanted even more money spent on recruiting a million-man army and on instituting universal military training. In a further instance of emotionalism on the part of its publisher, the *World* fell into the habit of questioning the patriotism of persons disagreeing with its views. The opposition to U.S. loans for the Allies, according to the paper, came from individuals "who call themselves Americans, but whose political sympathies are with Germany."[20]

In January 1917, Germany announced the resumption of unrestricted undersea warfare, previously suspended in response to the protests of neutral nations. Publication of the Zimmermann Telegram in February exposed the Kaiser's provocative meddling in Mexican affairs. Summoning a special session of Congress, President Wilson requested a declaration of war. Six senators and fifty House members, including Clarence Dill and William LaFollette of eastern Washington, voted in opposition. In a series of signed editorials, Rufus Woods specifically proclaimed Dill an embarrassment to "every red-blooded American" and a "near-traitor" to the United States. "May the Lord forgive this district," wrote Woods, "for electing to office a man so ignorant . . . unsafe, dangerous, [and] seditious."[21]

Already, intolerance dominated homefront America. In an earlier and more rational time, the *World* had preferred social justice to "spasmodic patriotism" as the best means of honoring the flag, and had denounced the Socialist Party only for its failure to endorse Theodore Roosevelt. Rufus Woods, along with Miles Poindexter and other leaders of the Washington reform movement, now demanded no-questions-asked loyalty to the government. "When a nation is fighting for its life," pronounced Rufus, "it cannot permit itself to be weakened by people who would paralyze its activities." There were but two classes of Americans, "those who are for the United States and those who are for Germany." Battling the trusts, progressives had viewed domestic affairs in good-versus-evil terms. The same absolutist tendency now animated the conviction that in a war to end all wars, nothing short of 100 percent Americanism would guarantee the triumph of truth and democracy over falsehood and imperialism.[22]

Woods also concerned himself with the war's benefits for North Central Washington. "Billions of dollars," he wrote, were going to be "shot away before this war ends." Most of these billions would be "expended in these United States and will be rolled about from one industry to another." Homefront spending provided Rufus with the opportunity to develop mineral deposits in the Cascades and bring industry to Wenatchee. On a visit to the nation's capital in October 1917, he met and fell under the spell of T.S. Elliott, the improbably named inventor of a revolutionary "Universal Compound" for welding copper and steel. Confident that this substance was "the kind of stuff that makes millionaires," Woods lobbied for contracts with the Army and the Navy and visited the headquarters of Bethlehem Steel in search of business.[23]

Hurrying home to make his millions, Rufus organized the Washington Chemical Company and acquired mining claims to supply raw material for the projected Wenatchee plant. Disastrous news soon arrived from the East: Elliott was the only person able to make the compound work and his claims were unwitnessed and obviously phony. Fortunately, Woods had rebuffed relatives and friends desiring to invest in the company. His own losses amounted to "about $1200 cash besides three months time." Worthless stock certificates remained as yellowing evidence of the failed speculation.[24]

Except for the sudden demise of the Washington Chemical Company, the local economy boomed in response to war demands, at home and abroad, for food. Despite rate increases and freight car shortages, growers had no difficulty finding buyers for their apples—from culls to extra fancy Winesaps—in 1917 and again in 1918. The latter year was "the most successful fruit season in the history of the Wenatchee district" according to the *World*'s accounting, with prices ranging between $2.50 and $3.50 a box. Apple earnings financed a number of manufacturing ventures. The Skookum Fruit Products Company was the first significant attempt to produce juice and other fruit by-products in Wenatchee. Woods, meanwhile, helped organize the Asbestomine Company, a producer of fireproof paint. The four-story plant, utilizing locally mined asbestos and silica deposits, marked, as the *World* stated, "the initial stages of . . . industry, correctly speaking . . . in Wenatchee."[25]

Prospering with the valley, the *Wenatchee Daily World* made what Woods called "a good clean up." Circulation reached 7,000 before newsprint shortages forced a cutback in both pages and subscribers. Profits allowed Rufus to retire the Cowles loan, freeing the editorial page of any influence from Spokane. Woods also bought another printing press. The *Anaconda Press* of Montana offered its Hoe press to Woods in 1918 "almost as a gift." Taking advantage of the opportunity, the *World* installed the Hoe in its basement, at a total outlay, freight included, of $2,500. The newspaper's technologically inferior Goss press was dismantled and sold for $5,000, a mere $500 below the original cost.[26]

"My business," Rufus wrote a relative in February 1918, "takes most of my time." He nonetheless had hours and energy enough left over to campaign, with mounting fervor, against any and all forms of homefront dissent. Individuals and organizations questioning America's war policies were guilty of "damnable . . . sedition." The condemnation applied to labor unions, including the mainstream American Federation of Labor. In particular, the radical Industrial Workers of the *World* deserved pariah status. Fearing an IWW strike in the orchards of the Wenatchee Valley, Woods advised growers to carefully screen pickers, so as to root out "agitators," and called for the creation of a state police force to intimidate the Wobblies.[27]

Preoccupied with the IWW presence in Wenatchee, Woods still sympathized with the problems of individual workers, especially those in the state's timber industry. In a July 1917 front-page editorial he addressed the issue of "Where Labor Has a Legitimate Kick." Recalling his own youthful, albeit brief, experiences in the logging camps of the Olympic Peninsula, Rufus maintained that laborers did, in fact, have legitimate grievances. After more than a decade and a half, he was still shocked by the danger, low pay, and living conditions he had encountered: "the bunk house[s] . . . were particularly vile." At most companies, showers and sanitation facilities were lacking and "the cooking . . . wouldn't do justice to a Kickapoo." These musings led to a conclusion applicable to current times. A great many employers "who think they are pretty good citizens," Woods pointed out, ". . . don't use even good sense when it comes to their treatment of the hired man." Workers, provided management was irresponsible, had every right to form unions and demand wage increases, shorter hours, and better accommodations.[28]

As it turned out, the timing, if not the sensible content, of this pointed editorial embarrassed Rufus. "Where Labor Has a Legitimate Kick" appeared literally on the eve of an IWW-led strike shutting down virtually the entire lumber industry of the Pacific Northwest. Beginning in the pine forests of eastern Washington and the Idaho panhandle, the walkout spread to the Douglas fir regions west of the Cascades in the second and third weeks of July. The basic Wobbly demand, the eight-hour day, was not exactly revolutionary in tenor or in impact, but the mill closure threatened, or at least appeared to threaten, the orderly flow of vital raw materials to the nation's defense effort. This aspect of the situation caused Woods to abandon the sympathetic tone just expressed in the *World* and to join employers in demanding government intervention to crush the strikers. "Labor agitators," he insisted, had "laid down conditions that it was absolutely impossible to meet." When the state of Washington attempted to arrange a compromise settlement, the *World* maligned Governor Ernest Lister's "halting, weak and generally unsatisfactory" performance in the crisis.[29]

Going back to work in the fall, the Wobblies adopted a "strike-on-the-job" slowdown as a more effective means of provoking the mill owners. Popular suspicion of organized labor, strikers, and dissenters, mounted with the success of the Bolshevik revolution in November. Russian communism, according to a thoroughly alarmed Rufus Woods, was "a much more deadly enemy" than Germany. The Germans would be defeated, sooner or later, but Bolshevism represented an insidious long-term threat to America, thanks in no small part to decades of unrestricted immigration from southern and eastern Europe. "We now have with us," wrote Woods, "men from European slums who . . . have wormed themselves into positions of power in labor unions." Together with native-born "rattle-brained college professors," the "riffraff" and the "off-scourings" of the Old *World* plotted the victory of the Kaiser as an immediate objective and, in the long run, the eventual triumph of Lenin's godless dogma.[30]

Considering the obvious danger to America, Woods insisted that all forms of opposition to the policies of the Wilson administration, even the mere expression of doubt, be crushed without regard to constitutional precepts. "Purveyors of sedition" in North Central Washington ought to be "tried by court martial and without ceremony . . . shot." With the enthusiasm usually devoted to better causes, Rufus endorsed all manner of supposedly patriotic acts. Individuals opposed to the war, if they could not be executed, should at least be deprived of the right to vote. Declaring an "open season" upon such miscreants, the *World* published the names of citizens refusing to buy Liberty bonds or contribute to the Red Cross. When the people of Cashmere painted a conscientious objector yellow, Woods approved the action. The victim was "a law abiding citizen, honest and unoffensive," but there was "no place . . . for the neutral" in wartime. The United States was "engaged in a holy cause and poor indeed is he who fails to perceive the GREAT UNSELFISH PURPOSE behind it all."[31]

Patriotism also necessitated the repudiation of "yellow office holders" at the polls in 1918. In particular, that most undeserving Democrat, Clarence Dill, must be defeated in his bid for a third term in Congress. *World* editorials denounced Dill as "a contemptible dirty cur" and a follower of the Kaiser. Although not himself a communist, the congressman had given aid and comfort to the underground conspirators against America. "Wherever you find a bolsheviki in this country," cried Rufus, "you invariably find a supporter of C.C. Dill." Instead of their votes, Wenatchee residents ought to give the incumbent "such a swift kick in his political parts that he won't recover till some time in the sweet by and by." Subjected to months of abuse from Woods and other editors, Dill lost to Republican J. Stanley Webster by 5,000 votes. On a visit to the *World* office after the election, Dill shook hands with Woods and, laughing, dismissed the campaign rhetoric as "just a dog-fight." Believing that a true American would have at least expressed anger, and probably resorted to fisticuffs over being called a traitor, Rufus was all the more appalled by Dill.[32]

In the final weeks of the red-white-and-blue election campaigns of 1918, Germany suddenly requested an armistice, bringing the war to an end. Forced by unexpected events into a consideration of "America's Duty in Peace," Rufus Woods had no doubt about the nation's proper course. The United States had preserved European democracy and defeated the Kaiser's attempt at imperial aggrandizement, but must now retreat to its traditional isolationist position, separate from and superior to the Old *World*. To be sure of avoiding unwholesome connections with its wartime partners—"which ultimately can mean only one thing . . . the absorption of our own independence"—the Wilson administration ought to immediately cancel the Allied war debt. "America—strong, virile America, whose abundant resources have scarcely been touched," argued Woods, "can lose every dollar that she has put into this struggle and scarcely feel it."[33]

As the leaders of the victorious powers assembled in Paris in early 1919, the *World* announced its opposition to the keystone of President Wilson's peace program, the proposed League of Nations. "In these days of parlor bolshevism and insipid internationalism," the paper noted, the idealistic impulse was to transform the wartime alliance into a means of resolving future disputes. The League philosophy, however, threatened the constitution and the very existence of the United States. With only one vote, America would be "obliged to participate in every war," even those opposed by its citizens or subversive of the national interest. Wilson's League was in reality "a *World* government" sure to be controlled by England and France, cynical powers happy to manipulate their naive North American ally.[34]

Rufus Woods was "a great fellow," an admirer once remarked, ". . . but ever[y] now and then he remembers that he is a Republican and seems to forget that Democrats also can do things." Once an admirer of Woodrow Wilson, Woods now found the President incapable of making sound decisions. At home, the Democratic administration had refused to allow Republicans, Theodore Roosevelt included, a part in the war effort, instead staffing defense agencies in debilitating partisan fashion. Abroad, Wilson, as the champion of the Versailles Treaty and the League of Nations, appeared to consider himself a messiah. Miles Poindexter and other Republican senators opposed U.S. membership in the League under the terms of the treaty, but the President refused to accept any revisions. In the aftermath of a stroke suffered while on a cross-country speaking tour in October 1919, he became even more intransigent. With no chance for a compromise, the Senate finally rejected the treaty in March 1920. A relieved Woods, convinced that a "bull-headed" Wilson had "set his personal will above . . . the laws," praised God as the entity ultimately responsible for seeing that the constitution provided for senatorial "advise and consent." The "mentally unbalanced" and "deranged" President was clearly unfit, physically and emotionally, for office and the Senate had acted responsibly to protect the "rights of 100,000,000 people."[35]

Homefront hysteria persisted in the form of the Red Scare of 1919. In Washington state, Woods followed the national example of Attorney General A. Mitchell Palmer, conducting his own campaign against suspect persons. The time had finally arrived, he announced, for retribution to be exacted upon those who had "failed this country in its hour of peril." Rufus endorsed the monitoring of public speakers by the Chelan County chapter of the American Legion. The refusal, on religious grounds, of a Russian immigrant colony to salute the flag was "a case of RELIGION GONE BUGHOUSE." The state should forcibly remove the children of the colonists "from the bonds of ignorance in which they live." The only thing wrong about the suspicious conviction of eight hapless Wobblies in Wenatchee, according to Rufus, was the fact that the jury required five minutes to render the guilty verdict.[36]

Woods himself became directly involved in the most dramatic event of Wenatchee's Red Scare. Founded in North Dakota in 1915, the Nonpartisan League called for public ownership of banks, grain elevators, and other enterprises blamed for the problems of rural America. The League rapidly gained support all the way to the Pacific Coast, where urban radicals and discontented farmers joined in forming a vigorous Washington chapter. Rufus might, under peacetime conditions, have sympathized with the organization, due to its condemnation of Eastern capital. By opposing the war, however, the Nonpartisan League became the evil twin of the IWW. The *World* regularly castigated national leader Arthur C. Townley, in jail for interfering with the defense effort, as a man "who showed up with the yellow streak when the country was at war." Chelan County friends of Townley complained, but Woods refused to repudiate his statements, demanding instead "a life sized apology" from all critics of the *World's* patriotic editorial stance.[37]

Ignoring a city council edict prohibiting the gathering, the Nonpartisan League convened an anti-*World* rally in Wenatchee in August 1919. Woods, in attendance as a reporter, challenged the speakers and, amidst considerable confusion, was struck over the head from behind. Knocked unconscious, he recovered in time to write the feature story on the incident for the next day's paper. Under the headline "League is Betrayed by Yellow Leaders," Rufus called the organization "the un-American division of the Socialist party" and charged his unknown assailant with cowardice.[38]

Despite its one-sided and brief nature, the Nonpartisan League affray reflected Rufus Woods's conviction that every town needed "a virile type of newspaper man." By reporting the news, provoking thought, and boosting the locality, the journalist served as "the throbbing heart of the average American community." The task was vital, the responsibility great, and the rewards often in the form of "knocks" rather than praise. "No class of people," claimed Rufus, "give more time and energy to matters pertaining to the general public welfare than does the . . . newspaper publisher." Based upon the concept that the well-being of society deserved first priority, progressivism drew new life via one significant wartime revelation. "A few years ago," Woods wrote in reflecting upon the armistice, "a project costing $1,000,000 would scare most everybody." In the course of the war, however, the United States had become accustomed to the idea of "shooting away the price of the Panama Canal every three weeks." Americans learned to think in big and expansive terms, a habit contributing to the rebirth of schemes for the large-scale reclamation of arid land east of the Cascade mountains.[39]

# Chapter Five
# The Land of Brobdingnag

WE OURSELVES ARE LIVING IN THE LAND OF
BROBDINGNAG. NOT BROBDINGNAG OF THE STORY BUT
IN REALITY THE LAND OF TREMENDOUS AND STRENU-
OUS PROJECTS—THE LIKE OF WHICH WOULD HAVE DE-
LIGHTED THE HEART OF NEBUCHADZEZZAR ... AN
IMMENSE RIVER IS TO BE DIVERTED ... TO THE THIRSTY
LAND. AND IT MAKES US LINK THE GULLIVER TRAVEL
STORY WITH THAT OF THE BIBLE WHERE IT SAYS, "AND
THERE WERE GIANTS IN THOSE DAYS."

*Wenatchee Daily World* [1]

AT THE END of the war Rufus Woods claimed that the opportune
moment had arrived for "MEN OF BRAINS, OF ENERGY AND
OF INITIATIVE" to attempt "the BIGGEST ENGINEERING FEATS
that have ever been undertaken." America's considerable and increasing
national wealth was once again available for productive investment. In a
special development series of articles published in the *Daily World* over a
two-week period, Woods called for the planting of alternative crops to
apples, the building of local industry, and negotiation of an interstate compact for utilizing the Columbia River drainage. The principal plank in this
program for regional growth was an enlarged version of the old Quincy
Flats scheme, taking in up to two million acres of land. The $250 million
cost, said Woods, was the same rate of expenditure required for "ten days'
warfare." A vibrant and forward-looking nation could easily afford to spend
such a relatively small amount of money in the interest of reclamation and
homes for worthy veterans and other citizens.[2]

After a decade of little or no rain, the countryside about Ephrata and Quincy was a parched scene of devastation. High winds blew away soil and seed. Even in the best seasons, when a few inches of precipitation fell upon thirsty crops, yields averaged only six bushels of wheat to the acre. Hundreds of families "that once farmed this land," reported one resident, "have pulled up and gone to, God knows where." Abandoned cabins and derelict windmills stood as sad monuments to failed dreams and broken homesteaders. Desperate people resorted to last-hope measures, including the expensive and ultimately unsuccessful importation of Charles Hatfield, America's most famous rainmaker.[3]

Settlers, with an understandably parochial view of such matters, believed that they had been betrayed by an indifferent federal government. In the early years of the century, the U.S. Reclamation Service had in fact studied the possibility of irrigating the Columbia Basin. One potential source of water, the Pend Oreille River, was summarily rejected on the basis of excessive cost. The government had printed a report on a potential Pend Oreille project, but in a press run so small that no person or agency in the state of Washington possessed a copy. Federal reclamation engineers, meanwhile, arbitrarily dismissed the alternative of storing water in the Grand Coulee. The lack of money and opposition from national farm organizations precluded serious response to the Big Bend drought on the part of the government. By default, local individuals and organizations assumed the lead in the fight for irrigation.[4]

Reclamation of the Big Bend, as a serious political cause, began in the depressed village of Ephrata. Country lawyer William Clapp, W. Gale Matthews, and other sweat-stained town leaders spent the summer of 1917 discussing the uncertain future of their region. The idea of building a dam on the Columbia at the mouth of the Grand Coulee had been proposed as far back as 1892. Clapp had also read studies by Professor Henry Landes of the University of Washington suggesting that an ice blockage had once diverted the river from its course, carving the great chasm. The lawyer suggested to his friends that nature's stupendous feat could be duplicated with construction of an 800-foot-tall dam, backing the Columbia up into Canada and providing the water for reclamation of a million-plus acres. Lacking any sophisticated engineering knowledge, the Ephrata group readily dismissed the technical difficulties inherent in the undertaking. Instead, they believed the primary obstacle would be political. "Our community is small and . . . without influence," worried Matthews, the owner of a local title company, and had virtually no chance of obtaining the proposed dam.[5]

In an autobiographical note, Rufus Woods recalled attending "about 1,000 meetings in this section of the state," the most significant being in Ephrata in July 1918. Arriving on one of his regular Traveling Office tours, Rufus called upon Billy Clapp and Gale Matthews for the latest news and gossip of the Columbia Basin. As Clapp outlined his Grand Coulee scheme, Woods began pacing back and forth within the narrow confines of the lawyer's tiny office. The lobbying organization thereafter known, with tongue-in-cheek affection, as the Dam University emerged from this casually arranged get-together. James O'Sullivan, a well-traveled and supposedly multi-talented promoter hoping to recoup a bad investment in land near Moses Lake, signed on at the urging of Rufus. So also did Clapp, Matthews, attorney W.E. Southard, and others from North Central Washington. The *Daily World*, because of its enthusiastic publisher and region-wide circulation, became the University's public relations arm.[6]

Returning to Wenatchee, Woods broadcast his newest and most enduring enthusiasm in the *World* on July 18, 1918. "First conceived by William Clapp," the proposed Grand Coulee dam was "the last, the newest, the most ambitious idea in the way of reclamation and . . . water power ever formulated." Considering the complete lack of technical evidence for this breathtaking assertion, the dimensions of the project were necessarily vague. "The height of the dam," according to Woods, "will approximate several hundred feet." A "practically unlimited" supply of water, meanwhile, would make possible the irrigation of between one and two million acres of land south and east of the coulee. The scheme's origin among promotion-minded visionaries, rather than among professional engineers, accounted for the innocent faith of the *World* article. "The . . . outstanding feature of the project is its immensity," concluded Rufus. "And . . . there seems to be no feature to make it an unworkable plan."[7]

Although lacking in specific detail, the *Daily World* account introduced Grand Coulee Dam to the public as a North Central Washington project. Grant County engineer C.W. Duncan issued the first expert commentary in late November. After "a hasty reconnaissance," Duncan recommended construction of a spillway 550 feet tall, "a dam . . . without precedent as to height and volume." The project was feasible from an engineering standpoint, reported Duncan, but considerable work remained before such vital matters as overall cost and exact location of the damsite could be determined. Because pumps would be required to lift water from the impounded Columbia River, the Grand Coulee scheme immediately became known, to friend and to foe, as the pumping plan.[8]

Between the publication of the Woods article and the submission of Duncan's report, E.F. Blaine, a longtime leader of the Washington irrigation movement currently in state employ, resuscitated the pre-war Bureau of Reclamation study of the Columbia Basin as an alternative to Grand Coulee. Under the gravity plan, water diverted from the Pend Oreille River at Albeni Falls on the Idaho border would be channeled to the Big Bend through some 130 miles of canals, tunnels, aqueducts, and reservoirs. In contrast to Grand Coulee, which depended upon electricity to run its pumps, the proposed Albeni Falls dam produced no power. Taking up Blaine's idea, the Spokane Chamber of Commerce secured the loan of engineers from the Washington Water Power Company to refine the proposal.[9]

Sponsors of each plan enjoyed particular advantages and faced specific obstacles. Rufus Woods, utilizing promotional talents honed over the years in various political and economic development campaigns, kept Grand Coulee constantly before the public. Editorials from the *World*, the only daily east of the Cascades supporting the dam, were regularly reprinted by the weekly newspapers of North Central Washington. This created an extensive network for the mobilization of opinion in a time when the printed word was far and away the principal means of circulating the news. Rufus also used his many personal friends in the four-county area to organize meetings, write letters, and raise funds. James O'Sullivan, meanwhile, quickly developed a devotion to Grand Coulee so pure and fanatical as to justify any means necessary for the securing of construction. No one else was willing to work for little or no remuneration. Together, Woods and O'Sullivan were the acknowledged leaders, for better or for worse, of the Dam University.

Contemporary interest in developing the Columbia River and in expanding regional energy production attracted serious attention to the Grand Coulee proposal. There were no dams on the river, as of 1920, and but a single power plant, a small facility operated by an irrigation company. The Stone and Webster trust, however, had plans ready for a $20 million dam at Priest Rapids. The Washington Water Power Company planned to build an even more costly structure at Kettle Falls, the ancient Indian fishing station close to the Canadian border. Demand for electricity was especially notable on the Pacific Coast, with per capita consumption at 50 percent above the national rate, providing the rationale for these and other projected undertakings. The increasing importance of hydroelectricity worked to the obvious advantage of Grand Coulee, since surplus energy from the pumping system could be sold on the open market, subsidizing construction and reducing the financial burden on water users.[10]

Blessed by the electricity connection, the Dam University still had to overcome considerable problems. Jim O'Sullivan habitually misrepresented facts, alienating individuals vital to the success of the dam and often doing more harm than help to the cause. Grand Coulee, moreover, lacked substantial support in the city most likely to benefit from construction. In 1919 Stone and Webster purchased the bankrupt Wenatchee Valley Gas & Electric Company and incorporated it into the operations of the Seattle-based Puget Sound Power & Light Company. The Wenatchee business establishment thereafter accorded Puget Power, which opposed Grand Coulee, the fawning devotion previously reserved for the Great Northern Railway. Grand Coulee's sheer magnitude, while thrilling to contemplate, was another weakness. The structure was taller, by far, than the biggest dam in existence, a fact readily exploited by the project's enemies. The inevitable collapse of the giant and obviously unstable dam would release floodwaters of mega-Johnstown volume to carry away farms, reclamation works, and entire towns. Washington's population was supposedly too small to ever absorb the huge amount of electricity to be generated under the pumping plan. Instead of subsidizing irrigation, argued the critics, Grand Coulee was sure to become a worthless drain upon taxpayers and settlers.[11]

Advocates of the Albeni Falls alternative, meanwhile, coped with their own vexing obstacle. The gravity plan, as first conceived, provided for storage of 3.6 million acre-feet of water in Idaho and Montana. Those states, to the consternation of Spokane, opposed the necessary raising of Pend Oreille and Flathead lakes. Idaho law prohibited the grant of water rights to non-residents, explicitly conflicting with an essential component of the plan. Albeni Falls backers complained of the selfishness exhibited by their neighbors to the east in refusing to accept, for the greater regional good, the flooding of towns, farms, highways, and railroad lines. Barring conclusion of an interstate compact dealing with utilization of the Columbia River drainage, reclamation via the gravity approach was, for all practical purposes, stymied. In uncomplicated contrast, Grand Coulee stored water only within the confines of the state of Washington.[12]

In the end, delays forced in part by the dispute over storage enabled the growing demand for energy in the Northwest to become a definitive argument in favor of Grand Coulee. At the outset, however, the lack of electricity at Albeni Falls was a source of strength, bringing to the project the support of the private utility industry in general and of the Washington Water Power Company in particular. Generating half the energy consumed east of the Cascades, Washington Water Power endorsed reclamation as an obvious means of increasing settlement and expanding business. But it opposed construction of competing hydroelectric projects. Preparing detailed construction plans for the gravity system, the firm's engineers deliberately left generators out of the Albeni Falls design. Working in close alliance with the Spokane Chamber of Commerce, the company secured support for the Pend Oreille dam from Puget Sound business leaders and transcontinental railroads, forming a powerful lobbying coalition.[13]

To much of the public, both plans for building the Columbia Basin Irrigation Project appeared to be the work of real estate speculators intent upon inflating land values and swindling unsophisticated purchasers of desert estates. Conceived at the local level, Grand Coulee and Albeni Falls were so monumental in scope and cost, variously and uncertainly estimated at between $100 and $300 million, that only the federal government could afford their construction. Unfortunately, the United States Reclamation Service expressed no interest in either project. Senator Wesley Jones, who might under other circumstances have worked aggressively on behalf of federal involvement, feared that he would antagonize influential constituents by favoring one or the other proposal. Despite prodding from both the Dam University and Spokane, Jones failed to advance his bill for a Reclamation Service study of the Columbia Basin to the floor of the Senate.[14]

Officials in Washington state, anticipating the Senator's failure, assumed the initiative. Responding to a proposal submitted by Governor Ernest Lister, the legislature established the Columbia Basin Survey Commission in 1919, appropriating $100,000 for necessary work. Grand Coulee supporters briefly, and innocently, expected the commission to make an objective examination and eventually endorse their plan. State hydraulics director Marvin Chase, a longtime friend of Rufus Woods, was, after all, the chairman. Chase, moreover, asked the Reclamation Service to assign an expert observer, D.C. Henny, to aid in the task. Henny was "the best engineer in the west" according to Billy Clapp and unlikely to approve anything but a fair and scientific appraisal.[15]

Chase, however, was only nominally in charge of the commission, which operated out of offices in Spokane. Henny had other Reclamation Service assignments to fulfill and, for the most part, observed from afar. The four commissioners appointed in addition to Chase either lived in

Spokane or, like Professor O.L. Waller of Washington State College, in communities dominated by that city. The Washington Water Power Company employed chief engineer Arthur J. Turner and other members of the professional staff prior to and after their work with the state. Commissioners and staffers alike viewed their real task as one of preparing an official justification of the gravity plan. Publicity director Fred Adams admitted to being "very luke warm" and unable to "get up any enthusiasm" on the subject of Grand Coulee. The supposedly exhaustive survey failed, as Waller conceded, to develop "a plan of procedure" for building the dam. Attending commission meetings when possible, D. C. Henny quickly concluded that the entire undertaking was a sham, controlled in the interest of Spokane.[16]

Unable to secure a serious hearing, the Dam University devised its own publicity to counteract the commission. James O'Sullivan drafted articles, editorials, and public letters for the *Daily World*. His own study of the rival projects, claimed O'Sullivan, provided absolute, if totally undocumented, proof that the basin could be watered from Grand Coulee at a substantially cheaper cost than by the gravity alternative. The "solid rock bottom and massive basalt walls" of the Columbia River made a superb dam foundation, sufficient to support a structure 600 feet high. Nature, moreover, had conveniently "blasted" a "great canal" in the form of the Grand Coulee. Electricity generation at the dam "would cut the Gordian knot" by reducing the financial burden on settlers. The pumping plan also had, according to O'Sullivan, enormous statewide implications. The dam guaranteed Washington's advancement to the first rank in manufacturing, while a reclaimed Columbia Basin automatically placed the state on an "equal footing with California" in terms of agricultural importance.[17]

Rufus Woods endorsed these "remarkable" findings. The original idea, Rufus admitted, was "so stupendous . . . that one hardly dared to discuss the matter seriously." O'Sullivan's painstaking investigations had now produced an impossible-to-refute case on behalf of Grand Coulee, a case sure to result in construction. Irrigation and electricity would together revolutionize North Central Washington, at least according to a heavily emphasized Woods outburst: "*SUCH A POWER . . . WOULD OPERATE RAILROADS, FACTORIES, MINES, IRRIGATION PUMPS, FURNISH[ING] HEAT AND LIGHT IN SUCH MEASURE THAT ALL IN ALL IT WOULD BE THE MOST UNIQUE, THE MOST INTERESTING, AND THE MOST REMARKABLE DEVELOPMENT . . . IN THE AGE OF INDUSTRIAL AND SCIENTIFIC MIRACLES.*"[18]

Nonetheless, the official survey report of 1920 dismissed Grand Coulee as an inviable enterprise. On the basis of guesswork and wishful thinking, the commissioners rejected the pumping plan for three reasons: there was no foundation for a dam anywhere near the Grand Coulee, no market for the power, and no prospect of Canada agreeing to restrictions upon its right to freely navigate the Columbia, supposedly guaranteed by the 1846 Northwest boundary agreement between the United States and Great Britain. Summarily consigning Grand Coulee to an apparently well-deserved fate, the report delivered a wholesale endorsement of the gravity plan. Its cost of $300 million was a reasonable expenditure considering the intent to irrigate 1.7 million acres of the Columbia Basin. The commission had, at least to its own satisfaction, fully resolved all technical matters and now looked forward to construction, provided a single remaining obstacle could be overcome. "The only question," wrote Professor O.L. Waller from his campus office, "is that of where the finances are to come from."[19]

Waller, of course, knew that the funding must come from the federal government, a realization that explained the commission's emotional reaction to a bizarre episode. Visiting Washington state in September, Reclamation Service Director Arthur Powell Davis agreed, at the behest of James O'Sullivan, to make a hurried visit to the Grand Coulee. In brief off-the-record remarks at the damsite, he commented favorably, if noncommittally, upon the plan's engineering features. O'Sullivan immediately wrote an overwrought account in the *Daily World*, claiming that Davis had thrown off his "red bandana neck scarf" in excitement and declared "emphatically that the construction of the proposed dam on the Columbia River . . . is perfectly feasible from an engineering standpoint." To Rufus Woods, who expressed skepticism prior to running the article, O'Sullivan affirmed that this forthright endorsement had been made "over and over again."[20]

Reprinted in a number of eastern Washington newspapers, the article set the Reclamation Service at odds with the state of Washington. Outraged officials demanded that Davis repudiate the supposed endorsement and upbraided him for participating in "a well planned effort . . . to discredit the Commission." Equally furious, the Reclamation Service director claimed that the *World* had published the account "without my knowledge or consent" and had irresponsibly magnified "casually mentioned . . . impressions" into a full-fledged statement of support. For his part, O'Sullivan blamed Davis for failing to speak with proper discretion. "I assumed," O'Sullivan told Woods, "that when he stated to me that certain statements were confidential that the other statements made so freely and unreservedly were for publication."[21]

Early on, Senator Jones had warned the survey commission of the dangers of a report unlikely to be "accepted by the United States as official." Belatedly acting upon this advice in the aftermath of the Davis affair, the state requested that a panel of federal engineers review its report. In December 1920, D.C. Henny, who had just been offered the job of building Grand Coulee by O'Sullivan, and two Reclamation Service colleagues delivered a major blow to Albeni Falls. The commission, they reported, had underestimated the cost of the Pend Oreille diversion and exaggerated the expenditure required for Grand Coulee. Pending a thorough investigation of the Columbia River dam, including genuine tests to determine foundation conditions, the board advised against government involvement in either proposal.[22]

Given the peculiar nature of the extant Columbia Basin report, this was a sensible recommendation, calculated to produce a final decision based upon factual observation. The survey commission nonetheless accused the engineers of unprofessional conduct and demanded Henny's removal as representative of the Reclamation Service. Following upon the Davis visit, the December review confirmed suspicions in Olympia and Spokane that the federal government, not the state, was biased in favor of the pumping plan. "Nearly all of the active Columbia Basin boosters," wrote one observer, ". . . believed the Reclamation Service to be prejudiced against, and . . . actively unfriendly to the . . . [gravity] Project." Practical circumstances, however, required that Henny's recommendation, no matter how offensive, be followed. The state legislature therefore responded with an appropriation of $50,000 for the requested Grand Coulee study.[23]

Controlling this fund as the successor agency to the functions of the now-defunct Columbia Basin Survey Commission, the Department of Conservation and Development intended to produce anything but an honest examination. In July 1921, the department named Willis T. Batcheller, a Seattle consulting engineer, to lead the investigation, at a fee of $25 per day plus expenses. According to the terms of his contract, Batcheller would examine the means and cost of transmitting power from a Grand Coulee dam. At the urging of D.C. Henny, the assignment was informally broadened to embrace the survey of alternative damsites, as well as certain other tasks unspecified in the surviving record. In a significant confidential aside, with Henny absent, Batcheller was orally instructed "to turn in an adverse report" on all questions likely to interfere with implementation of the gravity plan.[24]

Willis Batcheller, a prickly individual considered to be an extraordinarily capable and honest man, was, for the state, a most inappropriate appointee. Taking full advantage of the unofficial latitude allowed his operations, Batcheller had absolutely no qualms, as one official complained, about ignoring the interests of "those who employed and paid him." Finding Grand Coulee superior in both cost and feasibility to the gravity plan, he focused upon this finding in a 400-page draft report and in unauthorized speeches and newspaper interviews. The state response was decisive, if too late: it fired Batcheller in February 1922 and locked away all copies of his report in an Olympia safe. The information gathered, ordered Conservation and Development Director Dan Scott, must never "be permitted to reach either the public or [the] technical press for any purpose whatsoever."[25]

Gravity plan advocates were indignant, if somewhat compromised by their own less-than-honest behavior. The Department of Conservation and Development accused Batcheller of ignoring instructions, violating ethical standards, and even of embellishing "his name . . . in gold letters" on the spine of the report. Batcheller, claimed state engineer Ivan Goodner, had "faked up maps" and "prostituted his ability" in return for "secret compensation" from the Grand Coulee camp. Director Scott threatened a lawsuit and besmirched the professionalism of his former consultant. Scott, Goodner, and the others knew, however, that their damage control operations were insufficient, for Batcheller's findings were well known to all interested parties, including Henny of the Reclamation Service.[26]

At this embarrassing moment, the state of Washington diverted the remaining funds intended for Batcheller's work to yet another ill-timed master stroke in artless public relations. It engaged General George W. Goethals, the retired military engineer famed for completing the Panama Canal, to render the definitive verdict on reclamation of the Columbia Basin. The Spokane Chamber of Commerce also provided part of his $25,000 fee, along with the promise of employment as director of construction at Albeni Falls. Although he had been stationed on the upper Columbia as a young officer, the general knew little of the river and absolutely nothing about irrigation. Goethals was, in reality, engaged on the basis of his name, rather than for non-existent qualifications. He was expected, as one state official privately admitted, to "declare the [Albeni] project . . . feasible."[27]

The state certainly received little actual engineering work. Goethals spent less than two weeks on the scene, most of that in private conference with former members and employees of the survey commission. More than satisfying expectations, the general's report, issued in March 1922, recommended immediate construction of the gravity project. He pegged the cost, in a significant reduction from previous estimates, at $254 million. The pumping plan required even less money, the report advised, but reclaimed a much smaller acreage and therefore merited rejection. Besides, asserted Goethals on the basis of conversations with private utility executives, there was no "prospective market" for Grand Coulee electricity.[28]

Backers of the Columbia River dam immediately subjected Goethals to ridicule. The general had relied upon "faulty data furnished him by the [Washington Water] Power Company," stated Jim O'Sullivan, and, as a result, his study had "no value." On the basis of information from confidential sources in Olympia, Rufus Woods charged that Goethals had merely signed his name to a report written by state engineer Ivan Goodner. The gravity forces, said Rufus in a *World* column, were responsible for "the greatest hoax ever perpetrated on the people" of Washington.[29]

Dismissing Woods and O'Sullivan as sour grapes critics, Olympia and Spokane insisted that Goethals had delivered the final word on the rival plans. "The Grand Coulee site has been rejected," claimed Ivan Goodner, "and will not be given further consideration." The state, unfortunately, could not ignore the fact that Reclamation Service engineers agreed with the critique of the *Wenatchee Daily World*. The reduced cost estimate for the gravity plan, according to a confidential federal analysis, was based upon a figure of forty-eight cents an acre for annual operation and maintenance, an "absurd" calculation when the likely requirement was $2.70 an acre. In light of current trends in electricity consumption, Arthur Powell Davis termed the general's disbelief in a market for power "startling" and his reliance upon the utility companies intellectually suspect. Goethals recommended construction of the entire reclamation project at once, rather than unit-by-unit, but declined to reveal how enough qualified settlers could be recruited to take up the land. Privately, Reclamation Service personnel mourned the corruption of a revered colleague.[30]

A contemporary study, meanwhile, provided solid support of Grand Coulee. Appointed by the Federal Power Commission, a panel chaired by Colonel James Cavanaugh of the Army Corps of Engineers examined the question of developing the upper Columbia River in the combined interest of irrigation and electricity generation. Cavanaugh's illness resulted in

D.C. Henny, another of the panelists, writing the final report, released in June 1922. Ignoring the state's claim that Goethals had spoken "the last word necessary in the matter," Henny dealt at length with Grand Coulee. "Conditions for . . . construction may be regarded as unusually favorable," he wrote on behalf of Colonel Cavanaugh, basing this finding upon testimony from Willis Batcheller. The riverbed foundation was solid, the necessary pumping technology available, and more land than previously envisioned might be reclaimed. Even so, further investigation, including an in-depth examination of trends in electricity consumption, was necessary before "dependable estimates of cost" became feasible. Utilization of the Columbia, the Grand Coulee site in particular, for reclamation and energy production was inevitable, the FPC determined on the basis of Henny's work, but development must wait until an unknown future time, to be determined by the interplay of circumstance and planning.[31]

For the remainder of the decade, federal engineers followed the delay-and-study recommendation of the Federal Power Commission. Progress on reclamation, whether by gravity or by pumping, stalled on account of lack of interest in the nation's capital. Organized in June 1922, the Columbia Basin Irrigation League led a frustrating lobbying effort on behalf of Albeni Falls. The League, region-wide in membership, was headquartered in Spokane, sponsored by the local chamber of commerce, and funded in large part by the Washington Water Power Company. It spent much of its time in frustrating efforts to resolve the dispute over storage of water in Idaho and Montana. The Dam University lost all headway. James O'Sullivan moved to Michigan in search of a means to support his family and Rufus Woods temporarily shifted focus in response to a multitude of political, journalistic, and personal concerns.[32]

Columbia Basin legislation had no chance of passage in the face of continued opposition in Congress and in the federal bureaucracy. Eastern senators and representatives generally opposed reclamation on economy-in-government grounds. Western members, meanwhile, took pro- or con-positions depending upon whether or not specific projects were located in their districts. Crop prices fell and farm surpluses increased during the 1920s, to the extent that the Grange and other politically influential agricultural organizations fought all proposals intended to bring additional land into production. The Bureau of Reclamation, so renamed in 1923, devoted its energies to planning Boulder Dam on the Colorado River. "All that the friends of the Columbia Basin . . . are asking," complained the *Spokane Spokesman-Review* in bemoaning the lack of progress in developing the interior Pacific Northwest, "is a square deal." The problem was that the state of Washington had in the past dealt a crooked hand, compromising Grand Coulee and especially Albeni Falls with the Bureau and with Congress.[33]

Common aims and methods linked the pre-war progressive movement with the post-1918 campaign for a dam on the Columbia River. Grand Coulee was, in a literal concrete sense, progressivism poured into a stupendous framework of reclamation and power generation. The project perpetuated the Theodore Roosevelt faith in conservation as the intelligent utilization of natural resources. The Columbia currently flowed into the sea, its massive volume wasted so far as industry and agriculture were concerned. Rufus Woods saw the stream as an inexhaustible form of "white coal," ready to be harnessed for intensive economic development. Other regions had exploited their mineral and timber wealth in ruinous fashion, but Washington faced a different prospect, at least under careful management. "Our heritage of water power," asserted Woods, "will remain without depletion for thousands of years in the future and then some."[34]

River development made possible a sustained material yield for farms and factories dependent upon water and electricity. Reclamation lifted up the common man and woman, denied access to opportunity by the closure of nature's frontier. "The days of the free homestead have passed," the *World* pointed out. "Henceforth the American people must make their soil by irrigation." The pumping plan sought in the Columbia Basin a freeholding commonwealth independent of corporate influence, balancing agriculture and industry. A Columbia Basin Project based upon Grand Coulee was a sound public investment, an efficient and wealth-generating usage of taxpayer funds. Unlike navigation works and other expensive federal undertakings, which returned nothing to the U.S. treasury, reclamation paid for itself in the form of payments made by settlers. "If we could just have a little of the money that is sunk in the rivers and harbors," noted the *World*, ". . . my, what a country this west would be!"[35]

Fully convinced of the benefits of Grand Coulee, Rufus Woods had yet to resolve a major question. Only the federal government could finance construction of Grand Coulee, but the proper disposition of the completed dam remained open to debate. The Bureau of Reclamation might operate the project, producing and marketing electricity. Grand Coulee could also be leased or sold, perhaps to a reclamation district or even to the Washington Water Power Company. Here the pumping plan intersected with an emotional issue of Washington state politics. In the early years of the twentieth century, municipal plants in Seattle and Tacoma had demonstrated the value, in terms of reduced rates, of publicly owned generating facilities. Urban reformers and the Grange now sought to extend public power to all regions of the state, in the process wrecking the private utilities.[36]

On this issue, Woods was caught betwixt-and-between. His fear of corporate domination, transplanted from Nebraska to the Pacific Northwest, was undiminished. Although "somewhat afraid of getting into the grip of the big power companies," he also questioned the need for public utilities. The nation and the states might, in keeping with progressive tenets, make laws regulating capital, but to go beyond this socially necessary interference with the rights of property exposed American society to what Rufus termed "the vortex of . . . socialism." Experience demonstrated beyond reasonable doubt that "the government had better keep out of business." Public utilities, moreover, paid no taxes, imposing an extra burden on the owners of nonexempt properties and providing an apparently unfair advantage in the competition with private power.[37]

Rival measures before the voters in the 1924 general election forced Rufus to confront these divided sentiments. One referendum, written by Tacoma Representative Homer T. Bone, authorized municipal utilities to sell energy outside city limits. The other, drawn by Republican House leader Mark Reed, allowed such sales, but imposed a tax on the earnings of publicly owned plants. Opposed alike to big corporations and to intrusive government, Woods welcomed the defeat of both bills. Reed's version, while addressing the problem of tax-free municipal enterprise, did so, in his view, by imposing an excessive rate of taxation designed to throttle the expansion of public power altogether. The Bone alternative, meanwhile, was nothing but a "flim flam" proposition, promising inexpensive electricity and compelling "the man who owns his home" to pay higher property taxes. Bone's bill produced free power only in the sense "that it provides for an entirely too free use of the people's money."[38]

How to provide a sufficient supply of energy without becoming the victim of private utility avarice remained, at least for the time being, a fundamental and unanswered question. "We are inclined not to be greatly scared about this bugaboo talk about 'monopoly,'" wrote Rufus in October 1924, since popular opinion as shaped by watchdog newspapers like the *World* provided a guarantee against abuse. "Public sentiment," he asserted, ". . . can take a great big octopus, or a dozen octopi and simply lambast the daylights out of them all at once and at the same time." Placing his faith in the ability of concerned citizens to keep the corporations honest, Woods avoided explaining how Grand Coulee would be run in the aftermath of its construction. He also avoided dealing with the prospect that federal financing might entail federal ownership and management.[39]

# Chapter Six
# The Good, the True, and the Beautiful

For years it has been the hope of the publishers of the Daily World that in this city should be builded a newspaper which would be received in every family of the community with the knowledge that in its columns could be found those things which make for the good, the true and the beautiful and that as much as possible there should be suppressed those things which encourage the low, the mean and the contemptible.

*Wenatchee Daily World* [1]

O N A NOVEMBER evening in 1921, Rufus Woods climbed to the roof of Wenatchee's new six-story hospital and looked out upon a prosperous city. Through the haze of early winter chimney fires, the electric lights of the "little White Way" central business district illuminated Wenatchee Avenue and Mission Street. Beside the near bank of the Columbia, the loading of apples aboard Great Northern freight cars proceeded at the frenzied beat-the-freeze pace typical of the valley's annual defining rite. In the residential areas, trees planted a decade and more before had reached maturity, providing welcome shade in summer and a bright tone in fall. Thinking back to the rocks, the dust, and the tarpaper shacks of the early century, Rufus worried for a moment that the scene before his eyes was only a vision. "I pinched myself to see if I were dreaming—only dreaming," he wrote the next day in the *World*. "But I was not. And sez I to myself, sez I: 'Old Boy, this is Wenatchee—By George—WENATCHEE!'" [2]

With the first stage of the fight for Grand Coulee over, for the remainder of the 1920s Rufus Woods was preoccupied with matters having little to do with the dam. He suffered repeated political disappointment, managed the *World* to new prosperity, and fought, as in the past, for the advancement of North Central Washington. On a personal level, the birth of Wilfred in 1919 and Kathryn in 1921 completed the family of Rufus and Mary. Willa Lou, "naturally . . . precocious," joined her younger siblings in "play . . . the whole live long day." Wilfred, nicknamed "Old Timer," drew special attention, at home and among friends of his parents, for more than the usual number of childhood scrapes and for struggles with the rules of proper pronunciation.[3]

After years devoted to the art of fending off angry creditors, the *Daily World* emerged from debt in 1920. "Indications are that this . . . business will come near making us wealthy," Rufus informed a relative. He expected, at the least, to be "collecting interest instead of paying it" in the future. In addition to a favorable balance sheet, the *World*'s growing reputation for sober content well-suited to family reading was a source of pride. Woods claimed to devote more space to news of government and international affairs and less to accounts of "Bigamy and Divorce" and "social sewage" than America's premier big city dailies. His "In Our Own World" column, filling a permanent space on the front page, was a conspicuous new feature of the postwar era. Conceived as a "rag-bag," he devoted this personal outlet to autobiographical musings, political commentary, local history, and unadulterated rumormongering.[4]

Management of the *World* was not entirely trouble free. "It would be a very easy matter," Rufus wrote brother Ralph, his increasingly silent partner, "to throw out institution on the wrong side of the ledger." Close attention had to be paid to the cost of newsprint, an expensive and absolutely vital item consumed at the rate of 300,000 pounds a year. Breakdowns in the mechanical department occasionally delayed production or forced a reduction in the normal ten-page length of the paper. Other problems were editorial in nature. Prominent valley residents complained when news accounts included the names of family members involved in automobile accidents and drunken sprees. Republicans were irritated over the printing of Democratic letters-to-the-editor and Democrats were outraged by the failure to mention, much less mourn, the death of Woodrow Wilson in 1924. One subscriber claimed to have been personally libelled by a nationally syndicated comic strip and another, "with fire in his eye, and . . .

murder in his heart," berated reporters for condemning his favored pastime of spitting on the sidewalk.[5]

Woods now delivered his commentary from the perspective of a propertied man on the verge of middle age. He feared Wenatchee was, like the degraded empires of antiquity, well on the way to self-inflicted perdition. The evidence was everywhere to be seen and disturbing to contemplate. America emerged from the war in a big-spending, high-living, and damn-the-consequences mode, rejecting tradition and surrendering unconditionally to the pleasures of immediate gratification. The young men of Wenatchee were "lazy laggards" more interested in pool hall lounging than in books and honest labor. Women smoked in public and took up lewd dancing, following the debauched style of "the demimonde." The Chelan County courts supposedly failed to keep up with the shocking number of cases involving drunkenness and adultery. These "crimes," observed the *World*, "are the harvest, the reaping of the whirlwind, which Biblical authority states will follow the 'sowing of the wind.'"[6]

The *World* found that flickering entertainment wonder of modern times, the motion picture, a particular challenge, pitting the editor against the business manager. Movies distorted reality and stimulated unwholesome behavior on the part of impressionable viewers. The heavily publicized and invariably scandalous lifestyles of Hollywood celebrities tore at the nation's moral fabric. But the *World* profited from the advertising of Wenatchee's several theaters, which submitted copy prepared by big city agencies. Rufus Woods, as a result, found himself in an uncomfortable position. An advertisement promoting a Clara Bow picture, for instance, promised ticket buyers a look at the leading lady in "bathing suits and scanties!" The lip-smacking ad campaign for a Victor McLaglen adventure epic claimed that the hero had joined the Marines to "Get-A-Broad," then "left the Front Lines to play the Waist Lines . . . of the swellest set of sun and man-kissed babes a guy ever fondled."[7]

Other disturbing developments also compromised traditional American values in the postwar era. Labor unrest, Woods believed, threatened economic ruin and social dislocation. Locally, the attraction of high wages on Puget Sound depleted the ranks of harvest workers. Those remaining in North Central Washington, apple growers complained, tended to be lazy and malcontented, interested only in more pay for less effort. "Competent labor," the *World* observed, "is almost a forgotten commodity." The distinct possibility of strikes shutting down the nation's railroads, meanwhile, raised fears of an entire year's crop being left to rot beside the tracks of the Great Northern. The railway unions aroused further antagonism among Republicans east of the Cascades by targeting Senator Miles Poindexter and Representative J. Stanley Webster for defeat over anti-labor votes in Congress.[8]

Organized labor deserved ranking with the Eastern-based corporation as an enemy of the public interest. "In between the two," the *World* pointed out in September 1922, "is a great mass of people constituting 'Us Folks.'" Hardworking, property-owning Americans formerly sympathized with the unions, "in the belief that they had been instrumental in adjusting and ameliorating some bad conditions." Worker organizations, however, now thought only of higher wages and reduced hours, caring nothing for the inflated prices and inferior service inflicted upon society. Stranded in the upriver town of Pateros when a Great Northern train crew "sat down and loafed" in a convoluted dispute over work rules, Woods experienced at first hand the frustration of "folks" held hostage by an out-of-control labor movement: "*The pendulum is swinging and swinging fast and if the railroad boys don't change some of their ways of doing business, they are going to find themselves high and dry and their organization wrecked on the rocks of public sentiment.*"[9]

Woods saw further danger to society in the national response to prohibition. Taking effect in January 1920, the eighteenth amendment banned the manufacture and sale of alcohol throughout the United States. Right or wrong, prohibition was the law of the land and deserved, according to Rufus, complete support. Instead, however, came widespread lawbreaking, one more disheartening indicator of the collapse of order. High-powered automobiles sped south each day through the Okanogan Valley, smuggling good Canadian whiskey to thirsty customers in North Central Washington. Locally operated stills, including one concealed above a false ceiling in the Wenatchee Eagles' Hall, supplied an ever-expanding market. As a member of a federal grand jury impaneled in Spokane in 1924, a dismayed Woods listened to case after case involving violations of the Volstead enforcement act.[10]

Completing the impression of America in peril, shifting immigration patterns, bringing more southern and eastern Europeans to America, plus the sizable presence of Asians in the West, troubled Woods. The *World* called for the banning of "ignorant foreigners" and the admittance of only "the best blood" to the United States. The involvement of aliens in the anti-war movement and in post-Armistice labor disturbances appeared to confirm the paper's nativist argument. "The ships from Europe brought in a satisfactory class of home makers twenty, thirty, forty and fifty years ago," the *World* editorialized in February 1923. In recent years, however, "there has come into this country . . . a great horde of peddlers, of round heads, of people who are a problem as soon as they arrive." Pending a thoroughgoing reform of federal policy, intermediate steps of a practical nature seemed in order. Immigrants must be registered and closely supervised by the government. When Japanese American businessmen attempted to purchase a Wenatchee hotel, Rufus cooperated with the Chamber of Commerce to kill the deal. The *World* urged readers to vote Republican in congressional elections, since a national Democratic victory would make Representative Adolph Sabath of Illinois, "a native of Czecho Solvakia" who favored "letting all the scum . . . come into the United States," chairman of the House immigration committee.[11]

Unhappy with the general trend of American life, Woods was also disappointed by postwar political developments. With Theodore Roosevelt dead, Rufus hoped to see the 1920 Republican presidential nomination go to Miles Poindexter. The opportune scenario, a deadlocked convention, ensued, but the smoke-filled room decision went instead to Senator Warren G. Harding of Ohio. Although the nominee was "a standpatter of almost the reactionary type" and definitely "no superman," Woods considered his election preferable to a victory for James Cox, the equally depressing Democratic alternative. "Most of the followers of Roosevelt," he claimed in explaining the necessity of supporting an Old Guard paragon, "are of the opinion that the principal danger of late has been the tendency toward radicalism and are willing to help swing the pendulum back the other way for awhile till the country sobers up." In the aftermath of Harding's landslide triumph, Woods consoled himself with the expectation that the President-elect would appoint a cabinet "equal in strength and poise to Roosevelt's" and delegate to these statesmen the task of actually running the government.[12]

The fate of Miles Poindexter produced new political discomfort in 1922. Convinced of his own rectitude, the senator prepared to campaign for a third term by alienating the maximum possible number of voters. Internationalists bemoaned his role in the defeat of Wilson's League of Nations. Poindexter's advocacy of anti-strike legislation outraged organized labor. Falling wheat prices hurt him among farmers east of the Cascades. Their erstwhile leader's close relationship with Harding perplexed progressives. Rufus Woods stood out among former Bull Moosers by refusing to "ditch" Poindexter. "Fifteen or twenty years' clear cut record is good enough for me," he wrote in defending his friend. For opposing the League alone, the Senator deserved "a place in history" and another six years in the nation's capital.[13]

Friendship and past performance accounted only in part for the support Woods extended to the embattled incumbent. The Democratic candidate in 1922 was Clarence C. Dill, risen from the political graveyard. Operating upon the motto of boyhood idol John L. Sullivan to "never take a backward step," Dill had transformed himself into the champion of every individual and organization upset with Poindexter. Determined to thwart the comeback of his wartime nemesis, Rufus unleashed the *World* in an attempt to destroy the Spokane Democrat once and for all. Dill was a true hypocrite for all seasons, outfitted with "demagogic propensities" and "ready to promise most any old thing that will make him votes." The challenger, incapable of "sane leadership," appealed only to persons "of mighty strong stomachs." Should Washington turn out Poindexter in favor of his irresponsible opponent, the state would deserve the "contempt and scorn" of a truly scandalized nation.[14]

Rufus spent an unhappy election night with Poindexter in Spokane, listening as a crowd outside the Davenport Hotel followed the incoming returns on the *Spokesman-Review*'s special tally board. After surging to an early lead, Dill fell behind before finally recovering to secure a narrow victory on the basis of votes from Seattle and Tacoma. A morose Poindexter compared his repudiation to the death of a close family member. The senator's staff sat in silence with "sick" expressions on their faces. Unable to muster the energy for a reasoned analysis of the outcome, Rufus called the election a "disgrace." The closest thing to a positive prognosis, under the circumstances, was the hope that "the stigma may not be so great" as the victor's "past term of office would seem to indicate."[15]

Bested on the political front, Woods also experienced the frustration of his postwar plans for regional development. Although Rufus had made peace with the Great Northern, the railroad's local monopoly remained a permanent threat to Wenatchee's economic well-being. In the absence of competition, there was no incentive to lower rates or provide high-quality service. The line was unable to supply enough cars to move apples to market in timely fashion. "The annual increase of tonnage has reached a point," the *World* warned in April 1920, "where . . . North Central Washington is facing a calamity if something is not done." Backed by the paper, orchard interests launched a campaign for a locally financed railroad from Wenatchee south to Pasco and Kennewick, there to make connections with the Northern Pacific and the Union Pacific.[16]

More than $500,000 was raised to finance construction of the Wenatchee Southern Railroad. Local businessmen, carefully negotiating "billows of sand and dust," visited Pasco and Kennewick to generate additional support. Usually incapable of agreeing upon anything, apple growers pledged three cents a box for three years to guarantee the railroad's bonds. The promoters, unfortunately, had to secure a "certificate of necessity" from the Interstate Commerce Commission before beginning actual work. Calling present service more than adequate and claiming its would-be competitor was unlikely to earn sufficient revenue to pay creditors, the Great Northern contested Wenatchee's petition.[17]

Lengthy hearings and prolonged deliberation resulted only in a March 1923 announcement that the Interstate Commerce Commission intended further study of the matter. The news, asserted Rufus Woods, was "the greatest shock the people of Central Washington have had for a long time." Sputtering in indignation, Woods wrote that he intended to "get at something down at the national capital and proceed to turn it upside down, and wrong side out, and hit it in the face, and kick it in the pants, and pulverize it into powder." Over the continued protest of the Great Northern, the commission finally granted the prized certificate in August 1924. By then, however, the original financing arrangement had expired. Expanded storage facilities in Wenatchee relieved the pressure for rapid movement of the crop, removing the incentive for a new railroad.[18]

The rapid spread of automobile ownership, meanwhile, suggested that North Central Washington, with such scenic wonders as the high Cascades, Lake Chelan, and the Grand Coulee, might, given a little effective promotion, become "the great summer playground of the country." Unfortunately, the lack of suitable roads obstructed the realization of this ambition. Campaigning for completion of the Stevens Pass Highway, the key to development of tourism, Woods was again angered by the actions of Seattle. The Puget Sound metropolis intended to see "the lion's share of the state highway improvements" made west of the Cascades. The only exception to this policy was legislative authorization, at Seattle's behest, of a Columbia River bridge at Vantage, far to the south of Wenatchee.[19]

Efforts to complement the proposed Columbia Basin Project with smaller state water improvements also met defeat. The Banker Act of 1919 created a $5 million revolving fund for the state to purchase and sell irrigation district securities. The bill, in effect, resolved the principal dilemma facing the pre-war Quincy project: the lack of a public bond guarantee. An enthused Rufus Woods termed the measure "the most constructive piece of legislation passed . . . in recent years." The *World* singled out Representative E.F. Banker, Democrat of Okanogan County, for bipartisan praise. "Thousands of republicans," claimed Woods, intended to ignore party affiliation and vote him into statewide office.[20]

Although well intentioned, the Banker Act accomplished little beyond encouraging a series of ill-conceived and controversial projects. Woods expected the law to produce "a settled policy as to reclamation." Instead, it brought him profound disappointment. Marvin Chase, complained the *World*, was the only member of the commission appointed to supervise the revolving fund "who knows irrigation and ditch construction." Grange officials and leading citizens of the Yakima Valley, meanwhile, joined in opposing the expenditure of any money under the Banker Act. Outraged by this development, Woods reminded his readers that Yakima, Wenatchee's principal apple competitor, had received at least 90 percent of the federal funds spent on reclamation in Washington state. "Not being satisfied with this" record, Yakima now "lay in the way of any other section that comes in for a little money."[21]

Hoping to make productive use of the Banker Act in spite of adverse circumstances, Woods urged that immediate action be taken in the Okanogan Valley. Authorized in 1905, the federal Okanogan Project, covering 8,600 acres, was an embarrassing instance of governmental miscalculation and mismanagement. Much of the land was unsuitable for cultivation and the poorly constructed works suffered from persistent leakage. The sorry results included a 59 percent shortfall in the flow of water and a 255 percent increase in the annual charges imposed upon settlers. Rufus expected the newly conceived Methow-Okanogan project to provide a definitive solution, provided state assistance was forthcoming. Under the scheme, water stored behind a dam on the Methow River would be diverted to the Okanogan, irrigating 40,000 acres. Unfortunately, property owners, confused by a series of contradictory decisions on the part of the state reclamation board, refused to proceed with implementation of the plan.[22]

Rufus's other near-and-dear development scheme, the Greater Wenatchee project, was also still-born. A truncated version of the old Quincy plan, the promotion involved constructing a dam at the outlet of Lake Wenatchee in the Cascades, plus a canal and pipeline, in order to reclaim 42,800 acres east of the Columbia. Preliminary plans prepared under the state's supervision posited a staggering per-acre cost of $166. "Considering the character and value of the land to be irrigated," as well as the demonstrated worth of improved orchard tracts in the vicinity, the *World* advised landowners to accept this figure and proceed with the undertaking. The many property holders who disagreed with this assessment instead launched a petition drive for dissolution of the Greater Wenatchee District. Compelled to focus his time and energy on sidetracking the petitioners, Woods was barely able to keep the project "alive for future usefulness."[23]

Indulgence in travel provided solace for the frustrations of political defeat and failed promotion. Better automobiles and improved roads increased the range of Rufus's jaunts across the Pacific Northwest. Visits home to Nebraska became annual features of Woods family life. Always fascinated by technology, Woods took his first airplane ride in 1922. The flight featured an encounter with an air pocket over Ellensburg. The plane dropped 2,000 feet and made an emergency landing in a field outside Yakima. Rufus emerged from the harrowing experience as an aviation enthusiast. Foggy conditions along the coast, he argued in announcing a campaign for a local airport, would make Wenatchee the "terminus for transcontinental traffic," where Puget Sound-bound travelers would disembark for transfer to the Great Northern.[24]

At least once a year Woods visited New York and Washington on combined newspaper and political business. Recording his travel impressions in notebook "hyroglyphics" for publication in the *World*, Rufus wrote of the conviviality among transcontinental train passengers. Everyone, from the "bashful girl" to the "Old Bachelor," loosened up, exchanging life stories and making enduring friendships. On one trip Woods spent hours discussing Custer's Last Stand with an imposing "full-blooded Crow Indian." On another, he joined the other genuine Westerners in snickering over the "psuedo [*sic*] cowboy" attire of "a spoiled kid" on the way home from a dude ranch vacation. Wherever the train stopped, Rufus hopped off to purchase all available local newspapers—the best means, in his view, of keeping up with trends in small-town journalism.[25]

Refusing to make appointments while on his trips, Woods nonetheless called upon assorted leaders of business and government in quest of interviews and information. He would ask the receptionist to "tell Mr. Blank that there is a man out here who has come three thousand miles in order to see him!" Human curiosity (the movies, according to Rufus, taught urban dwellers to think of everyone from beyond the Mississippi as either a cowboy or an Indian) made this an effective ploy and the stranger from the West was usually admitted "without delay." When not crashing offices, he became the busy tourist. On one visit to New York Woods inspected the birthplace of Governor Al Smith, toured the Jewish "Ghetto," and sought out big city librarians for details on the reading habits of immigrants. His father's Civil War service led him to the battlefields of Pennsylvania, Maryland, and Virginia to gather cannonballs and other moss-covered souvenirs for mailing home to Wenatchee.[26]

Trained in the civics text version of American government, Rufus was disillusioned by personal observation of Congress in action. From the gallery he watched a senator orate upon the many-faceted subject of cotton to an audience of ten colleagues, only one of whom gave the slightest indication of actually listening. The speech nonetheless appeared in the next day's *Congressional Record* "punctuated throughout . . . with such words as (Applause), (Laughter) and (great Applause)." Members of Congress spent most of their time, Woods concluded, engaged in "a fine little old game of bunk" designed to fool voters at home. Rufus was also offended by Washington dinner parties, where seating was determined by the exact calculation of social status. If he were in charge, reflected the informally inclined visitor, he would draw seat assignments from a hat, then sit back and enjoy the "uproar among the . . . women folk."[27]

Press card in hand, Woods attended presidential news conferences whenever he was in the nation's capital. Face-to-face exposure made Rufus more appreciative of Warren Harding, the maligned victor of 1920. The President, he informed readers, exuded "strength and character," spoke in a "deep rich voice," and was, all in all, "one of the finest looking men I ever saw." Dazzled by charm, Woods ignored the gathering political problems of the Harding administration. At a May 1922 press session he failed, in a moment of defective hearing, to "catch" the presidential response to questions about "certain oil leases" and a mysterious place known as Teapot Dome.[28]

Back in the Pacific Northwest, Woods met Harding in Spokane and again in Seattle on the outward- and inward-bound legs of the President's ill-fated 1923 trip to Alaska. He stood close to the President as Harding addressed 32,000 people at the University of Washington and afterward attended an evening banquet in honor of the distinguished visitor. The latter affair was a final public appearance, for Harding took ill on his train that night and died several days later in San Francisco. Truly shocked, Rufus devoted his column and the *World* editorial page to extended praise of the fallen leader. "The country has lost a great and good man," he mourned, a President who had silenced the skeptics and more than adequately fulfilled the duties of his office. Personifying "the highest type of clean manhood and Christian citizenship," Harding had "lived a private life which any young American may emulate." Parents ought to read the late President's biography to their children as a lesson in the rewards of pure conduct: "His life sets a standard for the upright American even as the life of the Man of Galilee sets the standard of Christendom."[29]

Within months, a series of revelations destroyed Harding's well-crafted image, incidentally embarrassing the *World* in the process. As a Republican publisher, Woods delivered the news in the manner best-calculated to avoid damage to the new President, Calvin Coolidge. Rufus blamed Secretary of the Interior Albert Fall alone for the scandalous Teapot Dome affair and assigned sole responsibility for rampant corruption in the Veterans' Bureau to director Charles Forbes, a one-time resident of the Okanogan Valley. The real evil, according to the *World*, was to be found among the lobbyists and the Democrats, the former for tempting greed-inclined office holders and the latter for trying to persuade the American people that all Republicans were dishonest. The *World* ignored entirely lurid reports of presidential mistresses and illegitimate offspring.[30]

Nineteen twenty-four was an emotionally wrenching campaign year for Rufus Woods, ranking with 1896, 1912, 1932, and 1948. The drama had nothing at all to do with the austere Republican incumbent, Coolidge. (Attending the GOP convention in the dual role of reporter and Coolidge delegate, Rufus strolled arm-in-arm with boyhood hero William Jennings Bryan, who was on the scene as a journalist.) Emotion was definitely in short supply respecting Wall Street lawyer John W. Davis, the Democratic challenger. The story of that summer and the fall dealt instead with a third contender, Senator Robert M. LaFollette of Wisconsin, running on behalf of a new Progressive Party. Woods considered LaFollette, once an admired reformer, a national version of Clarence Dill. The senator had "played yellow" in opposing American involvement in the world war and survived politically only by exercising to the fullest the talents of the pure demagogue.[31]

Woods ignored Coolidge and Davis in order to devote the *World* to vilification of the Progressive candidate. LaFollette's claim to leadership of the reform movement, Rufus asserted, was "an act of dishonesty and effrontery without parallel in our political history." The nominee and his running mate, Burton K. Wheeler, dubbed "the two 'yellow boys,'" had absolutely nothing in common with Theodore Roosevelt, that "warmhearted . . . defender of the principles of Americanism." The old Bull Moosers of 1912, contended the *World*, had lined up "solidly [in] back of" Coolidge. If instituted, government ownership of the railroads, a key plank in the Progressive platform, would bring the immediate financial ruin of North Central Washington, since local taxes paid by the Great Northern supported public services in the four counties. The eventual bankruptcy of an apple industry subjected to bureaucratic decision-making was sure to follow. Although LaFollette finished second in Washington state, Coolidge's national triumph produced, on the part of Woods, renewed faith in the electorate: "The vote indicates that the country generally is tired to death of demagoguery and . . . rampant radicalism."[32]

Rufus ought to have paid more attention to state politics and less to national in 1924. On an embarrassing personal note, he neglected a promise to print literature for Ralph's congressional campaign in Tacoma and took the blame for his brother's narrow defeat in the Republican primary. When Governor Louis F. Hart declined to run for reelection and timberman-politician Mark Reed refused to seek the office, the gubernatorial door opened to Washington's most controversial Republican. Roland H. Hartley was an outspoken foe of radicalism and "the damnable practice of regulation, domination, dictation, and interference by governmental bureaus, boards, commissions and inspectors." Spending on public education beyond the level of rudimentary primary schools, he insisted, was "altruistic twaddle." He appealed to the tight-fisted and the unsophisticated, or, as an adviser frankly stated, "the moron vote." The *World*, with no other option and without conviction, endorsed state senator Edward French for the GOP nomination, but said little about the contest and avoided comment upon Hartley's primary and general election victories.[33]

Addressing the legislature in January 1925, Hartley asked it to adjourn until later in the year, allowing him time to conduct a thorough study of Washington's economic and social problems. The request was "Rooseveltian in . . . character" according to the *World*, which joined newspapers across the state in praise of the apparently businesslike proposal. With the legislature still in brief session, however, the governor vetoed a measure providing seed loans to drought-stricken farmers east of the Cascades. The veto might be "right in principle," complained the *World*, "but it is a mighty poor rule which cannot be broken when . . . necessary." The intended beneficiaries, after all, were "the most dependable class of settlers that any country ever saw," hard-working, property-owning people deserving assistance in their time of rain-short need. Responding to this criticism from Wenatchee, Hartley delivered a typically direct retort, heading a private letter to Woods with the expression "'Et tu Brutu.'"[34]

The governor was at war with eastern Washington by the time the legislature reconvened in the fall of 1925. "So far as this part of the country is concerned," Rufus advised Hartley upon learning of the latter's plan to curtail Banker Act spending, "you have committed political Hari Kari." Welcoming the legislators to Olympia in deliberately abrasive manner, the governor added to an already lengthy list of enemies by issuing a diatribe against every institution of state government not under his personal control. The *World*, in common with editorial opinion from the Palouse to the Pacific coast, promptly termed Hartley "a small town crank" and "a wild Injin." The governor had spent "his whole life . . . falling timber," the Wenatchee newspaper noted in reference to Hartley's background in the timber industry. He was therefore constitutionally incapable of recognizing "the necessity of building up the communities of the state" through irrigation and other positive programs.[35]

Hartley's wide-ranging attacks generated an angry coalition of threatened interests. "It is not one or two or a half dozen things," Woods observed of the governor's apparent love of carnage, "there are hundreds of things which show this man to be utterly unfitted for the job." The defining issue, for Wenatchee and North Central Washington, continued to be the threat to irrigation. Under Hartley, the *World* pointed out, "the state reclamation service is in the hands of its enemies." Out of regional self-interest, the paper again made common cause with Democrats, endorsing legislation introduced by E.F. Banker to remove reclamation from the governor's control. Backed by anti-Hartley Republicans from both sides of the Cascades, the bill narrowly failed to survive the inevitable gubernatorial veto.[36]

Emotions were literally at fever pitch as Hartley and the legislature, led by Mark Reed, battled to a standstill. The governor could not get his bills passed, while the hostile legislative majority fell just short of the strength needed to override vetoes. In a perfect moment of political symbolism, Hartley and the stolid Reed nearly came to blows on the floor of the house chamber in January 1926. This episode was followed by a vote of censure against the governor and by the issuance of an opposition bill-of-particulars condemning his "reactionary and destructive . . . philosophy." The *World* joined in the name-calling with a series of invectives apparently saved especially for the occasion. The paper called Hartley a "hornet in a bottle of bumble bees," a "mule," a "spoiled baby," the "Don Quixote of Washington" and a would-be Mussolini. His only support among legislators, claimed the *World*, came from a corrupt "little group who have received offices or are looking for something."[37]

Under the circumstances, the most famous imbroglio of the Hartley years was something of an anticlimax. The governor was not alone in desiring the removal of Henry Suzzallo, the president of the University of Washington. Over the years the educator had made many enemies by advocating improved working conditions in the lumber industry, securing a disproportionate share of state higher education funds for the university, and treating politicians with open contempt. Suzzallo served at the pleasure of the board of regents, forcing Hartley to wait until his appointees secured majority control of the panel. When Suzzallo refused to resign, the regents dismissed him in October 1926. The *World* termed "the ousting of a man of the mental equipment, attainments and exceptional capacity of Dr. Suzzallo" a scandal and the perpetrator of the deed "a man of low mental strain." Signing on with a statewide recall movement, Woods wrote of the "beginning of the end" of "the Hartley fiasco." Begun in indignation, the recall campaign lost momentum, in large part because of the former university president's genuine lack of public appeal. It failed to generate enough petition signatures to force a special election.[38]

Looking to the 1928 election, Woods contended that Hartley was nonetheless fatally weakened and had no chance of being renominated. Responsible Republican leaders, however, again failed to produce a worthy alternative. Mark Reed declined to run and the governor, facing only the undynamic Edward French, won the primary without difficulty. The opponents of Hartley must now vote for him or abandon the party and support Democrat A. Scott Bullitt. The dilemma was far from clear-cut in Wenatchee. Woods was offended when Bullitt attempted to "out-Hartley Hartley" in demagogic oratory. "He kept it up so long," observed the aggrieved *World*, "that even those who would like to have voted for him soured on his tactics." The paper refused to make an endorsement; Rufus Woods apparently cast no vote. Hartley's victory terminated a depressing campaign with the prospect of four more contentious years.[39]

Disappointed at the state level, Rufus's spirits revived considerably when he contemplated the 1928 presidential campaign. Democratic candidate Al Smith was, in his opinion, triply unqualified as a child of immigrants, as a "city man," and as a "wet" on prohibition enforcement. Born in Iowa, raised in Oregon, and based in California, Republican Herbert Hoover was, in contrast, a genuine man of the West, well-acquainted with reclamation and other pressing regional needs. As Secretary of Commerce under Harding and Coolidge, he had visited eastern Washington and endorsed the Columbia Basin Project. Woods extolled his party's standard bearer as the spokesman of "the whole American people" and as the most appealing nominee "since Roosevelt's day." Hoover's triumph meant that the White House would be occupied for at least the next four years, and probably longer, by a chief executive several cuts above the standard set by his immediate predecessors. Woods also dismissed the Democratic Party, after three consecutive landslide defeats, as a viable political entity. To win again, the *World* observed, the Democrats must somehow generate "a new leader, new causes . . . [and] in short a new deal."[40]

The national economic boom of the late 1920s, with Wenatchee participating fully, made Hoover's election inevitable and Hartley's survival easier to endure. The *Daily World* survived a confrontation with organized labor to become an even more prosperous business enterprise. Rufus had always viewed his newspaper as a family enterprise, a place where managers and employees worked together in "good fellowship" for mutual advancement. "Real effective work," he pointed out in succinct explanation of his concept of executive responsibility, "is done best not when men are driven but when they are sympathetic and desirous of doing their best." Complaints and disputes occasionally arose, but were resolved in face-to-face-fashion. This was the way of the West, the way of the small town, and the way to be followed in the future as in the past.[41]

Labor organizations naturally had different ideas about the proper relationship between employer and employee. The union must intervene between the two, taking the lead in formal negotiations on issues of pay and conditions of work. In February 1926 union members in the *World* mechanical department demanded a pay increase from $42 to $45 a week, matching the scale currently paid by the *Yakima Republic*. Resisting this imposition, Rufus appealed to the Pacific Northwest Newspaper Association for help. The organization immediately supplied the *World* with statistics showing that Woods would actually be "justified in decreasing the wage you have been paying" and recommended that employees wanting $45 should go to Yakima "and try to get a job." Backed by the trade association and by open shop publishers across the state, Rufus refused the increase and declined to sign a contract with the union. For the time being, at least, the organized labor movement was stymied as far as newspapering in Wenatchee was concerned.[42]

Happier developments diverted attention from the dispute. The *World* had long since outgrown its Mission-and-Orondo quarters. On Christmas Eve 1926 the paper moved a block north to a new brick-faced structure on Mission Street. The expense involved, much-inflated by a decision to avoid mortgaging the building, left Woods "clear down to last notch on cash." Early in 1927 newspapers began rolling off a high-capacity Hoe press, able to turn out editions of up to forty-eight pages, with consequences that soon demonstrated the soundness of the investment in expansion. Profits for 1927 were $23,000, the best twelve months "in the history of the business." Paid-up readership continued to grow at an impressive rate, reaching 11,000 by the end of the decade, an upward trend that all concerned expected to increase in the 1930s.[43]

Circulation increases, Woods observed, were the "natural result" of economic progress in North Central Washington. Without doubt, claimed the *World*, the most significant regional development of the decade was the "advent of the two greatest electric power companies in the Northwest into this territory." In 1924, the Seattle-based Puget Sound Power & Light Company assumed direct ownership of the Wenatchee utility operated since 1921 by another Stone and Webster subsidiary. The Washington Water Power Company purchased the previously unutilized Chelan Falls damsite in 1925. "Never again will the waters of Lake Chelan run to waste," enthused Rufus Woods as the Spokane firm installed a plant at the falls. Water Power, so known in most precincts east of the Cascades, also extended transmission lines into previously unserved parts of Grant and Okanogan counties. Puget, as that concern was ordinarily abbreviated, expanded its holdings, sending electricity across the Columbia into Douglas County. Power from Chelan Falls, meanwhile, enabled the Great Northern to electrify its trains running through the new eight-mile tunnel beneath Stevens Pass, opened in 1928.[44]

Agriculturally, the trend of the times in North Central Washington was encouraging. To be sure, drought and deflated wheat prices made life a bitter struggle in the ranching country east of the Columbia. Optimism prevailed, however, in the apple region along the river's profitable right bank. "The fruit harvest is a moving epic of progress," the *World* observed in late 1928, "which might well beguile the pen of a Kipling, or enlist the descriptive powers of a Washington Irving." Soaring with the post-armistice inflation, prices had attained a level of $3.50 a box for the top grades, before falling sharply in the ensuing recession. Serious frost damage inflicted upon the local crop in 1924, however, greatly enhanced the value of the surviving fruit and commenced a sustained upswing in earnings. In 1928 and 1929, the Great Northern shipped 41,000 carloads of apples out of Wenatchee, three times the rate for any previous two-year period. Booming Eastern and foreign demand easily absorbed this prodigious production at favorable prices.[45]

Despite the vast annual production figures, growers confronted a series of problems, some traditional and others newly developing. Profits were not equally distributed, but depended upon the variety of apple harvested in each orchard. Winesaps and Delicious, together comprising 55 percent of shipments, sold, on average, for between $1.29 and $1.80 per box between 1924 and 1928. Jonathans and Rome Beauties, a quarter of the crop, brought only 94 to 97 cents a box. Given the fact that the cost of producing and transporting fruit averaged $1.17 a box, orchardists producing large quantities of low-priced apples faced obvious difficulties in maintaining their operations.[46]

The railroad rate question became an enduring issue in North Central Washington. To the dismay of orchardists, the "temporary" $1.50 per hundred pounds charge imposed during the world war somehow attained permanent status upon the return of peace. "The cost of transportation," charged the *World* in 1925, "absorbs an unduly large portion of the actual selling price of apples . . . leaving little or nothing for the producers." At the risk of a quarrel with Ralph, who represented the Great Northern in such matters, Rufus backed an unsuccessful petition to the Interstate Commerce Commission for a reduction to $1.25. Growers confronted another persistent problem in the ongoing long-term shift of consumer taste away from apples to citrus fruits and bananas, heavily advertised products of California, Florida, and the Caribbean. The modern all-purpose grocery store also hurt by driving fruit markets and corner stands out of business, disrupting traditional patterns of distribution.[47]

In place of the cellars, sheds, and other makeshifts of the pre-war years, Wenatchee now had enough cold storage space to handle 1,800 carloads of fruit, stretching the shipping season for a significant portion of the crop to encompass the months between fall and spring. Most apples, though, still had to be sent east directly upon packing. Only the best-quality fruit, designated fancy and extra fancy, justified payment of the rates charged by the Great Northern. Unfortunately, many operators dumped C grades and culls upon an unsuspecting and unreceptive market, taking up scarce space in cars and driving down prices. Orchardists undertook a chemically induced shortcut to resolution of the quality problem, spraying growing apples with heavy dosages of sulphur and arsenic-laced compounds. The sprays controlled the coddling moth, but produced a new form of governmental interference. Regulations issued by the Food and Drug Administration and by apple-importing nations forced growers to institute expensive cleaning procedures for the removal of toxic residue.[48]

Straightforward thinkers easily settled upon the means of resolving these difficulties. "All cheap varieties must be eliminated," advised W.S. Trimble, Rufus's number-one man in the newsroom and himself a thriving orchardist. "Storage sufficient to care for a major portion of the crop" was also needed. Above all, the entire Wenatchee output must be placed in "the hands of a grower owned selling machine." The problem, as always, was the inherent one of persuading 2,000 growers to agree upon a single workable program. Neither the old Northwestern Fruit Exchange nor such rival entities as the Wenatchee-Okanogan Cooperative Federation ever represented more than a fraction of the industry. Good years, unhappily, removed the incentive for organization, and disappointing years sparked only after-the-fact efforts, too late for raising prices.[49]

Most growers still somehow made a profit. Annual net earnings for all district orchards, the bad with the good, averaged $65 an acre in the late 1920s, a sure indicator of the intrinsic value of fruit and irrigated land. Wenatchee, stable and genteel, abandoned the old "Home of the Big Red Apple" slogan in favor of calling itself the "Apple Capital of the World." Despite the heavy financial drain involved in funding the annual fruit crop, bank deposits stood at a record high. In a further measure of local prosperity, the town, though thirteenth in the state in population, ranked fifth in the monetary value of building permits issued in 1929. Groundbreaking for the highrise Cascadian Hotel marked what the *World* termed "the beginning of a new epoch in the history of this city."[50]

During the 1920s, Rufus Woods confronted the various troubling aspects of modern times, suffered political frustration, led the *World* to profit, had his appendix removed, and began wearing glasses. Following the designation of Wenatchee as the Apple Capital, Rufus announced a contest to rename North Central Washington. The winning entry, "God's Country," was never used for fear of offending churchgoers, but succinctly captured the publisher's feelings for his adopted homeland. No matter how troubling the political antics of Roland Hartley, no matter how disturbing the content of the movies or the blatant non-observance of prohibition, Woods drew solace from his natural surroundings and from the future prospects of the upper Columbia River. As 1928 passed into 1929, the *World* published occasional cautionary notes about the diversion of investment from "the regular channels of trade . . . to Wall Street and other speculative markets." Local people, raised in an apple commonwealth and, as a result, superior in character and intellect, fortunately preferred to invest their money in solid ventures like orchard land and the Cascadian Hotel.[51]

# Chapter Seven
## The Day of the Dam

The day of the Columbia river dam is nearly here.

*Wenatchee Daily World*[1]

Hɪɢʜ ᴀʙᴏᴠᴇ ᴛʜᴇ Columbia, the ranchers of the Big Bend looked down upon the blooming orchards of North Central Washington. Every day, from fall through spring, two Great Northern trains carried apples from Wenatchee to distant markets. A water-filled fault line, the Columbia River separated zones of boom and bust, euphoria and gloom. Atop the stream's volcanic battlements, depression was an early and persistent phenomenon of the terrible 1920s. Wheat prices declined by two-thirds, a statistic reflected in foreclosed mortgages, delinquent taxes, and failed dreams. Drought was a constant meteorological companion of economic distress. The rich soil, dried-out since Wilson's first term, lifted into the air with the strong spring winds, enveloping the countryside. Motorists drove at all hours with lights on, until their automobiles stuttered to a halt from dirt-choked engines. Storms, blowing in from east of the Columbia, forced the townspeople of Wenatchee, as the *World* reported, to "'eat' dust all summer."[2]

Salvation, even if some approximation of "normal" precipitation returned, depended upon construction of the Columbia Basin Project. The original sponsors of Grand Coulee dam remained convinced that theirs was the best, indeed the only practicable, means of reclamation. The structure, they maintained, would benefit every resident of Washington, west as well as east of the Cascades. The infusion of settlers and the creation of new markets for industry, claimed Ephrata attorney W.E. Southard, a charter member of the Dam University, "would quadruple the wealth of this state in less than 50 years." Billy Clapp advised James O'Sullivan to hold on to his Moses Lake land, no matter what the temptation to sell, in anticipation of the dam being built, as the eventual sales price "will justify all the expense you have ever put into [it] and a handsome profit."[3]

Rufus Woods, as in the past, thought of the dam in especially broad terms. Although Grand Coulee would provide farms for a quarter million people, the project, in his conceptualization, was far more than an agricultural undertaking. Leading the way into a new era of maximum river development, Grand Coulee meant nothing less than the industrialization of the Pacific Northwest, the transformation of an entire raw material-rich region into a manufacturing complex "which may in time equal that of Pittsburgh." The dam entailed "stability" and "balance" for North Central Washington, ending Wenatchee's dangerous concentration on a one-crop economy. All sorts of industrial enterprises—sawmills, chemical and fertilizer plants, aluminum manufacturers—would be drawn to the upper Columbia by the availability of cheap and abundant electricity, there to exploit the forested and mineralized wealth of the Cascades. Wenatchee itself would become the rich center of an imperial economic domain, the city proper assuming a size "as large or larger than Spokane."[4]

Grand Coulee energy made any comparison with the rival Pend Oreille gravity diversion plan ludicrous, at least in the opinion of Woods. "Don't you think," he asserted in one emotional outburst, "it is about time for the . . . people of Spokane to realize that the proposal of trying to dig a 134-mile main canal with 32 MILES OF TUNNELS with but little power, with complications among three states . . . is entirely out of the question." Spokane, and Olympia too, naturally thought otherwise, refusing to surrender political advantage to the superior engineering argument. Promulgated by the long-defunct survey commission and endorsed by General George Goethals, Albeni Falls remained the official policy of the state of Washington. Even Roland Hartley, otherwise hostile to reclamation, cooperated, placing Columbia Basin Irrigation League secretary Mark Woodruff on the public payroll as a means of subsidizing the organization with taxpayer dollars.[5]

Status as a quasi-official state agency was of little help to the Irrigation League in advancing its version of the Columbia Basin Project. The prime roadblock to implementation of the gravity plan remained the opposition of Idaho and Montana to storage of water in Pend Oreille and Flathead lakes. Albeni Falls supporters were particularly incensed by Idaho's obviously hypocritical recalcitrance. Reclaimed tracts in the upper Snake

River Valley, they pointed out, took water from reservoirs in Montana. Politicians and administrators in Boise supposedly intended to conclude a compact with Wyoming for the use of "all the water that can be impounded from the Snake," a stream flowing in its lower course through Washington. Idaho, though willing to inflict damage upon neighboring states, resisted the tiniest sacrifice on the part of its own people.[6]

On behalf of Spokane, the Washington congressional delegation secured an amendment including the state in legislation authorizing the Idaho-Wyoming water compact. "Idaho will now see that she must get our consent . . . on the Snake River," noted Roy Gill, chairman of the Irrigation League executive committee. Washington's representative on the commission negotiating the compact was Ross Tiffany, the pro-gravity plan state engineer. Bureau of Reclamation director Elwood Mead, the federal member, appointed Professor O. L. Waller of Washington State College to act in his place, adding to the expectation that Idaho must sooner or later agree to an accommodation allowing Pend Oreille diversion and storage.[7]

Roy Gill insisted that Idaho "cannot afford to be arbitrary in dealing with our water rights." Discussions between the two states, held at regular intervals beginning in 1926, revealed this expectation to be a considerable miscalculation. To the discomfort of their visitors from Washington, officials in Boise argued that Grand Coulee was the better means of irrigating the Columbia Basin. A public hearing at Sandpoint, the principal town on Lake Pend Oreille, was, according to the thoroughly intimidated Tiffany, "charged with violent antagonism against consideration of any storage whatever." Reflecting on the intense feeling in Idaho, Billy Clapp advised Dam University colleagues to rest easy, since Albeni Falls "can never be built."[8]

No matter what the state of public opinion in Idaho, other factors made federal action on behalf of the Columbia Basin Project unlikely. Meant to benefit agriculture, America's most influential farm organization opposed the plan. Vowing to "carry the fight into the halls of Congress," the Grange was on record against adding to land already under cultivation, so long as depressed prices prevailed. The nation's farmers, Washington State Master Albert Goss informed Senator Wesley Jones, "can not stand any additional production until some way is provided for caring for the surplus." The Bureau of Reclamation, moreover, was fully occupied with Boulder Dam. Elwood Mead claimed his agency had no funds available for a serious examination of either the gravity or the pumping plan.[9]

Opposition from the Grange and disinterest on the part of the Bureau provided Senator Wesley Jones with convenient excuses for his failure to secure Columbia Basin legislation. Sympathetic to the gravity plan in private, Jones proved unwilling to take any action in public that might cost him the support of the Grand Coulee group. The senator, elected to a fourth term in 1926, was on the brink of becoming chairman of the appropriations committee, a position attained in 1929. Seniority, though, was not an automatic indicator of legislative effectiveness. The Senate passed a measure to survey the basin in December 1928. Jones, however, refused to press his counterparts in the House GOP leadership for favorable action. An effort by Democrat Sam B. Hill, of Washington's Fifth Congressional District, to suspend the rules and bring the bill to the floor fell short of the necessary two-thirds vote, thanks to the opposition of Republican reclamation opponents.[10]

Grand Coulee supporters charged that the state's senior Republican was neither lethargic nor incompetent, but simply biased in favor of the Yakima Valley. Concerns about excessive spending and surplus farm production somehow lost their potency whenever legislation for the benefit of that locale came under consideration. Jones, at least, was able to secure continued appropriations for irrigation. "In the name of High Heaven, Senator Jones," blustered Rufus Woods in an unusually blunt letter of remonstrance, "hasn't Yakima been pretty well taken care of?" The time had arrived "to give a little to this part of the state." Yakima, of course, opposed federal spending on reclamation in North Central Washington, since such money would go to potential competitors in the agricultural marketplace. Adding to the aggravation in Wenatchee, the senator warned Woods against any attempt to divert funds from Yakima to either Grand Coulee or Albeni Falls, as the antagonism generated "would do nothing but harm to the project that you are . . . so greatly interested in."[11]

Despite his limitations, Wesley Jones was shrewd and experienced in the manipulation of obscure governmental processes. The political situation, as of early 1929, required an end-run around Congress and the Bureau of Reclamation. "Two or three years ago," the Senator reminded Roy Gill, "we adopted in the river and harbor bill a provision authorizing the appropriation of something over $7,000,000 to carry on a survey over the country . . . dealing with flood control, power development, and reclamation." The March 1925 congressional resolution in fact called upon the Corps of Engineers to prepare plans for multipurpose "improvement" of the nation's rivers. Published as House Document 308—the reason for designating subsequent Corps investigations of the river as "308 Reports"—the Army study list included the Columbia.[12]

The Army expressed no real interest in the study or in the speedy development of the Columbia. Responsibility for the river was divided at the mouth of the Snake River between the Portland and Seattle district engineering offices, with the North Pacific Division acting as coordinator. Portland was concerned primarily with the improvement of navigation upriver to Lewiston on the Snake. Seattle's Major John S. Butler, meanwhile, intended to concentrate on the Skagit River of western Washington, another stream listed in Document 308. Because of the paramount importance of irrigation east of the Cascades, he explained, the upper Columbia was properly the responsibility of the Bureau of Reclamation. The Army, said Butler, should avoid the "duplication of effort" involved in taking on a subject belonging to "another department of the Government." Rebuked by his superiors for this reluctance to interfere with another agency, the Major responded with a detailed plan for the examination of the river.[13]

To this point, nothing had suggested that the 308 investigation would result in preparation of the key planning guideline for construction of Grand Coulee and other dams on the Columbia. The study attained that level of significance only because of the behind-the-scenes handiwork of Wesley Jones. Although his Bureau of Reclamation survey bill was dead, the senator informed friends in January 1929 that "the survey is actually going on and we will probably get a report through the army . . . sooner than we might otherwise get it." Meeting Chief of Engineers General Edgar Jadwin, Jones asked that the Columbia River be assigned top priority. Eager to satisfy a senior legislator able to influence Corps appropriations, Jadwin promised to prosecute the work "with a vigor commensurate with its importance." At home, Roy Gill learned that Colonel Gustave Lukesh, the district engineer in Portland, and Major Butler in Seattle expected to receive "instructions . . . to proceed full speed ahead."[14]

A flurry of local organizational activity followed upon the sudden emergence of the Army study as a matter of prime importance. The Dam University had no intention of working with the Columbia Basin Irrigation League, which was "more or less dominated by the Power interest." To better push Grand Coulee upon the military engineers, the Columbia River Development League was formed in June 1929. Quoting Herbert Hoover, the League motto captured the still-vital essence of progressive conservation: "Every drop of water that runs to the sea without yielding its full commercial returns to the nation is an economic waste." Summoned from Michigan, Jim O'Sullivan assumed responsibility for day-to-day affairs as executive secretary, working out of a stifling office in Ephrata. Willis Batcheller, still a hero for exposing the state's Pend Oreille bias, became chief engineer.[15]

Rufus Woods assumed the Development League presidency when David McGinnis, his old friend from the early days in Wenatchee, resigned after a month on the job. Serving until 1933, Rufus devoted much of his time to raising money, a frustrating and generally unsuccessful task. The Wenatchee Chamber of Commerce contributed only a small amount, perpetrating what Woods considered "little less than a crime." The railroads, continuing to back the gravity plan, refused to give anything. The bulk of the funding came from the hard-pressed towns of Grant and Douglas counties and from such individuals as Billy Clapp, who overdrew his personal bank account at least once in order to make a contribution. Most of the money paid O'Sullivan's salary and expenses.[16]

Grand Coulee was, like a baggy suit, easily retailored to meet altered political conditions. It could, as the occasion demanded, be portrayed as an irrigation work, as an electricity-producing dam, or, in depressed times, as a marvelous source of public jobs. Of particular importance in 1929, Woods overcame the opposition of the state Grange to a Columbia Basin Project linked to Grand Coulee. The Albeni Falls plan called for complete construction at once and generated no hydroelectricity. The pumping alternative, though, could be implemented on a unit-by-unit basis, as justified by farm prices, and involved a massive addition to the regional supply of power. The latter was a prime goal of the Grange, while the reclamation-in-stages approach alleviated most of the concern over agricultural surpluses. Washington Master Albert Goss proclaimed his preference for Grand Coulee and privately assured Woods that he would not oppose authorization by Congress.[17]

Pressing senators Jones and Dill into action on this point, the League secured an indefinite postponement of Federal Power Commission action on Washington Water Power's application for a permit to build the proposed upstream Kettle Falls dam. If constructed, that structure would substantially reduce the maximum height of Grand Coulee, limiting electricity generation, increasing the lift required of the pumps, and adversely affecting the engineering and financial details of the project. In asking the FPC for rapid processing of its permit, the Spokane utility had this impact firmly in mind, at least in the view of residents of Ephrata and Wenatchee. For once, Wesley Jones and Rufus Woods were in complete agreement. "I . . . doubt very seriously," the senator wrote in the spring of 1929, "the wisdom of granting permits for the development of power on the Columbia River until there is a pretty definite determination with reference to the method of development of the Columbia Basin Irrigation Project." Supporting this assertion, Major Butler of the Corps of Engineers advised the power commission to set Kettle Falls aside, at least until completion of the 308 Report.[18]

Development League members believed that Butler, regardless of his public claims of neutrality, was privately on their side. The *World* regularly praised the engineer's professionalism, reminding readers that in his hands lay the fate of a project "many times greater than Boulder Dam." Butler had worked on the construction of Wilson Dam on the Tennessee River and was more willing than most of his military colleagues to think of rivers in broader terms than the traditional Corps of Engineers focus on navigation. Of equal importance to the Grand Coulee lobby, which based its hopes on the technical superiority of the pumping plan, the Major was a man of integrity.[19]

Certain developments detracted from the initial optimism in Development League ranks. The Army, unwilling to abandon its deliberate better-right-than-timely methods, even for Wesley Jones, set aside two years to complete the Butler and Lukesh studies. The Dam University had hoped to secure an advance contract for the sale of Grand Coulee power to City Light, the Seattle municipal lighting department. Unfortunately, City Light head J.D. Ross rejected the offer, for fear of encouraging competition with his planned expansion of hydroelectricity production on the Skagit River in the northern Cascades. James O'Sullivan, meanwhile, engaged in another damaging episode of misrepresentation, reading a noncommittal letter from Wesley Jones at public meetings in such a way as to make it sound like the senator endorsed the dam. Jones was horrified and the Irrigation League expressed outrage. Writing to the senator, O'Sullivan declined to apologize, insisting that his action was justified by Spokane's "deadly enmity to the Grand Coulee Project."[20]

Work on the 308 Report was fully under way by the time "Black Thursday"—October 24, 1929—signalled the beginning of America's descent into the Great Depression. The *World* responded to the Wall Street collapse with a mixture of unconcern and downright optimism. Stock prices, according to prevailing wisdom in the Pacific Northwest, had been artificially inflated by "gamblers and manipulators." The downswing, therefore, was nothing more than a healthy and much-needed readjustment. Wall Street's self-inflicted pain delivered a valuable lesson and offered genuine opportunity. Wenatchee residents learned anew the importance of investing only in "safe, sound home enterprises." Funds previously tied up in speculation, moreover, could now finance orchard expansion, reclamation projects, and dams. "This will . . . help carry on many essential enterprises," the *World* confidently proclaimed, ". . . give employment to labor and promote the welfare of all the people."[21]

Silly in hindsight, this positive analysis had a contemporary basis in reality, for Wenatchee was possibly the last place in the United States to feel the impact of the Wall Street crash. Nationally, 12 million people lost their jobs, 5,000 banks failed, and the gross national product declined by half in the three years after "Black Thursday." Chelan County, however, boasted the highest per capita income in the state of Washington. Financial institutions remained strong and the local building boom proceeded, with plans for an addition to the high-rise Cascadian Hotel. "While many other parts of the country are suffering from down right depression," the *World* announced in mid-1930, "the home community is enjoying a greater thrill than ever before." The town's widespread "reputation for prosperity" was the only cause for worry. "Other communities all over the Northwest," complained the *World*, "tell their beggars, their vagrants and their unemployed to 'go to Wenatchee, there is plenty of work there.'"[22]

To be sure, Big Bend wheat ranchers found that economic conditions could, in fact, grow worse, as prices tumbled to 38 cents a bushel. Apples, though, were "undisturbed and unaffected by the prevailing depression" according to the *World*. Despite a curtailed foreign market and falling domestic demand, heavy production kept overall earnings close to pre-crash levels. The 1930 Washington crop, a third larger than the previous year's, sold for $36 million, just slightly below the 1929 return. Street corner apple sales by unemployed urban residents absorbed 1,500 carloads from the Wenatchee Valley. This inventive approach to relief, said a pleased *World*, gave the "jobless a chance to help themselves" and provided a useful "added impulse to apple buying."[23]

By retaining a strong market position through 1930, apples helped insulate Wenatchee from the deflationary impact of the Depression. More important in this regard was the decision of the Puget Sound Power &

Light Company to build the first dam on the Columbia River, at Rock Island downstream from town. The plan, unveiled in November 1928, drew enthusiastic support from Rufus Woods as "one of the most vital projects that this part of the state has ever witnessed." Woods called upon the owners of property needed by Puget to immediately grant options, and defended the company against charges that the dam would interfere with navigation and harm fisheries. The enormous benefit to Wenatchee, he maintained, justified the sacrifice of such relatively minor interests to the greater good. "Numerous extensive industries," asserted Rufus, ". . . would be established in this vicinity as a result of the building of this dam." The local riverfront would be transformed into "a pond of still water," enabling pulp and paper and lumber mills to "bring down billions of feet of logs from the upper territory tributary to the Columbia."[24]

Reading the *World*'s numerous and enthusiastic pronouncements about the "far sighted policy" on display at Rock Island, members of the Dam University worried that the "power trust" had "forced Rufus into a corner" by requiring him to choose between Grand Coulee and the Puget project, between the interest of the region and the immediate prospects of Wenatchee. Concern that Woods had made a secret and obviously sordid deal with industry mounted when the paper opposed the 1930 state referendum authorizing creation of public utility districts. "I saw Rufus a few days ago," a relieved W.E. Southard reported in a letter meant to reassure mutual friends, "and he told me that the power companies would not control his attitude towards the big development when the time came to get in and work for it." The Woods alliance with Puget was, in fact, a temporary matter and in no way detrimental to the larger regional cause.[25]

Puget's dam, with construction fully under way in the aftermath of the Wall Street crash, was, in effect, a privately financed public works program. Depending upon the weather, employment at Rock Island fluctuated between 1,100 and 2,700 persons. The purchasing power of these individuals and their families produced an oasis of prosperity in the vast dispirited wasteland of the Great Depression. "Wenatchee," wrote a visitor in an appropriate play-on-words, "is having the damnest boom you ever saw." The Rock Island project, affirmed the *World*, "has prevented our feeling the depression which has prevailed generally throughout the country."[26]

Held at bay in North Central Washington, the Great Depression provided the general economic backdrop for preparation of the 308 Report. The Development League and the Irrigation League mounted strenuous lobbying efforts. Beset by uninvited and undesirable visitors to his Seattle office, Major Butler had to lock away sensitive documents for reasons of security. Butler, especially "peeved" with James O'Sullivan, accused the Grand Coulee champion of "pestering him to death" with unsolicited advice. Willis Batcheller, a more polished lobbyist, delivered a stern message to his Development League associate: "I have tried unsuccessfully to get you to see that you are doing the only thing which can wreck our plans and get an unfavorable report from the army." O'Sullivan must henceforth "imagine Butler is living on the moon and is not where he can be seen or communicated with." The advice, and similar attempts on the part of Woods to control the organization's secretary, had little, if any, impact.[27]

Military engineers working on the report concluded that neither the pumping nor the gravity plan enjoyed genuine outpourings of popular opinion. The Columbia Basin Project, Colonel Gustave Lukesh of the Portland Corps office observed in November 1929, was "the cherished hope of a small and active group who have apparently no direct personal concern in its consummation beyond the expectation of increased commercial activity for their communities." There was, in his view, no "great *general* public interest" in either reclamation scheme. "A limited number of people" wanted "the Federal Government . . . [to] finance an undertaking for them." Although considerably more sympathetic than his colleague, Major Butler agreed that the timing and the findings of their survey must remain untainted by special interest influence.[28]

Practical considerations sharpened the focus of the supposedly multipurpose study. Flooding, as far as the mainstream of the Columbia was concerned, was a serious problem only on the tide-water section below the Cascades. As for navigation, the vessel running between the Methow and the Okanogan rivers, the last vestige of the steamboat era on the upper Columbia, had ceased operation. Reclamation, meanwhile, was of limited interest to Oregonians along the lower Columbia, though retaining its paramountcy above the mouth of the Snake. Power thus became the principal factor in the Army development scheme. Installed hydroelectric capacity in the Pacific Northwest, as of 1930, was slightly in excess of 1.1 million kilowatts. Puget's Rock Island project and other dams currently under way would add significantly to the energy supply, requiring the engineers to carefully consider the question of demand, both at present and far into the future. On the basis of quantifiable trends in consumption, Major Butler estimated that in fifteen to twenty-five years of sustained growth the electricity generated by the Grand Coulee project would be fully absorbed into the regional economy, necessitating the construction of additional dams on the Columbia.[29]

Ordered, for reasons of budgetary economy, to rely upon previous dubious studies for his data on the gravity plan, Butler concentrated on the pumping alternative. His staff examined foundation conditions at six possible damsites: Grand Coulee, Foster Creek, Wells, Chelan, Rocky Reach, and Vantage. At Grand Coulee, the Major developed plans for two dams, one 220 feet high, backing the river up to Kettle Falls, and the other 330 feet tall, impounding the stream to the Canadian border. Engineers working in the Seattle office focused on spillway designs and other technical matters. The result, leaked to all interested parties well in advance of the report's official completion date, was a definitive argument endorsing the project backed since 1918 by Rufus Woods. "Our studies," Butler wrote in a supposedly confidential memorandum, "show that the pumping plan . . . is the more economical plan."[30]

Infuriated by the realization that the Army intended to resolve the long dispute between the competing plans for development of the Columbia Basin, the previously disinterested Bureau of Reclamation suddenly found the resources for its own bureaucratic initiative. Director Elwood Mead secured $50,000 for a competing, albeit less-detailed, survey of the river in 1930 and ordered H.W. Bashore, his man on the scene, to "stick to your job and let the Engineers complete theirs." Rufus Woods worried that the Bureau, by "get[ting] suspicious at the army," would deliberately produce a report favorable to the gravity plan. With contradictory findings, one for Grand Coulee and the other for Albeni Falls, Congress might then do nothing. Jim O'Sullivan made matters worse, "embarrassing" and angering Mead by including his name on a Development League list of persons supporting the Columbia River dam.[31]

Expecting the Bureau to side with Spokane out of agency self-interest, Grand Coulee boosters fortified their own de facto alliance with the Army. The Irrigation League "buys all the whiskey," as O'Sullivan observed of that organization's preferred lobbying device, but the Dam University relied upon flattery. "Your work of engineering on this Columbia intrigues my imagination," Woods wrote Major Butler in one of several heavy-on-the-praise letters. "You are doing the most important work in the whole country so far as future results are concerned." The *World*, delivered daily to the Seattle office of the engineers, lauded the military on every possible occasion and regularly published photographs of the Major. "Butler," reported Willis Batcheller in August 1930, "was tickled to death with the . . . [issue] for the fifth containing his picture and all of the other half dozen articles."[32]

Through news coverage, "In Our Own World" columns, editorials, and guest articles by O'Sullivan and other dam advocates, Wood stressed the case for Grand Coulee. Washington, he pointed out, lagged far behind its neighbors in the development of arid lands. The state had 500,000 acres under irrigation, compared to three million each for Oregon and Idaho and six million for California. The Columbia Basin Project, providing homes for 250,000 people, would close the gap. The *World* also answered the principal criticisms of the opposition. Reclamation on a unit-by-unit basis, in parcels of 100,000 acres, reduced concern over the current agricultural surplus in America. "It will probably be from 25 to 30 years before the Columbia Basin . . . comes into [full] production," the paper asserted, "and at that time the demand for farm products will doubtless be greatly increased." The same argument supported the contention that all the energy generated at Grand Coulee would be needed. Electricity use in Washington was presently increasing at a rate of 13 percent a year and "by the time . . . power is ready for delivery there will be a shortage . . . in this state."[33]

With his publicity machine well-oiled, Woods departed on a tour of Europe, his first trip abroad. In New York for the annual meeting of the Associated Press in April 1930, Rufus, literally on the spur of the moment, booked passage on the *George Washington*. He learned the night before the vessel's scheduled sailing that he needed a passport and that the processing of the necessary paperwork normally took ten days. He requested emergency intervention from Representative Albert Johnson. Within hours, the precious document arrived at dockside, courtesy of a cooperative State Department. Boarding the ship, Woods carried only a briefcase, filled with notebooks, shaving gear, two shirts, and three changes of underwear.[34]

Taking a slow train from Hamburg, the *George Washington*'s continental port-of-call, Rufus secured a room in an elegant Berlin hostelry. Although well-appointed, the place charged only "three dollars a day about the same as the cost of the Davenport Hotel in Spokane." A glad-handing innocent abroad, Woods struck up conversations with bemused Germans on the bus and on street corners, several times securing invitations home for dinner. He tapped out impressions gathered from ordinary folk in this fashion on a borrowed German-language typewriter and dispatched them by mail for the enjoyment of family members and subscribers in Wenatchee. The people of Berlin, Rufus concluded on the basis of his sources in the city, were gratified by the defeat of autocracy and militarism in 1918 and had no desire for the restoration of imperial glory or the resumption of conflict in Europe.

Berlin was only a waystation on the road east, for Woods's main purpose in visiting Europe was to learn more about the Soviet Union, that "outlaw and Pariah among nations," to quote a recent *World* editorial. The Russian Revolution was "one of the really great events in all history" and worth studying at first hand, even by a Republican. Carrying a letter of introduction from Hugh Cooper, the American engineer involved in construction of the massive Dnieper River Dam, the Wenatchee journalist flew to the capital of world communism. At Associated Press headquarters, an office heavily stocked with anti-religious literature, Rufus met Anna Louise Strong, the one-time Seattle radical now living and writing in exile. He quickly grasped the bureaucratic nature of Soviet government, writing that in Russia "it is a risky thing for one man to assume the initiative." Naively, however, Woods greatly understated the brutality of Stalinist rule and missed entirely the terror involved in the collectivization of agriculture.

Indeed, Rufus thought the collective farm "the biggest thing in Russia." Escorted by government tourist guides, he visited several collectives in an idyllic, albeit staged, excursion into a romantic countryside. Woods rode into one village atop a load of grain in a peasant wagon. Colorfully garbed women worked at their chores and modern farm machinery, no doubt hauled in for the occasion, stood by the path, polished and ready for inspection. Speaking through an interpreter, the impressed American addressed the assembled villagers and answered questions on such topics as America's refusal to recognize the Soviet Union. Russia under the communists, Rufus determined on the basis of such apparently spontaneous episodes of good cheer, was something of a socialist version of Nebraska.

Homeward-bound, Woods endured the mundane vexations and bizarre experiences of the tired and harried tourist. A Constantinople money changer cheated him out of $2.50. Visiting Rome, Woods watched from the gallery as Mussolini, resplendent in operatic-style uniform, delivered a hysterical address to the Italian senate. During a brief stopover in England, Rufus allowed an unwitting London matron to persist is mistaking him for a Hollywood actor. The great European tour ended on a sour note, however, due to the anti-American tone of an English press preoccupied, to the extent of forgetting India, with the alleged crimes of American misrule in the Philippines.

Back in the Pacific Northwest, Woods devoted a series of columns and speaking engagements to his experiences in the Soviet Union. "In no other country in the world," he enthused, "is there such tremendous possibilities for the future." The violence of 1917 and thereafter, excusable in part due to the circumstances, had given way to a responsible, forward-looking attitude on the part of Stalin. The introduction of universal suffrage and the beginning of efforts to fully tap the nation's natural resources were among the positive developments. "PEOPLE . . . THROUGHOUT RUSSIA," Rufus summed up in all-capitals emphasis, "HAVE HAD ALL THE REVOLUTION THAT THEY WANT AND THEY ARE LOOKING FORWARD TO EVOLUTION." Private enterprise was actually making a comeback in certain limited sectors of the economy. The United States, he advised, ought to immediately commence negotiations leading to recognition of the Soviet government. Unimpressed by his enthusiasm, conservative residents of Wenatchee feared that Rufus Woods had once again sped off the political rails, this time to the extent of becoming an apologist of communism.[35]

Rufus returned home during the final stage of the Army's work on the 308 Report. Meeting with Major Butler in early 1931, he learned that the study would be completed, in draft form, by mid-summer. Although the complete text remained a closely guarded military secret, the crucial findings were released to the public in September. (Official publication of the final version, in two volumes of 1,800 finely printed pages, was delayed until 1933.) The report presented nothing less than a comprehensive scheme for development of the Columbia River and its adjacent territory. "An effort was made," explained Butler in the introduction, "to combine the different features into a harmonious plan for the fullest possible use of the natural resources of the region; a plan which, if followed, would insure the ultimate complete use of those resources for the most beneficial purposes and without unnecessary waste." Future circumstances might require alterations in the basic framework, but, said the Major, "it is confidently expected that the plan suggested will be a safe guide."[36]

Factual data, examined objectively, revealed that the Albeni Falls gravity project, though technically feasible, would likely cost $750 million, more than twice the estimate submitted by General Goethals. The estimated expenditure for Grand Coulee, in contrast, was a comparatively modest $341 million, a figure that might be substantially reduced, in terms of the charges to be assessed landowners, through the sale of electricity. Subsidized by the dam, Butler calculated, settlement at an annual rate of 25,000 acres would result in repayment of all construction costs in sixty-eight years. Projected population growth, along with increases in the demand for food in the Pacific Northwest, justified the watering of the basin on a gradual unit-by-unit basis. As its most important immediate contribution, the 308 Report established the practicability of the Columbia Basin Project and resolved the long, contentious, and often dishonest argument over the relative merits of the gravity and the pumping approaches.[37]

Hydroelectricity was the unifying theme of the reports drafted in Seattle and Portland. To facilitate maximum utilization of the river, Army engineers based in those cities recommended construction of eight dams: Grand Coulee, Foster Creek, Chelan, Rocky Reach, Rock Island, Priest Rapids, The Dalles, and Warrendale. "With one exception," Colonel Gustave Lukesh pointed out, "each dam as planned will back water practically up to the dam next above . . . making available for power production about all the head that can be obtained at each site without interference with the next." The exception was the stretch of river, with a drop in elevation of seventy-five feet, between the foot of Priest Rapids and the mouth of the Snake. Unable to find a suitable damsite and unwilling to flood Pasco, the Corps of Engineers advised that this segment of the Columbia be left undeveloped.[38]

The draft report provided cost estimates and preliminary construction diagrams for each dam. Undecided between a "low" or a "high" dam at Grand Coulee, Major Butler supplied designs for both. The smaller structure, 360 feet tall from the base of the foundation, had a $114 million pricetag. The larger soared to a level of 490 feet and required an expenditure of $181 million. Both options included a fifteen-unit powerhouse, with turbines to be installed in stages. Ten giant pumps would lift water from the Columbia into the natural storage reservoir of the Grand Coulee. The river itself would be impounded for 151 miles upstream, all the way to the Canadian border.[39]

Because the dams, especially the six proposed for the upper Columbia, were located in remote and sparsely populated places, the means and cost of power distribution were of considerable importance. "Some industries," Colonel Lukesh noted, "may find it economical to locate close to the generating stations, but the bulk of the energy will require long-distance . . . delivery to the points at which it can be used most conveniently"— namely Puget Sound and Oregon's Willamette Valley. According to Army calculations, constructing a 250-mile transmission network would cost $10 million. Economic justification for the dams and the power lines depended upon urban demand, a fact reflected in the report's detailed accounting of trends in consumption. Electricity output in the Pacific Northwest had grown at an average of 9.5 percent a year since the war. "At this rate," Lukesh stated, "the business doubles in 7.6 years." Conceding that long-term projections of growth were inherently uncertain, the engineers nonetheless concluded that all the dams would eventually be needed to meet regional energy needs.[40]

In total, the 308 Report detailed an undertaking of awesome proportions, ranking with the Panama Canal. "The structures contemplated in the scheme of power development," wrote General Lytle Brown, the new Chief of Engineers, "are all on a large scale, some on a grand scale, and the conditions at some of them as to foundations and flood discharge over the dams are without precedent." The plan called for nothing less than the transformation of the wild, free-flowing Columbia River into "the greatest system for water power to be found anywhere in the United States." Though daunting, the engineering problems were capable of resolution, leaving only the major obstacle of financing to be overcome. The cost of the dams alone, from Grand Coulee to Warrendale, was a staggering $711 million.[41]

Publication of the Army findings produced dismay in Spokane and joy in North Central Washington. "The most important news that has come over the wires for a long time came in . . . yesterday," the *World* crowed in announcing the happy news on September 22, 1931. David McGinnis, still a supporter of Grand Coulee though no longer active in the Development League, had expected the engineers to couple an endorsement of the concept with opposition to actual construction. His anxiety on this point relieved, Woods's old friend was "simply delirious at the transcendent news." Rufus himself exercised diplomatic restraint in print, calling upon defeated gravity supporters to "unite . . . in one grand move in behalf of Grand Coulee dam."[42]

That united movement would have to be carried out in the context of the belated arrival of the Great Depression in Wenatchee. For a year-and-a-half, residents had boasted of their immunity from the national economic crisis, thanks to the Rock Island project and the relative stability of the trade in apples. Although one-fourth of the Seattle labor force, according to reliable statistics, was out of work, the *World* dismissed reports of suffering elsewhere in Washington as "greatly exaggerated," manufactured by communists and other troublemakers. "East of the mountains," insisted the paper, ". . . there is virtually no unemployment." On the west side, the number of people without jobs supposedly represented, at worst, a slight increase above the normal fluctuations of an economy based upon lumbering. Making light of the crisis, the *World* denounced schemes for unemployment insurance as "a variation of the English dole system," advised readers to ignore panhandlers, and called upon "itinerant families" traveling the state in search of employment to return home so that their children might enjoy the "advantages of an education."[43]

Wenatchee was not, after all, safe from the Depression. As Rock Island Dam neared completion in the spring of 1931, project payrolls dropped form 3,000 workers to 500. "For the first time since the present depression struck the country," the *World* conceded in May, "this part of the state is beginning to feel the unemployment situation." Even so, there was still no fear of impending disaster. The jobless, after all, were mostly laid-off migratory dam workers, not genuine resident sons and daughters of North Central Washington. In a further indication of a basically sound local economy, "only about half the applicants" for relief in Chelan County were "willing to work at anything they can get for the wages offered." More often than not, families receiving grocery vouchers attempted to "get these orders cashed so that they can spend the money for tobacco and other luxuries." The *World* lost "faith in human nature," not in the health of Wenatchee.[44]

Unfortunately, apples finally and completely fell victim to the Depression. "Every misfortune that could possibly happen to the apple deal has taken place," the *World* reported in October 1931. Enormous domestic production, a sharp decline in Eastern demand, and a total collapse of the foreign market combined to impose a 40 percent price reduction on growers. Orchardists again pressed the Interstate Commerce Commission to cut freight rates, from 75 cents to 50 cents a box. The Great Northern, pressed by its own fiscal problems, responded by asking for an *increase* in freights. Delaying action on both requests, the ICC added to local problems by suspending an earlier grant of lower rates on westbound fruit shipments to Puget Sound. Altogether, Woods summed up, "we are taking the best licking . . . that we have had for 19 years."[45]

Clyde Pangborn's record-breaking trans-Pacific flight from Japan terminated in Wenatchee on October 5, 1931, surpassing "Lindbergh in all essentials" according to the *World*. The sensation, however, only briefly diverted local residents from their preoccupation with the economic collapse. The railroads, denounced by the *World* in issue after issue as "unholy, ungodly and DAMNABLE," continued to reject pleas for a voluntary reduction in freight charges. In June 1932, the Interstate Commerce Commission, apparently eager to prove itself a "tyrant" intent upon "injur[ing] everything it touches," sustained the existing rate. An unusually small apple crop, the product of adverse weather and heavy insect damage, prevented another major reduction in prices, but the industry remained hard-pressed. The Wenatchee Apple Blossom Festival, held annually since 1920, was canceled due to the inability of area business and growers to provide financing. "People are eating all right," Woods informed a friend, "but it is surprising how many are without any money at all." Barely holding on, the banks refused to "loan a dollar."[46]

Financial stringency greatly reduced the ability of North Central Washington to capitalize upon the 308 Report. Continued struggle was necessary, since the Army study was not, as many observers had initially expected, the final word on the matter. Major Butler and Colonel Lukesh, according to the normal practice of periodically rotating the assignments of uniformed officers, were transferred to other posts. Their report became the responsibility of Colonel Thomas M. Robins, who supervised, under a temporary organizational arrangement, all Corps of Engineers activities on the Pacific coast. Robins was preoccupied with business in California, fiscally conservative, hostile to public power, and, said Jim O'Sullivan, "damnably rotten." Assuming that the 308 Report somehow passed muster with the Colonel, it then required approval by a board of senior officers, the Chief of Engineers, and the Secretary of War. At that point, the final Army recommendations, quite possibly with significant alterations from the original version, went to Congress.[47]

The *World* was therefore justified in warning that "the great danger now is over confidence." In public, the defeated gravity forces accepted

Grand Coulee as the only practicable means of watering the Columbia Basin. Judge L.C. Gilman, the Great Northern's influential Puget Sound attorney, informed Woods, on the basis of "a heart to heart talk" with Roy Gill of the Irrigation League, that "everyone is convinced that if the project is to go ahead at all it will go ahead on the Grand Coulee plan." Rufus and his friends, always suspicious, remained unconvinced, fearing that Spokane still intended to sidetrack the dam. Rumors circulated that the Washington Water Power Company had assembled a "warchest" to lobby against congressional acceptance of the 308 Report. "Loud protestations of impartiality" on the part of Gill and Mark Woodruff were "just so much bunk, misrepresentation and in short, lies," wrote Gale Matthews, the Ephrata title company owner. Jim O'Sullivan dismissed "the hue and cry about . . . harmony" as "a big joke." The Dam University, though momentarily victorious, expected to fight a protracted struggle against an implacable foe determined to have the gravity plan or nothing.[48]

Distrust and paranoia manifested themselves east of the Cascades. So far as the *World* was publicly concerned, the time had arrived for all interests to "quit squabbling and quarreling among themselves." Rufus Woods nonetheless thought little of the united campaign effort organized in the late fall by Judge Gilman. Woods reluctantly agreed to serve on the coordinating committee with Gilman and representatives of the Spokane, Seattle, and Portland chambers of commerce. Over his objection, the panel decided to send a trio of lobbyists, each man financed by his own organization, to Washington, D.C.: John Underwood of the Seattle Chamber of Commerce, Roy Gill of the Irrigation League, and Jim O'Sullivan of the Development League. "It is preposterous," Woods fumed with respect to Gill's appointment, "to send a man back there . . . who has fought the deal for 13 years." The movement for cooperation, he told O'Sullivan, "was lined up slick as grease," designed to place a well-funded enemy of Grand Coulee officially on the scene for the actual purpose of sabotage.[49]

Rufus, at his own expense, had already been to the nation's capital "for the purpose of getting the lay of the land . . . in the different departments." At the War Department, he read the complete text of the 308 Report for the first time. Visiting the Bureau of Reclamation, Woods discovered that Elwood Mead was "getting along in years" and was "somewhat shifty" in manner. The disturbing presence of Roy Gill in Mead's office added to his fear that the reclamation engineers were mainly interested in thwarting the Army. Even so, he considered Mead's agency the better choice for involvement in actual construction of Grand Coulee. "The big dams in this country," Rufus wrote home, "have [all] been built by the reclamation service." Although the Corps of Engineers had secured victory for the pumping plan, experience counted when matters progressed to implementation of the 308 Report.[50]

With a group of Republican leaders from the state of Washington, Rufus called upon President Herbert Hoover on the evening of October 8. From previous conversations with administration officials, he knew that "the political phase of this situation" was "paramount" at the White House. Woods therefore informed the President that Grand Coulee would provide work relief for thousands of the unemployed, demonstrate the federal government's genuine interest in the Pacific Northwest, and boost the party's chances in 1932. Ignoring his many past endorsements of the Columbia Basin Project, Hoover rejected these arguments as completely unpersuasive. There was no market for the power, he explained, the farm surplus problem would be exacerbated, and the public treasury was bare. Besides, construction of Grand Coulee could not possibly begin in time to help Hoover's reelection campaign. Concealing his disappointment, Rufus acted the part of the good GOP soldier upon returning to Wenatchee, making no mention in the *World* of the President's disturbing "Confidential and not for Quotation" remarks.[51]

Hoover's abrupt dismissal of Grand Coulee was by no means the sole piece of bad news. In December, the Corps of Engineers review board issued a negative preliminary assessment of the 308 Report. For one thing, three smaller dams ought to be substituted for the single "high" dam proposed for The Dalles. Of greater significance, the panel found the forecasted growth in regional power demand "unduly optimistic" and made clear its conviction that the United States "would not be justified at the present time in making any improvement of the [Columbia] . . . other than as authorized by existing [navigation] projects." These conclusions appeared to have suddenly ruined the prospects of Grand Coulee. "The report from the engineers rather bowled us over," confessed Rufus. A full-scale hearing was still scheduled for Washington, D.C., however, providing the opportunity to overturn the findings. Stressing this point, Woods called for renewed labor on behalf of the project. "No one interested in the construction of Grand Coulee dam," stated a determined *World*, "should expect for one minute that the . . . government is going to present the . . . dam like a big Santa Claus to the people of this district." Everything depended on Jim O'Sullivan and Roy Gill.[52]

Reaching Washington at the end of November, O'Sullivan rented a tiny apartment for living quarters and office space. On the basis of a promise from Rufus that his $300 a month Development League salary would be forwarded on a regular basis, he reunited his family, separated for many miserable months by Depression-related money problems. The better-financed Gill, meanwhile, occupied a suite at the posh Shoreham Hotel. Supported by an apparently lavish expense account, he entertained senators and congressmen "helpful to our cause" at dinners and drinking parties. "Those who do not care for a cocktail," Gill noted in explaining his careful adherence to Prohibition era protocol, attended special lemonade socials.[53]

Initially, O'Sullivan and Gill met each morning with John Underwood to plan the day's activities. Preoccupied with his regular activities on behalf of Seattle, Underwood soon dropped out of active involvement. Convinced that O'Sullivan was insane, Gill also went his own way. "I dont [*sic*] tell . . . any one here much about what I am doing," the Irrigation League representative privately admitted. Underwood was reliable, he conceded, "but I cant [*sic*] tell much to him as he might unthinkingly drop a word to O'Sullivan." For all his surface polish and ample reserves of cash, Gill was another paranoid on the loose, sure that "Rufus Woods and his followers would do most anything to hurt me."[54]

The Dam University expected Senator Wesley Jones to push Grand Coulee forward to success, no matter what the Corps of Engineers finally recommended. Since 1929, the senator had stressed the importance of waiting for the 308 Report. Now, however, he could no longer justify delay on this basis. "If we fail to secure favorable action . . . you [can] charge it up to Jones," O'Sullivan wrote Woods from Washington. In the past, claimed O'Sullivan, the senator "has actually told the [Army] Rivers and Harbors Board what to do and they have done it." At home, Grand Coulee supporters intended to hold Jones to strict account in 1932, when he would seek a fifth term. "There is a growing feeling," noted Rufus, "that if the old boy doesn't deliver we [might] just as well begin to look for a new senator."[55]

More convinced than ever that "things are not accomplished by fuss, noise and speeches," Jones resented the pressure applied from eastern Washington, especially the threat that he would be held responsible for the defeat of Grand Coulee. "I tell you Wood[s]," he complained to Rufus, "it is pretty tough when one is doing all he can to accomplish something to have his sincerity and his motives questioned." Blaming O'Sullivan for the "black-mail" attempt, Jones, according to one well-placed observer, shunned the

Development League secretary whenever he could. Unconcerned that personal antagonism might eventually prove counterproductive, O'Sullivan gloried in the senator's discomfort. "I only wish I could raise Hell with all our delegation," he reported to Woods.[56]

Rufus was horrified to learn that O'Sullivan had found a more congenial Washington associate in Senator Clarence Dill. Attempting to supervise the lobbying effort from afar, Woods warned that Dill was unreliable, entirely self-interested, and attempting to manipulate the dam issue for partisan purposes. O'Sullivan conceded that his newfound ally "may be trying to put Hoover in the hole out West," but for the moment persisted in accepting the Spokane Democrat's honorable intentions. "Regardless of politics," he argued in a series of unconvincing messages home, Dill was "sincere in trying to push the basin along" and "doing it for the sake of the project" alone.[57]

Influenced in particular by Frank Bell of Ephrata, Dill's adroit private secretary, O'Sullivan credited the senator with prodding Jones into jointly sponsoring legislation authorizing Grand Coulee as a Bureau of Reclamation project. The original text of the bill, though, produced an emotional outburst. "The conspiracy is now clear," O'Sullivan informed Woods in the first week of January 1932, for the wording was in actual fact "the entering wedge to overthrow the army report." The measure failed to specify the structure's height or the exact place at which irrigation water was to be diverted from the Columbia. Without explicit language on these vital points, said O'Sullivan, "I should not be surprised to see the gravity [plan] resurrected . . . and the Grand Coulee lowered so as not to interfere with Kettle Falls." Pro-Spokane bias on the part of the sponsors appeared to explain the deliberate oversight. Jones was "working hand in hand" with Roy Gill, claimed O'Sullivan. Clarence Dill, for all his suddenly apparent virtues, was "after all a Spokane man." Even Sam B. Hill, the respected former Douglas County judge whose Fifth Congressional District extended from the Cascades to the Idaho border, was "damnedly afraid . . . of the Spokane vote."[58]

Rising to the challenge, O'Sullivan "cuss[ed] and threaten[ed]" for two days before Jones and Dill agreed to change the bill. O'Sullivan claimed that Republican Representative Ralph Horr of Seattle, a Grand Coulee supporter and possible challenger of Jones in the 1932 senatorial primary, intended to introduce legislation authorizing construction under the terms of the 308 Report. Sidestepping that threat, Jones and Dill amended their measure in accordance with Dam University wishes. Their proposal now called for a spillway "of the greatest practical and necessary height" and required diversion of water at the damsite. Victorious at the cost of "a real row," O'Sullivan anticipated further inventive challenges to Grand Coulee. "If anybody out there thinks things are on the square here, let him forget it," he observed in a report to Woods. "Believe me, they will lower our dam if we don't look out and they will work back to the gravity [plan]."[59]

After stiffening the resolve of Washington's congressional delegation, O'Sullivan turned to his other major assignment, the formal Army hearings on the 308 Report. "We cannot pass a bill without the engineering reports," he explained in another message home. O'Sullivan visited Corps of Engineers headquarters "every day," waylaying officials and examining documents. Much of the intelligence gathered on these forays was discouraging. By happenstance, he discovered a confidential memorandum from Colonel Robins disparaging the Butler-Lukesh forecast on future markets for electricity. Colonel William Barden, the chairman of the Army engineering board and the presiding officer at the coming hearing, gave every indication of being "a tool of the power trust." The board members in general, O'Sullivan reported, were "hard boiled" and "don't seem to give a damn for facts."[60]

Testifying at the January 18 hearing, O'Sullivan read a detailed brief based upon the draft 308 Report and called upon the board to endorse the fieldwork of Major Butler and Colonel Lukesh. Roy Gill, apparently without ulterior motive, testified on behalf of the recently completed Bureau of Reclamation study, which actually recommended a larger dam than the report prepared by the Army. Secretary of Agriculture Arthur Hyde, speaking for the opposition, forcefully claimed, on the basis of incoherent statistical analysis, that farm land currently under cultivation in the United States could meet the nation's food needs until at least 1950. There was no need for the Columbia Basin Project. The board's only recorded response to the testimony was a complaint from Colonel Barden that the Jones-Dill bill before Congress called for construction by the Bureau rather than the Army.[61]

By early February, the basic outline of the board's decision had become public knowledge. The verdict reaffirmed the December conclusions on the issues of power markets and the farm surplus. Finding no economic justification for federal involvement in dam construction, the panel sustained the 308 Report only as a planning guide for private development projects on the Columbia. "The situation . . . has driven me almost wild," O'Sullivan wrote of the "deviltry" perpetrated by "those pirates on the Board." The dimensions of a vast conspiracy against Grand Coulee had, in his view, finally been revealed. President Hoover and the Washington congressional delegation, Clarence Dill included after all, headed the list of the plotters acting on behalf of the private utility industry. The Army was merely "the safe instrument to kill off the project before it gets to Congress—thus relieving the whole bunch from any blame." In a summation dispatched to Woods in Wenatchee, O'Sullivan mixed metaphors in comparing his poorly paid and tireless lobbying effort to "an uphill battle with the cards stacked against you."[62]

One slender hope remained, so far as the Army was concerned. The engineering board findings had to be endorsed, pro or con, by General Lytle Brown, the Chief of Engineers. Badgered by O'Sullivan, Brown promised an independent judgment and even volunteered the opinion that Senator Jones needed Grand Coulee in order "to win out at the next election." Fully attuned to this vital point, Jones himself, noted O'Sullivan, "has been doing some work to straighten out the army report." At the end of March, however, Brown approved the board's assessment, causing the 308 Report, in its final official form, to render a negative opinion on the building of Columbia River dams by the federal government. Issuing a hysterical denunciation of the Corps of Engineers, O'Sullivan complained of being "doublecrossed" and charged that the "densely ignorant" General Brown "did not know if the Grand Coulee dam was on the Columbia or in Timbuctoo."[63]

Belittled in the *World* as "Swivel Chair Engineers," Brown and the Army board delivered a crippling blow to the dam. But the blame, according to O'Sullivan, belonged to Senator Jones and Roy Gill. "If I was not here watching every move, making a fight for the project at every turn, and arousing public opinion," claimed the Development League lobbyist in another of his vivid accounts to Woods, ". . . we would be nowhere today." For all the energy expended, however, the fact of the matter was that Grand Coulee had advanced but a short distance beyond nowhere status. The final Army report ended any hope of securing a favorable vote in Congress. O'Sullivan nonetheless insisted upon proceeding with formal House and Senate hearings, to "establish the merits of the project . . . and save time making a record later on." With the Hoover Administration and the Democratic-controlled House of Representatives both working on public works programs, the one to operate through the Reconstruction Finance Corporation and the other to be financed by a federal bond issue, Grand Coulee might yet be resuscitated, possibly in the next session of Congress.[64]

Under arrangements made by Representative Sam Hill, O'Sullivan appeared before the House reclamation committee in June. Major Butler, flying in from Omaha for the occasion, was, however, the principal witness on behalf of Grand Coulee. "God bless him . . .," wrote O'Sullivan. "He came right down the line for the big dam even though there might be a . . . reprisal from his superiors." Without time to prepare in advance and forced to depart immediately afterward, the Major asked O'Sullivan to read and, where necessary, edit his testimony before publication in the official hearing record. Taking full advantage of this opportunity to modify Butler's arguments, O'Sullivan advised in a confidential message to Wenatchee that the Major "will find himself making statements . . . that will surprise him."[65]

Even a doctored transcript proved unavailing, at least under prevailing political circumstances. Major Butler's unwittingly exaggerated testimony was the final stroke on behalf of Grand Coulee. "We have probably gone as far as we can," O'Sullivan reported at the end of June. Senators and congressmen were eager to adjourn for the presidential nominating conventions and the approaching 1932 campaign season. "The project is now in excellent shape to be shoved ahead . . . at the next session," claimed O'Sullivan, especially considering the probable impact of the Depression on the partisan makeup of the Congress to be elected in November. He lingered on in Washington through the summer and into the fall, issuing unread public statements and pestering those officials unable to escape his attentions.[66]

Frustrated by the rejection of the 308 Report, ignored in Washington, and apparently forgotten at home, O'Sullivan saw himself as a martyr to a lost cause. His paychecks, except for a token $150 received from Woods in July, failed to arrive. "Unless I get some money soon," he wrote in August, "I will be out on the street, with my family, without any food or shelter, and no means to get anywhere." The Development League, at this low point of the Depression, was, however, simply out of money. Billy Clapp advised that his law practice rarely generated income in excess of $20 a month and that the drought-ravaged residents of Ephrata were incapable of making further contributions. Wenatchee, too, was "broke," Ed Southard observed after a visit to Chelan County. Rufus Woods confirmed this bleak intelligence. Subjected to hectoring and other forms of "high pressure," Wenatchee merchants gave $42 to the cause, "but told us not to come back again."[67]

Ignoring these reports of dire conditions at home, O'Sullivan blamed his plight on Woods, who failed to honor, no doubt from habitual inattention to detail, the promises of financial support. Rufus was, in fact, preoccupied by the death of the aged Lebbeus Woods in August. Letters and telegrams from the nation's capital to Wenatchee went unanswered as he attended the Nebraska funeral and handled, with Ralph, problems associated with initial disposition of the family estate. Finally, on October 5, Woods wired O'Sullivan enough money, drawn from his own pocket, to pay outstanding bills and purchase a ticket home to Washington state. The likelihood of O'Sullivan receiving any more funds, including past-due salary, was close to nil. "It is just a matter of how much can be raised," explained Rufus, "and you will have to accept it that way." O'Sullivan's ignominious return to the Pacific Northwest, one step ahead of the creditors, signalled the apparent end of the fight for Grand Coulee Dam. The hopes raised by the draft recommendations of the 308 Report had been dashed. The Hoover Administration opposed construction, Congress was disinterested, and, as long as the Great Depression persisted, there appeared to be no chance of building new dams, public or private, on the Columbia River.[68]

Addressing a convention of the U.S. Chamber of Commerce in Spokane in December 1931, Rufus Woods maintained that the proposed Grand Coulee Dam represented "the spirit and genius of the American people[,] which more than anything else has made possible in our land a better human life."[69] The bitter struggle for the project also reflected the national propensity for waste, confusion, and political intrigue. The introduction of the Corps of Engineers as a major institutional force on the upper Columbia resulted in the crucial 308 Report, but also initiated years of bureaucratic conflict between that agency and the Bureau of Reclamation, interfering with efficient and economical work in the Pacific Northwest. The fate of the report in Washington in 1931 and 1932 suggested that dams might be more readily secured through the Democratic than through the Republican party, a point dimly grasped by Jim O'Sullivan through his work with Clarence Dill and Sam Hill. In the future, Rufus Woods would have to work closely with Democrats, would have to make Grand Coulee a bipartisan, indeed an apolitical, undertaking. Born of progressive Theodore Roosevelt conservation, the project was stalled by the increasingly conservative nature of a Republicanism oriented toward the farm belt and the corporation. O'Sullivan's mission to the nation's capital also exposed the limitations of the conventional engineering mindset. On the basis of supposedly objective facts, the Army and President Hoover, the "Great Engineer" of the 1920s, rejected the recommendations of Major Butler and Colonel Lukesh. If Grand Coulee was to be secured—a highly doubtful proposition as of the summer of 1932—pedestrian calculation of cost and benefit must give way to vision; political genius must replace naysaying.

# Chapter Eight
## For Ten Thousand Years

It is a remarkable thing to have both a president and a governor who are in sympathy with the construction of the Grand Coulee Dam. The big job will be a monument to both of them, and it will be a monument that will last for ten thousand years in the future and then some.

Rufus Woods[1]

AFTER ELEVEN uncomfortable months in Washington, D.C., Jim O'Sullivan returned to a Pacific Northwest fully involved in the final crisis of the Great Depression. Genuine misery, rather than any failure on the part of Rufus Woods to honor financial commitments, explained the lack of support provided his lobbying mission. West of the Cascades, the timber industry ran at less than a fifth of capacity, with production and payrolls down by two-thirds since 1929. In Seattle, 50,000 people received some form of public or private assistance. The unemployed marched in the streets of the city, demanding work, and hundreds found shelter in a Hooverville built of packing crates and salvaged lumber. Along the Columbia, meanwhile, orchard owners followed the wheat ranchers into economic ruination, and the banks, holding worthless mortgage paper and harried by fearful depositors, closed their doors.[2]

Rufus Woods frankly admitted, after intense personal reflection on the Depression, that "the question of the remedy . . . is one which stumps about all of us." His discussions with members of local service organizations suggested that residents of the Wenatchee Valley agreed upon the need for public works projects and upon a requirement that the unemployed take any job offered, even if room and board was the only remuneration. Use of the negative word "depression" must also be avoided, since "constant . . . reference to it is detrimental to all concerned." Wenatchee certainly opposed any tinkering with the basic tenets of capitalism. "Experience . . . shows that natural laws govern in these matters," noted Woods in agreeing with these sentiments. Americans, he argued, must give up the debilitating habit of "yelling for Uncle Sam to come to our rescue whenever we get into trouble."[3]

Since the normal cyclical workings of the economy would eventually bring about recovery, the intelligent course was to avoid measures that might actually delay the return of prosperity. "Unemployment is a local condition," affirmed the *World* in August 1931, "and should be handled by the various communities." Taking action in accord with this philosophy, North Central Washington chambers of commerce issued identity cards to out-of-work local residents to insure that jobs were filled only by such persons. They warned "outsiders" to "keep away." Sharp reductions in taxes and public spending were also traditional approaches to depressed economic conditions. A new Wenatchee city administration, voted into office in 1931, slashed spending by one-third. Chelan County, also under pressure from the *World* and from angry taxpayers, eliminated $100,000 from its budget. Following the defeat of Wenatchee's school levy in 1932, teachers had to accept substantial salary reductions. These measures only partially relieved the burden upon property owners. "Instead of a pruning knife," the *World* contended, "we will have to . . . use the axe if we expect to make our expenses balance our sadly depleted income."[4]

Calling for a "new deal" on taxes and spending, Woods also favored old candidates and traditional party alignments, in effect endorsing the very system responsible for the high rates of taxation. He believed the re-election of Herbert Hoover in 1932, more than any other action, was essential to economic recovery. The President had faced the national crisis with Theodore Rooseveltian vigor and, if not already in the White House, would have been "the one man above all others to whom people of all parties would naturally turn and choose as a Moses to lead them out of the . . . wilderness." The Reconstruction Finance Corporation, Hoover's most innovative anti-Depression measure, already offered loans to banks and railroads and might eventually provide credits to apple growers. The 1932 presidential campaign, observed Woods, must be decided by principle, not by personality: "The Republican party has always been the party of stability, and never has there been such a need for steadfast adherence to common sense . . . as at present."[5]

Hoover's stature was enhanced by comparison with Democratic nominee Franklin D. Roosevelt. The governor of New York, a cousin of the great TR, deserved praise for fighting back against terrible illness, but he was still a pitiable figure of modest and limited personal dimension. Forgetting that Roosevelt had visited the Columbia Basin while campaigning for vice-president in 1920, the *World* ridiculed him as another out-of-touch Easterner, an aristocratic Al Smith. "If Roosevelt has ever been in the west," the paper noted, "we never heard of it." Reminding readers that "the job of president is a man-killer," the *World* not so subtly drew attention to FDR's paralysis as another disqualifying factor.[6]

The selection of a weak and undeserving challenger by the Democrats apparently guaranteed another four years of Hoover in the White House. The *World* was also relieved by the victory of Wenatchee's own John Gellatly in the Republican gubernatorial primary. Roland Hartley, who had burnished his reputation for total irresponsibility by refusing to call a special anti-Depression legislative session, was thereby removed as a drag on the ticket. The Democratic Party was bound for destruction in the state of Washington, judging from the caliber of its candidates. Cheney miller Clarence D. Martin, nominated for governor, was the only dependable and businesslike person on the opposition slate. Among other obviously unfit characters, Seattle band leader Vic Meyers, ridiculed by the *World* as a player of "provocative" music, received the nomination for lieutenant governor. The chameleon-like challenger to Wesley Jones was Homer T. Bone, at various times in the past a socialist, a Farmer Laborite, a LaFollette Progressive, and a Republican. "A comparison of the tickets," summed up a confident *World*, ". . . cannot but impress the thinking voter with the distinct superiority of . . . the Republicans."[7]

In the third week of September, Rufus Woods crossed the Cascades to attend and report on a Seattle rally for Roosevelt. A raucous standing-room-only throng jammed the city's Civic Arena, drowning out an attempted introductory speech by Clarence Dill. Ninety minutes late, Roosevelt made his appearance, cane-in-hand and assisted by a son. "He is much more handicapped than any one had dreamed," wrote Rufus in an attempt to undermine confidence in the candidate's health. A "feeling of pity and hushed silence" supposedly fell upon the assembled Democrats. FDR waved and smiled, but otherwise appeared "tired and worn out" as he carefully crossed the stage. The New York governor's address, dealing with the Democratic position on the tariff, "disappoint[ed] . . . his followers." The speech was "the talk of an affable, tired man, without any points to carry conviction" and, more than ever, made Hoover look like a winner.[8]

Unfortunately, considering the historical significance, Rufus ignored Roosevelt's next campaign appearance, in Portland on September 21. The Democratic candidate's speech that day focused on the potential economic and social impact of electrical energy. Already, said FDR, the public interest had been advanced in three of America's four geographical corners. On the St. Lawrence River, at Muscle Shoals on the Tennessee, and at Boulder Dam, hydroelectricity provided, or would soon provide, "a national yardstick to prevent extortion" by private industry. The time was now at hand, according to Roosevelt, for the Pacific Northwest to share in this freedom from dependence on corporate monopoly. "I state in definite . . . terms," he pledged, "that the next great hydro-electric development to be undertaken by the Federal Government must be that on the Columbia River."[9] The promise amounted to a resurrection of the 308 Report, to a realization of the dreams of those who had fought for dams on the stream. By failing to cover the Portland speech, Woods avoided facing the emerging dilemma of his political life: Democrats, as a rule, supported and Republicans, in general, opposed Grand Coulee.

Republican faith in the American people was sorely tested on election day. As but one small component of his national victory, Roosevelt secured 57 percent of the Washington vote. Clarence Martin won with a similar percentage, carrying all but two counties. The Democrats obtained a 70-29 majority in the state house of representatives and, except for the staggered nature of senatorial terms, would have taken more than the 25 of the 46 senate seats they did secure. Homer Bone defeated Wesley Jones by a wide margin, a rebuff so personally devastating to the veteran senator that he died a few days later. Rufus Woods was also devastated. Aside from briefly commenting upon the decisive impact of the urban vote on the Democratic triumph, the *World* published no post-election observations.[10]

Political upheaval opened new opportunities for Grand Coulee, at the national and at the state level. According to prevailing constitutional guidelines, Roosevelt would not take office until March 1933. Hoover remained in the White House for four increasingly bitter months, discredited and neither willing nor able to initiate new policies. Wesley Jones was gone and Clarence Dill, now Washington's senior senator, was, as a vocal critic of the administration, despised by Hoover. Operating in this political vacuum, Senator Charles McNary of Oregon and Colonel Thomas Robins of the Corps of Engineers launched a campaign for a federal dam on the lower Columbia, either at Umatilla Rapids or at Bonneville, the latter a damsite now favored over Warrendale. "It looks as if, through the appeal of navigation," warned Jim O'Sullivan, ". . . they might box us out and isolate the demand for Grand Coulee to a section of the State of Washington." All commentators agreed that the United States was unlikely to undertake two dams on the Columbia River at the same time. Without immediate action in the nation's capital, noted Roy Gill, an apparently sincere convert to Grand Coulee, "we will be set back thirty years, or more."[11]

Clarence Martin and the Democrats assumed power in Olympia in January 1933, two months in advance of the national changeover. Since the rejection of the 308 Report, the Dam University had focused on the possibility of the state building Grand Coulee. "I have no more hope of our Federal Government doing the job," asserted Ephrata attorney W.E. Southard, "than I have [of] Mahatma Gahndi [*sic*] doing it." Under a scheme pushed by Southard, an expressly designated sales tax would finance construction of the dam. Agreeing that the plan had merit, Rufus Woods advised that it be kept under wraps for the time being, to keep open the option of money from the federal government. Southard restrained his enthusiasm, at least in public, despite considerable annoyance over the cautious approach advocated by Woods. "I am as loyal to you as a dog Rufus," he thundered, "but great Heavens, we are going to sit here and let Congress play with us for a quarter of a century, and let Oregon get in with a big power plant down the river and shut us off." The only sensible course was for the state of Washington to "tell Congress to go to h—l, and do this thing ourselves."[12]

McNary's aggressive campaign for a dam on the lower Columbia made the state option more attractive. Several weeks before taking office, Governor-elect Martin announced his support for Grand Coulee and recommended formation of a new Columbia Basin Commission. Under the terms of a measure drafted by E.F. Banker, who would lead the Democratic majority in the 1933 legislature, the commission was empowered to "employ any and all means . . . to secure the early construction of the Columbia Basin Project." Visiting Wenatchee, Martin conferred at length on these subjects with Rufus. Setting aside their recent partisan differences, the

Democrat and the Republican established a cross-party political alliance, based upon common interest in river development. Woods, quipped Martin, "has almost had a change of heart and is really a Progressive Democrat."[13]

On the eve of his inauguration, Martin observed that "this [Columbia Basin] matter is going to assume a state aspect this year," with the commission handling the subject. Plotting a course for the legislative session, Grand Coulee supporters conceded that Oregon was far ahead in the quest for a federal project. "You can imagine how far we will get trying for both dams at one time," Southard wrote to Woods. Washington state had alternatives. Martin, Woods, and O'Sullivan wanted the Columbia Basin Commission, once organized, to secure funds from the Reconstruction Finance Corporation. Willis Batcheller favored another course, which avoided all federal involvement by using Martin's proposed $10 million relief bond issue to begin construction.[14]

Woods and O'Sullivan, in close contact with Martin, recognized the political drawbacks to any proposal devoting the statewide relief fund to a single public works venture. Advocating a politics-be-damned approach, Batcheller warned that federal financing inevitably entailed federal control of the project. Federal control, of course, threatened his own ambition of becoming chief engineer at Grand Coulee. "You have promised me during the last few years," Batcheller wrote Rufus, ". . . that when the Grand Coulee project is ready to be started, you would assist in every way possible to insure my employment to take charge of the enterprise." The reward was justified, insisted the engineer in a revealing moment of megalomania, by "the fact that it is my plan, others merely approving and amplifying it."[15]

Batcheller's all-state approach was fine in theory, his erstwhile friends in the Dam University conceded, but faltered in its reliance upon the $10 million relief fund. "To finance the project," Jim O'Sullivan pointed out after calculating the total cost of construction, "would [eventually] require either taxation or a bond issue of at least $150,000,000." Carrying this burden, a state-financed dam would never be completed and Olympia would, in the meantime, have "close[d] the door to Federal authorization." Legislation drafted by Batcheller passed in the senate but died without a vote in the house, to the relief of those favoring a more roundabout means of securing the dam. Responding to Governor Martin's call, the legislature established the Columbia Basin Commission, with five unpaid commissioners, a full-time executive secretary, and an appropriation of $50,000.[16]

As finally constituted by Martin, the commission joined Inland Empire and North Central Washington wheat and fruit producers in a deliberate balancing of interests. E.F. Banker, who became director of the Department of Conservation and Development at the close of the legislative session, served as chairman, endorsed for the position by Woods. According to arrangements previously worked out with the governor, Rufus himself was appointed a commissioner. State Grange Master Albert Goss, another commissioner was, like Woods, a Republican. Moses Lake orchardist Harvey Smith, a Democratic state senator, and Spokane insurance man J.E. McGovern filled the remaining seats. According to O'Sullivan, the commission had a built-in four-to-one majority in favor of Grand Coulee, with only McGovern, one of "the deadliest enemies of the dam," in opposition as the representative of the Columbia Basin Irrigation League position.[17]

Meeting in Spokane on April 5, 1933, the Columbia Basin Commission renewed the fight for Grand Coulee. "The main theme was to get action," Rufus stressed in advancing $300 from his own pocket so that business could proceed pending receipt of the funds appropriated by the legislature. With this cash-in-hand, the commission named James O'Sullivan its secretary and leased the office space formerly occupied by the Irrigation League. Rubbing out a longtime nemesis, O'Sullivan personally painted over the League's name on the office door. Further satisfaction came from the discovery of a file of Roy Gill letters, inadvertently left behind, detailing the lobbyist's liquor-soaked efforts to influence members of Congress.[18]

With the commission at last in operation, O'Sullivan hoped to "hold the road open to either State or Federal development." Ideally, Franklin Roosevelt would honor his Portland campaign pledge by calling for congressional authorization of Grand Coulee. The problem, as Senator Clarence Dill reported, was the President's preoccupation, in the first hundred days of the New Deal, with assorted political and economic emergencies. "We have never had the project adopted," the senator added, "and the minute that we propose that, we run up against the opposition of the . . . farm states." Considering the prevailing hostility to reclamation on the part of senators and congressmen, the most that Dill expected was possible approval of Grand Coulee "within the next year or so." This negative prognosis forced the commission to concentrate on state construction, financed by a portion of Governor Martin's welfare fund and by a loan from the Reconstruction Finance Corporation (RFC).[19]

As the first step toward obtaining funds from the RFC, the Columbia Basin Commission sent Albert Goss east to "seek an interview with President Roosevelt to urge him to include the Grand Coulee dam . . . in his public works program." Goss had been ready, on election eve the previous fall, to deliver a radio address in support of FDR in the event national Grange officials endorsed Hoover. Recognizing that the White House owed Goss a favor, Woods and O'Sullivan congratulated themselves upon the "masterstroke" involved in persuading the farm leader to serve as a commissioner. Departing for Washington, Goss remarked that he would, as a matter of courtesy, ask Senator Dill to arrange his appointment with the President.[20]

Unfortunately, Dill, who also had favors coming as the result of his early endorsement of FDR's presidential candidacy, proved to be a dilatory guide. The senator had already promised J.D. Ross of the Seattle municipal lighting department that he would support the City Light application for a RFC loan to fund the Skagit River project. The RFC was unlikely to contribute to two expensive Washington state dams, so Dill had to betray Ross in order to help Grand Coulee. While deciding how best to proceed, in his own political interest, the senator delayed making a White House appointment for the representative of the Columbia Basin Commission. A decade later, Goss still seethed over "how hard it was to get him to do a thing when I came back here."[21]

Pressed by the Washington Grange Master, Dill finally arranged a meeting with the President for April 17. Although the Senator was present, Roosevelt and Goss did most of the talking. FDR's "first comment," wrote Goss later in the day, "was that he knew very little about the project except that he carried the impression that it was too large to finance at this time." The current $160 million cost estimate for the dam alone, plus the bill for reclaiming the Columbia Basin, made Grand Coulee, in the President's words, "too big a proposal to handle . . . in Congress." Roosevelt was nonetheless enthused over the general concept, eager to develop the Columbia, and happy to repay the obligation owed his political supporters in the Pacific Northwest.[22]

Under certain conditions, Roosevelt assured his guests, he would support a Reconstruction Finance Corporation loan to build Grand Coulee. The plans must be revised to provide for a "low dam . . . with foundations sufficiently strong for [a] higher dam later." This program of "step development" entailed the expenditure of "probably fifty or sixty million dollars during [the] next four years," substantially reducing the federal government's obligation. Reliance on the RFC also meant that the project did not have to be submitted to Congress. The "low dam," moreover, would not raise the Columbia high enough to economically pump water into the coulee reservoir. As a result, Roosevelt wrote in an informal letter of agreed-upon principles, reclamation must be "deferred until such time as existing lands suitable for agriculture have been taken up." Although pleased on this point, Goss objected to the low dam, fearing that it would increase the cost of power generated to unmarketable levels. The Columbia Basin Commission depended on the President for funding, however, and Goss advised his colleagues at home that "there was nothing further to do except to follow out his suggestion."[23]

Albert Goss left the White House "disappointed in the President's attitude" respecting the size of the dam. Clarence Dill, though, was "quite elated." Previously a skeptic so far as Grand Coulee was concerned, the senator now "dream[ed] dreams" and saw "visions that are truly wonderful." In particular, Dill thought the Columbia Basin Commission could be transformed into a region-wide energy-marketing agency, the Columbia River Power Company, producing "enough revenue to pay all the taxes of the State." The individual responsible for this stupendous undertaking, obviously Dill himself, would "write . . . [his] name forever in the history of the Northwest" and also be the clear choice for appointment as manager of the publicly owned power firm. "We simply must have somebody at the head of this work," said the senator, "who can not be reached by the big power interests, and who at the same time understands their methods and their far reaching activities, all of which will be used to . . . cause [the] failure of this great development."[24]

Dill's contemporaries had little doubt as to the reasoning behind his late conversion to all-out support of the dam. The Columbia Basin Project was "a degenerate real estate scheme" according to J.D. Ross. The senator's longtime associate Frank Bell, recently appointed director of the federal marine fisheries bureau, was, claimed Ross, the head of an "association" owning at least 20,000 acres in the Big Bend. Information gathered by detectives on the City Light payroll confirmed that Dill himself was "a partner of that association," as well as a participant in other speculative ventures. Members of the Dam University indirectly confirmed the accusations. Personal letters referred to the "dead cat in Senator Dills[*sic*] closet" and to his "personal activity" in the Columbia Basin. "This is Frank Bells[*sic*] old town," W.E. Southard wrote from Ephrata, "and we have Dills[*sic*] measure." Reporting to Jim O'Sullivan, Rufus Woods made no attempt to refute rumors that the senator was involved "in a gigantic land speculation scheme."[25]

Woods and his friends treated Dill's claim to be the father of Grand Coulee with scorn. According to the senator's subsequent and oft-repeated account, he had, beginning in January 1931, regularly informed Franklin Roosevelt of "our hopes for a President who would build the great dam." The two men supposedly discussed the project on many occasions prior to the 1932 election. "He often said to me," recalled Dill, "if we succeeded in electing him, 'I'll build your dam.'" These statements were simply untrue, as demonstrated by the contemporary record. Reporting upon the crucial Roosevelt-Goss conference, Dill wrote that FDR was "studying the Columbia Basin project for the first time" and had previously been given no "definite or official information about it." The senator himself admitted at the time that "I have never been convinced until now that this project could be built." Dill had a negative attitude toward Grand Coulee as late as April 1933, remembered Albert Goss: "he was not only not pushing it but he was doing his best to discourage it."[26]

Accepting appointment as head of the federal farm loan bank, Goss removed himself from active involvement in the Grand Coulee campaign, leaving Senator Dill as the vital link between the Columbia Basin Commission and Franklin Roosevelt. Aware that Dill was selfish and believing the reports of his involvement in land speculation to be true, members of the Dam University were far from enthused over this dependence on an old antagonist. In recent times, the *World* had attacked Dill for opposing U.S. intervention in Nicaragua, made fun of his proposal for broadcasting Senate debates, and accorded him high rank among the "many pygmies in the political life of the country." Circumstances now required a shift, at least in print, from expressions of disgust to unadulterated praise. Dill "has grown wonderfully in the past few years," Rufus abruptly announced, to the amazement of readers of his column. In letters of encouragement to the senator, Woods revealed the rationale behind his support for the one-time "traitor" to America: "one of the most important things in connection with this whole affair is the elimination of red tape, by President Roosevelt and yourself."[27]

Private discomfort with Clarence Dill was as nothing compared to the appalled reaction of Woods and other Grand Coulee supporters to the design changes mandated by the White House. The people of Ephrata and Quincy, not to mention hardscrabble dryland ranchers outside those towns, objected to the indefinite postponement of reclamation. The principal criticism, though, focused on the low dam policy. Recording the response of the Columbia Basin Commission, E.F. Banker noted that "the members . . . were not satisfied with this idea." According to quick calculations by Jim O'Sullivan, the level of funding acceptable to the President was sufficient to build a structure only sixty feet above low water mark. The headgates, intakes, penstocks, and generators suitable to a project of this limited height "would have to be junked" upon commencement of the "high" dam, Willis Batcheller pointed out, greatly increasing the final cost. The unit method, moreover, allowed time for Washington Water Power to build its Kettle Falls project, which would forever limit Grand Coulee to modest dimensions. "The low dam," cautioned Gale Matthews of the Dam University, "is the old power company idea for the purpose of giving them an opportunity to build private dams further up the river."[28]

Roosevelt's insistence that the state employ the Bureau of Reclamation to draw detailed construction plans was an additional irritation. The problem with the President's demand, wrote Woods, was that the "Reclamation Service [is] too dilatory and has always had to be pushed into action." Relief for the unemployed would be delayed, probably by a year or more. "We have plenty of engineers that can do the job," Ed Southard reminded the Columbia Basin Commission, "and they are out of work." Of particular concern, involving the Bureau might be the first step toward eventual federal control of the project, an eventuality likely to cost North Central Washington many, if not all, of Grand Coulee's benefits. "This dam should be built as much as possible from this end," Woods urged of the only policy likely to protect local interests.[29]

Further problems arose upon consideration of the practical methods available to the state of actually building a federally funded project. Aware that a local contribution was necessary in order to secure the RFC loan, Dill pledged, without any authority to do so, half the $10 million bond issue. This promise "impressed" President Roosevelt "considerably," but horrified officials in Olympia. The fund, currently under challenge in the courts, was supposed to be expended on a statewide basis, keeping the unemployed at home and forestalling criticism in the legislature from neglected communities. "It was not our intention to use this [$10 million] for any major project," Governor Martin reminded the senator, "but rather to use it on many smaller projects in the various counties." Dill's commitment "would not meet with general approval" and the most that Martin was willing to contribute, with extreme reluctance, was "two or three million dollars."[30]

Practical considerations, meanwhile, restricted the construction options available to the state. The Quincy Irrigation District, still in legal existence, was too small, too weak, and, in any event, committed by its charter to the use of Lake Wenatchee as a water source. The Columbia

Basin Commission was authorized to "employ any and all means" to secure the project, a mandate apparently allowing the agency to handle construction. A significant proviso in the enabling act, however, required that the means employed not obligate the state for a sum in excess of the amount appropriated by the legislature, a mere $50,000. A special legislative session—the next regular session was scheduled for January 1935—must be called if the commission's powers were to be suitably expanded. The Dam University opposed utilization of this device, except as a last resort, for fear of giving the Spokane and Seattle delegations an opportunity, as Willis Batcheller warned, to "kill the entire deal." Governor Martin, moreover, had no intention of exposing his precariously balanced budget to big-spending legislators. The commission, he ordered, must "exhaust every resource possible to avoid a special session."[31]

Supporters of the dam therefore found themselves without a viable means of doing the job, even with federal funds. Hoping to find a way out of this trap, preferably one that preserved local control of the project, the Columbia Basin Commission sent Jim O'Sullivan to Washington in May. En route, O'Sullivan visited the Denver regional office of the Bureau of Reclamation, where technical work was under way on the Roosevelt version of the dam. The engineers believed that a structure 145 feet high could be erected for $60 million and that eventual completion of the dam to a height of 371 feet was probable "in about 15 years." Reaching the nation's capital, the CBC secretary immediately fell under the influence of Clarence Dill, especially with regard to the absolute necessity of working closely with the President. "We cannot dictate to the Federal Government which will put up the money whether . . . John Jones or Tom Smith are to be the engineers," O'Sullivan reported, "[or] whether we are to build all the big dam now or not but we have got to do what Roosevelt wants." At home, O'Sullivan received considerable criticism for so readily falling into line with Dill. Rufus Woods, advised Ed Southard after a visit to Wenatchee, "is pretty much concerned over what he thinks you have done in the matter of getting the Reclamation Engineers on the job."[32]

Whatever the purity of his motives, Senator Dill maintained a shrewd view of the entire situation. Speed, in his view, was of the essence. "We have a man in the White House who wants to help us," Dill reminded Governor Martin, "and if we are delayed in getting a specific proposal before him . . . conditions might be such that he could not help us as he can now." The state of Washington, despite the complaints from Wenatchee and Ephrata, "simply must get this dam started while there is a possibility of getting federal funds." Knowing that projects once begun regularly become all but immortal, the senator considered the concern over Grand Coulee's initial size both naive and irrelevant. "Once we place that dam in that river," he argued, "I care not if it is only 50 feet high, and we get the federal government interested in it financially, the development will go on and on for the next hundred years."[33]

Helped by O'Sullivan, Dill continued to work with the President, refining the details of the dam. Passed by Congress in mid-June, the National Industrial Recovery Act opened a new source of funds for Grand Coulee. Among several major anti-Depression initiatives, the legislation created the Public Works Administration, with authority to spend a total of $3.3 billion on projects of enduring merit, including highways, bridges, and dams. Directed by Secretary of the Interior Harold Ickes, the PWA had, over the next several years, an enormous impact on the Pacific coast, funding such ventures as Grand Coulee and Bonneville dams and California's Central Valley Project. The Bureau of Reclamation, the conduit through which much of the money was expended, became, with little doubt, the most influential federal agency in the western United States. The attraction for the Columbia Basin Commission was easy to comprehend, since the PWA granted, rather than loaned, funds. For obvious reasons, Senator Dill lost all interest in dealing with the Reconstruction Finance Corporation.[34]

Between hurried trips home to confer with the commissioners, Dill worked to obtain a PWA grant for Grand Coulee. Detailed planning, plus core drilling, to be carried out by the Bureau of Reclamation, involved an expenditure of $377,000 and both Roosevelt and Secretary Ickes expected the state of Washington to pay the bill. "It will be necessary," advised Dill, "that it be paid . . . before the President will begin to spend money on the dam." Pressed by the senator, Governor Martin agreed to tap the $10 million relief fund for this purpose, on the understanding that most of the money would be used to employ out-of-work state residents at the damsite. On June 30, the Bureau and the Columbia Basin Commission concluded a contract for the necessary work by the federal agency.[35]

President Roosevelt, with Dill present, instructed Harold Ickes on July 26 to approve the Grand Coulee project. Three days later, Ickes officially allocated $63 million in PWA funds for construction of the dam. Despite the fact that the state's initial $377,000 contribution paled in comparison to this commitment on the part of the federal government, the Dam University hoped to somehow retain control. Willis Batcheller, for one, still intended to be appointed chief engineer by the Columbia Basin Commission. "I am expecting you to stand squarely back of me," Batcheller demanded in a letter to Woods, as "your only insurance of having a good job . . . is dependent upon my having charge." The commissioners themselves were overwhelmed with thousands of applications for work at Grand Coulee.[36]

Responding to a suggestion from Senator Dill, the commission hired appraisers to begin the difficult task of determining the monetary value of land required for the project. Disputes over the compensation due displaced settlers were certain to be numerous and expensive. Woods, for instance, was presently engaged in "a little set too" with his old Dam University friend Ed Southard, the attorney for the owners of the damsite. "Rufus argued that the land had laid down there all these years," Southard grumbled in recounting the argument, "and was not worth anything and that what they get would be simply velvet." The prospect of undeserved profit motivated a number of ingenious speculative schemes. Certain officials of Grant County filed townsite plats on the floor of the Grand Coulee, expecting to force the government to buy out their spurious urban developments. Landowners hammered shacks together, intending to demand payment for the loss of their family homes.[37]

The Commission let contracts for core drilling and the digging of test pits to determine the quality of locally available sand and gravel on September 2. Shortly thereafter, Frank A. Banks, previously engaged in Reclamation Bureau work in Idaho, arrived at the damsite to take charge of the preliminary stages of the project. Posing in front of the white marks painted on the cliffside by Army surveyors to designate the spillway's center line, Banks proclaimed the commencement of work to an audience of reporters and curious desert residents. The nearby flyspeck communities of Wilbur, Almira, and Coulee City turned into instant boom towns. "Hotels are full to the eaves," a visitor reported at mid-month, "lumber yards [are] reopening, [and] all available store buildings [have been] leased." Business activity was especially pronounced in the restaurant trade, with "a flood of eating places, good, bad, and indifferent" opening to serve incoming contractors, engineers, and laborers.[38]

Financed by the state, work at the damsite began prior to the receipt of a single dollar from the federal government. In mid-September, the Public Works Administration allotted $1 million to build a bridge across the Columbia, but declined, at least for the moment, to turn additional funds over to the project. A worried Columbia Basin Commission approved in

advance "any plan" Senator Dill "may be able to make with the President
. . . that will result in the construction of the Grand Coulee Dam." Dill
met again with Roosevelt, only to find that the problem came from a source
outside the White House. Harold Ickes was in fact, as Rufus Woods learned
from the senator, "one of the hurdles . . . and really one of the obstacles to
the Grand Coulee Dam."[39]

The Secretary of the Interior was determined to live up to his "Honest Harold" reputation. Ickes intended to use the $3.3 billion in PWA
funds under his control only for "honest work at honest wages on honest
projects." Of particular importance to the Pacific Northwest, the secretary,
who surely had heard the rumors of land speculation in the Columbia
Basin, concluded that federal control was the only means of insuring hon-
esty and efficiency at Grand Coulee. "This is to be a Federal project . . .
constructed, operated and maintained by the Bureau of Reclamation," Ickes
announced in early October. The Columbia Basin Commission must therefore agree to the building and management of the dam by the Bureau.
Under the terms of a contract drawn in Washington, D.C., the state of
Washington was granted an option to acquire the "entire power output"
for a sum equivalent to 70 percent "of the estimated cost of the . . . first
unit dam." If the state failed to act according to the terms of this provision,
as was certain under prevailing financial conditions, "the United States
shall retain all rights in the said dam, power plant and transmission line
and the power output thereof."[40]

Reaction to the Ickes demand was immediate and furious. The arbitrary, take-it-or-leave-it contract, Jim O'Sullivan pointed out, "eliminates
the State entirely of any control, except in an advisory capacity." Should
the Bureau of Reclamation decide to build "a low dam that cannot be
completed to full height . . . it can do so." The contract contained no
prohibition against the expenditure of Grand Coulee revenues outside Washington and allowed the Bureau to ignore the advice of the Columbia Basin
Commission. "The future of the State is jeopardized," warned O'Sullivan.
Rufus Woods hoped that some vestige of control might still be retained "in
the hands of the State of Washington for the reason that it is closer to
home," but was unable to devise a practical means of thwarting Ickes.
"Under present conditions," summed up Senator Dill, "there does not seem
to be any way to retain the state's interest."[41]

Meeting in Governor Martin's Olympia office on October 31, the
Columbia Basin Commission bit the poisoned bullet. Senator Dill, supported by Martin, argued that there was no alternative to acceptance of the

contract, since the state was "in an impasse until the Legislature meets." A defiant Woods voiced the only outright opposition. The agreement "constituted an abdication of rights by the Commission representing the State," he contended, and established a distasteful "policy for the coming generations." Accepting the terms with reluctance, the commissioners also voted that "no publicity relative to the said contract be given out to the public or to the press." Afterward, Rufus explained the decision to Willis Batcheller: "Time is an element of much importance and it is necessary to get started just as quickly as possible." The state "had already received two million dollars [*sic*] without the scratch of a pen" and the time had therefore arrived "to get down to some bases" of formal operation.[42]

Woods remained angry for the rest of his life about the events of October 1933. Harold Ickes, Rufus believed, was "an outstanding man" who had done much to develop the West in general and the Columbia Basin in particular. The Secretary of the Interior was close to being the ideal public servant, hard working and impossible to corrupt. Yet Ickes had, in the "stroke of a pen," robbed Grand Coulee of its meaning, at least for longtime supporters in the Dam University. An undertaking conceived as the means of encouraging regional independence became, thanks to the hard fact that federal dollars came attached to federal strings, an instrument of dependence on Washington, D.C.[43]

As of the fall of 1933, people only partially comprehended the significance of a federalized Grand Coulee. The immediate loser was Willis Batcheller, deprived by Ickes of his dream of personally building the dam. While Batcheller was embittered, other participants in the struggle for Grand Coulee attained immediate profit. Commissioner J.E. McGovern secured the contract for insuring state vehicles assigned to the project. E.F. Banker obtained a franchise for his son to run a bus line between Ephrata and the Columbia River. In addition to representing the damsite owners, W.E. Southard handled the legal arrangements for Banker's transit company. Gale Matthews invested in land, and Billy Clapp defended local clients in condemnation suits.[44]

Grand Coulee placed Washington at the forefront of a rapidly developing contentious relationship between the West and the federal government. Washington ranked ninth among the forty-eight states in per capita New Deal spending between 1933 and 1939 and at the top of a list limited to states with populations in excess of one million. One of four federal water project dollars appropriated during the 1930s went to Washington. The Columbia Basin Commission and the Dam University, along with individuals and organizations from the Mississippi River to the Pacific coast, were compelled by practical circumstances to surrender cherished ambitions in order to attain other equally important goals. Money flowed out from the nation's capital in a great engulfing wave and political power returned upon the incoming tide.[45]

New Deal dams—Grand Coulee, Bonneville, Shasta, Boulder, Fort Peck—generated, by their very construction, currents of political change. Those who had fought for Grand Coulee since the Great War expected to drain population and industry from the center to the hinterland. With one-sixth of the nation's potential hydroelectricity, said Rufus Woods, Washington possessed an advantage "over all other states in the union." As long as local interests retained control of the Columbia, the stream would be developed in accordance with the dreams and aspirations of state residents. "This heritage of yours, and of your children and your children's children," Woods proclaimed in a 1933 speech, "will last hundreds of years in the future and . . . should be properly handled to do the most good for the people." Now that Grand Coulee was a federal project, a new struggle began for the preservation of as many benefits as conditions allowed.[46]

# Chapter Nine
# Ups and Downs, Ins and Outs

A newspaper records the ups and downs, ins and outs of daily life which go to make up the passage of a year. Without the newspaper, which in reality is but a mirror of events, only a sorry and incomplete picture of a community or city could be presented, and that not enduring.

*Wenatchee Daily World* [1]

S EATED AT HIS newsroom desk, behind piles of correspondence, books, magazines, and clippings, Rufus Woods observed the day-to-day business of the *Wenatchee World*. Every twenty-four hours, the press turned out "papers by the thousands" for door-to-door delivery in town and shipment by train and bus to distant subscribers. Organizational "marvels" in production and distribution allowed Rufus to focus on the various editorial tasks of the responsible publisher. Objective news reporting and reasoned expressions of opinion were bound up in a package that was both attractive and literate. Dealing with North Central Washington, with the struggle for Grand Coulee Dam, and with the benefits sure to follow from development of the Columbia River, the *World* told what Woods liked to call the "saga of the sage."[2]

Tragedy rather than romance prevailed in the long winter of 1933, as Roland Hartley and Herbert Hoover faded out in favor of Clarence Martin and Franklin Roosevelt. Apple prices, averaged across all varieties, fell in February to 49 cents a bushel, an all-time low. A 62 percent delinquency rate in tax collections forced Chelan County to drop 389 families from the local relief rolls. Across Washington, daily and weekly newspapers resorted to barter arrangements in desperate attempts to maintain circulation and stave off bankruptcy. The *World* performed better than most, but still suffered from the loss of advertising and readers. "We newspaper men," Rufus Woods observed in early 1933, "are simply going down the toboggan at a terrific rate financially speaking."[3]

Governor Martin's $10 million relief fund became available only in the summer of 1933. There was little the state could do in the meantime to relieve the suffering. The 40-mill limit initiative, approved by the voters in 1932, mandated a sharp reduction in property taxes, the traditional mainstay of the Washington revenue system. The income tax, also authorized at the polls in November, was immediately subjected to legal challenge and eventually declared unconstitutional by the state supreme court. The legislature thus had great difficulty maintaining even the regular functions of government. Democrats and Republicans, Rufus Woods included, praised the governor for persevering under these conditions. Facing down the advocates of increased spending in his own party, Martin demonstrated his commitment to fiscal responsibility and businesslike methods. With common interests to promote—namely Grand Coulee Dam, economy in government, and opposition to organized labor—Woods and Martin became close and across-the-board political allies. From 1933 on, Rufus was an important adviser and the governor's unofficial representative in North Central Washington.[4]

Following the inauguration of Franklin D. Roosevelt, Woods, in a further instance of bipartisanship, endorsed the man he had formerly considered a weakling inferior in body, mind, and character to Herbert Hoover. "When such an emergency exists as that which confronts the American people today," the *World* contended, "the President of the United States is entitled to the support of every intelligent and patriotic member of congress regardless of party affiliation or personal prejudice." As his first dramatic act, Roosevelt proclaimed a national Bank Holiday in an attempt to stop panic-driven runs on financial institutions across the country. Three of Wenatchee's four banks, ruled safe and sound by federal examiners, quickly reopened, but for several days normal business came to a cash-starved halt. The *World* and other Wenatchee enterprises issued scrip, providing the town with its own circulating medium. The irregular currency had an immediate positive impact, since the saving of "play" money was hardly prudent. "People are inclined to pass them on freely," one observer noted of the scrip. "Bills are paid . . . goods purchased and business stimulated all along the line."[5]

Rufus had no time for contemplation of this successful experiment in local moneymaking. The *World* had instituted a 20 percent pay cut on March 1. Printers belonging to the typographers union demanded immediate reinstatement of their previous 80 cents-an-hour rate, threatening otherwise to walk off the job. "I told them," Woods reported, "that . . . the way things were breaking it might be a condition not of salaries, but of getting something to eat." The closure of the banks and the lack of alternative employment certainly made the timing inopportune. The printers nonetheless walked out on March 9. Aided by reporters from the newsroom, Rufus published a reasonable facsimile of the *World* that day. "People generally would not have known anything about it," he claimed of the dispute, "if a lot of circulars had not been distributed by the strikers." The next morning, two experienced print shop workers arrived from Walla Walla, on loan from that city's antilabor publisher, J.G. Kelly. A third new hand showed up shortly thereafter, dispatched by the *Spokesman-Review*, resulting in a complete victory for management.[6]

Triumphant over the strikers, Woods focused his full attention upon the political drama of the New Deal's first Hundred Days. "Never before in any similar period of time . . . since the government was organized," the *World* enthused, "has such a stupendous and revolutionary program of . . . reform been set in motion." Appreciating the magnitude of the task at hand, the paper pledged itself to "stand by the President until a fair trial has been given to all his measures."[7]

In personality, in program, and especially in preferring action to contemplation, the Democratic Roosevelt became in 1933 the legitimate heir of his cousin, the great Theodore. The President, said Rufus Woods, was "100 per cent right in wishing to properly conserve the resources of this country" through the Civilian Conservation Corps, the Tennessee Valley Authority, and development of the Columbia River. Grand Coulee and Bonneville dams, in particular, revealed Roosevelt's "understanding of the West." On visits to Washington, Woods attended White House press conferences to view the man at close range. FDR was "all affability and smiles," he reported after one session in the oval office. "That Roosevelt . . . hand clasp is in a class of its own."[8]

Although much of Roosevelt's popularity in North Central Washington derived from his support of Grand Coulee, other New Deal programs also had a significant impact on the region. The apple industry, for instance, faced a desperate crisis. Established in the last year of the Hoover Administration, the Regional Agricultural Credit Corporation, referred to locally as the RACC, offered growers long-term federal financial assistance, but came on the scene too late in the harvest season to be of immediate help. Despite a 50 percent cut in wages, orchardists were unable to reduce expenses below the rate of prevailing income. This fact compromised hopes for the future, as the amount of money to be loaned by the RACC was determined by current prices. Unless a blight or a Siberian freeze intervened to reduce anticipated production by at least a third, the *World* pointed out in February 1933, apple interests must endure record low returns.[9]

In an entirely unanticipated benefit of the national confidence generated during the Hundred Days, growers suddenly found themselves on an upward track. Despite what the *World* termed the "glutted condition" of the market, prices for the final carloads of the 1932-33 season made a "sensational advance." Per-box returns for Winesaps and Delicious, the varieties most in demand, soared to $1.10 and $1.40, double the rate prevailing at the "zero hour of March 1." Local businessmen revived the spring Apple Blossom celebration as a "festival of joy and thanksgiving" for the "demise of 'Old Man Gloom.'" The sole negative factor was the unfortunate happenstance that most of the valley's apples had been shipped prior to the price surge. Wenatchee was "one of the last places . . . to feel the depression," noted the *World*, and "may be slower than the rest of the country to recover."[10]

Thinking observers worried that the rise in prices was only temporary, the product of a politically inspired inflationary trend. The inherent shortcomings of an economic endeavor broken into thousands of component units continued. "The fruit industry," advised the *World*, ". . . needs a dictator or czar with authority to correct . . . flagrant abuses," in particular the selling of inferior quality apples and the shipping of unsold carloads for sale at auction. The RACC proved to be a genuine helpmate in this regard. In addition to providing loans, it refused credit to growers attempting to sell low-grade fruit. The National Recovery Administration and the Agricultural Adjustment Administration, meanwhile, gave growers a genuine opportunity to, as one observer wrote, "put our own house in order" through the organization of trade associations for the control of production and prices. Rufus Woods believed that the industry's historic destabilizing tendencies might finally be overcome. "Competition has been the 'life blood of the trade,'" the *World* observed, "but controlled and regulated competition would produce still better results."[11]

Practical implementation of "controlled and regulated competition" was, unfortunately, an exceedingly difficult matter. A midsummer conference in Chicago attempted to draft a national code for the fruit industry, but foundered upon opposition from Washington and Oregon. "Conditions vary so much in ... different parts of the country," the *World* pointed out, "that what will fit the situation in New York ... would not be applicable ... [to] the Pacific Northwest." Regional operators, meeting in Spokane, also failed to reach agreement. Representatives of packing houses and existing marketing agencies insisted upon a system of strict enforcement, with themselves in charge. Wenatchee and Yakima producers rebelled, demanding an equal role in administering the proposed Northwest code. "The fruit growers ... are not Bolsheviks, agitators, obstructionists or malcontents," insisted the *World* in defense of the argument that power belonged in the orchards. "An association without representation," after all, was "as unfair today as it was back in 1776."[12]

By the time a Pacific Northwest apple marketing code was signed in October, the year's harvest was already under way. The final terms were so badly written, moreover, that the exact meaning escaped most observers. "No one knows exactly what the terms ... are," confessed the *World*, "but it is believed that ... objections will be overlooked rather than plunge the industry into another period of discussion and disagreement such as took place when the code was first proposed." Growers, finding no reason to behave otherwise, persisted in sending fruit to market in haphazard fashion. Although prices, especially for Delicious apples, continued to climb, improved orchard earnings had more to do with RACC financing by the Interstate Commerce Commission's instituting an emergency $1.25 freight rate than with the code.[13]

The failure of the National Recovery Administration (NRA) to get "to first base" also disappointed Woods. Administration of the many industrial codes was lax and enforcement virtually impossible. The *World* nonetheless retained its early confidence in the Democratic occupant of the White House. "No other president," Woods pointed out in an assessment of the administration's first year, "ever threw more enthusiastic energy into his task than Franklin D. Roosevelt, no man ever tried harder, none ever seized opportunities with greater zest." The Agricultural Adjustment Administration (AAA) and the NRA may have floundered, but the impact of New Deal public works measures, crop reduction programs, and RACC loans had been "felt in every line of trade and business" in North Central Washington. The *World* itself experienced its first gain in advertising inches in over two years in November 1933.[14]

Still enthusiastic over Roosevelt, Woods found certain negative tendencies in the New Deal. For one thing, Americans were encouraged to think of government as "some sort of magnificent Santa Claus," a habit bound, if not soon checked, to destroy self-reliance and initiative. "Entirely too many people," moreover, were "willing to see the Constitution . . . mutilated if not entirely destroyed." Channeled by the Depression, power flowed from the states to the nation and, in the capital, from Congress to the presidency. "Hardly realizing it," warned Woods in August 1933, "we are currently now in a dictatorship," albeit a benevolent one under the well-intentioned FDR. The profusion of new governmental agencies also increased the danger of rule by bureaucratic appointees who "cannot be curbed or removed," no matter how incompetent or destructive. "It is Hitlerism and Czarism at their worst," noted the *World*.[15]

Early on, New Deal bureaucrats subjected apple growers to "restrictions, requirements and limitations," providing a close to home example of the dark side of the Roosevelt Administration. Past controversies over the spraying of trees had led to installation of expensive cleaning machinery to remove chemical residue from harvested fruit. At the specific urging of Rexford G. Tugwell, late of Roosevelt's campaign Brains Trust and now number two man in the Department of Agriculture, the government took action against the industry in the fall of 1933. A federal lawsuit charged Yakima growers with poisoning workers and with selling tainted fruit. Rigorous inspections of orchards and packing houses became the norm in the Yakima and Wenatchee valleys. Congress introduced stringent pure food legislation, drafted by Tugwell. Orchard owners, complained the *World*, were under unprovoked attack from "autocratic" officials who "make their own rules, set up their own standards, and then condemn any product without any recourse on the part of the . . . seller." Tugwell himself was accorded the title of "the Jonah of the administration."[16]

Rex Tugwell made a convenient target, diverting criticism of the New Deal that might otherwise have been focused directly upon Roosevelt, endangering Grand Coulee. At the end of 1933 circumstances appeared to be highly favorable for the Coulee project, even with the loss of control to the Bureau of Reclamation. Clearing of the damsite began in December and proceeded ahead of schedule through the following spring. Touring the construction boomtowns and observing the "big shovels at work," Jim O'Sullivan found the entire bustling scene "like a new frontier." Serious challenges, however, must still be overcome. Although Elwood Mead pledged that the low dam would be built in such a manner "that the high dam could be added to the . . . foundation with the least possible cost," the Dam University placed little faith in the Bureau. O'Sullivan, Woods and company worried that the federal engineers really intended to prevent completion of a high dam project. "Any layman can see," O'Sullivan explained to Rufus, "that the mass contained in going up in the high dam . . . will have a tendency to slide on the downstream surface of the low dam."[17]

Federal officials, for their part, doubted that the Columbia Basin Commission really had the public interest at heart. To verify assorted reports of improper conduct, Harold Ickes dispatched detectives to the Pacific Northwest. The investigators assembled information about land speculation and other instances of alleged insider profiteering. One detective followed Rufus Woods about the region for several days, failing in this particular case to uncover any derogatory intelligence. Federal agents even burglarized a Spokane motel room in quest of evidence implicating the firm clearing the damsite. The contractor was, in fact, actively "gouging everybody" at Grand Coulee, according to a confidential report from O'Sullivan to Woods.[18]

Unable to work on a mutually respectful basis with the Bureau, the Columbia Basin Commission had to act in circumspect fashion respecting its ultimate goals. Any public agitation for a high dam was regarded as political suicide. "We simply must not attempt to change the allocation," advised Senator Clarence Dill in February 1934, "and we must build the dam to whatever height it is possible to build it with . . . the $63,000,000." Otherwise, the bargain with President Roosevelt would be broken and the opposition of farm states aroused. "If those who are opposed to it," Dill pointed out, "could make it appear that this dam is to irrigate more land . . . in the immediate future, they might . . . prevent expenditure of even the $63,000,000." Jim O'Sullivan, normally a practitioner of bashing-over-the-head lobbying methods, agreed with the senator. "We have got to be awfully careful," he mused, "or we may upset the whole works."[19]

Widespread public criticism of Grand Coulee, as currently constituted, confirmed the necessity of careful behavior. National magazine articles portrayed the project as a New Deal boondoggle bound to produce

unneeded electricity and disastrous additions to the country's farm surplus. *Newsweek*, for instance, reported that the Pacific Northwest was already "overpowered." J.D. Ross, still attempting to boost the Skagit River
at the expense of Grand Coulee, stated belief that the Columbia River dam
would founder upon the lack of markets. New Corps of Engineers studies
provided apparently objective support for this negative forecast. "On account of uncertainty as to how long it will take . . . to absorb the very large
blocks of power" from Bonneville and Grand Coulee, Colonel Thomas
Robins recommended postponing all preliminary work on dams scheduled for Umatilla Rapids and the lower Snake River. Even if built, these
projects ought to serve primarily as aids to navigation, providing for safe
year-round trade between Portland and Lewiston. "Further development
of the Columbia River in the interests of power," said Robins, "will not be
required for many years to come."[20]

Danger also appeared in the form of the Pacific Northwest Regional
Planning Commission, established under the auspices of the Roosevelt
Administration's National Resources Planning Board. The commission's
initial region-wide plan, made public in December 1934, appeared to reflect personal bias, rather than scientific criteria. Colonel Robins, an opponent of Grand Coulee, chaired the important committee on power,
providing him with an opportunity to undermine the dam. In a report to
the commission, Robins questioned the existence of a market for Grand
Coulee power and insisted that the dam was justified, and barely so, only
as a work relief measure. "What is the matter with your man, Colonel
Robins?" Woods protested in an angry letter to commission chairman
Marshall Dana.[21]

First proposed in 1934, the Columbia Valley Authority was another
source of provocation for those individuals described by Woods as "the real
friends of the Grand Coulee Dam." In addition to distributing power produced by Bonneville and Grand Coulee, the CVA was supposed to direct
all future development of the river basin. The problem was that the proposed administrative setup called for one director each from Washington,
Oregon, and Idaho, raising the possibility of two-to-one votes against the
Evergreen State. The CVA, asserted Rufus, "would turn the scepter over to
Idaho and Oregon," resulting in the high dam being "delayed indefinitely"
in favor of a "steady grind for an open river" between Portland and Lewiston.
The better idea, Woods informed his readers, was for Oregonians to "closely
watch their Bonneville development" and for the people of North Central
Washington to "watch jealously the Grand Coulee development."[22]

In accord with this advice, the *World* continued to serve as the leading protector of Grand Coulee. Rufus Woods eagerly responded, usually with emotional outbursts, to criticism of the project in Eastern newspapers and magazines. A June 1934 *Collier's* article targeting reclamation in general and the dam in particular as wasteful expenditures of taxpayer money, drew a heated response requiring two front-page and three inside columns of the *World*. *Collier's* author Owen White had perpetrated a "virtual libel," Woods charged, a "contemptible fling at the West." Instead of "whining," suggested Woods, the enemies of Grand Coulee ought to retarget their investigative zeal on the "billions . . . being spent all over the United States" on navigation and flood control, "with nothing to show for it" in terms of monetary return to the government. "Why, oh why," asked Rufus, "are there so many writers in the East . . . who don't know a doggone thing . . . [but] who continue to snap and snarl about the way things are done in the West."[23]

Grand Coulee was also highly flexible, in the sense that positive arguments on its behalf could be easily altered to meet changing political requirements. Originally conceived as a reclamation project, the dam was under construction as a generator of electricity, with no irrigation features. Touting the dam's many and varied benefits for the region and nation, Rufus devised assorted and appealing developmental goals. Grand Coulee was a giant economic pump-primer, employing hundreds of laborers in the preparatory stage and thousands once actual work began. Filtered through the paychecks of the formerly unemployed, infusions of cash would revive the local economy and end the Depression, at least in North Central Washington. Woods also expected the building of the "biggest thing on earth" and the "eighth world wonder" to attract large numbers of tourists, creating a profitable new industry for the interior Northwest.[24]

Between 1931 and 1937, with 1934 and 1935 the worst years, drought turned the Plains states, from the Dakotas south to the Texas panhandle, into the Dust Bowl, handing the Dam University what the *World* called "a weapon of the highest order." Tens of thousands of families joined in what the paper described as "an exodus . . . comparable to the westward movement . . . following the discovery of gold in California." Watching for a few hours from a Wenatchee street corner, one observer recorded the passing of vehicles bearing license plates from North and South Dakota, Kansas, Nebraska, and Oklahoma. A reclaimed Columbia Basin would provide well-watered homes for the dispossessed, making the high Grand Coulee dam the obvious solution to the natural and human disaster of the Dust Bowl. "No finer example of the . . . necessity of reclamation," the *World* pointed out, "could ever have been prepared than is furnished by the searing sun of the middle west." Completion of the basin project, claimed Rufus Woods, would cost the federal government less than all the programs devoted to the relief of those suffering from drought in their home states.[25]

If Grand Coulee was to provide work for the unemployed, attractions for tourists, and homes for Dust Bowl refugees, it must be protected against all manner of threats, real and imagined, from inside and from outside the government. Although the worksite was cleared by the spring of 1934, the Bureau of Reclamation delayed letting a contract for construction, stoking the suspicions of the Dam University. The problem was that stiff requirements, including the filing of a $5 million bond and the assumption of liability should the river break loose during construction, gave pause to prospective bidders. "If no bids are received . . . or if the bids received are excessively high," Jim O'Sullivan worried, "I cannot conceive of anything better calculated to give the Grand Coulee project a black eye." Indeed, "a wonderful excuse for dropping Grand Coulee" would be presented opponents of the dam. Hurrying to Washington, O'Sullivan discovered, at least to his own satisfaction, that the restrictive contract provisions were designed to "throw the dam to the Six Companies," the politically astute firm organized by Henry Kaiser, Warren Bechtel, and other contractors that successfully bid on Boulder Dam in 1931.[26]

Shifting from metaphor to metaphor as he reported the unsavory details, O'Sullivan wrote that "lots of gravy" was "mixed up in the Six Companies' bid" and that "a big melon was to be sliced up" once the firm secured the job. Dispatched to Rufus and other friends, his version of events provided an unwholesome insight into the methods used in securing government contracts. One associate of Senator Dill worked behind the scenes for the Six Companies after arranging to sell Kaiser gravel from his landholdings near the damsite. Another "grafter" close to the senator offered to help the rival Mason-Walsh-Atkinson-Kier conglomerate, known as MWAK, secure the contract in return for a $100,000 fee. A member of the Columbia Basin Commission apparently sold inside information to the Kaiser group, causing the latter, in a fatal blunder, to increase its bid by $5 million. "The gnashing of teeth" was audible on the part of Six Companies representatives, O'Sullivan reported to Woods when the contract was awarded MWAK in July 1934.[27]

Plots to ruin or take advantage of Grand Coulee seemed to arise on a regular basis. A referendum approved in 1934 authorized the condemnation of private utility operations and the extension of public transmission lines across the state of Washington. The Dam University immediately detected an insidious connection between the referendum and the proposed purchase—announced on the eve of the election—of the Puget Sound Power & Light Company by Seattle City Light. The transaction, viewed from Wenatchee and Ephrata, seemed a possible mortal blow to completion of the Coulee dam. If successful, O'Sullivan pointed out, J.D. Ross "will shut out the Puget Sound market to Grand Coulee power." Taking up the challenge in a series of *World* columns, Woods warned that Seattle intended to dominate "the power industry of the state," to the detriment of all competitors. Rufus claimed that, in return for Wall Street financing of his Skagit River project, Ross had agreed to "an understanding that he was to fight Grand Coulee." Writing to Ross directly, Woods accused City Light of "carrying on a definite program of opposition to Grand Coulee dam." Concluding a lengthy disquisition on the merits of the project, Rufus expressed doubt "that this letter will do any good," since Ross was "certainly running true" to the "reports I get" respecting sordid connections with "New York bankers."[28]

Moribund since the election of Roosevelt, the Columbia River Development League was revived in 1934 for the express purpose of countering City Light. Ashley Holden, the organization's aggressive new secretary, believed that J.D. Ross was "drunk with power" and intent upon assembling "an electrical empire." Unless stopped, Ross would "for all time to come . . . be an obstacle to the development of Grand Coulee." Operating out of a Seattle office, Holden prepared literature critical of the Puget purchase and worked to defeat city council members friendly to the public utility in the spring 1935 municipal elections. Although complex political and economic questions stalled, and eventually killed, the sale, the Grand Coulee group continued to fear Ross as an intractable enemy. The man's capacity for mischief was enhanced in the summer of 1935 when he accepted, without giving up his City Light post, an appointment to the Securities and Exchange Commission.[29]

Far from the scenes of political contention, construction of the dam proceeded at a rapid pace. Railroad and paved highway connections were opened to the construction site in the fall of 1934 and a power line from Lake Chelan made round-the-clock lighting of the project possible. The "amazingly efficient" MWAK organization—so described by the Columbia Basin Commission's resident staffer—had nearly 3,000 workers on the scene by February 1935. Enormous steam shovels fed 40,000 cubic yards of dirt per day into an intricate system of conveyor belts. Crews of lifejacket-clad men worked against the eight-mile-per-hour current, driving piles into the streambed for the left bank cofferdam.[30]

MWAK transformed its headquarters, Mason City, from a sagebrush-covered wasteland into what an admiring visitor described as "a modern, up-to-date city of almost one thousand people." Houses, barracks, and dining halls catered to the needs of company management and professional employees. On the left bank of the river, the well-tended community of Coulee Dam provided engineers and other Bureau of Reclamation workers with green lawns, shade trees, and a freshly painted schoolhouse. Looking down on the damsite from the swollen lip of the coulee, the privately developed town of Grand Coulee provided twenty saloons and a half-dozen houses of ill-repute for construction personnel. Prostitution was the dominant form of business, a commercial fact reflected in the socially revealing report that half the prescriptions filled in local pharmacies were for treatment of venereal disease.[31]

If the labors on the Columbia River were to pay a maximum return, work on the low dam must lead directly to construction of the high dam. Elwood Mead pressed upon Secretary of the Interior Harold Ickes the absolute necessity of a smooth transition. With irrigation postponed and no likelihood of navigation on the upper river, the entire cost of construction must be charged, under government accounting methods, to power. Grand Coulee, as currently authorized, was therefore at a distinct competitive disadvantage with the Bonneville project, which was outfitted with locks and bound to benefit commerce in a substantial manner. A high dam, though, would generate greater revenue and provide sufficient storage for reclamation. "From being a dubious enterprise," Mead informed Ickes, "it becomes an attractive one." Mead hesitated to make his arguments public, however, for fear of provoking opposition from the congressional enemies of irrigation. For attribution, he said only that the government intended to complete the low dam in a fashion calculated to "get the best economic and social results."[32]

Unaware of Mead's efforts for the high Grand Coulee project, Dam University members worried constantly over the state of affairs in the nation's capital. Jim O'Sullivan feared that his friends, lulled into a false sense of security by the performance of MWAK, were "falling down" and "loafing" in the belief that Grand Coulee would be "handed out on a silver platter." North Central Washington must "watch every move and every detail," agreed Rufus Woods, or else the private utilities and the farm organizations would "submarine the entire . . . program." Clarence Dill's decision not to run for a third term in 1934 cost the Dam University its vital link to the White House. Lewis Schwellenbach, Dill's successor, joined Senator Homer Bone and the state's three west-of-the-Cascades congressmen in the most tepid endorsement possible of Grand Coulee, drawing a complaint from Woods that they had "just about broken their pick." Rufus spluttered that "if the High Dam goes over it will be in spite of . . . these men."[33]

Attempting to fill the vacuum created by the retirement of Dill, Rufus Woods went East in January 1935 on behalf of the state of Washington. Working closely with Representative Sam Hill, Rufus devoted himself to behind-the-scenes work on Grand Coulee, seeking diversion only in the occasional White House press conference. Ignoring criticism from Ephrata that he behaved "cowardly" for not aggressively pushing the high dam and irrigation, he met with dozens of congressmen and officials of the Bureau of Reclamation. "I have been sliding around quietly," he wrote home, "without even one piece of news even for my own paper." He intended to subtly reinforce the argument for completion of the entire dam. "We are sitting pretty," Rufus noted at the end of the trip. Challenges must still be overcome, though, for "the east and middle west are trying to get at us both from the standpoint of POWER as well as of IRRIGATION."[34]

Good and bad tidings followed Woods on the road back to Wenatchee. Rufus knew, apparently from Harold Ickes himself, that the Bureau of Reclamation would, at the opportune moment, issue a change order approving construction of the high dam. The long-hoped-for action finally took place in June 1935. A new development, however, threatened completion of even the low structure. The Supreme Court ruled in April that the Roosevelt Administration had acted unconstitutionally in authorizing work at Parker Dam on the Colorado River, another New Deal public works project. Only Congress, according to the court majority, could authorize the obstruction of navigable waterways. Considerable legal debate ensued over whether the decision applied to Grand Coulee, Bonneville, and other Western dams, but the action of the Supreme Court represented a clear danger. "It would be a very easy matter to lie down and let them lick us at this stage of the game," Woods confessed to Governor Martin. Fortunately, the spirit that had animated the fight for Grand Coulee over the years remained alive. "I suppose," Rufus wrote O'Sullivan, "it is just another hurdle we have to pass."[35]

Regardless of the legal technicalities, the Parker Dam decision eventually forced the Columbia River project into the hazardous congressional arena. "The prevailing opinion," Sam Hill informed Woods, ". . . appears to be that there is authority for the Grand Coulee dam but in order to be on the safe side it is well to have specific authority from Congress therefor." At the urging of Hill, the Wenatchee publisher undertook another trip to Washington in late May. The situation was grave, for the dam was now fully exposed to the political opposition so neatly avoided in 1933 by Senator Dill and President Roosevelt.[36]

Forces more insidious than farm state congressmen must now be overcome. J.D. Ross, according to Woods, was personally responsible for the increasingly critical media coverage of Grand Coulee and for encouraging Harry Hopkins, the powerful Federal Relief Administrator and Roosevelt confidante, to oppose the dam. Ross was also blamed for the mounting concern in the nation's capital over speculation. The President was "greatly exercised" by the activities of "certain prominent persons in the Columbia Basin area," advised Sam Hill after a White House conference. The Grand Coulee project, Harold Ickes warned Woods, would be terminated "if the government is going to be held up." The Dam University fretted over how best to counter the suspicions, especially in light of the fact that Roosevelt and Ickes had good reason for their concern. "There are quite a number here in Washington," Rufus wrote Clarence Martin, "who have been buying the land at $20.00 an acre and expect to get $1,000.00 an acre out of it."[37]

Woods arrived in Washington on May 28, the day following announcement of the Supreme Court decision overturning the National Industrial Recovery Act, the Roosevelt administration's principal means of stimulating economic recovery. For a week, regular business came to a standstill as people gathered in corridors and hotel lobbies for postmortem analysis of the failure of the New Deal's most prominent anti-Depression effort. Operating out of Sam Hill's office, Rufus relieved the harried congressman of the detail work involved in promoting the dam, working as a self-described "errand boy" and "good hound dog . . . scent[ing] out trouble." Acting upon Hill's suggestion, he assembled the congressional delegations from states threatened by the Parker Dam ruling and arranged the release of publicity critical of Harry Hopkins for apparently preferring leaf-raking to genuinely productive public works projects.[38]

Thanks to Rufus, Hill could focus his energies upon a genuinely daunting task. The annual rivers and harbors bill had passed the House prior to the Parker Dam decision. The Senate approved amendments authorizing construction of Parker and Grand Coulee dams, introduced after the court ruling by Hiram Johnson of California, Carl Hayden of Arizona, and Lewis Schwellenbach of Washington. House negotiators, however, insisted upon the removal of Grand Coulee from the bill finally approved in conference. Unless he could somehow reinstate the Columbia River project on the floor of the House, reflected Hill at this gloomy moment, "it was a certainty that . . . the Grand Coulee dam would be lost." To accomplish this feat, he had to overcome the tradition that decisions of the House-Senate conference were final and best the "strongly organized group" opposed to "reclamation in general."[39]

Preparing for the live-or-die House debate, scheduled for August 19, Hill labored "single handed and alone" on behalf of his amendment restoring Grand Coulee. Courting potential supporters, he insisted that the dam was first and foremost a power project, with reclamation only to come at some later date. Hill stressed that the professional courtesy due a colleague of long and convivial standing entitled him to votes on an issue of maximum back-home importance. On the day of reckoning, the congressman's friends stood at the doors to the chamber, telling late arrivals that "it was Sam Hill's project and we are voting for Sam Hill." The final tally was a surprising 200 to 126 in favor of Grand Coulee. "But for my . . . bloodsweating efforts," Hill recalled in later years, "there would be no Grand Coulee dam."[40]

Hill's hard-fought victory, coupled with the Ickes change order, brought late-summer relief to North Central Washington. The complete Grand Coulee Dam, as now planned by the Bureau of Reclamation, would soar to a height of 500 feet above the streambed. Impoundment of the Columbia to the Canadian border and the filling of the coulee increased reservoir capacity to 9.6 million acre feet, twelve times the figure for the low dam. The power plant, once fully installed, was rated at 2.5 million horsepower, a three-fold increase. The pricetag also tripled, from the $63 million approved by Roosevelt in 1933 to an estimated $196 million. Meanwhile, MWAK made rapid progress toward completing what was now a mere, albeit imposing, foundation. Work on the left bank cofferdam was finished and the river diverted in August 1935. At the coulee, Rufus Woods, in a moment of great personal satisfaction, "walked on the granite bottom of the Columbia," 110 feet beneath the former surface level of the stream.[41]

Because of Grand Coulee, Woods continued to hold the national Democratic administration in general high regard. At the state level, however, Democrats—Clarence Martin excepted—appeared intent upon promoting immorality, unionism, and political radicalism. Rufus had watched in despair as the voters repealed Washington's state prohibition law in 1932 and as Congress, the following March, legalized the sale of beer and wine. "Cheap beer," a disgusted *World* soon reported, was available in "almost every store" in Wenatchee. Ratification of the 21st Amendment in December 1933 brought national Prohibition to an ignominious end. A special legislative session, summoned expressly for the purpose by Governor Martin, responded by establishing a state monopoly on liquor sales. Woods believed the "pesky question" of alcohol to be "more pernicious than ever." Taverns were hardly model social institutions, young people ignored repeated warnings from the *World* that "this stuff is HABIT-FORMING," and arrests for drunk driving mounted at a terrifying rate. The half million dollars spent in North Central Washington liquor stores during 1934 were "taken out of the regular channels of trade and lost forever" to legitimate business.[42]

Meanwhile, New Deal legislation, in particular Section 7a of the National Industrial Recovery Act and the National Labor Relations, or Wagner, Act of 1935, produced a revolution in the work place. The federal government now guaranteed the right to form unions and the obligation of management to bargain with organized labor. The result in the Pacific Northwest was indeed revolutionary, at least in the eyes of a horrified Rufus Woods. Longshoremen, led by the Australian-born Harry Bridges, shut down Pacific coast ports in 1934. Strikes closed the sawmills of Washington and Oregon the following spring and summer. The newly assertive union movement, complained Woods, pitted the selfish interests of the few against the welfare of the many. "Shall the public representing 95 per cent of the people," he asked, "be held up or inconvenienced by the other 5 per cent?" The "malignant condition" on the docks and in the mills threatened "the prosperity of the Northwest" by retarding recovery from the Depression. Rufus applauded Governor Martin for ordering the national guard and the state police to end picketing in the lumber industry: "He took the stand that when the majority . . . want to go to work, they are entitled to work without being molested by those who do not work."[43]

Coddled, if not encouraged outright, by Democratic leaders other than Martin, the unions also had designs on the country east of the Cascades. The attempt by remnants of the old Industrial Workers of the World to organize farm workers in the Yakima Valley in 1933 was, said the *World*, "a warning to orchardists" in Wenatchee. A more resourceful and determined opponent than the Wobblies appeared on the upper Columbia in the form of "chislers," the *World*'s favorite epithet for the Seattle-based

Teamsters headed by Dave Beck. Operators hauling apples to Puget Sound by truck found that they must hire an unnecessary union co-driver to avoid harassment. Despite threats of vigilante reprisals, Beck's representatives organized several Wenatchee packing houses in 1936, forcing the owners to increase wages and growers to pay higher handling fees.[44]

Held responsible for the longshoremen, the timber strikers, and the Teamsters, Woods also accused Democrats of imposing radicalism upon the state of Washington. Fiscal stringency alone stood in the way of social and political upheaval. In 1934, Washington assumed the obligation of paying pensions to the indigent elderly. The voters also endorsed continuance of the 40-mill limit on taxation of real estate and defeated a constitutional amendment establishing an income tax. As a result, the state was placed in "the embarrassing position," the *World* noted, of being "without funds to make good its promise to the aged." The solution, pushed through the overwhelmingly Democratic legislature of 1935, was the sales tax. Although the need to carry tokens for fractional tax payments on purchases under 35 cents aggravated consumers, the measure resolved the immediate budgetary crisis and spread the burden of government across the widest-possible segment of the population.[45]

Endorsed by Woods as the fairest means of addressing the state's revenue shortage, the sales tax, by generating new income, presented Democrats with the opportunity to spend money on assorted programs. Public expenditures must still be "trimmed and trimmed deeply," insisted the *World*, while "reforms" should be "held in abeyance until the people are in a position to foot the bill without ruin." The legislative majority instead gave serious consideration, in 1935 and afterward, to "poorly considered, poorly written, and immature" social welfare measures. Such, at least, was the regularly expressed conviction of the Wenatchee newspaper. "Utopia-bringers" favored state-owned gasoline stations, a state-operated bank, and a production-for-use commission with power to levy taxes. No wonder, observed the *World*, that "substantial, thinking citizens" got the "jitters" at the "mere mention" of the legislature. The bizarre behavior detailed in Mary McCarthy's famous 1936 *Nation* article on Washington's "Circus Politics" was, Rufus lamented, "more or less true."[46]

Celebration over the pouring of the first concrete at Grand Coulee on December 6, 1935 was short-lived, for assorted enemies of the dam continued to assault it. The newest danger arose from the death of Elwood Mead in February 1936. The problem was not so much Mead's demise as the possibility that J.D. Ross might become his successor. "I would not put it beyond Ross," wrote an alarmed Jim O'Sullivan, "to attempt to get this appointment in order to stop Grand Coulee." Warning Woods that the "forces" behind the City Light director "are quite a power," Representative Sam Hill called for "a barrage of protest from home." Responding in a series of signed editorials, Rufus contended that "the naming of Ross would be about the least satisfactory [choice] to those in this part of the Northwest." The man's recent assertion of support for the Columbia River dam was a shameless manifestation of cynicism: "To speak frankly, everyone who has been watching out for the interests of Grand Coulee dam . . . knows that J.D. Ross has been . . . trying to slug it in a sly way." The eventual appointee, John C. Page, was considered a tool of the Six Companies, but his selection was greeted with relief east of the Cascades. "It would not be wise," admitted O'Sullivan, "to have a company which is doing a great deal of construction work . . . succeed in naming the next Commissioner." If the alternative was Ross, though, Page was entirely acceptable.[47]

Like J.D. Ross, opposition on Capitol Hill was a never-ending obstacle to completion of Grand Coulee. Sam Hill's amendment authorizing the dam made no provision for money, since funding was already secured through June 1936. (Grand Coulee was allotted $15 million by the PWA for the 1935 fiscal year and $20 million in emergency relief funds in 1936.) Annual congressional appropriations would thereafter be required for construction to proceed at an orderly pace. Any attempt to secure at once the "entire amount necessary to complete the dam," said Woods, would be "a whale of a mistake," sure to result in rejection. The preferable course, despite the danger of exposing the project to its enemies on an annual basis, was to "slide . . . along and take a chunk of money as we can."[48]

The burden, as work began on the federal budget in 1936, fell once again upon Sam Hill. Angered that the Interior Department had requested only $250,000 for work in his state, Representative Edward Taylor of Colorado, the chairman of the appropriations subcommittee handling Bureau of Reclamation spending, deleted the $22 million for Grand Coulee from the bill sent to the House floor. Over several exhausting weeks, Hill negotiated a complex arrangement under which Taylor agreed to a Senate amendment restoring funding for Grand Coulee. Two million dollars were taken from the Columbia River and enough money from other projects, Hill informed Woods, "to make up a pot of about five million . . . to give to

Colorado." Broken in health by the time the budgetary process was completed in June, the congressman gladly accepted appointment to the federal tax court in Washington, D.C. "Our people owe . . . Sam Hill a debt of gratitude," Jim O'Sullivan properly noted. Indeed, the representative from North Central Washington had saved Grand Coulee twice, securing its authorization in 1935 and the initial congressional appropriation in 1936.[49]

Rufus Woods was not on hand to again serve as Hill's "errand boy" in 1936. To the chagrin of colleagues in the Dam University, Woods instead fell victim to another bout of wanderlust, departing on a new tour of Europe. In spite of the publisher's curiosity about other countries and cultures, the *World* had maintained an isolationist stance since the end of the world war. Italy's attack upon Ethiopia in 1935 produced the paper's first detailed commentaries in years upon events beyond America's shores. Ethiopia's Haile Selassie, the victim of Italian avarice, deserved sympathy, according to the *World*, but not active support from the United States. Although the European powers seemed intent upon expanding the Ethiopian crisis into a full-blown international conflict, the *World* noted, "we will not allow ourselves to be entangled in any foreign brawl."[50]

Americans had sensibly "profited by the bitter experience of our thankless participation in the last folly." The lessons derived from that experience were clear and enduring. Protected by "thousands of miles of blue ocean," the United States need fear no threat from abroad. Trade with belligerents, especially in munitions, must be avoided, for the years between 1914 and 1917 had demonstrated that the country could not "profit from a war between other nations without becoming involved in the fracas." What seemed, in the immediate postwar period, "the worst ignominy of all," the failure of the Allies to pay their debts, had turned out to be "the best thing that could have happened." Memories of "those unpaid billions" helped America avoid involvement in a new round of "quarrels and squabbles." The willingness of European statesmen to "ruthlessly" abandon "every covenant solemnly made and signed" proved that the U.S. had been wise to remain out of the League of Nations. The essential *World* philosophy was summed up in "two short words, 'never again.'"[51]

There was no reason, however, for Americans to be uninformed about the affairs of the world; hence the Woods trip to Europe in the spring of 1936. Rufus accompanied a cargo of Wenatchee apples across the Atlantic, intending to study the marketing of the home valley's export crop. Upon landing, he immediately abandoned this plan in favor of a hectic cross-continent journey. His principal destination, as in 1930, was the Soviet Union. Arriving in Moscow, Woods was impressed by the obvious material achievements of Stalin's "benign dictatorship." The city's subway, new government palaces, and huge factories, all currently under construction, testified to the enormous progress made in recent years.[52]

Russia was clearly "on the up-grade," reported Woods after an extended excursion west of the Urals. Families still crowded into one-room apartments, but the quantity and quality of food had increased considerably since 1930. Illiteracy, even among adults, had been "virtually wiped out" through the regime's emphasis upon education. Rufus wrote of soldiers of the Red Army—"they remind me of some poor downtrodden boys that I have known"—studying their lessons, and of enthusiastic school children blessed with "an opportunity never before given in their land." The Dnieper River dam, built with the assistance of the American engineer Hugh Cooper, was, in dimension and in significance, a Soviet Grand Coulee. And Stalin's proposed constitutional reform, which included the promise of a freely elected parliament, would make the dictator "one of the great men of this age in which we are living."

Massive construction projects and grandiose five-year plans, however, failed to conceal certain disturbing undercurrents of Soviet society. The people, so friendly in 1930, were now "afraid to talk to strangers." Everyday Russians, met in the depots and on the trains, refused to believe that the photographs and advertisements in a weeks-old *Daily World* accurately portrayed life abroad. Rufus purchased books from vendors flabbergasted to learn that Americans could lawfully read communist literature. "To them," Woods wrote, "America is a land of oppression."

Stalin's government was at least stable and capable of planning the country's long-range future. The situation in Germany, Woods discovered in the course of a visit to Berlin, was just the opposite, for Hitler was "riding a rocky road," beset by internal opposition and foreign suspicion. The Nazi attempt to blame German Jews—a mere "one per cent of the people . . . when Hitler came into power"—for losing the war was both "pathetic" and counterproductive. A quarter of the Jewish population, including journalists, professors, and physicians, had already fled, further weakening the country. In one instance only did the government have a sensible approach to the problems of the day. Relief payments, unlike the dole system prevailing in England, came in the form of loans, allowing the recipient to avoid "feeling and acting like a pauper."

After weeks in the lands of the dictators, Woods rejoiced at the openness of "old England." Visiting Hyde Park on a Sunday afternoon, he was enthralled by London's famous and rambunctious "free speech" corner. Some orators spoke to a hundred listeners and one disturbed "lone wolf" shouted only to himself. Coming upon a toothless gentleman declaiming upon the wonders of the "Workers Paradise" in Russia, Rufus could not restrain himself. Mounting a chair, he delivered an impassioned address, arguing that what the Soviet Union most needed was "a decent government such as that in . . . America." Onlookers eager to learn the latest about conditions in Moscow mobbed Woods following his talk.

Pleased with his oratorical triumph over one of Stalin's English apologists, Woods left Europe with a sobering thought uppermost in his mind: "There is a feel of war in the air." Attempting to recover from the world-wide economic collapse, European nations had adopted policies of self-sufficiency, throwing up tariff walls and increasing military expenditures. "Armies, armies, armies," Rufus reflected, "and armaments, armaments and more armaments!" Fortunately, "the memory of the last war" still preoccupied "those of middle age and older." Woods expected one of the powers, motivated by domestic desperation or expansionist zeal, to eventually "make the break that means trouble," probably within "another five or six years."[53]

The disturbing impressions produced by the trip began the dismantling of Rufus Woods's isolationist position. The United States must avoid involvement in foreign wars, he still believed, yet the chances of remaining aloof appeared evermore problematical.

Barely unpacked, Rufus immediately became embroiled in the tumultuous 1936 campaign. The Republican presidential nominee, Governor Alfred M. Landon of Kansas, had no record on the issues of importance to the Pacific Northwest. Colonel Frank Knox, the vice-presidential candidate, published the *Chicago News*, a paper opposed to federal water projects. On the way east in March, Woods had paid a disappointing call upon Landon in Topeka. Asked to comment upon Grand Coulee, the governor said only that he would abide by the Republican platform, a straddle that was anything but reassuring. "Landon is dead against our reclamation of the West," Rufus immediately warned friends at home in a confidential report.[54]

Circumstances, particularly the need to protect the dam, dictated a bipartisan stance for the *World* in 1936. "Good" Democrats—those favoring reclamation—deserved support and "bad" Republicans—the enemies of development—merited rejection. Clarence Martin had disregarded party lines, supporting the Basin Commission, standing up to strikers, and fighting the Democratic "radical element." His administration, said Rufus, made a definite "contrast with the incompetence, the waste of public funds, [and] the political pettiness" of the eight Hartley years. Under the state's new blanket primary, which allowed voters to pick and choose without regard to party affiliation, Woods recommended that Democrats like Martin ought to "draw votes" from responsible Republicans.[55]

Franklin D. Roosevelt merited the same consideration. The *World* questioned the President's tendency to "minimize constitutional restraints" and bemoaned the "many fool ideas" conceived by Rex Tugwell and other ardent New Dealers. Attempts by state Works Progress Administration director George Gannon to apply a political means test to job holders merited censure. Still, FDR's contribution to the Columbia dam project entitled him to a second term, especially in view of Landon's flinty hostility. Under fire from the Republican Party, Woods announced that he intended to "vote for Landon and Knox." Attentive readers recognized that the casting of an individual ballot lacked the force of a forthright endorsement and understood the publisher's real preference to be the head of the Democratic ticket. [56]

Woods thus became a Clarence Martin-Franklin Roosevelt Republican. He also became an outright Democratic activist. Sam Hill's efforts had confirmed his belief that the district must be represented by a champion of Grand Coulee. Unfortunately, the likely nominee for Hill's former House seat, in a year when nomination was tantamount to victory in the general election, was E.F. Banker, who had resigned from state government to make the race. His friendship with J.D. Ross and lack of enthusiasm for the high dam made the retiring Basin Commission chairman "a tricky spinner of yarns" in the view of the Dam University. To solidify his support in Spokane, Banker had engaged in the ultimate sellout. "There is no question," reported Jim O'Sullivan, "but that the pretender is backed by Washington Water Power Company money." Should Banker be elected, "we will have a Power Trust man in Congress representing Grand Coulee," a prospect that justified immediate and drastic action. "The die has been cast," O'Sullivan told Rufus, "and . . . you and I must cross the Rubicon."[57]

Entering the political stream, Grand Coulee supporters rode the candidacy of Judge Charles Leavy of Spokane. Woods worried about the jurist's long association with Clarence Dill and endorsement of expensive old-age pension schemes, but recognized that support of the dam made him the best alternative to Banker. "Better a clean man, even though a little off-color to the left," O'Sullivan agreed, "than a subservient tool of the interests that have fought this dam for many years." O'Sullivan delivered speeches "exposing" Banker's untrustworthiness and joined Rufus in canvassing the towns and weekly newspaper offices of North Central Washington. The *World*, meanwhile, proclaimed Leavy the only pro-Grand Coulee Democrat in the race.[58]

Thrown on the defensive by the unexpected assault from his former Columbia Basin Commission colleagues, Banker responded in a series of vitriolic radio addresses. Woods, he contended, was "carrying on an under-cover campaign" and O'Sullivan was both dishonest and "crazy." Still, posing as the foremost advocate of Grand Coulee proved to be a difficult chore, in light of the countervailing fact that virtually all prominent project supporters declared in favor of Leavy. Overcoming pro-Banker expenditures estimated at $15,000, Leavy won the nomination, with an especially large margin in Chelan County. Hearing that the governor intended to reappoint Banker to his old state positions, Woods immediately met with Martin to successfully argue that such a step would open a rift with the Dam University. "We certainly trimmed the power trust this time, Rufus," an ebullient O'Sullivan wrote from Spokane.[59]

In the general election, Woods worked hard for Governor Martin. A series of bizarre campaign appearances, featuring rambling oratory, sudden screams, and chilling Indian war-cries, convinced most observers that Roland Hartley, running for governor again on the Republican ticket, had progressed from eccentricity to downright lunacy. "Governor Martin is entitled to an endorsement for the job as he has handled it in the past four years," Woods advised readers of the *World*. "In one hundred different situations . . . he has played the part of a real governor." On election day, he stated with the utmost confidence, "there is no doubt in my mind where the votes of central Washington ought to go."[60]

Greatly offended by the endorsement, the Chelan County GOP took out a quarter-page ad in the *World* on October 27 to accuse Rufus of "touting the cause" of "New Deal Democrats" and of plotting to "sell . . . Republican candidates down the river." Woods, the advertisement suggested, was "indebted" to Martin for his appointment to the Columbia Basin Commission. Responding in the same issue of the paper to these "silly" accusations, Woods noted that he was entitled to $10 a day when the commission was in official session and that he had actually billed the state only $30 over the past year: "Out of that comes board and hotel charges . . . and board when on the way to and from the meetings." His endorsement of Martin was not purchased by this "great sinecure," but given freely out of the simple fact that the incumbent "has made the best governor in twenty-five years."[61]

Franklin Roosevelt's positive Grand Coulee response and Alf Landon's negative made the Democratic top-to-bottom sweep in November acceptable to the *World*. Woods credited the FDR landslide to the President's "compelling personality" and to the failure of his dull challenger to "ring the bell with the public." The voters also sensed that the incumbent had "done everything possible to break the depression." The Administration had "square[d] away . . . the bank credits of the United States," taken "care of millions of people on relief" and curbed the "tremendous big combinations of wealth." Post-election economic indicators, from an upswing on Wall Street to an increase in Wenatchee Valley apple prices, affirmed the wisdom of the verdict delivered at the polls. Congressman-elect Charles Leavy, meanwhile, was a worthy successor to Sam Hill. And the reelection of Clarence Martin amounted to a deserved rebuff of both reactionary Republicanism and the radical wing of the state Democratic Party.[62]

Every resident of Washington, observed one prominent Democrat, "should be a 100 per cent New Dealer" in gratitude for Grand Coulee and Bonneville dams. Crossing party lines in 1936, directly and by the flank, Rufus Woods revealed himself to be a New Deal Republican on the crucial issue of river development. The Roosevelt Administration, following the Dam University guidebook, had gone where Hoover feared, and Landon refused, to tread. The story of Grand Coulee's construction, wrote Rufus, was "one of the greatest dramas ever enacted in the West." A small group of obscure men had devised a plan, then "kept at it when hearts less courageous would have quailed at the immensity of the task." They had won in the end by adhering to the old adage that success eventually comes to those "who hang on after all the rest . . . let go." The victory also depended on the intervention at a critical moment of an interested President of the United

States. All citizens of the interior Northwest, regardless of party preference or personal philosophy, owed much to the leader of the Democratic Party.[63]

Key events since 1929 resolved for Woods the question of whether public or private development was the best course to follow on the Columbia. "A wise and benign government can be most useful to all of its citizens," he pointed out in July 1935. Some tasks, including the building of great dams on wild rivers, were too large and too costly for business to undertake. Assorted investigations in the aftermath of the Wall Street crash, moreover, exposed to ridicule the notion that utility interests could be trusted with matters of the general welfare. "The people of this country are not against wealth," Rufus observed. "But what they are against is the way these holding companies have been used to bilk . . . the public" through excessive rates and watered stock. "When private enterprises develop corporations so large that they dominate or attempt to dominate the government itself," he noted in a series of essays on the subject, "then it is time for the government to take a hand at regulation." Regulation had failed to curb the utilities and the only remaining option was "public ownership."[64]

Even so, public projects—particularly Grand Coulee—regrettably came with a price. Deploring the "mad scramble" of states and localities to "share in the unprecedented . . . bounty" of the New Deal, the *World* warned that "in the long run, nothing is free." Funding all manner of things, the federal government insisted upon building and operating the major projects undertaken with its resources. Acquiescing out of necessity in this centralizing tendency, the Dam University still hoped to preserve a measure of autonomy for North Central Washington. "Whole sections of the United States . . . have been LOOTED and the people robbed of their birthright," Woods contended. The Pacific Northwest could avoid a similar fate only by resisting outside political and economic control: "It is for us to decide whether the billion dollar wealth of the resources of the Columbia shall be looted and decimated, or whether . . . we shall have a program of ORDERLY DEVELOPMENT."[65]

An anonymous "twenty-one year subscriber" took Rufus brutally to task for devoting so much of the *World*'s space to Grand Coulee. "When a person thinks and talks about the same object continuously," complained the disgruntled reader, "he is mentally unbalanced and headed for the insane asylum." Publishing the letter, Woods refused to apologize for "chasing moonbeams." He could, in actuality, never write too much about the project, for it was the "key" to the development of an entire region, "a piece of statesmanship" rather than a mere structure of concrete and steel.

The work under way at Grand Coulee represented the start of "a PRO-GRAM, which must go down for the next 50 years and thence be extended for a thousand years in the future." No one was more qualified, or more obligated, to speak on behalf of the plan than were genuine longtime residents of the counties abutting the Columbia. "It is . . . up to those who live on its banks," Rufus lectured the nameless complainant, "to develop and publicize the policies which make for the proper control of this greatest of all power streams of the world."[66]

# Chapter Ten
# The Land of Folks

Central Washington. Land of folks—folks who are owned by no man.
Folks of the independent type who can look any scoundrel in the face
and tell him where to go. Leaders—men of initiative and energy, home
builders who are willing to start out with a small shack and then line it
with flowers.

Rufus Woods[1]

NINETEEN-THIRTY-SEVEN, the nineteenth year of the fight for Grand
Coulee, was a time of significant change in the life of Rufus Woods.
Daughter Willa Lou, graduating from the University of Washington, joined
Wilfred, just out of high school, and the teenaged Kathryn at work in the
*World* office. All three, according to a private diary entry, had become "delightful" young adults. Concerned for the Constitution and for private
property, Rufus abandoned his flirtation with Franklin Roosevelt and returned to the old Republican fold. The breakup produced no check on
regional progress, for the letting of the high dam contract marked a major
advance toward completion of Grand Coulee. The highlight of the year,
though, was neither familial nor political in nature. At the age of fifty-
nine, Rufus Woods, solid citizen and a leader of his community, satisfied a
boyhood dream by joining the circus.[2]

"It has been a long, long wait," Rufus informed readers of his column
in late August, "forty-five years of it, waiting for my heart's desire–waiting
and waiting and waiting some day to run off with the circus." The opportunity came at last with the arrival in Wenatchee of the Cole Brothers
entertainment extravaganza, featuring animal-tamer Clyde Beatty and cowboy hero Ken Maynard. The aerial artiste Madame Reta de la Plata horrified onlookers, on schedule, by falling from a "broken" trapeze, only to be

hauled up short of the ground by a concealed safety harness. Rufus, though, considered the seventeen clowns, exploding props, and outrageous gags the main attraction. The entire circus was a big and eccentric family, living and working in harmony.[3]

When the circus departed Wenatchee, Woods went along as the guest of the proprietors and a genuine performer. Made up in grease paint, with putty nose, shaggy wig, oversize clothing, and flapping shoes, Rufus, billing himself as the "Mayor of Seattle," joined his new friends in antic misbehavior. He paraded through the streets of Tacoma, with Otto, Skinny, and the other clowns, arm-in-arm with brother Ralph, also costumed for the occasion. Persuading a bewhiskered hobo to join the march, they laughed when townspeople, watching the procession from the sidewalk, failed to distinguish between the "Weary Willie" and professional circus troupers. The *New York Times*, *Time*, and *Life* published photographs of the grinning, middle-aged Republican journalist in clown garb. "This is what a fellow gets," wrote Rufus, "for doing something just a little bit differently."

Matters political assumed a different aspect in the closing years of the 1930s. The reelection of Clarence Martin in 1936 signalled, for Woods, the beginning of a conservative trend in state affairs. Fortified by his triumph at the polls, the governor stood as a rock against the final surge of the radical current in Olympia, vetoing every unsound budget-busting measure to emerge from the legislature. As a result, claimed the *World*, he ranked "higher in the estimation of the people . . . than ever before." Against all odds, Washington was, thanks to Martin, "the best-governed of our 48 states." The victory of Arthur Langlie, leader of the New Order of Cincinnatus, in the 1938 Seattle mayoral race appeared to be further proof that the voters were "through with slapstick politics."[4]

From the perspective of the Wenatchee Valley, national affairs underwent a contrary shift to the left. After carrying forty-six of the forty-eight states, FDR moved against the Supreme Court, the institution responsible for killing the NRA, AAA, and other key New Deal initiatives. In early February 1937, Roosevelt called for a reorganization of the federal judiciary to, among other things, allow appointment of up to a half dozen additional justices. "The builders of the Constitution," Rufus pointed out in immediately attacking the so-called court-packing bill, " . . . were very emphatic in their opinion that there should be checks and balances in government." If the President succeeded in taking effective control of a rival branch of the federal government, he warned, "then you and I will be . . . thrown under a dictatorship." In a shrewd retreat, the Court began issuing pro-New Deal rulings, while months of emotionally draining congressional debate ended in the defeat of Roosevelt's reorganization proposal. The entire affair convinced Woods that FDR was a fundamentally untrustworthy politician.[5]

Defending itself against Roosevelt, the Supreme Court approved the constitutionality of the Wagner Act. Originally passed by Congress in 1935, the law guaranteed the right of workers to organize and created a National Labor Relations Board to monitor union elections and check unfair employer practices. East of the Cascades, the decision was viewed as an encouragement to urban sit-down strikers and as a portent of trouble for small towns and rural areas. The *World* complained of the "epidemic of strikes . . . spreading all over the country," threatening recovery and leaving the national economy "tottering on the brink of a volcano." Locally, the Teamsters were increasingly active in the packing houses and growers feared they would attempt to unionize orchard hands. Rufus Woods bemoaned the failure to concede that management also had rights, that excessive demands would only bankrupt business, to the detriment of all concerned. "There is such a thing," he contended, "as an even keel and common sense and moderation in all of these relationships in life."[6]

Armed with the Wagner Act, New Dealers swung entirely, according to conservatives and old-time progressives, into the anti-business camp. "The whole labor situation so far as our national government is concerned," proclaimed Woods, "is in a MUDDLE and a MESS, both spelled with a big M." Rules and procedures devised by lawyers, professors, and other suspect experts in the employ of the government gave no leeway to "the payroll makers" and were biased in favor of "the man who doesn't want to work." The actions of the National Labor Relations Board in supervising a prolonged dispute among sawmill employees in the Okanogan Valley proved to the *World* that the agency was guilty of "prejudice, unfairness and rank injustice."[7]

Passage of the Fair Labor Standards Act in 1938 produced new aggravation, establishing for industries engaged in interstate commerce an hourly minimum wage of forty cents and, after three years, a maximum workweek of forty hours. The *World* objected to "hard and fast rules adopted by a committee in Washington . . . familiar only with industrial operations where production can be . . . controlled to the last one ten-thousandth of an inch." Once again, outsiders had acted in ignorance of regional distinctions, for "when harvest time comes in the fruit industry . . . rules and regulations have to be discarded temporarily." Although agriculture was specifically exempted, the Labor Department ruled that the act applied to packing houses. This determination interfered with the traditional frenzied handling of the fall apple crop and drew a renewed protest from the *World*: "The law has so many loop-holes that a crack-pot board has been able to use its autocratic powers in such a way as to strangle industry and scare capital."[8]

Summing up, the second term indictment of the New Deal focused on two principal concerns. Despite the defeat of his court packing plan, Roosevelt had gone far toward dismantling the Constitution. The executive branch of the federal government, Woods pointed out in 1939, was now responsible for "dictating the planting and marketing of crops, dictating labor relationships and the hours of work, dictating the mining of coal, dictating business activities, [and] dictating local and state . . . activities." The proliferation of legislation, rulings, and alphabetical agencies, moreover, confused business owners, retarded investment, and delayed the return of prosperity. "There are so many of these queer regulations," confessed Rufus, ". . . that it is hard for us to understand the why and wherefore thereof." No wonder FDR wanted an expanded judiciary, given the "additional bureaus, additional laws and central control of so many corporations, persons and things."[9]

Rufus Woods noted that foreign observers of the United States often thought, incorrectly, that "when we are opposed to some of the issues, we must be opposed to all." Increasing animosity over the New Deal certainly failed to interfere with continued cooperation with the Roosevelt Administration on Grand Coulee and other matters related to the Columbia River. The breakup on this vital topic was not between Woods and FDR, but between the Dam University and certain officials of the state of Washington. The Columbia Basin Commission had met only infrequently of late and was singled out, at the beginning of the 1937 legislative session, as a political target by E.F. Banker's revenge-minded friends. Meeting with Governor Martin, Woods, weary of the animosity left over from the previous fall's Democratic primary in the Fifth Congressional District, agreed to abolition of the agency, provided that Jim O'Sullivan was retained in state employment. The arrangement allowed Rufus and the governor to maintain their friendship and had the added virtue of preserving an old friend's much-needed paycheck. Reluctantly acquiescing in the decision, O'Sullivan privately blamed Rufus for engineering what he considered to be a humiliating demotion to "some clerical position."[10]

Political machinations of this sort appeared to have little import for Grand Coulee, with the dam securely on the road to completion. The appropriation secured by Sam Hill in 1936 funded the final stages of work on the foundation. "After that it will be just a question of pouring concrete," Woods believed. Persistent reports that the project would be stalled, or even halted, at this stage made for occasional sleepless nights, especially because of the presence in Washington of J.D. Ross. As a member of the Securities and Exchange Commission, Ross had an opportunity to directly contact and influence New Deal officials. Returning from a White House reception for new members of Congress, however, Charles Leavy dispelled the rumors. President Roosevelt, he reported to Rufus, "freely discussed the Coulee Dam and did not hesitate to show his deep interest in seeing it finished." Leavy noted that FDR was particularly concerned to avoid the waste of money bound to result from a prolonged interruption in construction.[11]

Events nonetheless confirmed Woods's fear that "there will be a snag somewhere along the line as usual." The Interior Department caused momentary consternation by briefly claiming, on the basis of a literal reading of Hill's 1936 amendment appropriating funds, that Congress had inadvertently repealed authorization of Grand Coulee. Frank Banks, the chief government engineer at Grand Coulee, requested $20 million for 1937, but the Bureau of the Budget reduced the figure submitted to Congress to only $7.2 million. President Roosevelt, moreover, continued to be concerned over land speculation in the project area. The Dam University believed the problem was greatly exaggerated, especially in relation to the vast acreage to be placed under water. "You would think that there were a thousand real estate men running a wild campaign," exclaimed O'Sullivan. Nonetheless, the President's concern had to be addressed in order to avoid jeopardizing the necessary annual appropriations for the dam.[12]

Work in the nation's capital proceeded on two tracks, one aimed at securing the highest possible Grand Coulee appropriation in 1937 and the other headed toward a curb on speculators. Along the latter course, Senator Homer Bone introduced anti-speculation legislation drafted by the Bureau of Reclamation. Under the measure, water recipients were limited to owning forty acres if single, and eighty acres if married, and had to sell excess holdings at a government-appraised price. Landowners, moreover, must form an irrigation district and sign a contract with the Bureau before work could begin on the canals.[13]

Rufus spent March and April in Washington, "thinking of nothing morning, noon, and night but Grand Coulee Dam." He met daily with Charles Leavy, who had secured a seat on the appropriations subcommittee responsible for Interior Department spending. Although inexperienced and "already worked to death," Leavy gave every sign of "being able to fill the shoes of Sam B. Hill." Woods also conferred on a regular basis with Hill, now on the federal tax appeals court, with Albert Goss at the farm loan bank, and with Frank Bell at the marine fisheries bureau. Despite the problems caused by his alleged involvement in land speculation, Bell was, according to Rufus, "the best behind the scenes worker I have ever seen." Aware that the "average Congressman is mighty cherry [*sic*] about these lobbyists," Woods pretended to be nothing more than a visiting journalist, circulating among members of the House and Senate with notebook always in hand. Politicians, craving publicity, were eager to talk with reporters. Even a vehement critic of reclamation like Representative Francis Culkin of New York welcomed the newsman from Washington state.[14]

His own inclinations on this point reinforced by cautionary advice from Hill and Goss, Rufus downplayed or ignored the reclamation aspects of Columbia Basin development. "To hitch this project to irrigation at the present time," he reminded Governor Martin, "is dangerous." There was, however, "a strong combination favorable to power in the House" willing to fall behind Grand Coulee as a generator of hydroelectricity. Woods cultivated what must have been a bizarre relationship with Representative John Rankin of Mississippi, a racist, anti-Semitic advocate of federal dam construction. To Rankin and others offering to help, Rufus stressed that Grand Coulee would pay for itself from power sales and was already so far advanced that a halt to construction meant the waste of the large sums invested. "This SELF LIQUIDATING IDEA together with the fact that the dam is HALF COMPLETED are the strongest points I find in discussing it," he reported to Martin.[15]

At the request of Woods, Jim O'Sullivan came east on behalf of the state to help with lobbying chores. Convinced that the Power Trust hoped to purchase Grand Coulee "at considerably below . . . cost" once work on the low dam was completed, O'Sullivan eagerly undertook the mission. Prior to departing, J.B. Fink—E.F. Banker's successor as head of the

Department of Conservation and Development—ordered O'Sullivan to "avoid any controversy with the power interests" and to withhold all data "showing that Grand Coulee power could be sold cheaper than that charged by the private utilities." Woods and O'Sullivan, the latter simply ignoring his instructions, prepared a detailed brief in support of Grand Coulee and testified before Leavy's subcommittee. O'Sullivan, unfortunately, embarrassed Rufus and offended most of the congressmen present by violating the strict time limit imposed upon witnesses, holding the microphone for over an hour as he delivered a detailed monologue.[16]

Senator Homer Bone, Rufus reported on the eve of the House hearing, had "shot some hot talk over the phone to the president's secretary, telling him that the bill providing for elimination of speculation was ready as requested . . . and now would the president send the word down the line to jack up that appropriation." Acting upon FDR's quickly expressed wishes, the Budget Bureau approved an additional $6.75 million for the dam. Favorable action in the House and Senate allowed Grand Coulee to emerge from the session with nearly $14 million in new financial support. "This changes the entire situation," wrote a relieved Rufus Woods, "and sets us [up] pretty well for another year."[17]

The mission to Washington resulted in more than additional money for Grand Coulee, as a long and close friendship ended in a display of irrationality. Through the years, Rufus had never pretended to be anything more than "one of the organization." Many individuals, he pointed out, deserved credit for their vital contributions to the dam. The key to victory, though, was the unified approach followed from 1918 onward. "Every problem which has come up," reflected Woods, "has been threshed out and agreed upon and then all went to work to do their respective bit for the big job."[18]

His newspaper background and outgoing personality made Woods a natural focus of Grand Coulee coverage in the national press. A "Cavalcade of America" radio broadcast prepared in the spring of 1937 focused on his role in the construction of the project. *Fortune* magazine called Rufus the individual most responsible for Grand Coulee. Stopping off in Chicago on the way home from Washington, he appeared on the Edgar Guest radio program in the role of a twentieth century "frontiersman." Outraged by the apparent slight to his own role, O'Sullivan erupted in fury. "Rufus is deliberately building himself up as the Father and Putter-over of the dam," the angered lobbyist wrote, to the extent of actually soliciting laudatory news coverage and "fixing up" the "Cavalcade of America" documentary. "What a H-ll of a lot of gall," charged O'Sullivan in one of his more lucid moments.

Piling petty accusation upon petty accusation, O'Sullivan spread rumors that Rufus had dated young women while in Washington and, in an even more debauched act, used Columbia Basin Development League stationery for his personal correspondence. O'Sullivan demanded that the "Cavalcade of America" cancel its Grand Coulee broadcast and spent several days in New York belaboring *Fortune* editors with "proof" of his own responsibility for the dam. A disinterested Woods had supposedly been "warmed up" over the years by the real supporters of Columbia River development. Claiming to have examined all back issues of the *World*, O'Sullivan asserted that the paper had not even mentioned Grand Coulee between 1920 and 1929.[19]

Only partially comprehending O'Sullivan's bitterness, Woods defended himself against the accusation of glory-hogging. He had credited everyone involved with Grand Coulee in interviews for the "Cavalcade of America" broadcast, but the producers had, unbeknownst to him, ignored historical accuracy in editing the final version. The minor roles assigned to other individuals, moreover, resulted from their failure to sign releases in time for the mid-June program. "We all in the Northwest recognize," he reiterated in the *World*, "that the Grand Coulee dam is no one man's or no two men's job." O'Sullivan refused to be mollified, producing an open breach in the ranks of the Dam University, a breach kept fresh by his enduring resentment of old comrade Rufus Woods.[20]

Ignoring the role played by the Wenatchee publisher in saving his state job and in arranging for the trip east, O'Sullivan accused Woods of responsibility for the "deal to kill the [Columbia Basin] commission" and of attempting to "keep me away from Washington." J.B. Fink, supposedly at the bidding of Rufus, "heaped insult and injury" upon O'Sullivan, cutting his salary by 50 percent. Looking for more congenial employment, the embattled lobbyist considered writing an unexpurgated history of the struggle for Grand Coulee. Stressing the damage that this tell-all literary enterprise might inflict upon the quest for future appropriations, Representative Charles Leavy successfully urged abandonment of the "extremely interesting" yet "detrimental" book project. O'Sullivan eventually left Olympia for a stint as a researcher with the Bonneville Power Administration, courtesy of J.D. Ross, before accepting the secretaryship of the Quincy-Columbia Basin Irrigation District.[21]

O'Sullivan's unhappiness had no bearing upon the progress of construction on the Columbia. In 1937, said Woods, Grand Coulee became "a dam that is a dam." On an October visit, President Roosevelt praised Grand Coulee as "the largest structure so far as anybody knows that has ever been undertaken by man." With the low dam nearing completion, project supporters worried about the slow progress of the Bureau of Reclamation in concluding a contract for the high dam. Although the Bureau finally scheduled the opening of bids for December 10, a new concern threatened the orderly transition from the first to the second stage of construction. If the bids submitted exceeded the confidential cost estimates prepared by federal engineers, there might be no contract, stalling Grand Coulee at the foundation stage for at least a year, if not permanently.[22]

Interested contractors had similar concerns, given the large sum of money at stake. A MWAK executive asked O'Sullivan, "if it isn't too much out of order," to procure the secret cost specifications from his sources in the Interior Department. Believing that the entire project was at stake, O'Sullivan obliged. "I was able to . . . give the information to MWAK Company," he advised Billy Clapp. "I also found out that if the bids exceeded the estimate of $35,000,000 very much they would be rejected." Provided with this helpful intelligence, Mason-Walsh-Atkinson-Kerr joined with Henry Kaiser and other participants in the Six Companies to form the Consolidated Builders, Inc. On December 10, CBI submitted a suspiciously close-to-the-mark bid of $34.4 million, several million dollars below the nearest competitor. Aware that some form of "collusion" was involved, the Bureau of Reclamation nonetheless awarded the high dam contract to CBI.[23]

Assuming that Congress continued to annually appropriate funds for construction, the high dam contract settled the issue of Grand Coulee's final dimensions. Attention now focused on selection of a method for distributing power. Bonneville Dam would be completed in 1938, so this matter needed prompt resolution. J.D. Ross reminded his friends in the Roosevelt Administration that the public was threatened by "a tremendous amount of inconvenience." The Corps of Engineers wanted to sell the electricity produced at Bonneville and the Bureau of Reclamation expected to do so at Grand Coulee. To forestall this duplication of marketing effort, pending expected creation of a permanent Columbia Valley Authority, Congress devised a temporary expedient, establishing the Bonneville Power Administration in August 1937 as "provisional" sales agency.[24]

The appointment of J.D. Ross as BPA administrator produced considerable unease in eastern Washington, since Grand Coulee was sure to be placed under his jurisdiction. "It is entirely incongruous," pronounced Woods, that a man "whose loyalty to the dam was questioned while the fight was on, should now want to boss the job." Transformed into an enthusiastic advocate of developing the Columbia, Ross admitted that his previous opposition had been entirely political in nature, designed to advance the interest of City Light. He was now ready with a revised power forecast, based upon timely recognition of an upward trend in regional energy consumption. "Our demand here doubles every 5-1/2 years," Ross informed President Roosevelt in December 1937, "so by the time the 800,000 or 900,000 kilowatts of firm power is furnished at Coulee, there will be another 1,600,000 kilowatts needed." Sounding exactly like his old Wenatchee antagonist, he maintained that electricity, by its very availability, automatically generated markets, hence "no great hydro plant ever goes begging."[25]

Despite their meeting-of-the-minds on the issue of power demand, Woods had no intention of falling in behind the leadership of the BPA administrator. Upon assuming office, Ross secured approval for a transmission line linking Bonneville Dam with Grand Coulee, bringing about the "consolidation of the two Federal plants into one." His goal, an aim largely achieved by the early 1940s, was creation of a regional intertie combining public and private generation facilities in a Pacific Northwest energy grid. "That is a more ambitious plan than ever was dreamed of by our . . . dam enthusiasts," admitted Rufus. As far as North Central Washington was concerned, the plan was also inherently dangerous, for the transmission lines enabled the draining-off to distant points of electricity that might otherwise be consumed in the local four-county region.[26]

Arguing that common sense called for sending electricity to industry rather than requiring industry to go to the power source, Ross also devised the basic BPA "postage stamp" rate structure. Regardless of distance from the generating station, customers paid $17.50 per kilowatt year for primary power. Manufacturers therefore had no incentive, complained a bitterly disappointed Woods, to build plants in Wenatchee. Local residents stood to lose the benefits of "their" dam. Operating from a new institutional base, J.D. Ross remained an enemy of North Central Washington.[27]

Provided Grand Coulee was protected from such enemies, Rufus Woods had a fully matured forecast ready for the future of the Columbia Basin. In terms of agriculture, Grant County would undergo a dramatic transformation. After three decades featuring "lack of water, lack of rain-fall . . . and lack of almost everything else," a new reclamation empire neared realization. This new domain, however, would be no clone of the Wenatchee Valley. The orchard areas along the right bank of the Columbia had been nearly "ruined by . . . success and prosperity," in the opinion of the *World*. "A few years of good crops and higher prices for apples in the early days resulted in apple trees being set out wherever there was a foot of soil capable of holding the trees in place." The result was a regional economy that "carries all its eggs in one basket." Growers, as well as the seasonal work force and small-town merchants dependent upon apple profits, suf-fered when markets were overstocked and prices driven down to—and below—the cost of production. The paramount requirement of the day was, therefore, crop diversification.[28]

Noting the relative stability of the Yakima Valley, where only half the value of farm production came from fruit, the *World* suggested that the person responsible for bringing to Wenatchee a "workable" complement to apples ought to be awarded the title of "the real 'Moses' of . . . this district." Woods believed that he, in fact, knew the way to the promised land of Columbia Basin prosperity: the sugar beet. Possessing "the world's finest soil," the 400,000 acres adjacent to Quincy, Ephrata, and Moses Lake ought to be planted in beets as soon as water became available. The first unit of the Columbia Basin Project, Rufus pointed out, "would support eight to ten sugar beet factories." Apples west of the river and beets to the east made a good fit, satisfying the historical demand for agricultural diversity.[29]

Balancing agriculture, Woods also anticipated a rapid expansion of local industry, centering on the extraction and processing of metals. North Central Washington, in his view, held abundant wealth, resources previously unexploited because of the selfishness of outside capitalists. The Holden copper mine at the head of Lake Chelan, then producing 2,000 tons of copper per day, was a small harbinger of things to come, claimed the *World*, once cheap electricity from Grand Coulee became available for the efficient handling of minerals from the Cascades. The paper predicted that over the next half century "an epic drama of production and wealth, surpassing the most fabulous dreams of the pioneer prospectors" would unfold. And Wenatchee, still the place where the river met the railroad, could expect to rise with the hinterland, maintaining itself as the regional urban center. Woods expected the city to become a manufacturing center, with "a population of 50,000 to 75,000," all depending upon the degree to which the benefits of Grand Coulee were preserved for local benefit.[30]

There would, of course, be nothing to preserve if Congress failed to provide regular appropriations to complete the dam. Arriving in Washington in early 1938 on another lobbying foray, Jim O'Sullivan immediately grasped the significance of "the tremendous economy drive" currently underway in response to the "Roosevelt Recession," the severe national economic downturn under way since the previous fall. The Bureau of Reclamation asked for $13 million for Grand Coulee in the coming fiscal year, half the amount required to maintain a speedy construction schedule. The Budget Bureau, moreover, supported this request only because of the President's continuing personal interest in the project. Through "delicate" work, Representative Charles Leavy maneuvered Grand Coulee funding through the House and, with assistance from Senator Homer Bone, the conference committee. "We should have had several million dollars more," Leavy told Woods, "but to have attempted to get them . . . would have jeopardized the entire appropriation." Except for his membership on an influential subcommittee, the congressman noted, the money for the dam "would have suffered a substantial reduction, if not an elimination."[31]

Matters grew more difficult the following year, in large part because of the Republican comeback in the 1938 congressional elections. The approaching end of the Roosevelt Administration—few observers believed that FDR would break with the two term tradition—reduced the influence of the White House. Correctly anticipating "a real fight to secure Coulee appropriations for next year," Charles Leavy managed to secure $12 million in new funding. The Budget Bureau threatened even this level of spending—although barely sufficient to keep work going at steady pace—when it sought a 50 percent cut for all federal construction projects so that money could be shifted to the administration's preparedness program. The outbreak of the war in Europe in September 1939, however, worked to Grand Coulee's advantage, since the dam, when completed, would make a major contribution to defense industry. Meeting with President Roosevelt in January 1940, Leavy secured an exemption from the budget reduction order, plus an allocation of an extra $7 million, making possible an actual speed-up in construction.[32]

Although the approach of a new international conflagration naturally focused attention on the strategically important electricity Grand Coulee would generate, Congress also funded preparatory work for the long-delayed irrigation aspects of the project. The Bureau of Reclamation surveyed the entire basin, prepared detailed topographical maps, located the land susceptible to agricultural exploitation, and assessed the value of these tracts. "About one-half of the total area"—slightly in excess of a million acres—"is . . . suitable for farming," the *World* reported in May 1939, "in fact it is exceptionally rich, deep and fertile." Upon completion of its preliminary studies, the Bureau organized the Columbia Basin Joint Investigations for detailed study of such technical matters as ideal farm size, the cost of water and the anticipated income of settlers. Rather than wait for completion of this time-consuming work, reclamation advocates in Ephrata and Quincy, along with Rufus Woods in Wenatchee, favored an immediate start to excavation of the necessary canals and ditches.[33]

Timely construction, unhappily for water-hungry landholders, proved impossible under the restrictive terms of the federal anti-speculation law. According to the Bureau of Reclamation reading, the statute required that a single irrigation district, incorporating all irrigable acreage in the Columbia Basin, must be formed and a contract with the government negotiated prior to the turning of a shovelful of earth. This approach, though substantially correct in a legalistic sense, ignored the fact that the basin was actually composed of distinct subregions. On the west, the mostly absentee property owners in the old Quincy Irrigation District favored Grand Coulee and believed themselves entitled to priority treatment in the apportionment of water. On the east, dryland wheat ranchers opposed the acreage restrictions imposed by the government and were unwilling to proceed prior to completion of the Joint Investigations. Wheat producers to the south, near the mouth of the Snake River, shared these concerns and bristled over being, by dint of geography, last in line for water.[34]

Aware of the danger involved in organizing a single district, including the possibility of a negative vote by landowners, Jim O'Sullivan assigned himself the task of "leading the fight for a square deal in irrigation." Strict construction of the anti-speculation measure, in his view, threatened the basin subregion responsible for the success of Grand Coulee. "If this super-district is formed," he warned, "the control . . . will be on the East side," with the first canals, thanks to the political influence of nearby Spokane, built to serve the wheat ranching country. Pressed by the Great Northern and other interests expecting to benefit from population growth in the Big Bend, the Bureau of Reclamation abandoned its original position. The Quincy-Columbia Basin District, employing O'Sullivan as its secretary, was organized in October 1938 and validated by an overwhelming vote of the landowners in February 1939. In December, property holders approved creation of the East-Columbia Basin and the South-Columbia Basin districts.[35]

Except as a cheerleader-from-afar, Rufus Woods was not involved in these essential organizational developments on the reclamation front. In March 1938 he sailed for Europe aboard a Belgian steamer, accompanying a cargo of Northwest apples. After attending the Antwerp fruit auction, Rufus considered revisiting Moscow, the focal point of his 1930 and 1936 tours. "To have witnessed Russia in travail while trying to give birth to new ideas in government," was, after all, ". . . to me one of the great events of my life." But the dramatic story was now in central, rather than in eastern, Europe. Upon the proclamation of the Anschluss, the union of Austria with Germany, Woods caught the first train to Vienna, arriving minutes before Adolf Hitler entered the city. Displaying his Associated Press card, notepad, and pencil, Rufus talked security officers into allowing him to stand a few feet from the dictator's swastika-decorated route. When the motorcade came into view, he briefly looked Hitler squarely in the face.[36]

Seeing Hitler up close was a "compelling event," precipitating a series of dispatches to the *World*. The dictator deserved censure for the murderous methods used in attaining and consolidating power and for encouraging the worship of his person. Still, Woods had positive things to say about the Nazi leader. Through personality and showmanship, Hitler had "enthused the German people" and restored political stability to the country. "As a speaker," he was "nothing short of a marvel," the equal of the "most magnetic religious exhorter I have ever heard." Building upon traditional German culture, the Nazis had also achieved a number of things worthy of emulation. Americans exercised at second-hand, watching "the baseball players, the basket and football players work out," but the youth of Germany engaged in hiking, skiing, and other healthy out-of-doors activities. To develop character and encourage respect for work, the government made national service mandatory, outlawed strikes, and provided the unemployed only with modest stipends.

To his credit, Rufus also reported upon the vicious aspects of Nazi rule. A "heavy blanket of oppression, depression and repression" lay upon Germany. The number of newspapers and magazines had declined by a third since 1933 and the survivors were nothing but "pure propaganda sheets." Government censors cleared radio broadcasts and even "the letters which go out and come in." With Ralph McGill of the *Atlanta Constitution*, Woods called upon a Jewish acquaintance in Vienna. "Frightened" by the knock upon his apartment door, the man was "much relieved when he saw that it was not an officer." Rufus was present when a newspaper friend in Berlin was dismissed because of his marriage to a Jew. All over Germany and Austria, he reported, jobholders "have found it necessary to check back [on] their ancestry." The Nazis had produced order, but only by introducing a sickness into German life. "Let no one say that the stories of terror are propaganda," Woods wrote home. The brutality viewed at first hand made him "ashamed."

Sailing for home, Woods was convinced that America must provide "moral support" for "those nations standing for peace" and opposed to the designs of Hitler. In September 1938, Germany's demand for the Sudetenland confirmed his fear that the Anschluss was a preliminary to further aggression. If war started over the fate of Czechoslovakia, Rufus noted, there must be no repetition of 1914 so far as Americans were concerned: "Hitler can expect at least the sentiment of the United States against him from the start." Although the Munich agreement resolved the crisis, at least for the moment, the folly of isolationism was now readily apparent. "America is no longer a disconnected nation," Woods observed, "standing by itself with no regard for what is taking place in other parts of the world."[37]

"Anything that can happen there," Woods wrote of Europe, "may happen here." Americans must therefore "gird our loins" in defense of the national interest. The accelerated preparedness program proclaimed by the Roosevelt Administration at the end of 1938 was, according to Rufus, the policy best calculated to make ready for war without surrendering the freedom of independent action. "Nothing that the present administration has proposed ever won such support . . . as the rearmament program," the *World* noted in commending Roosevelt's national defense activism. "The soundness of the plan for preparing to meet the threat of a war-mad world . . . appeals to all sensible, sane, right-thinking people." Absorbing what was left of Czechoslovakia in March 1939, Germany violated another international agreement and proved, once and for all, that force was the only argument likely to deter Hitler.[38]

Diverted by events in Europe, most Americans ignored the equally dangerous situation in the Far East, especially the ongoing Japanese attempt to conquer China. Seeking personal knowledge of Asia, Woods sailed from Vancouver aboard a British cargo vessel in January 1939. (Ralph McGill teased his Pacific Northwest friend for traveling the globe at a moment's notice: "I wish I were a bloated successful publisher instead of a grubbing newspaper man.") At Yokohama, officials boarded the ship to examine travel documents and determine the views of the passengers on the Chinese conflict. Rufus turned what might have been a difficult encounter into "a delightful visit and parley" by taking out his reporter's notebook and "interviewing" the astonished security men.[39]

Observations gathered in Tokyo and Osaka provided Woods with the material for reports home. Japan's "amazing progress" was most evident in the building of a modern industrial economy. The entire country was electrified and "tremendous holding companies" planned the details of financing and production in "cooperation with the Japanese government." The dormant volcanoes of the home islands provided the visiting American with an apt metaphor. "In those peaceful looking cones," observed Rufus, ". . . there lie the potential forces of Nature which rip and tear asunder and send great masses of earth by the cubic miles into the air." The increasing regimentation of society was "emblematic" of a national landscape poised on the verge of violence. Students, from elementary schools through the universities, drilled under the supervision of army officers. Loyalty to family was transformed into blind devotion to the emperor and the military.

Moving on to China, Rufus saw in appalling scenes of devastation and cruelty the product of the erupting Japanese volcano. At Shanghai, most of the city outside the International Settlement had been destroyed by bombs and artillery shells. One hundred thousand refugees, by conservative estimate, crowded into the foreign quarter. Severed heads impaled upon fenceposts and corpses floating in the river reflected the hazards of speaking out against Japan. Meeting with the faculty at a university run by American missionaries, Woods learned that their president had been murdered by soldiers of the invading army. "It's a war," he informed readers in Wenatchee, "where there is NO QUARTER—NO PRISONERS—A WAR TO THE DEATH."

Departing for home in late April, Rufus spent the voyage reflecting upon the course of events in Asia. Clearly, Japan had adopted a Hitler-like strategy of "tak[ing] one place at a time." During a stopover in Manila he interviewed Emilio Aguinaldo, the hero of the Filipino struggle for independence. The meeting brought home to Woods the widespread fear of Japanese expansionism. The dignified old gentleman desired a free Philippines, but recognized the need for America's "protecting arm." Japan's imperial aspirations, fortunately, appeared to be entirely focused, at least for the time-being, upon China. Heavily dependent upon imports of oil, scrap iron, and other essential items, Tokyo could ill-afford a confrontation with the great powers. Although Woods had seen much suffering, he returned to Wenatchee convinced of one thing: "Japan wants no war with the United States."

His concern remained focused on Europe, where Hitler's latest demands threatened Poland. The state of affairs reminded Rufus, writing in August 1939, of the annual forest fire season in the Pacific Northwest. The "tinder" was the "driest it has been for years, and all that is needed for a terrible conflagration is a start." As the final crisis neared, Woods abandoned the last vestiges of his old isolationist faith, reasoning that if war was inevitable, "we might as well get into it at the start and on the right side." Modern means of transportation and communication had erased protective barriers of time and space and made continued adherence to America's traditional foreign policy "unsound and . . . dangerous in the extreme." The *World* called, in vain, for immediate repeal of the Neutrality Act, which prohibited arms sales to all belligerents and limited non-military trade to a "cash-and-carry" basis. Hitler and Mussolini, the paper suggested, might back away from the brink if they knew that "the great resources of this nation will be available to their enemies."[40]

Hitler invaded Poland on September 1, provoking English and French declarations of war against Germany. Listening to the "click, click, click of the electric printers hammering out the . . . news," Woods thought for a moment of his many German friends, good and decent people, and of their problematic fate. Unable to do anything for these individuals, he shifted to a concern for the policies of the United States. The country must increase defense expenditures to insure readiness should the nation become involved in the war. More than ever, the case against the Neutrality Act seemed perfectly clear. The "irony" of the present situation, said Rufus, was that "the sympathies of the American people are with France and Britain, but the invoking of the law . . . helps Hitler." To applause from Wenatchee, Congress passed and Roosevelt on November 4 signed a new law allowing sale of munitions on the "cash-and-carry" principle.[41]

Preparedness had obvious domestic consequences for the nation and for the Pacific Northwest. Since 1929, the *World* noted, political debate in the United States had been a "constant battle" between the advocates of reduced government spending on the one hand and the supporters of increased "prime the pump" expenditures on the other. Committed to spending billions of dollars on defense, the Roosevelt administration submitted the second approach to the "supreme test," for "never before in peace time has any nation attempted to force so much money into the channels of business in such a short time." Woods intended to take every possible local advantage of the situation. He endorsed the demand of that "scintillating young congressman from Seattle," Warren G. Magnuson, for construction of a military highway between Washington state and Alaska, with Wenatchee as the ideal "starting point" for the road. Rufus also called for the use of "waste land" near Moses Lake as an Army bombing range.[42]

On a larger scale, Bonneville and Grand Coulee dams, the former already on line, made possible a preparedness-related transformation of the regional economy. At the outset of the war in Europe, most Pacific Northwest wage earners labored in the timber industry and in agriculture, activities dating back to the earliest days of pioneer settlement. Large-scale manufacturing was limited to the production of lumber, pulp, and paper. Aircraft factories and shipyards together employed a mere 6,000 persons in Washington and Oregon. The closest aluminum plant was in California. Beginning in the fall of 1939, the winds of war, driven by a mighty current from the Columbia River, swept away this traditional setting.[43]

"The Boeing plant . . . is being expanded in a big way," Woods informed his readers after a trip to Seattle in December 1939. Responding to the demand for light metals by the aircraft industry, the Aluminum Company of America announced plans that month for a manufacturing complex at Vancouver on the lower Columbia, to be run by Bonneville electricity. For years, critics had predicted an embarrassing, if not scandalous, white elephant fate for the river's two federal dams. Suddenly, aluminum producers and other interests intent upon profiting from the defense boom were, as Rufus wrote, "positively avid for cheap electric power." The preparedness drive guaranteed the economic success of Grand Coulee and Bonneville and set the stage for further development of the Columbia.[44]

If North Central Washington was to benefit from defense production, Grand Coulee must be pushed to completion at the earliest possible date. Under the direction of Consolidated Builders, the speedup became standard operating procedure. "They built the biggest this and the biggest that," noted one observer, "and the words 'world's record' were bandied about until they became commonplace." The Roosevelt administration's loosened financial purse strings kept the work going at a frantic pace. By early 1940, the mammoth Roosevelt Lake reservoir was well on the way to formation. Hillsides had been deforested, roads relocated, and small towns drowned. Terrifying rapids and the ancient Indian fishing station of Kettle Falls disappeared beneath the placid surface of the growing lake. A "new world . . . is in the making," Rufus informed his readers in a burst of pride.[45]

Still, Grand Coulee was only the foremost of several factors boosting confidence among North Central Washington's residents. Wenatchee opened a junior college in 1939, providing local students with an affordable stay-at-home alternative to the state university. The Stevens Pass Highway was at long last completed, due to the discovery of the pass by Seattle skiing enthusiasts. Apples, the regional economic mainstay, made a surprising recovery during the winter of 1939-40, even though it looked for a time like another miserable year. The crop was heavy, but the railroads increased their freight charges and Hitler's attack upon Poland temporarily closed foreign markets. "No . . . season ever opened under more discouraging and disheartening conditions" according to the *World*. Impending disaster quickly became opportunity under the pump-priming impact of federal defense spending. Domestic demand absorbed output and prices nearly doubled by spring. Fancy Delicious apples increased from $1.25 a box to $2 and Winesaps advanced from 80 cents to $1.60.[46]

Better times in Wenatchee accounted to a certain extent for Rufus's reversion to partisan Republicanism upon the eve of the 1940 campaign. The emotional strain of a prolonged and disturbing labor dispute, moreover, convinced him that the New Deal had become "a wormy apple." Although the *World* was an open shop operation, some of its workers belonged to a Seattle union local. The Pacific Northwest Newspaper Association advised Woods in 1940 to grant all "reasonable" requests to these workers, including the eight-hour day, because union leadership was "itching" to mount a strike. Wage negotiations took on a personal aspect in June when Rufus decided his son Wilfred needed experience in the paper's blue collar functions. The *World* did not displace any of the regular employees, but labor delegates from Seattle demanded that the younger Woods be dismissed. Publication of the *World* was temporarily halted before Rufus, pending final resolution of the dispute, agreed to remove Wilfred as a gesture of conciliation.[47]

A fundamental issue was at stake, for both Woods and the union. "It was a question," brother Ralph wrote from Tacoma, "of whether . . . you were to run the shops or whether the Unions were to run them for you." In defense of the first of these propositions, Rufus returned his son to the mechanical department in August, resulting in a sit-down strike on the part of the unionized employees. Refusing, as long as Wilfred remained, to go back to work, Rufus fired them for "insubordination." In the past, the dispute would have ended at this juncture, awaiting only the hiring of new workers. The New Deal, however, offered the union an effective means of response. Until September 1941, when the case was finally dropped, the *World* had to defend itself in hearings and in meetings before the National Labor Relations Board. For Woods, the affair demonstrated, in a personally frustrating manner, the dangers inherent in the New Deal, which presumed to give unions the right to tell him whom he must hire and whom he could fire. Federal officials even presumed to interfere with the training of his son.[48]

No wonder, then, that the Republican Party seemed a safe haven in 1940. Victory was possible, even against FDR, claimed Woods, "depending entirely upon who carries the banner." The stature of the leading contenders for the presidential nomination drove home the importance of this qualifying statement. Senator Robert Taft of Ohio had visited Wenatchee in 1939 and left absolutely no impression, positive or negative, upon the citizenry. New York district attorney Thomas E. Dewey sought office upon no qualification beyond a heavily publicized record for rackets-busting. "There isn't one in ten thousand people who knows what Dewey stands for," reflected Rufus in a column examining the New Yorker's unaccountable popularity. Woods escorted Dewey on a tour of Grand Coulee in February 1940 and covered his campaign appearances in Washington and Oregon. As a result, Woods became firmly convinced that while Dewey was "plenty smart," the party's chances depended upon discovery of a "dark horse" alternative.[49]

Heading for Philadelphia and the GOP convention in June, Woods hoped to avoid a choice between Dewey and Taft. The prospect of either man at the head of the ticket left him feeling "a sort of gloom of foreboding disaster." In a genuinely amazing development, fortunately, a formidable darkhorse actually became available in the person of Wendell Willkie, the Indiana farmboy turned New York utility executive. Riding what Rufus termed "a veritable blitzkrieg" of professionally generated publicity, Willkie appealed to those who found Dewey callow and Taft a head-in-the-sand isolationist. Experienced in business, he was a much-needed practical-minded alternative to New Deal experimentalism. His internationalist views on foreign affairs, moreover, meant that the nation would be in sound hands in terms of the world crisis. Nominated on the sixth ballot, Willkie was a Rufus Woods dream-come-to-life.[50]

Writing in the "cold gray dawn of the morning after," Rufus admitted to being "dizzy yet." The Willkie triumph was "one of the most dramatic things I have ever witnessed." In background and in personality, the Republican candidate was bound to appeal to the Wenatchee publisher. "He is a big man, approachable and with a friendly air about him," Woods reported after a convention meeting. Rising from rural youth to the ranks of the corporate elite, Willkie had remained a country boy at heart and was "no high hat." Listening as the nominee addressed the delegates on the evils of the New Deal and the perils of the current international scene, Woods was "half-mesmerized" and on the verge of tears. Willkie, he summed up in the last of a series of columns from Philadelphia, was "the most dominating personality, in a public way, that we have seen since the days of William Jennings Bryan."[51]

Popular appeal and manifest ability only partially concealed the glaring, perhaps fatal, weakness of the Willkie candidacy, a shortcoming sure to be exploited by the Democrats. The nominee was head of the Commonwealth and Southern energy combine and a vocal opponent of public power. Intending to help the candidate develop a more politically viable stance regarding federal dams and river development, Woods questioned Willkie on these matters at press conferences and in a private interview, without eliciting a direct answer. "This won't do," he complained to Senator Charles McNary of Oregon, the party's selection for vice-president. To avoid losing pro-Grand Coulee voters to Roosevelt, Rufus suggested that Republicans adopt a squatter sovereignty approach to the electricity issue. Willkie should announce that "he would leave the question of private ownership versus public ownership up to the people themselves in the different communities." Supporters of federal dam building in the Pacific Northwest could then vote for the GOP ticket with the same enthusiasm as utility corporation stockholders.[52]

Moving on to the Democratic convention in Chicago, Woods found the proceedings dominated by the "shadow" of Willkie. The latter's freshness and energy made for a telling contrast with the worn-out image of a party too long in power. Roosevelt's appointment of GOP elder statesmen Henry Stimson and Frank Knox to the cabinet was "a wonderful stroke," but otherwise the President seemed tired and his party support perfunctory. The principal task of the convention was the "spontaneous draft," described by Rufus as "a carefully worked out piece of political chicanery," of FDR for a third term. Talks with delegates convinced him that "probably a third" actually opposed the administration, a percentage that increased steeply on the subject of the nomination of Secretary of Agriculture Henry A. Wallace for vice-president. The politicians prevailed over the public will at Chicago, according to Woods, a travesty ripe for exploitation by Willkie, a true man of the people.[53]

Partisanship, even in the emotional context of the 1940 campaign, extended only to the limits of the nation's borders. Throughout the summer and fall, Rufus supported the Roosevelt foreign policies with a fervor matched only by his denunciation of the administration on domestic issues. The selection of Stimson and Knox to head, respectively, the War and Navy departments meant that FDR had avoided the mistake of a Democrats-only approach to war government. Woods also endorsed the draft, the President's most controversial act of the year. "Conscription is a real democratic way to handle an army," he pointed out, insuring that all classes shared in the burden of mobilization. Preparation in advance to fight was "just good common horse sense," bound to result in the smallest possible sacrifice of life and treasure.[54]

At home in Washington state, meanwhile, the September primary brought the two-term Martin-Woods alliance to a doubly unsatisfactory end. The governor not only lost by a decisive margin, but his defeat was also at the hands of Clarence Dill, making a political comeback. Rufus had difficulty explaining the outcome, finally deciding that Republicans had crossed party lines to vote for Dill as the weakest possible Democratic contender. Disappointed, Woods was at least free to support Republican nominee Arthur Langlie, the mayor of Seattle. Intent upon preventing Dill's return to public office, he launched an all-out assault upon the former senator's integrity. The Democrat, Rufus claimed, had promised alcohol manufacturers and restaurant owners that he would, in return for large campaign contributions, secure approval of liquor-by-the-drink if elected.[55]

Rufus's emotional reaction to Dill was matched only by his enthusiasm for Wendell Willkie. When not bashing the former's candidacy, he argued the case for the latter's election to the presidency. The central national issue, Woods maintained, was the question of "whether or not we are for an INTERMINABLE TENURE of office for the president." Once the two-term tradition was violated, "we have . . . opened the flood gates for a fourth, fifth, and a LIFE TERM" for Roosevelt. To prevent residents of the Pacific Northwest from concluding that virtual "dictatorship" was a worthy tradeoff for development of the Columbia, Willkie clarified his belief that cancelling Grand Coulee was "inconceivable." Adopting a course suggested by Rufus, the nominee argued that local inhabitants ought to determine for themselves whether power should be distributed by public agencies or by private corporations. Energy was in any event a "minor" concern, asserted Woods in elaborating upon the Willkie position, when compared to "the question of turning the entire American government over to one man."[56]

Roosevelt's relatively easy reelection triumph terminated what the *World* called "one of the most unique, the most spectacular and the most hair-raising" campaigns "in all . . . the history of this country." Woods credited the outcome to the world crisis, to "the billions of dollars . . . now being expended in defense industries," and to the unfortunate Republican identification with big business. In a more pleasing development, Arthur Langlie won a narrow victory over Clarence Dill, apparently administering final defeat to "the most skillful, clever and efficient campaigner that the state has ever known." Dill, however, contested the official tally. Forty-five Democratic members of the legislature supported a resolution endorsing his claim and reversing the result of the election. Majorities in both house and senate, however, condemned this effort on the part of what Rufus called "the lowest strata of the political life of the state" to overturn the will of the people. Resolved on the eve of the inauguration, the dispute ended with Langlie safely installed in office and Clarence Dill exposed again, in Rufus's view, as a charlatan.[57]

At the age of sixty, Rufus Woods looked back over the events of his life and was reminded of an old saying: "The magic spirit of willing men accomplished more than the MIGHT OF MONEY or the MARVELS OF MACHINERY."[58] Will and spirit had certainly produced many diverse rewards in the final years of a tumultuous decade. Rufus satisfied an old dream by becoming a circus clown and, like a small-town Walter Lippmann, traveled to and reported upon distant foreign trouble spots. At home, Grand Coulee, the great work of his career, neared completion, made secure by the high dam contract and the approach of the Second World War. The national preparedness program brought the expansion of Boeing, the reopening of shipyards, and construction of the first Pacific Northwest aluminum plant. The long debate over the necessity of Grand Coulee and hydroelectric development on the Columbia River had been answered in clear and undisputed terms.

# Chapter Eleven
## The Spirit of the River

For a quarter century the name Wenatchee has been associated with apples. We have grown apples, talked apples, sold apples and sold the nation on apples as a delicious food and a healthy food. But this city has a distinction of far greater import. Wenatchee is the chief city of the Columbia river. No other city . . . lives and breathes the very spirit of this great river as does Wenatchee.

*Wenatchee Daily World* [1]

ON JANUARY 22, 1941, Bureau of Reclamation engineer Frank Banks opened a penstock gate and set in motion the turbine blades of a small generator, producing electricity to run the Grand Coulee power-house. Two months later, Governor Arthur Langlie and other dignitaries gathered to witness the first transmission of power to the outside world. Pushing a button, Jim James, leader of the Nez Perce tribal members residing along the Columbia's right bank, sent current to an Indian electric cooperative on the Colville Reservation. Through this ceremonial gesture, claimed one observer, the "descendants of northeastern Washington's first inhabitants gave their approval" to Grand Coulee. This proposition was open to doubt, considering the flooding of Kettle Falls and other fishing places and the destruction of the annual upper Columbia salmon migration. There was no doubt, however, upon another significant point. Although considerable work remained, including the fine-tuning of mammoth generators and the completion of power lines, the great Columbia River dam was at last in business.[2]

A major undecided question, as of 1940, involved the means of selling Grand Coulee electricity to maximum advantage. President Roosevelt issued an executive order in August establishing the Bonneville Power Administration, headquartered in Portland, as the project's marketing agency. Leaders of the upper Columbia River counties, unhappy about being permanently governed "at so great a distance . . . by men so little known here," viewed the presidential order as a short-term expedient, made necessary by the lack of definitive congressional action. "*They have no authority to sell power production at Grand Coulee dam,*" Kirby Billingsley of the *Wenatchee World* wrote of the BPA, "except questionable authority given them by the president." What was needed, from the perspective of North Central Washington, was legislation creating a separate organization for Grand Coulee, authorized to combine and spend the revenues from the sale of energy and water.[3]

Drafted by Roosevelt administration lawyers in 1941, legislation sponsored by Representative Knute Hill of Washington provided for a Columbia Power Authority (CPA) headed by a single director, appointed by and subordinate to the Secretary of the Interior. A rival bill backed by Senator Homer T. Bone created an agency managed by a three-person board of Pacific Northwest residents. Another measure introduced by Bone required Senate confirmation of the BPA administrator, as a means, noted Rufus Woods, of giving "the Northwest a little say through its senators" in the selection of management. Woods and others successfully opposed Hill's version of the CPA because they worried that "the power of the Columbia River [will] be administered from Washington, D.C.," with Secretary of the Interior Harold Ickes as the "chief." The private utility industry, meanwhile, fought any strengthening of government, or public, control over the Columbia River, frustrating attempts to pass the Bone bills. The "unfortunate" result, as Representative Charles Leavy observed, was perpetuation of "the temporary legislation and executive orders under which we are now acting." A July 1942 directive establishing the Northwest Power Pool, linking the BPA with existing public and privately owned operations, ended all consideration of permanent "reform" for the duration.[4]

No matter how unsatisfactory or controversial the means of administration, cheap Columbia River power drove regional industry to unparalleled heights. The basic BPA rate of $17.50 per kilowatt year served as "the chief drawing card" attracting new aluminum plants to the Pacific Northwest in 1941, according to the National Resources Planning Board. The production of a single ton of aluminum required 17,000 kilowatt hours, meaning that inexpensive Bonneville electricity more than offset the cost and inefficiency of transporting bauxite ore from distant mines. Despite opposition from the monopoly conscious Aluminum Company of America (Alcoa), the government funded manufacturing complexes at Spokane, Longview, and Tacoma, to go with Alcoa's original Vancouver facility. The valley of the Columbia, enthused Rufus Woods, "soon will be the aluminum capital of the world."[5]

An actual energy crisis loomed in the Pacific Northwest by the fall of 1941. New generators were already on order to supplement the three 108,000-kilowatt units scheduled to come on line at Grand Coulee. Congress authorized construction of a second powerhouse at the coulee. The original belief that it would take fifteen years to absorb the project's electricity gave way to a call from Paul Raver, who had succeeded the late J.D. Ross at the Bonneville Power Administration, for at least one new Columbia River dam. The BPA and the Federal Power Commission initiated studies to determine which of the sites recommended by the 308 Report should be accorded priority. On the basis of these investigations, Raver advised in February 1942 that planning work be started at Foster Creek Rapids, downstream from Grand Coulee, and that Puget Power complete its Rock Island Dam to design capacity.[6]

Despite all this activity along the Columbia, North Central Washington failed to secure a serving from what a *World* staffer termed "the first big war gravy bowl." The various defense mobilization agencies located plants in urban areas on the lower river and on Puget Sound, where large supplies of electricity were already available. "Virtually all the small communities of our state . . . are being depleted of man power," Woods complained to Harold Ickes in August 1941, "while the metropolitan centers are taking . . . the big defense projects." So long as the $17.50 postage stamp rate structure remained in force, moreover, completion of Grand Coulee was unlikely to reverse this trend. "We have gone right smack into centralization," Rufus unhappily observed, as federal money and rural residents gravitated to the cities. Indeed, the only significant impact of the preparedness campaign on Wenatchee was "a crisis . . . in the apple harvest," due to the departure of pickers for jobs in coastal industries.[7]

Woods himself was preoccupied throughout 1941 with foreign affairs and with the increasing likelihood of American military involvement in the world conflict. The United States was "in it so far as our manufacturing is concerned," he noted in January, and "on the edge of it" in terms of active participation. At the end of February, Rufus departed on a tour of Latin America, the last of his pre-war trips to exotic and troubled overseas points. Traveling by airplane, Woods carried an old portable typewriter, planning to "pitch it overboard" if fellow passengers were annoyed by his use of the instrument. After a visit to Mexico City and an excursion to Aztec ruins, he moved on to the Panama Canal Zone. There, the government-owned hotel reflected the business incompetence of a seedy federal bureaucracy: the overpriced $10 room had no working light fixture and was furnished with a desk at which "one might write if there were . . . envelopes and paper."[8]

On the principal leg of the journey, Rufus visited Colombia, Ecuador, Chile, Argentina, and Brazil. Despite heavy German political and economic influence, he found public sentiment unfavorable to Hitler. The Roosevelt Good Neighbor policy had placed Nazi sympathizers "on the defensive." His reports home, though, included more travel accounts than political commentary. Everywhere, the cost of first-class lodgings and fine food was unbelievably low. The beautiful Cali Valley in Colombia was a "dream land" worthy of the designation "Shangrila." Crossing the Andes, Woods was reminded of the pictures and text of a favorite boyhood schoolbook. "It was one of those far off regions," he remembered, "which I could never, never hope to see." The trip turned out to be a vacation, the last before the long years of war.

Despite his hostility to the New Deal—that sorry Panama Canal hotel was a perfect symbol of Democratic maladministration—Rufus continued to advocate a nonpartisan approach to the conduct of foreign policy. "Roosevelt is president and commander in chief," he reminded Republican readers of the *World* in July, "and we've got to trust him in this international emergency, much as we might fight him in some of these domestic issues." Ignoring complaints from isolationist subscribers, Woods endorsed the Lend-Lease Act, which provided direct arms assistance to Britain and other nations fighting Hitler. Following the German attack upon the Soviet Union in June, he called for all-out aid to Russia. Over the summer, the *World* publisher backed FDR on extension of the draft and on the maintenance of a firm stand against Japan in the Pacific.[9]

America's movement toward active involvement in the war coincided with a momentous development in the interior Pacific Northwest. On the first

Saturday in October, Grand Coulee began producing electricity for regional industry. "This event," wrote Sam Hill, the former Fifth District congressman, "marks the beginning of the translation into economic utility of the greatest single natural resource known to man." The layout of the BPA transmission network, however, suggested that the transformed Columbia was unlikely to benefit local interests. A second power line ran alongside the original J.D. Ross connection to Bonneville. The first of four lines projected for Spokane was near completion and placement of a line across the Cascades to Puget Sound was under way. "Millions of dollars are spent to take the power away," mourned the *Wenatchee World*, "and apparently it's all going to be taken away."[10]

The key point, for the moment, was not so much the bypassing of Wenatchee as the "fortunate" timing of Grand Coulee's completion. Rufus Woods was in Seattle on December 7, the day of Japan's Sunday morning attack on Pearl Harbor. Through the afternoon and evening, he sat in the *Seattle Times* office, reading bulletins. Woods awoke the next morning "somewhat stupefied, in a sort of a haze, wondering just what will be next." In common with many observers, he feared that Japan would next assault the Northwest, bombing, among numerous inviting targets, Bonneville and Grand Coulee dams. Although emotions were high and spies probably active, Rufus urged that Japanese Americans be protected in the full exercise of their rights. The eventual decision to remove persons of Japanese heritage from the Pacific coast, made by the Army in the spring of 1942, was to the *World* a regrettable necessity. In "another surprise attack," asserted Woods, "no one would know whom to trust and the result might be [a] terrible slaughter of innocent people."[11]

While Japanese Americans experienced the grim exigencies of war ("for their own safety" in the words of the *World*), owners and employees of defense plants enjoyed homefront prosperity. Building upon the industrial base erected by the pre-Pearl Harbor preparedness campaign, the federal government expended billions of dollars in Washington and Oregon. Shipbuilding employment passed the 200,000 mark by 1944 and 50,000 workers toiled at Boeing. A half dozen aluminum plants produced, depending upon the study consulted, between 37 and 45 percent of the nation's supply of strategic metal. A quarter million people migrated to the Pacific Northwest in search of defense work. Within the region, cities grew at the expense of small towns and farms. Despite significant growth in Ephrata, the site of a military training facility, Grant County lost half its inhabitants. Two out of three persons in

Douglas County, along the east bank of the Columbia, left for the coast and jobs in defense plants.[12]

Electricity from the Columbia, from Grand Coulee in particular, made these developments possible. Pending installation of the fourth, fifth, and sixth generators, two units were shifted north from California's Shasta Dam in 1942, allowing for a major boost in output. The statistics, Rufus Woods noted later in the war, reflected a performance that was "little less than astounding." In 1944, Grand Coulee produced, at minimum, a third of the energy consumed in the Pacific Northwest. With Bonneville downstream, it drove the aluminum plants of Washington and Oregon and met the needs of the shipyards. Two of every five planes turned out during the war were credited to the Columbia dams. Overall, claimed Paul Raver of the BPA, "fully 85 per cent" of the power generated by the federal dams went into the defense effort. Local boosters claimed that Grand Coulee was responsible for victory over Germany and Japan.[13]

Even so, losing both population and power, North Central Washington remained outside the mainstream of regional economic change. Traditional business activities prospered, albeit under the strain of war-induced dislocation. Wheat prices increased to $1.19 a bushel in 1943, several times the rate prevailing at the outset of the New Deal. Riding the pre-Pearl Harbor upswing in consumer demand, the 1941 fruit crop yielded $20 million, two-and-a-half times the 1939 return. "From a condition of utter despondency and hopelessness," the *World* observed, ". . . growers have taken a new lease on life." Apple prices mounted by 40 percent in 1942 and advanced again in 1943, making up, with margin to spare, the losses of the Depression. Operators planted new trees, paid off mortgages, and retired debts. "The old country is reveling in money these days," reported Rufus Woods, who thought apples a more valuable commodity than gold.[14]

War-related problems prevented unrestrained celebration of prosperity in Wenatchee. The government, to deny useful information to the enemy, banned publication of weather forecasts, incidentally preventing growers from preparing for early season frosts. The RACC financing system fell under the control of incompetent homefront bureaucrats and was suspended altogether in 1944. Federal price ceilings were imposed on fruit in 1943, an unwelcome decision exacerbated by the failure to take into account the high quality of Wenatchee Valley apples.[15]

Growers traditionally recruited seasonal help from among a mixed force of valley residents and itinerant "fruit tramps," laborers now lost to the armed services and to defense plants. A serious, indeed calamitous, labor shortage threatened orchardists in the aftermath of Pearl Harbor. Chelan County schools ran six days a week in winter and spring, in order to release students for work in the fall harvest. Wenatchee merchants took to the orchards with their employees. Undergraduate contingents from Washington State College and the University of Washington arrived by special train in 1942, helping to minimize crop losses. The collegiate assistance was a one-time-only proposition, though, for a few of the orchardists, as Woods described matters, "put the entire country in bad" by providing filthy accommodations and stomach-turning food. For the duration, the *World* speculated, the employment of Japanese American detainees or German prisoners of war might be the only alternative to ruin.[16]

Responding to the labor problems of Western agriculture, the federal government recruited Hispanics from Colorado and Texas and concluded a diplomatic agreement for the importation of bracero workers from Mexico. Eight hundred Mexican pickers arrived in Wenatchee in time for the 1943 harvest. (Of the 47,000 braceros employed in the Pacific Northwest during the war, approximately 6,000 worked in the Wenatchee and Yakima valleys.) Orchard operators complained that the newcomers lacked mechanical aptitude, and townspeople grumbled that the workers sent wages to families at home rather than spending them in local stores. Such criticism was the mark of ingratitude, considering that the Hispanic hands were, as the *World* forthrightly pointed out, the salvation of the apple industry.[17]

Prosperity for growers, even if burdened by assorted grievances, meant profits for the *Wenatchee World*. Circulation increased to 13,000 and the paper enjoyed its highest earnings since the Coolidge Administration. Homefront pressures nonetheless compelled a "rather ragged" style of operation. Forty employees, including Wilfred Woods and cousin Warren's son Bob, served in the military or took defense plant jobs. (Aided by a portable Dictaphone, Rufus maintained a steady correspondence with the departed staffers, providing news from home and promises that jobs were being held for their return.) Three dozen persons did the work normally handled by fifty-five men and women. Newsprint was also in short supply, due to a cutoff of imports and the diversion of pulp to defense industries. The *World* suspended publication on holidays, turned away would-be subscribers, and rejected new advertising accounts.[18]

Newspapering failed to divert Woods from larger promotional projects. The residents of North Central Washington had "gone to sleep over our own potential resources," he observed in February 1942, with the result that defense plants and Grand Coulee energy went to distant urban centers. "Disgusted with the way that Columbia River power is being handled," Rufus launched a campaign for industry and for the recovery of electricity. The Columbia River Development League was revived for the express purpose of securing government funding for local economic growth. Kirby Billingsley, a *World* employee since 1918, acted as day-to-day all-purpose lobbyist for Woods, spending much of the war in Washington. Billingsley, formerly head of the paper's news department, agreed entirely with the goals of his employer and exceeded the zeal of even Jim O'Sullivan in the pursuit of federal money. "I have tried to explain to Mr. Billingsley," one exasperated official complained, "that after all our first job is to win the war, but in his enthusiasm he ignores 'small' things like that."[19]

The Columbia Basin Commission (CBC) was also reborn, as the result of pressure from Wenatchee. "There must be an over-all functioning agency with an official status," Billingsley advised Governor Langlie in June 1942. Rufus Woods was one of the six commissioners named to the new CBC in early 1943. The principal task before the commission, he contended in a series of *World* columns, was to preserve for "the people . . . some say in the development of our own resources." The federal government might be "used like a machine to work in our behalf," Woods noted, providing funds and engineering expertise. Washington, D.C., though, must never be allowed to "become the master of the Northwest." Short-term aims to be pursued by the state of Washington included revision of the BPA postage stamp rate, decentralization of war industry, and the allotment of Grand Coulee power to the upper Columbia.[20]

Internal divisions prevented the Basin Commission from functioning in the manner Woods envisioned. At his urging, Jim O'Sullivan was appointed to the staff as a reward for past services. (Billingsley passed on the advice that the veteran lobbyist "be taken into a room" and warned against "letting himself get out of control.") Ungrateful and unrepentant, O'Sullivan complained of his lack of real responsibility and inferior salary, undermining morale and disturbing relations among the commissioners. The three Columbia Basin irrigation districts each had a representative on the commission, a device supposed to insure that reclamation received equal consideration to power in the deliberations of the panel. The conflicting interests of the districts, however, snarled the CBC from the outset in what one observer called "fighting factions."[21]

On his own initiative, Rufus Woods made the case for overcoming North Central Washington's retarded wartime development. "This great old Columbia valley," he argued, "is now at the cross roads." Down one path lay a course devised by the federal government, which had already seized control of Grand Coulee and placed its power in the hands of the BPA. Down the other might be found independence, to be attained by "keep[ing] a handle on this tremendous potential resource of the future." Under current conditions, grumbled Rufus, the coulee project "is being made just the tail on the kite of the Bonneville dam." Grand Coulee dwarfed the latter in size and capacity, "yet it is Bonneville, Bonneville, Bonneville." Decisions, including those dealing with rates and the construction of transmission lines, were made in Portland, to the disadvantage of Wenatchee. Unless this trend was soon reversed, Woods predicted, the upper Columbia "will be in the same fix" as the American South, an impoverished land exporting cheap raw materials and importing expensive manufactured products.[22]

Three-fourths of the Columbia's potential energy lay within sixty-eight miles of Wenatchee "by the way the crow flies," asserted Rufus. North Central Washington had a right to demand better treatment, including separation from the BPA. Present and future development "should be guided by the people of the immediate area concerned," Woods explained to Paul Raver. "The people who are vitally interested . . . will do a better job because it is before them by day and by night." Grand Coulee was "our dam," promoted by and built on behalf of local organizations, a fact that went far to explain the betrayal felt when the benefits went instead to Portland, Spokane, and other distant places. "Those cities still laugh at us," wrote Kirby Billingsley, "they take the power and thumb their noses at us in [the] Columbia Valley." The Bonneville Power Administration, exclaimed another associate of Rufus, was guilty, in both the figurative and literal sense, of "selling Grand Coulee down the river."[23]

Wartime considerations, Woods conceded, prevented a grant of independence from the BPA, at least for the duration. He concentrated instead on making the best of a bad situation by securing defense industries for Wenatchee. The campaign for local contracts, unfortunately, was only partially successful. A proposed air base was scuttled because of Wenatchee's supposed vulnerability to attack by Japanese planes flying undetected through Stevens Pass. The quest for an aluminum plant foundered upon the refusal of the BPA to build a transmission line from Grand Coulee. "You have given power to all these other communities," Woods protested to Paul Raver, so North Central Washington was "certainly entitled" to a share. The government "plant site crew," meanwhile, declined to visit the upper Columbia on a "final once-and-for-all site check-up" tour. Personal lobbying by Rufus secured congressional authorization of an electro-metallurgical laboratory for the Pacific Northwest. Oregon won the project, however, when Washington State College contested Wenatchee's claim to the facility.[24]

On the positive side of the developmental ledger, Wenatchee was awarded a ferro-silicon plant in 1942. Built by the federal government on the east bank of the Columbia, an Ohio alloys corporation leased the mill. This time the BPA cooperated, allocating electricity from the Northwest Power Pool and extending a transmission line from Rock Island Dam. Once up and running, three furnaces produced a compound used in the harden-ing of steel and in the manufacture of magnesium. "The only war plant in the entire upper-Columbia region" was for Rufus Woods a significant ad-vance toward the industrialization of North Central Washington.[25]

Another war-related enterprise represented the realization of a long-time dream for a Wenatchee byproducts industry. At a November 1942 meeting in Seattle, Rufus and state Grange Master Henry Carstensen agreed that development of manufacturing must accompany the expansion of ir-rigation in North Central Washington. Woods and the Grange soon be-came partners in the Northwest Chemurgy Co-operative, formed to produce glucose and starch from wheat and potatoes, offsetting the wartime sugar shortage. A plant opened at Lynden, west of the Cascades near Bellingham, and work began on a facility in Wenatchee. Despite shortages of machin-ery, the local outlet handled a carload of grain a day by the end of 1943.[26]

Potential additional business for Wenatchee appeared in March 1943. Karl Stoffel, the secretary to new Fifth District Republican Congressman Walt Horan and a former *World* staffer, informed his friends at the news-paper of a "mysterious" contract just awarded by the Corps of Engineers. "This thing is so big and so secret," advised Stoffel, "that the orders on it which went from the President . . . on down left that space blank which told what it was all about." The *World*, meanwhile, reported on the surge of activity under way in the desert between the Columbia and the lower Yakima River. "The DuPont people and the Army have taken over 650,000 acres," Kirby Billingsley wrote from the scene, ". . . and . . . [the] people of White Bluffs, Hanford and other communities have been given 30 days to evacuate."[27]

Discussing the situation, Woods and Billingsley concluded that the government and DuPont must be building a giant smokeless powder fac-tory. Wenatchee, they also agreed, ought to be given a phosphate plant or "some other phase of the munitions deal." In reality, the reports from Stoffel and the frantic activity downriver were manifestations of the Manhattan Project, America's top-secret program for construction of the atomic bomb. The inhospitable countryside about Hanford proved an ideal site for plutonium production. The resident ranchers and orchardists were easily removed, the Columbia River flowed past the site in mighty volume, and Grand Coulee Dam met the demand for power.[28]

Regional newspapers, the *World* included, covered the initial movement of laborers and equipment-laden trains into the eastern Washington wasteland. Rufus Woods also spoke on behalf of the displaced inhabitants of Hanford, evicted and paid "ridiculously low prices" for their homes. Appealing to the patriotism of Rufus and other publishers, Colonel Franklin Matthias, the officer in charge of construction, soon instituted a voluntary self-censorship. With rare exceptions, the press never mentioned Hanford. Private discussion continued, though, focusing on the unhappy fact that the project, whatever its exact nature, harmed rather than helped Wenatchee. "They will immediately take all the surplus power from Grand Coulee Dam," warned Billingsley after an off-the-record conversation with DuPont engineers. Once in operation, the plutonium works absorbed the entire output of two coulee generators. As a result less electricity was available for possible diversion to local users.[29]

Compounding the enormous energy drain created by aluminum mills, Hanford threatened to exhaust the energy capacity of the interior Pacific Northwest. Existing defense plants, Woods pointed out in August 1943, "require service night and day, week in and week out and month in and month out," producing "a 100 percent power load" on Grand Coulee. Wenatchee's only hope, therefore, must be the building of new dams. Releasing a Corps of Engineers study, the War Department endorsed earlier findings by the BPA documenting the existence of an electricity emergency in the region: "The construction of Bonneville and Grand Coulee . . . and the development of war industries utilizing electric energy generated at these projects has demonstrated the need for the ultimate development of the full water resources of the entire Columbia River Basin." Supported by the Dam University and by Representative Walt Horan, a Woods-like advocate of federal work on the Columbia, Rufus initiated a campaign for the building of the proposed Foster Creek dam.[30]

Expanding upon data gathered in previous surveys, the Corps of Engineers began serious planning work at Foster Creek in the fall of 1943. The site, fifty-one miles below Grand Coulee and several miles above the mouth of the Okanogan River, was a virtual desert. South of the Columbia, the land featured broken hills scattered among sand-filled depressions. On the north bank, sage-covered terraces led across the Colville Indian Reservation toward distant mountains. The closest approximation to civilization, Bridgeport, had once prospered as a steamboat landing for Big Bend wheat ranches, but was now a derelict beyond-the-end-of-the-line remnant of bygone times.[31]

Although the *World* contended that "Foster Creek dam cannot be built too soon," shortages of personnel compelled the Corps of Engineers to proceed in deliberate fashion. The Corps did not complete engineering studies until late 1944 and the survey report finally appeared in August 1945. Colonel Conrad Hardy, the officer in charge of planning, designed a structure 220 feet high, the maximum height compatible with Grand Coulee. Installation of fifteen generators, with a total capacity of 960,000 kilowatts, was planned, reflecting the fact that "production of electric power" was "the primary function of the proposed project." Up to 15,000 acres along the lower Okanogan River could be irrigated by Foster Creek, but the Army, unwilling to create an opportunity for the Bureau of Reclamation to claim the project, advised that this acreage was best watered from other points of supply.[32]

Officially endorsed by the Chief of Engineers in October 1945, the Hardy plan drew a skeptical reaction from the Dam University. The lack of irrigation, local advocates of Foster Creek feared, reflected bureaucratic politics rather than rational calculation. Hardy's $104 million cost figure more than doubled the estimates submitted in the 308 Report and in a recent BPA study, increasing the difficulty of securing congressional authorization. "Disturbed" by the "ballooning of these costs," Representative Walt Horan suggested on the basis of a "layman's reasoning" that $55 million was a sufficient amount for the project. The Army's explanation that suspect foundation conditions required expensive counter-measures to prevent "seepage" failed to satisfy the critics. That old Grand Coulee opponent, Thomas Robins, now both a general and the second-ranking officer in the Corps of Engineers, appeared to Woods and Horan as the villain of the piece, the author of a plot to scuttle Foster Creek in favor of projects elsewhere in the Pacific Northwest.[33]

A "definite effort," suggested Horan, "should be made to find out what factors" lay behind the Corps' plan. There was no need, answered Rufus, since the costly Hardy design obviously reflected the Army's preference for the proposed Umatilla dam below the mouth of the Snake. "The army boys are pretty tightly tied up to the Umatilla project," Woods believed, and intended only that Foster Creek "will come on later." The downriver dam was an integral component of the navigation-oriented scheme long favored by General Robins. Deliberate bias explained why the Corps released the Foster Creek study only after Congress had authorized the Umatilla project in 1944. The timing, asserted Kirby Billingsley, "was largely [the result of] fast footwork on the lower river which had an element of trickery in it." Political considerations and budgetary constraints supposedly meant that the federal government could build only a single dam at a time on the Columbia. "The action of one man," noted Billingsley in a bitter reference to Robins, had therefore caused Foster Creek to be "pigeonholed for years to come."[34]

What Billingsley called "this Umatilla versus Foster Creek situation" preoccupied the *Wenatchee World* for several years. Unwilling to have the Army make the decision on spurious grounds, the newspaper fought a continuous war on behalf of the upstream project, spilling over from wartime into peacetime. "The next dam to be built on the Columbia river," Woods contended, "should be the best and [the] cheapest." Objective analysis, in his view, affirmed the obvious superiority of Foster Creek. "Here," Rufus maintained, "power may be produced at $50 per horsepower—an amazing low figure." In addition, the high-head feature of the project would improve the efficiency of all downriver plants. "Those people down there," warned Woods of efforts in Portland to secure Umatilla, ". . . are playing a precarious game so far as the Columbia . . . is concerned." If built first, the more expensive Umatilla project, poorly calibrated with existing and prospective dams, would mean "trouble in Congress" when funding for other parts of the "river program" came under consideration.[35]

Homefront planning for the future use of the Columbia involved more than the controversial debate over Foster Creek and Umatilla. The efficient operation of existing hydroelectric plants could be substantially increased through the storage of water upstream for release during natural low-flow periods, allowing maximum year-round power production at all downriver points. The construction of upstream storage dams was, wrote a military engineer in the closing days of the war, "the key to complete development of the Columbia River." Energized by the concept, Rufus Woods recognized that the principal obstacle was more political than technical in nature, since the selection of damsites would be controversial. In common with the Corps of Engineers, Rufus was particularly interested in the Columbia north of the international border, and in the Kootenai, the Clark Fork, and other tributaries on the U.S. side of the line.[36]

To insure the largest possible benefit, storage must ignore international and state boundaries. Yet plans formulated by the Corps on this basis produced an immediate diplomatic conflict between the United States and Canada. Although only 15 percent of the land drained by the Columbia lay in British Columbia, a third of the river's water came from north of the border. "The heavy runoff and mountainous topography of the headwaters," reported an early American study, "make the Canadian portion of the Columbia River favorable for large storage reservoirs." Woods favored construction of a dam at the outlet of the Arrow Lakes, on the mainstem, providing ten million acre feet of storage. Endorsing this site, the Army also recommended building a dam at Libby on the Kootenai River in northwestern Montana, a project necessitating cross-border impoundment of that stream.[37]

British Columbia, to the chagrin of American planners, met its current and prospective power needs from existing plants and had little to gain from the proposed dams. Acting upon a 1943 request from the United States, the International Joint Commission (IJC) convened a series of hearings on the issue of storage and engaged a panel of engineers to examine the initial Army plans in detail. After prolonged and contentious deliberation, the IJC eventually accepted the "basic principle" that "the boundary is to be ignored in setting up the physical elements of the best plan" and endorsed the American proposal for development of the Kootenai. Actual construction, however, was delayed for years due to continued protests from Canada. Rufus Woods, attempting to arrange substantive talks between Washington state and British Columbia for use of the Arrow Lakes, also met frustration.[38]

Similar political differences between upstream and downstream governments postponed the implementation of storage on even those waters that lay entirely within the United States. For example, the same opposition from Idaho and Montana that had helped defeat the gravity plan in the 1920s now thwarted the designs of Rufus Woods. "Full of rocks, rapids and falls, and . . . utterly unnavigable," to quote a nineteenth century survey, the Clark Fork drained western Montana and northern Idaho before entering Pend Oreille Lake. Exiting the lake and renamed the Pend Oreille River, it dropped over Albeni Falls, flowed north through remote Washington canyons and passed into British Columbia. The Bureau of Reclamation's Hungry Horse project, already authorized by Congress, would provide significant storage on the Flathead River. Kerr Dam, owned by the Montana Power Company, could be enlarged to store a million acre feet in Flathead Lake. A dam at Albeni Falls, the site once favored by Spokane for the Columbia Basin Project, might raise the level of Pend Oreille Lake by up to twenty-five feet.[39]

As the official representative of the Columbia Basin Commission, Woods attended federal hearings in Montana and Idaho in June 1943. He found Kalispell literally up in arms, with farmers threatening violence to prevent the flooding of land adjacent to Flathead Lake. One irate witness castigated Rufus as the personification of downstream greed in Washington and Oregon. The anger of Pend Oreille Lake property holders also became clear at a hearing in Sandpoint, Idaho. The testimony, Woods reported upon returning to the safety of Wenatchee, was "cantankerous, and serious, and humorous, and uproaring, and savage." In "forty years of newspaper experience," he had never experienced "anything compared to this."[40]

There was "a ghost of [a] show," Rufus realized, "that the waters of Flathead lake will be raised . . . in the face of local opposition." The state of Idaho, meanwhile, claimed the entire outflow of Pend Oreille Lake and threatened a lawsuit to prevent construction at Albeni Falls. Woods blamed the emotional reaction in part upon misleading propaganda issued by private utilities opposed to increasing federal energy production through storage. He also conceded that much of the hostile sentiment was the product of legitimate bitterness against outsiders and therefore akin to Wenatchee's own long-running battles. The angry witnesses at Kalispell expressed "the love of the folks for their beautiful lake and the thought that it might be taken from them." Still, the hard fact remained that efficient operation of the Columbia River dams necessitated up to fifteen million acre feet of stored water. The opposition of Idaho and Montana must somehow be overcome if the overall regional economy was to continue its present healthy expansion.[41]

Neither Foster Creek nor the storage dams would be needed if the pace of wartime economic growth tailed-off substantially upon the return of peace.

Defense plants were "mushroom industries," noted the *World*, and sure to be cut back, if not eliminated outright, in the reconversion process. Federal planners predicted a 90 percent drop in shipyard employment in the Pacific Northwest and a major work force reduction at Boeing. On a more optimistic note, though, the National Resources Planning Board forecast an increase in aluminum output, thanks to the release of pent-up consumer demand for automobiles, home appliances, and other civilian goods. Two things were necessary, Rufus Woods believed, to justify the building of new dams. War industry, especially the energy-draining light metals sector, must be preserved to the greatest extent possible. And construction of the Columbia Basin Project must begin promptly upon the end of the war, providing jobs for former military personnel and defense workers and markets for hydroelectricity.[42]

Prosperity depended, first and foremost, upon retention and expansion of aluminum manufacturing. The late 1943 announcement that the federal government intended to reduce regional production, closing at least one mill, therefore provoked a heated reaction. The Aluminum Company of America, supposedly intent upon reasserting its traditional monopoly, was blamed for this ambition-crushing decision. "Alcoa," fumed Representative Walt Horan, "shows a premeditated disposition to treat the defense plants in the Pacific Northwest something like battle ships, as necessary in the heat of battle but to be sent to dry dock at the first opportunity." The *World* blasted the "queer game" played by the "dollar-a-year men" in Washington, D.C., who were ready to "shut out the Northwest as soon as possible to assure the post-war operations of their own eastern plants."[43]

Anger mounted when Northwest residents learned that the Reconstruction Finance Corporation (RFC) had funded development of the Shipshaw site in Quebec by the Aluminum Company of Canada, an Alcoa corporate cousin. Commencing operation in 1943, the 970,000 horsepower plant produced aluminum for sale south, as well as north, of the international boundary, serving markets that might otherwise have been supplied from the Columbia River. From the outraged perspective of Wenatchee, the RFC arrangement appeared to be a gigantic swindle, perpetrated by "dollar-a-year men" more interested in the profits of their peacetime employers than in the public welfare. Honest and competent federal bureaucrats would not attempt to retard domestic production while at the same time encouraging foreign competition. Denouncing Shipshaw as a "smoothie job," Rufus Woods claimed that the war had provided a convenient "subterfuge" for subsidizing Alcoa with taxpayer dollars at the expense of Washington and Oregon.[44]

Wenatchee had trouble enough retaining its modest defense industry, much less dealing with the machinations of distant corporations and governments. The Rock Island ferro-silicon plant was, according to all accounts, the third in size and the cheapest to operate in the United States. Federal officials nonetheless ordered a two-thirds cut in production in early 1944 and then, at the end of the year, closed the facility. "There is something inherently wrong with this kind of a deal," protested Woods, for the shutdown represented another sacrifice of local interest to outside greed, another instance of Wenatchee residents losing jobs so that others might profit from diminished competition. Frantically and with little prospect of success, Rufus sought a means of reopening the plant.[45]

The other vital component of long-term growth in the demand for electricity, the Columbia Basin Project, underwent a series of war-time starts and stops. Congress authorized the project in March 1943, but provided no funding. The Department of the Interior insisted that all three Big Bend irrigation districts conclude contracts with the government before it would undertake construction. Complex computations, moreover, must be made prior to the making of the agreements. James O'Sullivan spent close to two years in Washington, working on a formula for the allocation of Grand Coulee's costs. The BPA wanted to write off a substantial portion of the expenditures on the dam to unemployment relief and the war effort, making a reduction in power rates possible. The Bureau of Reclamation feared, though, that cheaper electricity would force settlers to pay more than the annual irrigation costs of $85 per acre already promised. An early compromise foundered upon the issue of whether or not the 3 percent interest charge assessed electricity sales could be used to subsidize irrigation. The prolonged and highly technical debate finally concluded in a September 1944 decision under which the interest was applied to reclamation, without a reduction in the $85 water user obligation.[46]

Secretary of the Interior Harold Ickes, meanwhile, released the terms of the government water contracts in March 1945. The provisions were needlessly complicated, complained Rufus Woods, tangled in enough red tape "to scare any landowner out entirely unless his land is valueless without water." A more important shortcoming related to the requirement that all three districts must approve the agreement. By "forc[ing] land owners to take water who do not want it at this time," Rufus feared that the Bureau of Reclamation would secure a negative vote from wheat ranchers, currently prospering under wartime demand for food, killing the project for all concerned. "As long as the . . . growers are making money as they are today," said Woods, "they don't want irrigation." Fortunately, the Columbia Basin Act allowed the hostile wheat producers to opt out of the project. By July 1945, over 300,000 acres had been removed, upsetting overall cost estimates and other technical calculations. The removals, however, were responsible for the overwhelming vote of approval that month by the remaining property holders.[47]

Family developments intruded upon Rufus in 1944, for a time distracting him from promotional and political business. He had remained close to Tacoma-based brother Ralph. The latter's shrewd advice and willingness to debate "all kinds of questions" were the central features of a lifetime relationship. Ralph's visits to Wenatchee became more frequent in later years as he sought emotional relief from the demands of an invalid wife. Ralph had diabetes, which produced physical debilitation. A prolonged family dispute over disposition of the Lebbeus Woods estate in Nebraska brought mental stress. A vacation east of the Cascades in the first days of 1944 apparently provided a much-needed restorative. "He rested and read and . . . looked much better than on his arrival," reported Rufus.

Always an optimist, Rufus was shocked to learn that his brother had suffered a stroke soon after returning to Tacoma. Without regaining consciousness, Ralph died on January 17. "It was just such a blow as struck us when we lost the two babies at one time," wrote a stunned Rufus in a rare reference to past tragedy. He was "awfully dazed" and "disorganized in a mental way," unable to write and incapable of composing an obituary column on Ralph's life. In a manner peculiar to identical twins, Rufus had literally lost part of himself. "I still get very lonesome indeed for Ralph," he confessed in later years.[48]

Although Ralph's passing opened the 1944 political season on a distressing note, the principal issue confronting Washington voters—public power—soon revived the publisher's aggressive instincts. "We are up against the fight of those boys," Rufus declared of the private utility executives, "and they are going to continue to fight as they have for the past twenty-five years." The industry demanded the right to purchase electricity at the Grand Coulee powerhouse, rather than from the BPA transmission network.

Such a policy, charged Woods, would squeeze out competition and "turn over the entire Columbia River to an eastern outfit to dominate." The utilities also attempted to defeat Walt Horan's campaign for the Brewster feeder, the first transmission link between the dam and "the little fellows . . . in the northern part of the central part of the State." The National Reclamation Association, dominated by the utility interests, fought all irrigation proposals involving government development of hydroelectricity. At home, Washington Water Power and Puget Power rejected the attempts of local public utility districts to acquire, by sale or by condemnation, their holdings.[49]

The private utilities, according to Rufus, dispatched public relations specialists "getting $500 a month with expenses" to Washington state to secure defeat of Referendum 25, the most controversial issue on the 1944 ballot. Originally passed by the legislature as Initiative 12, the measure authorized the joint purchase of private power companies by combinations of public utility districts. Such combinations, presumably, would be able to finance large-scale transactions of the sort necessary to acquire Water Power and Puget. Endorsing the referendum, Rufus maintained that the venerable question of "whether or not we are going to be continually thwarted every time a move is made to develop the resources of the Columbia" was again at stake. Approval by the voters, encouraging a shift from outside to local control, was the ideal means of "lifting us out of a colonial status." The importance of the fight was reflected in editorial rhetoric reminiscent of the early century campaigns against James J. Hill and the Great Northern. The utilities, asserted Woods, were as "ruthless as crocodiles" and, like the Nazis after D Day, had "their backs to the wall." For stalling legitimate development, private enterprise deserved to be "brushed aside."[50]

Focusing on the power question, Woods had considerable difficulty reconciling his traditional concerns with current local development requirements. "We have had too much equivocation with the republicans on this matter," he complained. Among the party's major candidates, only eastern Washington's incumbent congressmen, Walt Horan and Hal Holmes, merited endorsement on the issues. The national ticket of Thomas E. Dewey and John Bricker supported the purchase of power at the busbar, ignoring a warning from Wenatchee that preservation of the federally owned transmission system was "absolutely necessary" to prevent monopoly. Governor Arthur Langlie, apparently intent upon maintaining the support of the utilities in his bid for a second term, opposed Referendum 25. The Democrats, in contrast, called for the takeover of private firms, the building of more dams, and early construction of the Columbia Basin Project. "Roosevelt and Rufus and Ickes," Kirby Billingsley noted, ". . . are pulling right down the line for the same things."[51]

Good-soldiering the situation in print, Woods in public gave priority to his Republican connection. The *World* endorsed Langlie, although a disappointment, as "a clean-cut and high-minded public official," especially in contrast to the Democratic gubernatorial candidate, Senator Mon Wallgren. Dewey, meanwhile, had matured and gained valuable experience as governor of New York, making him a worthy successor to FDR. Besides, insisted Rufus, the real issue to be addressed in the national election was "the fact that one man has been president of the United States for twelve years." Attempting to capitalize upon rumors of Roosevelt's failing health, Woods pointed out that three terms were "enough to deplete the physical capacities of any man." The choice, therefore, was really between Dewey and the President's obscure running mate, Harry S Truman. While professing confidence in the outcome, Woods privately worried over the Republican/utility relationship. "The power boys," he wrote, "have rolled in a vast amount of money in order to beat Referendum 25," in the process becoming the "worst liability" borne by Dewey and Langlie.[52]

Roosevelt's fourth term victory was a foregone conclusion, given the nation's involvement in the world conflict. The President "was elected," said Rufus, "to lead the people in the finish of the war, and the making of the peace." By making a credible effort, Dewey at least solidified his claim to the Republican nomination in 1948. At home, voters defeated Referendum 25 by a solid margin, due, apparently, to the influence of utility money and propaganda. In a somewhat illogical expression of opinion, however, the voters, according to Woods, endorsed public power in virtually every other contest. Governor Langlie, though "an upstanding . . . man and strictly honest," lost to Mon Wallgren. "It was Langlie's own fault," reflected Woods, for following the line of "the gang in Spokane." The state Republican Party, he wrote the defeated incumbent, "spent too much time fighting Referendum 25 instead of fighting for . . . your administration." The fact that congressmen Horan and Holmes were the only Republicans to win major state races clarified the failure of other candidates to grasp the popular mood. Their position on power was "just 100% right," Woods pointed out. "If it had not been for that, they too would have been swept aside."[53]

Democrats generally supported, and Republicans invariably opposed, federal river development, so the 1944 election was anything but a local disaster. Although Mon Wallgren quickly filled every available state job with a deserving party member, the new governor was more interested than his predecessor in the work of the Columbia Basin Commission. Wallgren even retained that self-confessed "cantankerous republican," Rufus Woods, as commissioner. "We were being held back" by Langlie, Rufus conceded. But the CBC now had genuine backing from Olympia. Warren G. Magnuson, meanwhile, succeeded the retiring Homer Bone in the U.S. Senate, promising more aggressive action on behalf of federal water projects. Another rising and quite liberal Democrat admired by the *World*, Hugh Mitchell, formerly Wallgren's private secretary, was appointed to serve the two years remaining in the governor's own senatorial term.[54]

By the spring of 1945, major changes had transpired in the state of American affairs, domestic and foreign. Roosevelt was dead and Truman occupied the White House. The latter, though little-known, counted Senators Magnuson and Mitchell and Governor Wallgren among his close political friends, a definite plus in the campaign for development of the Columbia River. Germany's surrender ended the war in Europe and made possible the full concentration of Allied might upon Japan's crumbling empire. American victory soon was complete and the time at hand for building dams and reclamation works on a large scale.[55]

Foster Creek and the Columbia Basin Project had "been engineered to death," Rufus noted in a letter to Walt Horan. "What we want is some action." Unfortunately, forces set in motion by the federal takeover of Grand Coulee, by the BPA, and by the war worked against action on behalf of North Central Washington. "This whole section," Woods complained to Paul Raver, "has been treated as though it were a scrub." The treatment accorded Wenatchee was undeserved, especially because "there wouldn't have been any Bonneville Administration . . . if it hadn't been for this gang of battlers here in Washington," the Dam University. "Three fourths of the power of the Columbia," in current or potential service, came from above the mouth of the Snake River, but decision-making was centralized in Portland, a situation "just as wrong as it can be."[56]

Grand Coulee was built in a river of ironies. Designed to protect local interests from outside economic and political domination, the structure emerged from the developmental process as the property of the United States, constructed and operated by one federal agency, the Bureau of Reclamation, and subject to the dictates of another, the Bonneville Power

Administration. "As long as this Columbia River is controlled by the people who live in the Northwest," Woods postulated, "all will be well and good." Under prevailing circumstances, however, self-sufficiency was denied and democracy compromised. Absent corrective measures, Washington stood to share the fate of other looted states, stripped of basic raw materials and controlled by unsympathetic outsiders.[57]

Immediate alterations in course were essential to counter this loss of control. Disputing Paul Raver's assertion that "the basic principles which underlie the postage stamp . . . theory are fundamentally sound," Woods demanded a "limitation" upon application of the harmful rate philosophy. "A certain percent" of Grand Coulee's power must be reserved, via a lower charge, for use in North Central Washington. The BPA, moreover, ought to be renamed, moved to Wenatchee, and "loaded up with people from this section." Decisions would thereafter be based upon genuine need and objective analysis, rather than upon the subjectivism of Portland. The goal of a Grand Coulee regained, so far as the benefits of the dam were concerned, represented a declaration of postwar independence.[58]

# Chapter Twelve
## This Rip-Roaring Old Columbia

This ferocious, rip-roaring old Columbia whose millions of acre feet are wasting away their energy on their way to the sea, is to be properly harnessed and to be put to work.

Rufus Woods[1]

T HE FRONT PAGE headline in the *Wenatchee World's* extra edition for August 6, 1945 announced the opening of a new and uncertain age: "TERRIBLE ATOMIC BOMB LOOSED AGAINST NIPPON." The secret of Hanford, where plutonium production had commenced the previous fall, was at last revealed to the public. The reaction was in part euphoric, for the attack upon Hiroshima appeared well-justified and certain to hasten the end of the war. Thoughtful observers, Rufus Woods included, also took alarm, realizing that, as a product of science, the atomic bomb was as readily exploitable by bad as by good governments. Currently spending a few days cruising along the "peaceful shores" of Lake Chelan, Woods was overcome by "a sort of cold chill" as he read the first reports of Hiroshima. The weapon was "wonderful" and "awful" and should make every American "jittery," even in the moment of victory.[2]

In spite of the disturbing premonitions, the end of the war brought "great days." On V-J Day, the people of Wenatchee gathered in the city park for a moment of silence in memory of "the dead, the mangled and the broken" and then paraded through the streets behind the American Legion band. Woods sat in his backyard that evening, listening to the honking of automobile horns and dictating the next day's column. "We have won a great war for humanity and for the world of the future," he pointed out, defeating, "at least for the present," the international "hosts of evil." Grand Coulee had "contributed more than any other one thing to winning the war." Conceived for the advancement of peaceful pursuits, the dam had instead become an integral component of the government-industry win-the-war alliance, its electricity transformed into metal and plutonium. Mixed with science at Hanford, water power had given birth to what the popular author John Gunther soon called the "demonic child of the Columbia."[3]

America's new superpower responsibilities were a prime subject for the daily Rufus Woods column. Pearl Harbor had "knocked the props out from under" the nation's traditional isolationist position. "We can no longer withdraw behind our shorelines," proclaimed the *World*, "hold our hands to our ears, close our eyes, and say that nothing of what goes on in the rest of the world concerns us." The airplane and the radio made the United States the near neighbor to "all places and all things." A vitriolic critic of Wilsonian internationalism after the First World War, Rufus Woods declared himself, as early as 1943, in favor of the proposed United Nations.[4]

In the spring of 1945, Rufus attended the founding conference of the UN in San Francisco. Although 3,000 delegates were on hand, representing four dozen countries, along with 2,000 reporters, Woods managed, through audacity, to become the subject of feature stories from coast-to-coast. Arriving without credentials or hotel reservations, he was briefly denied admission by fancy-pants functionaries. "I simply slammed down two Wenatchee Worlds and said 'Do I get a ticket?'" Rufus wrote of his brazen response. "I got the tickets and from there I went to the hotel, assuming of course that I could get a room, which I did." Watching the diplomats in action, the gate-crasher was convinced of the possibility of a firm and enduring peace, provided that the United States, Russia, and England maintained their wartime alliance.[5]

On the key foreign policy problem of the time, Woods urged that every possible step be taken to preserve harmonious relations between America and the Soviet Union. "The present regime," he claimed with un-Republican respect to the Communists, "has done a lot for Russia," leading the country from "the ox team days" into the middle of the twentieth century. The United States must avoid antagonizing Moscow "for the next 10 or 15 years." The alternative was inevitable military conflict, "the most futile war ever waged." Regarding Asian affairs, Rufus refused to allow his relationship-by-marriage to Representative Walter Judd of Minnesota, a leader of the China Lobby, to deflect him from a common sense position on the

Chinese civil war. "We don't have to like it," the *World* observed of the likely Communist victory, "but we had better learn to get along with it."[6]

Common sense also required an activist approach in genuine crisis situations. The Greek civil war of 1947 and the fall of the first eastern European states to Communist rule convinced Woods that "appeasement" of Stalin had failed. The U.S. and the Soviet Union had come to "a parting of the ways." The *World* endorsed the Truman Doctrine, proclaimed by the President to justify military and economic aid to Greece, as "an expanded interpretation of the Monroe Doctrine." The *World* greeted the Marshall Plan, involving billions of dollars in American obligations, as the ideal means of rebuilding Europe and exposing the deficiencies of the Soviet system: "Russia cannot afford to see peoples in countries around her enjoying a higher standard of living than their [*sic*] own people." American intervention abroad "in time of peace" was preferable to the loss of lives and money "in time of war."[7]

Although he considered Harry Truman to be untutored and undignified, especially in contrast to FDR, Woods avoided criticizing the President's conduct of foreign affairs. Bipartisanship was, more than ever, the correct patriotic attitude when the national interest was at stake. The *World* accorded "great man" status to Secretary of State George Marshall and found Dean Acheson, Marshall's successor and a favorite target of Republicans, to possess "insight . . . and understanding." Except for an occasional swipe at Democratic Congressman Hugh DeLacey of Seattle, Rufus avoided the Red-baiting tactics increasingly favored by the GOP. Roosevelt's mistakes at Yalta, if mistakes they were, arose, in his view, from ill health rather than from treason. Congressional investigations of domestic subversion followed "Nazi methods" and were based upon the faulty assumption that former Communists, having once sworn allegiance to a creed favoring deceit, were now telling the truth. Communism was an ideology "and you fight ideas with a better one—an idea that comes from a free people with common objectives and aspirations," from a people devoted to the Constitution and to freedom of expression.[8]

For Rufus, the real "ENEMIES . . . in our own ranks" were the politicians in Washington and the corporate executives in New York opposed to federal development of the Columbia River. This conviction led Woods home to his lifelong preoccupation, the economic advancement of North Central

Washington. The *World* came out of the war in a strong position, fortified by the return of experienced employees and by an upward trend in advertising revenue. Rufus resolved a lingering newsprint shortage in the spring of 1946 by purchasing a Cascades timber tract and sending *World* staffers into the forest to assist the loggers in removing trees for manufacture into paper at a Spokane mill. The aging and now portly publisher set to work himself with a crosscut saw, at least long enough to allow the snapping of publicity photographs. Continuing profitability made possible the acquisition of yet another new press and a fleet of delivery trucks. The expense, though considerable, placed the *World* in a position to operate efficiently, as Woods boasted, "until a circulation of 50,000 to 65,000 is reached."[9]

Newspapering, unfortunately, was the only local business to prosper immediately following the war. Shortages of civilian goods and labor, following upon the "hard pull" of the Depression, left Wenatchee, in the succinct observation of the *World*, "run down at the heels." Poorly stocked shops and unrepaired streets reflected a series of disappointing economic developments. The apple industry experienced another of its periodic downturns, with markets glutted and prices reverting to pre-Pearl Harbor levels. Northwest Chemurgy, expanding rapidly under the aggressive stewardship of Henry Carstensen and Rufus Woods, recorded strong earnings in 1946. The decision to expand, however, was unwise and the profits misleading. Lack of capital, shortages of raw materials, and a declining demand for artificial starch soon bankrupted the overextended firm.[10]

Wenatchee's lone defense industry, the Rock Island ferro-silicon plant, remained closed. Instead of converting the facility to peace-time purposes, the government decided to dispose of the machinery at auction. "It would be a crime," protested Woods, "to tear down this plant located as it was all ready to go and on the biggest power pool in America." The usual corporate suspects, bent upon retarding the industrialization of the Pacific Northwest, appeared responsible. The stakes were high as Rufus mounted a campaign to prevent demolition and then find a buyer. "This is the only power-using plant in the electric power section of the Columbia," warned his close associate, Kirby Billingsley, "and it will take 50 years to ever get another if that one is taken out." With Woods directing strategy and Billingsley handling the details in the nation's capital, an arrangement was finally concluded in 1948 to sell the building and fixtures to the Keokuk Electro-Metals Company, a firm interested in exploitation of nearby mineral deposits.[11]

Stagnation appeared to be the fate of the entire Pacific Northwest as of 1945. The closure of defense plants would likely produce, in the view of most observers studying the reconversion problem, a return to some approximation of depression conditions. Testifying before the Columbia Basin Commission, utility executives forecast a massive energy surplus, to prevail for at least a decade. "No market for power, no market for power!" a scornful Rufus Woods wrote of the hand-wringing on the part of the representatives of private industry. "These men . . . were just like a bunch of old magpies singing their same song." Disinterested experts nonetheless agreed that troublesome times lay ahead. The Bonneville Power Administration predicted that a million persons in its service area would be unemployed by 1947. The principal and almost hopeless problem facing the region, according to former Senator Homer Bone, was how to develop enough civilian demand for electricity to make up for the lost consumption of abandoned war-time factories.[12]

Confounding expectations, the brief postwar slump was followed immediately by a regional economic boom. Continuing population growth and the frenzied purchase of automobiles, refrigerators, and other civilian goods, available in quantity for the first time since Pearl Harbor, accounted for much of the stimulus. So too did the collapse of harmonious relations with the Soviet Union, preventing the expected wholesale cutback in the armed forces and defense manufacturing. Hanford, growing in top-secret fashion, maintained a steady drain on Columbia River power. Instead of being decommissioned, the aluminum industry was reorganized under government auspices, with Reynolds and Kaiser introduced as major competitors of Alcoa. Forty percent of the energy from Grand Coulee and Bonneville dams went into producing aluminum, increasing the demand for hydroelectricity. By August 1946, a year following the Japanese surrender, the BPA was ready to declare an impending and deadly serious power shortage in the Pacific Northwest.[13]

A rational approach to the planning, construction, and management of water projects appeared to be necessary to meet the emergency. Twenty federal agencies in three cabinet departments claimed some degree of responsibility for the Columbia River. The states of Washington, Oregon, Idaho, and Montana insisted upon involvement in making decisions, adding to the administrative complexity. Journalist Richard Neuberger observed of the confused result, "duplication of governmental units has become a fine art." Democrats and Republicans agreed in theory upon the obvious remedy. "To insure the greatest possible development of the basin," stated Senator Warren Magnuson, "it is necessary that inter-agency jealousies be submerged and the efforts of all pooled." That meant the "inevitable" creation of a single river authority, according to Representative Walt Horan.[14]

Discussion had begun in late 1944 on the means of rationalizing development of the river. "There needs to be an overall Authority to harmonize and coordinate," explained Rufus Woods. "We have seen the good in Bonneville and we have seen the evil," Kirby Billingsley informed Horan after an in-depth talk on the subject with Rufus. "We decided that if the Authority could be in the right place with the right men . . . it was our best course." The Wenatchee publisher saw "no reason why it should not go through," provided the state of Washington, and the upper Columbia in particular, received appropriate protection. Pending that guarantee, Woods advised Jim O'Sullivan, "we ought not to go on such a program until we have some understanding as to how this thing is to be manned."[15]

On behalf of the Columbia River Development League, Rufus toured the Tennessee Valley in February and March 1945. Dressed in "old roustabout clothing," he interviewed administrators, scientists, and laborers, seeking every bit of information possible about the advantages and the pitfalls of the TVA approach to river basin management. Director David Lilienthal, praised by Woods as a "great big country boy from Indiana" with "a mind like a steel trap," provided advice and encouragement. The TVA had succeeded, Rufus concluded, for two basic reasons. Jobs, from top to bottom, were filled on "a non-political standpoint" and the organization was authorized to take action "without continually referring to some Bureau Head in Washington." Effective local control was the correct solution to developing a truly beneficial Columbia Valley Authority (CVA) in the Pacific Northwest. "Rufus arrived home," Billingsley wrote Senator Hugh Mitchell, ". . . thoroughly sold on the Tennessee Valley Authority and convinced that we should have such an agency in this region."[16]

Drafted by the Department of the Interior, Senator Mitchell's Columbia Valley Authority bill greatly exceeded the limits Woods envisioned. Introduced in the spring of 1945, the measure provided for a presidentially appointed CVA answerable to a National River Basin Development Board. The latter was to be chaired by the Secretary of the Interior, a proviso establishing Harold Ickes, still the occupant of that office, as the ultimate arbiter of the Columbia's fate. "I . . . certainly do not think that Rufus should worry too much now about the final form of the bill," Mitchell assured Billingsley, since amendments reflecting the views of local critics were anticipated. Although friendly to the senator as a genuine supporter of federal water projects, Woods reacted with a heated and blunt protest. "That matter of turning the Columbia over to . . . Washington, D.C. is all wrong," he fumed. Unless significant changes were made in the bill, advocates of local authority would wage "a ferocious fight."[17]

Also opposed to any arrangement whereby "the initiating impulses come from Washington, D.C. rather than from the people of the states involved," Representative Walt Horan provided the principal alternative to Mitchell's measure. Unveiled in April, after consultation with Woods, the Horan bill created a Columbia Valley Cooperative Authority, managed by five directors appointed by the president upon the recommendation of the governors of Washington, Oregon, Idaho, and Montana. "My bill," claimed the congressman, "brings the *control* of the Columbia as *close* to the people as it can be brought," given the federal government's constitutional responsibility for navigable streams. The measure provided for the maximum practicable "local autonomy," agreed Rufus, and was "absolutely" the course favored by those desiring genuine development of the river.[18]

Lobbyists, journalists, and politicians focused on the Mitchell concept of complete federalization. New Dealers, the White House, and Harold Ickes supported the senator's bill. All-out opposition to a CVA in any form came from the utility industry and from federal and state agencies fearful of losing projects and funding to the proposed authority. Rufus Woods and Walt Horan were opponents of a different sort, linked by circumstance to reactionaries and turf-defending bureaucrats. "The main idea in issue," said Woods in attempting to separate himself from the rabid and the irresponsible, was whether or not the "Authority shall be handled locally just the same as the T.V.A."[19]

Concerned about losing influence, the Corps of Engineers undertook a long-delayed review of the 308 Report in order, as one high-ranking official admitted, to keep "pace with . . . the CVA." The new study presented a Master Control Plan for "coordinated . . . long-range . . . development" of the "largely unused" Columbia drainage. As the focal point of the plan, the Army recommended completion or construction of 10 dams: Hungry Horse and Glacier View on the Flathead, Libby on the Kootenai, Albeni Falls on the Pend Oreille, Hells Canyon on the Snake, and Foster Creek, Priest Rapids, Umatilla, John Day, and The Dalles on the Columbia.

Funding problems delayed completion of the study until 1948, submission of a final draft to Congress until 1950, and publication of the finished report until 1952. The effort therefore served more as an in-progress delaying stratagem than as a direct assault upon the Mitchell proposal.[20]

Hoping to immediately outflank the CVA, the Corps, Bureau of Reclamation, BPA, and other federal agencies joined the drainage states, including Nevada, Utah, and Wyoming, in forming the Columbia Basin Inter-Agency Committee. The organization conducted studies, convened regional planning conferences, and accomplished absolutely nothing of substance because it required a unanimous vote for action to be taken on any given issue. "It is like the United Nations," quipped one critic. "The . . . Committee can air grievances but does not make decisions," noted Walt Horan. The failure of the committee left the hodgepodge managerial situation on the Columbia unchanged, unwittingly making the case for a genuine river authority.[21]

With opinion on the CVA so divided, no legislation passed. "They are just eating up Mitchell's bill," Woods wrote of the prevailing view in Washington state. The senator, by attempting "to tie us on to the Secretary of the Interior," had "just about . . . wrecked" the chances of securing an authority based upon the concept of local autonomy. Horan's alternative was lost in the furor. Kirby Billingsley reported from the nation's capital in early 1946 that the CVA movement had, in actuality, "gone backward."[22]

Woods remained the captive of counter-productive forces. Electricity from Grand Coulee "should be used right here along the Columbia River," he insisted. "Otherwise, if this power is shipped out, it will never be brought back." Under the $17.50 per kilowatt year BPA charge, North Central Washington continued to be sold down the river, deprived of any benefit from its own dam. "What I am trying to study out," Rufus announced in a series of commentaries, ". . . is how to LIMIT the postage stamp rate." While the remedy was uncertain, "an open out and above board fight" with the BPA appeared absolutely necessary. The problem of securing no-strings-attached federal funding, meanwhile, remained beyond resolution. The construction of mammoth dams was "too long winded a job and too important," not to mention too expensive, for private enterprise. The difficulty of "get[ting] the government to do it" and "at the same protect[ing] the interest of the locality" continued to bedevil Woods.[23]

All the "talk of a Columbia Valley Authority," Rufus noted in September 1945, ". . . has started both the U.S.B.R. [Bureau of Reclamation] and the U.S. Army Engineers to some action." Local residents ought to take advantage of the anti-CVA drive to secure authorization of Foster Creek and funds for construction of the Columbia Basin Project. Woods had several advantages in renewing the fight for development of the river. National security, particularly with the onset of the Cold War, depended upon the avoidance of power shortages. President Truman, Harold Ickes, and Paul Raver, among high-placed federal officials, agreed the country needed more dams. Walt Horan, as a member of the minority party, lacked the influence of his Democratic predecessors Sam Hill and Charles Leavy, but his position on the House Appropriations Committee was still an asset. Washington's senators, moreover, supported the cause with enthusiasm. Warren Magnuson, especially, understood "the importance of timing," observed Kirby Billingsley, of knowing when to avoid confrontation and when to push legislation.[24]

Numerous obstacles, though, stood in the way of new development work. The utility industry, according to one account, had "oodles of money" and hundreds of lobbyists available to fight proposals involving the generation of electricity by the federal government. The National Reclamation Association, heavily subsidized by the utilities, opposed new power dams. The Bureau of Reclamation, out of institutional jealousy, intended to prevent the Army from constructing Foster Creek. The Corps of Engineers, preoccupied with its own bureaucratic interest, preferred to build Umatilla dam first and apparently intended to proceed with work at The Dalles and at Albeni Falls before turning to Foster Creek. Except for fending off the Reclamation Bureau, the Corps exhibited little genuine interest in the latter project. Budget Bureau attempts to impose substantial reductions on federal spending, the one Columbia River dam at a time argument, and the contention that Washington state had received "preferential treatment" dating back to 1933 also worked to the disadvantage of Foster Creek.[25]

Great public works, Woods believed, were bipartisan in nature. "Development projects do not constitute a political question," he lectured the leaders of both parties, for nothing less than the national interest was at stake. "Republicans and democrats should unite no matter who is at the head of the administration," limiting their quarrels to matters of comparative small import. Working hard to conceal his private opinions respecting certain politicians, Rufus maintained a common public front as far as the Columbia River was concerned. The *World* regularly praised Governor Mon Wallgren. The paper also downplayed such examples of President Truman's ineptitude as Harold Ickes's messy departure from government and the dramatic dispute over Soviet-American relations between Henry Wallace and Secretary of State James Byrnes. When Walt Horan publicly criticized Truman and Senator Magnuson, Rufus strongly advised him to "go easy on fighting men individually." Restraint was the key to success, since the alienation of even one well-placed ally could prove fatal to Foster Creek.[26]

The wisdom of suspending party politics was demonstrated, according to Woods, by the relative ease with which funds for the Columbia Basin Project were finally obtained. "All we need is cash," Rufus had noted upon acceptance of the federal contracts by the reclamation districts in 1945. Congress provided $6 million for construction in 1946 and, later that year, a $10 million deficiency appropriation. Morrison-Knudsen, the Bureau of Reclamation contractor, began "throwing the dirt" on the first 400,000 acre unit in June. Work in the Ephrata-Quincy area focused on excavating the main canal and impounding dams at the northern and southern ends of the Grand Coulee and at a site near Moses Lake.[27]

Foster Creek, meanwhile, appeared to have little chance of approval, especially with McNary Dam (the Umatilla project, renamed in honor of the late Oregon Senator Charles McNary) already authorized. "We know that Foster Creek will not be built until there is some demand for it," conceded Rufus. Cold War defense spending, happily, supplied the requisite need in 1946. "With the aluminum industry beginning to reopen and with other industries coming in at the same time," observed Woods, "we must . . . look for more and more power from the Columbia." The dam planned for the upper river was needed "quickly" to "keep ahead of industrial expansion." Traveling to Washington, Rufus joined Kirby Billingsley and other representatives of the state in testifying on behalf of legislation authorizing Foster Creek. A last-ditch attempt by the Bureau of Reclamation to secure the project was thrust aside and Congress in early July approved construction of the dam by the Corps of Engineers.[28]

Until Congress actually provided funds, Foster Creek remained open to counter-attack by its enemies. Except for a small allocation of planning money provided by the Corps of Engineers on a "not for publication" basis, no financing was available in 1946. A Budget Bureau directive ordering federal agencies not to submit spending requests for "projects on which the ground has not been broken" forestalled any likelihood of funding in 1947.[29]

Rufus felt compelled to support Foster Creek, even though it was unlikely to benefit Wenatchee. "There is very little object in building these dams," Kirby Billingsley wrote, "if they do not help develop the areas in which they are located." Under the postage stamp rate system, electricity generated at the dam would, like the output of Grand Coulee, be lost to distant metropolitan centers. The project's only possible advantage for North Central Washington was reclamation, a usage precluded by the Corps plan. Two hundred thousand acres between Wenatchee and "the Canadian line" might be watered, complained Woods, if common sense prevailed over the Army's fear of the Bureau of Reclamation. Project supporters must, in addition to lobbying for construction funds, somehow fortify Foster Creek, securing the addition of irrigation to the prevailing design.[30]

National political developments, in particular the Republican victory in the 1946 congressional elections, further complicated the Foster Creek situation. Although personally disappointed over the defeat of Hugh Mitchell, Woods at first welcomed the rejection of the "Roosevelt New Deal policies." Talk of a national "renovation" soon gave way, however, to genuine concern for the future. Grand Coulee, Bonneville, the Columbia Basin Project, McNary, and Foster Creek had all been approved in times when the Democratic Party controlled both Congress and the White House. The collapse of this equation therefore threatened continued funding of public works in the Pacific Northwest. The new chairman of the House Appropriations Committee, John Taber of New York, advocated wholesale cuts in federal spending and was bound to be a "problem." Senator-elect Harry Cain of Washington was uninformed on matters relating to the Columbia, worried Rufus, and prone to relying on advice from "fool friends."[31]

What Rufus termed "A GIGANTIC CONSPIRACY" against the Columbia River on the part of "sinister factors and elements" in the Republican Party took the form of a direct assault upon the economic well-being of the Pacific Northwest. Jim O'Sullivan, his paranoid eagle eye unaffected by rapidly failing health, warned that the new congressional majority intended to see that "the present Bonneville rate structure is raised." Warren Magnuson advised "everyone interested in low-cost power" to "have no illusions" about the "over-all private utility strategy." The utilities intended to improve their competitive position by substantially reducing, through various means, the difference between their rates and those charged by the

BPA. Among the side effects acceptable to Eastern-oriented management and investors were a slowdown in the rate of industrialization, delayed dam construction, and destruction of the Columbia Basin Project.[32]

"The number of bills introduced during this Congress aimed at our Federal Power policy," Senator Magnuson noted in a June 1947 report to his Wenatchee friends, "indicate that private utilities are mobilizing for an all-out fight." Provisions of the Reclamation Act of 1939 dealing with the allocation and repayment of project costs provided a major opening for exploitation by industry. Although the Interior Department had ruled in 1944 that the 3 percent interest assigned to power revenues could be used to subsidize irrigation, the complex legal argument defied comprehension. "Astute attorneys" devoting "HOURS OF STUDY" to the opinion, Rufus Woods noted, admitted confusion. Claiming perfect comprehension of both the law and congressional intent, Seattle Chamber of Commerce secretary Floyd Hagie insisted that the department's position was illegal. Congress clearly meant, asserted Hagie, for the interest to be paid into the U.S. treasury. The fact that Hagie was in the employ of interests hostile to public power and determined to force an increase in BPA rates had no influence, of course, on his objective analysis of the situation.[33]

Relying upon Hagie's legal brief, congressional Republicans attempted to overturn established federal policy by legislative fiat. A bill introduced by Representative Robert F. Rockwell of Colorado expressly banned the use of interest for subsidies and required that project costs be repaid within 50 years, rather than in the "reasonable period" then allowed. The government would, as the sponsors intended, have to choose between reducing support of irrigation—thereby placing an extra burden upon settlers—or increasing electricity rates to generate additional revenue. "Such increased revenues, of course," the Bonneville Power Administration noted with respect to an additional dilemma, "would be based upon the questionable assumption that the same quantity of power could be sold at the higher rates." Under the Republican approach, Paul Raver estimated his agency would have to hike rates by "from 20 to 30 per cent," with disastrous economic consequences for the Pacific Northwest.[34]

Genuinely apoplectic, Rufus Woods watched as his own party attempted to undermine the present and future prosperity of an entire region. "I have . . . given you up as a hopeless cause," he wrote the president of the Seattle Chamber of Commerce, on account of "the rotten job" involved in sending "that man Hagie" to Washington in support of the campaign for higher BPA rates. Woods threatened to "tear" the Seattle

Chamber "all to pieces" should it persist in a policy of "monumental mistakes." Senator Harry Cain, meanwhile, added to his conservative reputation by siding with Hagie and launching an oratorical assault upon the Bureau of Reclamation. For the first time in memory, Rufus protested, a member of the state's congressional delegation was "shooting from behind the lines," ignoring the welfare of his constituents. In attempting to "kill . . . the West," Woods charged in a letter to the chairman of the Republican national committee, the party was engaged in a "wild and crazy and UNPOLITIC" effort to advance the interests of corporate monopoly.[35]

Although Congress defeated the anti-BPA measures favored by GOP leaders, the drive against public power kept development advocates on the defensive, fighting to preserve cheap electricity rather than battling for new appropriations and new projects. Concerted effort on the part of the Washington and Oregon delegations, Senator Cain excepted, produced additional money for the Columbia Basin Project, but only after a shutdown by contractors in the fall of 1947. Foster Creek, though, received no construction funds in 1947 or 1948. Drawing upon another analysis supplied by Floyd Hagie, Republicans argued that the authorized single-purpose project was illegal. Ignoring this contention, the Truman Administration nonetheless refused to endorse a War Department request for money from Congress. "We . . . are asking quite a bit," Walt Horan observed, and must therefore avoid "jeopardizing" the Columbia Basin Project by pushing too hard for Foster Creek.[36]

Supporters of the dam blamed the Corps of Engineers for lethargy and bias toward Portland. "Somewhere between the Seattle office and the Washington D.C. office this project has been sidetracked several times," Kirby Billingsley pointed out. "Some of those fellows," he wrote of the officers willing to dismiss the interests of the upper Columbia, "think they are Gods." Institutional pique compounded the unwarranted arrogance of an intrenched bureaucracy. The military, Jim O'Sullivan reported after conversations at the War Department in February 1948, intended to punish the residents of North Central Washington for daring to suggest that the project ought to be "turn[ed] . . . over to the Interior Department." Frustrated at the lack of progress, Woods concluded that the "United States Army Engineers have rather foxed us regarding the Foster Creek dam," giving priority to McNary while supporting the upriver project only when there was a danger of its being lost to the Reclamation Bureau.[37]

Virtually comatose in early 1948, Foster Creek quickly revived, stimulated by a series of dramatic events, foreign and domestic. Resuming his pre-war habit of overseas travel, Rufus witnessed the first of these developments. Sailing from New York at the end of May aboard a cargo vessel bound for Bremerhaven, he landed in Germany just as the Soviet Union closed down overland access to Berlin. The U.S., Britain, and France hastily organized an airlift to the besieged city and a new world war became a distinct possibility. Waiting for an opportunity to visit Berlin, Woods traveled "up and down, criss cross and round about" the defeated country. He found the condition of the German people, three years after V-E Day, deplorable. Their "fantastic" currency consisted of American cigarettes, purchased at eight cents a pack and convertible into all manner of goods and services. One person in three lacked decent clothing and the only shoes available were homemade makeshifts. The schools lacked books and supplies. *Stars and Stripes*, the Paris edition of the *Herald-Tribune*, and a few local sheets, heavily censored by the occupation authorities, provided the only source of news.[38]

Despite genuine distress over "the sad faces" of his pre-war friends, Woods had no sympathy for the German population. "I thought in swear words," he wrote after observing a group of workmen dressed in tattered S.S. uniforms. Reporting at length upon the "queer psychology which exists all over Germany," Rufus noted that he had met few individuals honest enough to "admit that they were followers of Hitler." Most people, to their discredit, denied "any sense of responsibility whatever for the excesses" of the Nazis. A sobering tour of Dachau convinced him that the "known facts" were sufficiently "sickening" to condemn the nation's wartime leaders as the worst "monsters . . . known to history."

Unable to get into Berlin, Woods drafted personal reflections on the crisis for publication under the title "Hair Trigger Days in Europe." Observation of the Soviets in action erased the last positive opinions regarding Stalin left over from the war. The attempt to starve Berlin into submission reflected, in his view, the weakness, rather than the strength, of Moscow. Failing to satisfy the most basic domestic needs of Russia's own population, the Communists hoped to "unite the people against some foreign foe." Anyone doubting that America should "stand pat on the line as now established," ought to consider this fact and also the desire for freedom exhibited by the tens of thousands of displaced persons currently in flight from the Soviet satellite states. Europeans found the U.S. "about as welcome as the proverbial wet pup is in a home." The "shaggy" creature, though, was "willingly borne in preference to a Mad Dog from the East."

Rufus returned to America in August, fully aware that the German crisis would likely produce increased appropriations for the Columbia River. Proof that the Cold War was no short-lived phenomenon, Berlin demonstrated that a sustained defense buildup was the only means of thwarting Stalinist expansionism. "War talk," as Walt Horan noted, was an extremely effective means of "point[ing] up our power shortage." Instead of fighting over federal appropriations, as in the past, Oregon and Washington now stood a good chance of securing increased funding for both McNary and Foster Creek.[39]

Nature proved as helpful to the development cause as Joe Stalin. Drought had prevailed east of the Cascades in 1947, ruining crops and producing prayers for rain from the faithful of all denominations. An overly generous response fell upon the region in the spring of 1948. "Flood Waters Rip Northwest to Shreds," proclaimed a *World* headline on May 24, after days of heavy precipitation. Three thousand acres were flooded by the Kootenai River near Bonners Ferry in the Idaho panhandle. Flowage over the Grand Coulee spillway was 50 percent above normal. The Columbia had risen four feet in the previous week at Wenatchee, washing out the highway at Rock Island Dam. Far downstream, the river stood at six feet above floodstage at Vanport, the war-time boomtown outside Portland, threatening to overflow protective dikes.[40]

Once the rain stopped, temperatures soared above 90 degrees, melting the heavy snowpack in the mountains above the Columbia and its tributaries. Already swollen rivers, unable to handle the enormous volume of water, surged out of their channels. Levees gave way at Bonners Ferry, inundating the town. Grand Coulee set spillway records daily, and Rock Island Dam actually disappeared beneath the surface of the roiling Columbia, with only a ripple to mark the location of the structure. On Memorial Day, the river wrecked Vanport, destroying the community, noted a witness, "as completely as a mashed toy village." From the Canadian line to the sea, at least thirty people were killed, including fifteen at Vanport, and 50,000 left homeless. Property damage exceeded, by the most conservative estimate, $100 million.[41]

North Central Washington, overlooked in the national attention accorded Vanport, suffered a full measure of destruction. Omak was flooded in the Okanogan Valley and Twisp isolated by the washing out of bridges on the Methow River. "Wild waters . . . ripped down the narrow river bottom" of the Entiat River, sweeping away fifty homes. The Wenatchee River, backing up from its mouth, covered hundreds of acres of orchards, threatened Cashmere, and overflowed the Great Northern mainline. Engorged by new cloudbursts, the Columbia punched a hole in the floor of the Wenatchee pumping plant, cutting off the city's water supply.[42]

Absent in Germany, Rufus Woods missed the most dramatic local story of his newspaper career. Reading wire service accounts with a mixture of alarm and excitement, he expected the disaster to increase the pressure on Congress to construct more dams. Already, the BPA had called for implementation of "adequate flood control" measures. The policy of "mumbling, stumbling and fumbling . . . piecemeal development," Paul Raver exclaimed in an Ephrata speech, must give way to an "integrated system" of multipurpose dam building. Senator Warren Magnuson demanded that the federal government take prompt action to tame the rampaging Columbia. Members of Congress, responding to the reports of destruction, missed the salient point that Foster Creek, with limited reservoir capacity, would contribute little to protection against flooding. The Vanport disaster also sparked renewed interest in the storage concept studied during the war. Together, the Reclamation Bureau's Hungry Horse project, currently under way, and the proposed Army plants for Albeni Falls and Libby represented nine million acre-feet of storage, with obvious benefits for regulation of downstream flowage.[43]

Woods returned from Europe to a nation caught up in the "confused, fluid and puzzling" presidential campaign of 1948, another key factor in determining the future course of Columbia River development. Convinced by his party's mishandling of the Columbia that "the times demand a change in Republican leadership," Rufus had favored either California Governor Earl Warren or Minnesota's Harold Stassen for the nomination. Thomas E. Dewey's habitual refusal to "speak up and tell where he stands on some of these red hot issues" made the New Yorker "a second rate . . . standard bearer." Despite this considerable weakness, the Dewey march toward the White House appeared unstoppable, especially considering the selection of the progressive Westerner Warren as running mate. An over-confident Woods spent a good deal of time drawing up lists of probable cabinet appointments in the GOP administration-to-come and reflecting upon the confrontation sure to take place between a President Dewey and the Republican Old Guard in Congress.[44]

Dewey was bound to win because Truman was doomed to defeat. Henry Wallace, regularly excoriated in the *World* as an "idealistic and high-principled" apologist for Moscow, drew liberal Democrats to his Progressive Party candidacy. Governor Strom Thurmond of South Carolina provided an alternative for Southerners opposed to the President's civil rights program. Fatally weakened by defection on his left and on his right, Truman deserved to lose anyway for vetoing the "reasonable" restrictions upon the right to strike in the Taft-Hartley Act. By ignoring "the dictates of the people" on such a vital matter, the incumbent disqualified himself from continuation in office. Truman's "entirely too savage" conduct on the campaign trail further indicated his fundamental unfitness.[45]

Truman won anyway, in a stunning upset. "What an election it was!" Woods exclaimed in a series of flabbergasted columns. Responsibility for the Republican defeat, asserted Rufus, belonged with the party's reactionary congressional leadership. Dewey deserved censure for his less-than-scintillating campaign, but was merely the "scapegoat" for those attempting "to stand on the old issues that long ago disappeared and no longer have meaning." Instead of listening to the people on such matters as federal water projects, the GOP had followed the lead of a "gang of lobbyists" and, as a result, had lost control of Congress. Woods readily admitted to feeling "happy" about the reassertion of Democratic strength. "It looks as though we're going to have some real funds to work with in the next four years," he informed readers of the *World* in summing up the significance of the election.[46]

As if to clinch the case for renewed river development, abnormally low streamflow, the product of an early winter freeze, imposed a post-election electricity brownout on the Pacific Northwest. Lights were switched off, business operations curtailed, and laborers thrown out of work. The situation, according to Rufus Woods, was scandalous: "here we are in the greatest power pool in America . . . and talking about [a] shortage of power." Common sense held that dams should be built "SOMEWHAT IN ADVANCE OF DEMAND," yet "foolish, foolish" advocates of the private utility line had "opposed construction of Foster Creek" and other much-needed projects. The Corps of Engineers would not complete McNary Dam, the only plant currently under construction on the Columbia, until 1954, adding to the sense of dire emergency. Backed by Woods, Senator Warren Magnuson and Representative Henry M. Jackson, the ambitious young congressman from west of the Cascades, demanded immediate commencement of work at Foster Creek.[47]

In early 1949 the Democratic Congress provided $2 million for preparatory work at the Foster Creek damsite in a supplementary appropriation bill. Additional money, from the regular federal budget for the coming fiscal year, was briefly threatened when navigation interests on the Snake

River attempted to secure an early start on the proposed Ice Harbor dam. The measure finally signed by President Truman in October, however, appropriated $5 million for road building and excavation. Although less than the original administration request, the sum was "nothing to sneeze at," reported Kirby Billingsley, particularly considering the dam's lack of "flood control or transportation features." The project also had a new name, Chief Joseph Dam, after the legendary Nez Perce leader exiled to the Colville Reservation in the late nineteenth century.[48]

*"Chief Joseph is on the way,"* Billingsley wrote from Washington in mid-1949. *"It won't be stopped now."* Firm support from Senator Magnuson insured the funding of construction in subsequent sessions of Congress. Trailer parks, shanty dwellings, and what one visitor described as "enough empty beer cans to erect a mountainous monument to the infinite thirst of dam builders" testified to the sweat-stained rebirth of Bridgeport as a government boomtown. To maximize production, the Army enlarged upon its original plan, providing space for twenty-seven generators, sixteen to be installed in the project's initial phase. The Eisenhower Administration, however, postponed completion of these first generating units from 1955, when the powerhouse went on line, until 1958. Meanwhile, legislation passed in 1954 authorized the use of water stored behind the dam for irrigating 5,680 acres of land, partially fulfilling a prime objective of the dam's North Central Washington sponsors. The reservoir itself was, years later, officially named Rufus Woods Lake, in honor of the Wenatchee publisher and his work on behalf of the project.[49]

The dam at Foster Creek propelled the Pacific Northwest into what Woods called "the Age of the Epoch of Super-development." Chief Joseph was by no means the only result of the Berlin crisis, the 1948 flood, and the Truman upset. New generators, the tenth and eleventh overall, were installed at Grand Coulee in 1949. The Corps of Engineers began constructing a low dam at Albeni Falls, completing the project in 1952. Responding to the damage at Bonners Ferry, the Army also got ready for work at Libby on the Kootenai, pending resolution of the cross-border storage issue. Oregon's congressional delegation launched a campaign for a dam at The Dalles and organizations promoting the development of the Snake River did the same on behalf of Ice Harbor and Hells Canyon. Core drilling and other exploratory investigation began above Wenatchee at the Rocky Reach and Wells sites, the latter replacing the Chelan location recommended in the 308 Report. Alert to any and all means of exploiting the Columbia, Rufus Woods pressed for resumption of negotiations on use of the Canadian Arrow Lakes, and publicized the supposed merits of Moses Coulee as a storage reservoir.[50]

The Bureau of Reclamation also made substantial progress on the Columbia Basin Project. The mammoth Grand Coulee pumping station was completed in 1949. Excavation on the main canal route from Ephrata to Quincy began that year, under a $6 million Bureau of Reclamation contract. Woods drove to the flats on a regular basis to watch "those gigantic earth movers . . . rolling the dirt and rock out of the big ditch." A midsummer design adjustment was required when the Atomic Energy Commission, worried about possible soil contamination from Hanford, ordered the removal of 173,000 acres from the Wahluke Slope area of the project. The truly significant development, though, was the announcement that reclamation of 87,000 acres in the Quincy-Columbia Basin District would begin in 1952. Thereafter, assuming all went according to schedule, 80,000 additional acres would be watered each year.[51]

Full-speed-ahead work on reclamation and power again brought to the fore the issue of a central planning agency and the obvious need for coordinated development. Woods had once expected the Columbia Basin Commission, which Arthur Langlie retained after winning a second gubernatorial term in 1948, to serve this function, at least for the state of Washington. Factionalism and personality conflict, however, limited the panel's effectiveness. The east side irrigation district, for instance, wanted to drop out of the federal reclamation project, since "twenty to thirty years" were likely to pass before water from Grand Coulee became available in that sector. Secretary Charles Cone, disagreeing with the vision of an industrialized North Central Washington, referred to a manufacturing proposal as "Rufus' Crazy Idea" in the minutes of a 1948 commission meeting. Woods responded that he "appreciate[d] a man who talks out frankly and abruptly," but other commissioners forced Cone to resign over the indiscretion. Succeeding to the secretaryship, Kirby Billingsley became the focus of prolonged squabbling, especially after he inadvertently mailed a letter to a strong supporter of developing the Snake detailing how federal funds meant for the Snake River might be transferred to Chief Joseph. Although Woods blocked the removal of his friend, he was unable, in part because of this very act, to restore harmony to the commission.[52]

President Truman's call in January 1949 for a TVA-like approach to the nation's river basins restored momentum to the drive for a federal valley authority in the Pacific Northwest. The need seemed apparent to all concerned about the prevailing inefficient state of affairs. The Bureau of Reclamation and the Corps of Engineers, observed Clarence Dill, a member of the Columbia Basin Commission, were engaged in a "race to present their plans to the public, each fearing the other may get the job of building these dams." Herbert Hoover's commission on the reorganization of the federal government indicted the agencies for wasting billions of dollars in senseless duplication of effort. Senator Magnuson and Representatives Henry Jackson and Hugh Mitchell, meanwhile, introduced legislation for a Columbia Valley Administration. The new CVA would absorb the BPA and the regional power and irrigation functions of the Army and the Reclamation Bureau. To insure that "the people of the area concerned should have a major voice in the operation," Magnuson informed a constituent, two of the three directors must be residents of the Northwest. Believing that this provision offered no more than a "semicolon of improvement," Walt Horan resurrected his own postwar bill. The Columbia Interstate Commission, as his authority was now named, "retain[ed] . . . power in the hands of the resident population."[53]

Although committed in theory to a CVA, Rufus Woods became more convinced than ever of the need for local control. The danger inherent in an authority run by outsiders was graphically demonstrated by a new threat to the Columbia. Beginning in 1947, Paul Raver proposed an energy intertie between the Pacific Northwest and California, allowing the BPA to sell surplus electricity in the southern state. On an equally disturbing note, the Bureau of Reclamation announced plans to study the feasibility of diverting water from the Columbia River drainage to agricultural areas in California. The proposals set off "a big roar" east of the Cascades. "This section of the country has not been stingy about its power," Woods protested, "but . . . there is too much of the power now going out." Even more would be lost under a valley administration subject to the dictates of officials in the nation's capital. The Columbia River "will be turned over to the people of California," Rufus warned. "That would leave us as a way station here in the state of Washington."[54]

There was "a growing fear of this Columbia Valley Authority out here," Woods informed Walt Horan in January 1949, "due largely to . . . the threat of taking the power out of the Columbia into the other states." Because Washington's future depended upon exploitation of the cheap energy within its borders, he told Senator Magnuson, "we should not turn over our patrimony . . . to be shipped elsewhere." Rufus nonetheless bemoaned the failure of critics to "distinguish . . . one kind of a C.V.A. from another kind." The Northwest needed a workable authority to free it from the "stooges of selfish organizations" and to "permit steady construction dam by dam as needed." The essential aim, for Woods, remained the securing of "government help to go ahead with our river development without TURNING OVER FOR ALL TIME THE IMPERIAL COLUMBIA." The proper methodology was genuine regional management of the river, giving paramount consideration to the needs of residents. For the moment, unfortunately, political conflict between those favoring rigid federalization and those defending the muddled status quo prevented approval of a CVA in any form.[55]

One means of securing steady development in lieu of the CVA arose as the result of unexpected bureaucratic initiative. The Corps of Engineers and the Bureau of Reclamation continued to work at cross-purposes. Completed in draft form in 1948, the Corps' 531 Report presented a main control plan for the Columbia, with no role for reclamation. The Bureau Blue Book, meanwhile, detailed a series of projects to be funded under a "pooling plan." Interest applied to repayment of power costs on federal dams, agency engineers argued, ought to be used as a direct subsidy for irrigation. The idea was well-received in North Central Washington, where Rufus Woods and friends saw the built-in subsidies as the first step toward sustained dam building, each project financing the next in line. "We wouldn't have to ask for anything," Kirby Billingsley pointed out in an early assessment of the advantages to be attained under a sustained growth system.[56]

Despite the conflicting focus of the two reports, intense negotiations began for interagency peace. "As a result of all this CVA talk," Billingsley wrote from Washington in March 1949, "the Army and [the] Bureau appear on the verge of getting together in a way which would mean much to us." The agreement, announced in April, apportioned responsibility for all proposed dams in the Columbia Basin, depending upon whether irrigation, flood control, or navigation was the principal complement to power generation. The Army also endorsed the "pooling plan" concept and agreed to incorporate the Bureau Blue Book in the final draft of the 531 Report. The arrangement, charged Henry Jackson, was a "shotgun wedding," forced upon bitter rivals whose hatred for one another was exceeded only by common fear of the CVA. Slapdash in nature, the "division of territory" created a new opportunity for securing regional independence.[57]

Bills introduced in June 1949 by Warren Magnuson in the Senate and by Tacoma Republican Thor Tollefson in the House authorized construction of the multipurpose projects specified in the Army-Bureau accord. This comprehensive plan adopted the "pooling" approach in the form of a basin account. "The objective towards which we have all been working for years," Billingsley wired Woods from Washington, "is almost in our grasp." Together, the comprehensive plan and the basin account insured sustained economic growth. "The more power development there is in a region the greater the interest on power . . .," Billingsley explained, "and there is so much power . . . in the Columbia watershed, present and future, that it will take care of all future irrigation." Dams and reclamation works would be self-financing, protected from private utilities and obstructionist politicians.[58]

Introduced with considerable fanfare, the legislation provoked an unexpectedly hostile opposition. Republicans immediately attempted to delete the basin account feature. Farm organizations, still preoccupied with visions of unending agricultural surplus, also fought the provision. Some members of the Columbia Basin Commission thought that Washington power should finance only projects within the state. "At various times," Magnuson wrote Woods in March 1950, "the Plan has been either dead or badly mutilated." Billingsley spent months in the East, trying to hold support together for the measure as originally conceived. "We *cannot* be for the Comprehensive Plan without being for the basin account," he argued. Most of the projects were simply "not feasible" without the "hundreds and hundreds of millions of dollars" collectively available in the projected subsidies. By summer, unfortunately, Congress was preoccupied with the outbreak of the Korean War and with the sudden controversy over the communists-in-government charges made by Senator Joe McCarthy. Any chance of the bill securing a favorable hearing, much less a majority vote, vanished amidst overseas crisis and domestic political upheaval.[59]

Unsuccessful in Congress, individuals and organizations seeking independence from outside forces made significant progress at the state level. The belief that private utilities could not keep up with the rising demand for electricity had given new impetus to Washington's public power movement during the war. Public utility districts actually took over the holdings of the Washington Water Power Company in Grant and Okanogan counties.

Puget Sound Power & Light Company rejected a complex 1944 arrangement under which the company's properties would be sold to, and apportioned among, Seattle City Light, several utility districts, and the federal government. The defeat of Referendum 25 in the fall election—which would have authorized cooperative purchases of private companies—was a blow to future ventures in cooperative purchasing. The resourceful New York financier Guy Myers responded, however, with a $135 million plan for the acquisition of Puget by the Skagit County Public Utility District.[60]

Woods believed that the private utilities operated on borrowed time. "I suspect it will be all public power in this State within the next few months," he noted in January 1945, "which is as it should be." Rufus denied that the utility districts were engaged in either socialism or in extortion, even when condemning property. They were, in fact, merely "RETRIEVING THE POWER BUSINESS back into the hands of the people of the state." Stockholders, moreover, received a fair price for their holdings. Endorsing the Myers plan and defending the financier against charges of taking exorbitant commissions, Woods expressed a single caveat: any transaction involving Puget must, sooner or later, involve the transfer of Rock Island Dam to the Chelan County PUD. "It is right at our door without [the need for] expensive transmission lines," he pointed out, and could be easily expanded to support Wenatchee industry. "Under no circumstances," asserted Rufus, "should this [dam] go into the hands of those outside this community."[61]

Considering their frequent complaints about the unfair competition of public power, the utilities "should be happy" to be "relieved of all these burdens," quipped Clarence Dill. The industry nonetheless mounted a legal challenge to the Myers scheme. The state supreme court devoted several months in 1947 to a muddled and controversial handling of the appeal of a circuit court decision affirming the legality of the Skagit takeover. Justice Matthew Hill, who had organized the anti-Referendum 25 campaign in 1944, prepared a draft opinion overturning the ruling, but the vote was a four-four tie. The ninth jurist, William Millard, hesitated for weeks before casting the decisive tally negating the acquisition of Puget. Outraged by the entire episode, Woods suggested that Hill must have taken a bribe and, building upon earlier allegations by the *Seattle Post-Intelligencer*, published a *World* series exposing Millard's connections with gambling interests.[62]

Suspicious behavior on the part of certain supreme court justices forced new strategies upon the advocates of public power. Myers devised a grandiose proposal for the purchase of both Puget and Washington Water Power. Rufus, meanwhile, focused on obtaining Rock Island for the Chelan County PUD, thwarting in the process designs on the dam by Seattle City Light. As a result of ineffective corporate management, he charged, the plant's current capacity was only 80,000 kilowatts. Under local control, however, financing was available through Myers for installing six 20,000 kilowatt generators. This addition to the Rock Island output, argued Woods, was crucial to the prevention of "a BROWNOUT or a COMPLETE BLACK-OUT OF THE POWER POOL."[63]

Legislation allowing joint public utility district purchases passed the state house of representatives in 1949, but was bottled up in a senate committee controlled by Spokane Republicans. "Connivance and smooth dealing and underground politics" were to blame, exclaimed a furious Woods. With Kirby Billingsley in tow, Rufus spent several days in Olympia, working on a replacement bill with Governor Langlie and with sister-in-law Eva Anderson, a member of the house. Their "three-way" power measure, signed by Langlie, made possible the PUD takeover of Rock Island. The action regained "SOME LOCAL CONTROL of this Majestic Columbia," observed Woods of the triumph for Wenatchee. Confounding the expectations of public power advocates, however, Puget and Washington Water Power survived in truncated form. Washington was left with a multi-party energy system, composed of private plants, PUD facilities, the municipal operations of Seattle and Tacoma, and federal dams—all linked by the BPA.[64]

Since Ralph's death, Rufus had paid increasing attention to questions of his own mortality. Frequent medical consultations revealed a series of disturbing signs. Woods, substantially overweight, learned that he too suffered from diabetes, albeit in relatively mild form. Cataracts obstructed his eyesight. Under doctor's orders he gave up sweets, cut back on meat and starch, and dropped fifteen pounds. Although Rufus arranged for the handling of the *World* upon his death, he saw no reason to reduce the hours spent at the office. "Regarding the pace that I have been going," Woods informed a friend, "it has been so enjoyable that I did not realize that I was going any pace."[65]

After a late evening at work in January 1950, Rufus retired for the night, only to be awakened at 3:30 in the morning by intense pain surging through his chest and down both arms. The sensation was "like a streak of lightning." Summoned to the house, a doctor stabilized Woods before sending him to the hospital in an ambulance. Though only partially conscious, Rufus was typically curious about the various aspects of this new and life-threatening experience. From the medical staff, he learned that "about 40% of those who get a blood clot finish off then and there," a statistical fact that left him "thankful" for being in the 60 percent survivor category.[66]

Rufus spent four weeks in the hospital, claiming to be "just as comfortable as a bug on a rug." Returning home at the end of February, he endured another month of recuperation, mostly on a library couch with a Dictaphone and a pile of books close at hand. In early April, the patient was allowed to spend an hour a day at the *World*, walking downhill to the office and riding back in a car. Incapable of continuing at an invalid's pace, Woods resumed his usual frenetic schedule at the earliest possible moment. "The old hoss . . . has been in the stable now for about three months," he announced upon the restart of his daily column, but was once again "feeling like a colt." In mid-May, Rufus joined President Truman and Governor Langlie in officially dedicating Grand Coulee Dam. The great structure had been "born out of a terrific battle of politics," he reminded readers of the *World* in reflecting upon the long-delayed ceremony, a battle that "still goes on."[67]

Searching, as always, for the best means of protecting North Central Washington, Rufus, accompanied by wife Mary and son Wilfred, headed east after the Grand Coulee dedication to study and report upon power in the Canadian province of Ontario. Founded in 1906, the provincial Hydro Electric Commission financed energy development and avoided the postage stamp philosophy of the BPA by charging "what it actually costs to transport the power to . . . different communities." After taking delivery of a new automobile in Michigan, the travelers crossed into Canada, visiting Windsor and London before arriving in Toronto on May 28. That evening, Rufus was felled by a heart attack while crossing the street in front of his hotel. During the night, he regaled nurses with stories of the faraway Columbia River. Another attack occurred at 6:15 in the morning and a half hour later Rufus Woods died, a dozen days past his seventy-second birthday.[68]

That afternoon, the Monday *Wenatchee Daily World* appeared with its front page bordered in black. The headline "PUBLISHER RUFUS WOODS DIES" and the accompanying photograph of Rufus posed before Grand Coulee Dam violated a "standing rule" that his name and picture never appear in the paper. Referring to the mission to Ontario, the obituary observed that Woods had "died . . . as he had lived, in the main current of power development." Rufus was "both a stable landmark of the past and a youthful proponent of the future." In his lifetime, Wenatchee had advanced from a gathering of shacks to the status of a thriving small city, the center of an apple empire. The Columbia River, once fearsome and free-flowing, lay contained behind barriers of concrete, its energy made into aluminum and airplanes and its water about to moisten an arid land. Taking over as publisher of the *World*, Wilfred Woods penned a personal and perceptive epitaph: "The wilderness transformed! Glorious opportunities ahead!"[69]

Rufus Woods, said the *Spokane Spokesman-Review*, was "a man of vision . . . and a man of action." Remaining true to "old and trusted ideals"—individual initiative, hard work, public spirit—he was also "unafraid of new ideas." A personality built upon the traditional American foundation of the family farm and the small town was open to the transformed America of industry and urbanization. Woods was best understood, wrote Kirby Billingsley, as a lifelong "progressive in every way," as a "Bull Mooser" following in the giant footsteps of Theodore Roosevelt. In the early days of Wenatchee, he utilized what John Gellatly called the "institutional megaphone" of the *World* to fight Eastern corporations and Olympia politicians intent upon restricting the economic advancement of North Central Washington. Campaigns for direct democracy, for lower railroad rates, and for Miles Poindexter were meant to release pent-up energies and allow the upper Columbia country to realize the full potential of abundant orchards and imperial rivers.[70]

Progressivism also drove the fight for Grand Coulee Dam and for the Columbia Basin Project. Theodore Roosevelt-style conservation demanded the efficient use of natural resources in the general interest of society. "It is better than any oil belt, better than any coal field or any gas field," Rufus claimed of the Columbia. "For this gigantic producer of both wealth and happiness will be running along here for 10,000 years and a lot more." Government-financed dams served the public first, without regard to distant management and anonymous stockholders. "This program," the *World* exclaimed in a summation of the Woods development creed, "is of, by and for the people." Properly utilized, the Columbia guaranteed regional independence, protecting Wenatchee and its hinterland from outside corporations and bureaucratic agencies. What Rufus termed the "dove-tailing" of industry and agriculture provided local markets for farmers in the reclaimed Big Bend and promoted the self-sufficiency of North Central Washington.[71]

Woods found obvious meaning for his home region in the aphorism that "the destinies of the nations have been written by the rivers." Destiny, though, must be helped along, especially when the obstacles were many and the opposition well-financed. Rufus also believed in a dictum he attributed to the Republican Roosevelt: "It is all very well to be good, but organized goodness is the thing that counts." With respect to development of the Columbia, Woods reminded those inclined to think only in terms of sound ideas and pure intentions that "things have been made to happen."[72]

The Dam University had assembled to support Grand Coulee and it remained united behind—despite latter day personality clashes—Columbia Basin reclamation, Foster Creek, and other projects essential to regional progress. Considerable time and emotion has been wasted in attempting to single out one individual, be it Billy Clapp, Rufus Woods, Jim O'Sullivan, or Clarence Dill, as the "father" of Grand Coulee Dam. The truth is that the project was built only through the collective efforts of these individuals, joined at various points by the likes of Willis Batcheller, Wesley Jones, Major John Butler, Albert Goss, Franklin Roosevelt, and Sam Hill.

Still, Rufus Woods deserves the credit he has received for his role in promoting the dam. There was no need for a statue of Woods, maintained original Dam University member Gale Matthews, since Grand Coulee "will . . . for ages to come be a living memorial to his . . . unceasing labors." By 1950, the coulee project was a phenomenal success, work was under way on Chief Joseph, and settlers on the Columbia Basin Project would soon have water. Woods nonetheless died knowing that his crusade had been frustrated in a fundamental way, that the fight for Grand Coulee had, at least for the moment, resulted in disappointment. "The Battle for the Columbia has only just begun," he remonstrated in March 1949. The problem "now looking us in the eye here in central Washington," Rufus elaborated, "is how to get the power that we need, even though we live in the very center of the power belt of America."[73] Grand Coulee, after all, was supposed to promote local interests through the expansion of agriculture and the introduction of large-scale industry. Unforeseen factors, however, brought a loss of local autonomy. Federal financing, the BPA postage stamp rate and transmission network, and the Second World War perpetuated Wenatchee's subjection to outside economic and political forces. Electricity became, like big red apples, a prime North Central Washington export, produced at home and consumed at a distance.

Rufus Woods died, but the Columbia River continued to be a major factor in the political and economic life of the Pacific Northwest. Under the direction of Wilfred Woods, the *Wenatchee World* persisted in advocating the utilization of the stream for energy and irrigation. By the early 1960s, the development scheme originally presented in the 308 Report was, for all practical purposes, fully implemented. In addition to completing the Chief Joseph and McNary projects, the Corps of Engineers constructed John Day and The Dalles dams. The Grant County PUD developed the Priest Rapids and Wanapum sites. Further upstream, the Chelan County and Douglas County public utility districts built, respectively, the Rocky Reach and Wells dams. The Columbia, in a profound environmental irony, flowed in some approximation of its natural state only in the stretch adjacent to Hanford, where fear of "adverse effects" upon the nuclear reservation prevented the Army from building the high Ben Franklin dam near Richland.[74] The Columbia Basin Project, meanwhile, was a dream partially fulfilled, with slightly in excess of 550,000 acres under irrigation, substantially less than the acreage contemplated under the 1918 pumping proposal. Much remained to be done, Rufus would have said. Yet the increasing complexity of public affairs in the late twentieth century, most notably the rise of a regional environmental movement focused upon the negative impact of dam construction, prevented further work along the Rufus Woods line. Left outside the orbit of industrialization, Wenatchee, albeit somewhat larger in population, was still the pleasant apple-producing center of earlier times, still the place where the river met the rails.

Rufus Woods typically spoke with great enthusiasm about the need to dam the Columbia River.

Wenatchee initially prospered as the place where the river met the rails. *Upper left:* The steamboat landing on the Columbia River. *Lower left:* Great Northern Railway bridge under construction at Rock Island, early 1890s. *Above:* A self-confident Rufus Woods on his first newspaper job with the *Republic* in his new hometown of Wenatchee.

Identical twins Rufus and Ralph Woods were, except for contrasting hat styles, difficult to tell apart.

*Above:* The first office of the *Wenatchee Daily World.* *Below:* Once he took over the paper, Woods organized a large contingent of delivery boys to insure prompt service for *Daily World* subscribers.

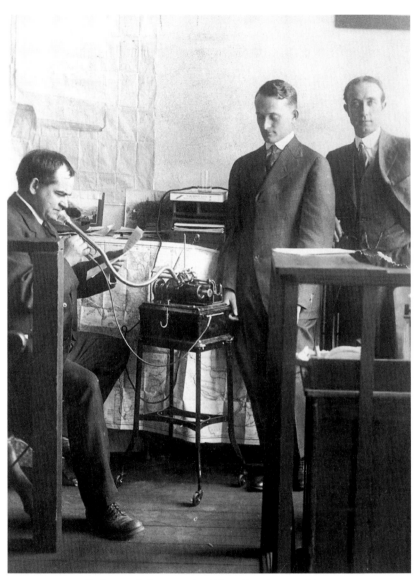
Rufus, on left, at work with a dictating machine.

*Above:* Woods poses in front of the *World*'s "traveling office," used in his tours of north central Washington. *Below:* Rufus, an early aviation enthusiast, sits in the cockpit on the left.

Woods with Billy Clapp, the originator of the Grand Coulee Dam idea.

Rufus and Mary Woods pose with pipe-smoking James O'Sullivan, the fervent lobbyist for Grand Coulee Dam.

*Above:* Government surveyors at work at the Grand Coulee damsite. *Below:* Senator Clarence C. Dill breaks ground for Grand Coulee, July 1933. Courtesy Eastern Washington State Historical Society.

*Above:* Governor Clarence D. Martin, shown when the railroad to Grand Coulee Dam was completed and turned over to MWAK, 1935. *K.S. Brown photograph, courtesy Eastern Washington State Historical Society, #L84-286.185. Below:* Franklin Roosevelt addresses a crowd on one of his two trips to Grand Coulee.

Rufus, with fellow Dam University members W. Gale Matthews and Billy Clapp, on a winter visit to Grand Coulee.

Woods posed before the Grand Coulee spillway.

*Left:* A middle-aged Rufus Woods, on the right, escapes from the daily routine by running away with the circus. *Above:* Woods, here shown in a publicity photo "logging," solved a post-World War II newsprint shortage by purchasing a tract of timber in the Cascades.

The distinguished newspaperman Rufus Woods near the close of his long career in Wenatchee.

# Endnotes

## Endnote Abbreviations

*ARCE—Annual Report of the Chief of Engineers*
Batcheller Papers—Papers of Willis T. Batcheller, University of Washington
Billingsley Papers—Papers of Kirby Billingsley, North Central Washington Museum, Wenatchee
BR19-29—Bureau of Reclamation Project Files, 1919-1929, RG 115, National Archives
BR30-45—Bureau of Reclamation Project Files, 1930-1945, RG 115, National Archives
Burke Papers—Papers of Thomas Burke, University of Washington
CBC—Columbia Basin Commission Records, Washington State Archives
CBIAC—Columbia Basin Inter-Agency Committee Records, University of Washington Library
CBSC—Columbia Basin Survey Commission Records, Washington State Archives
Chittenden Misc.—Collection of H.M. Chittenden, University of Washington
DC—Department of Conservation Records, Washington State Archives
DI07-36—Department of the Interior Records, Office of the Secretary, 1907-1936, RG 48, National Archives
Gill Papers—Papers of Roy Gill, Washington State University
Hartley Papers—Papers of Roland H. Hartley, Washington State Archives
Hoover Letters—Letters of Herbert Hoover, Washington State University
Horan Papers—Papers of Walter Horan, Washington State University
Jackson House Papers—Papers of Henry M. Jackson while he was a member of the U.S. House of Representatives, University of Washington
Johnson Papers—Papers of Lon Johnson, Washington State University
Jones Papers—Papers of Wesley L. Jones, University of Washington
JOS—James O'Sullivan
KB—Kirby Billingsley
Langlie Papers—Papers of Arthur Langlie, University of Washington
Magnuson House Papers—Papers of Warren G. Magnuson while he was a member of the U.S. House of Representatives, University of Washington
Magnuson Senate Papers—Papers of Warren G. Magnuson while he was a member of the U.S. Senate, University of Washington
Martin Papers—Papers of Clarence D. Martin, Washington State University
May Papers—Papers of Catherine May, Washington State University
Mires Papers—Papers of Austin Mires, Washington State University
Mitchell Papers—Papers of Hugh B. Mitchell, University of Washington
Myers Papers—Papers of Guy C. Myers, University of Washington
NPD—North Pacific Division Records, U.S. Army Corps of Engineers, RG 77, Federal Records Center, Seattle

NRPB—National Resources Planning Board Records, RG 187, Federal Records Center, Seattle

OCE1943—Records of the Office of Chief of Engineers, 1943, Washington National Records Center, Suitland, Maryland

O'Sullivan Papers—Papers of James O'Sullivan, Gonzaga University Library, Spokane

*PHR—Pacific Historical Review*

*PNQ—Pacific Northwest Quarterly*

Poindexter Papers—Papers of Miles Poindexter, University of Washington

Reed Papers—Papers of Mark E. Reed, University of Washington

RG—Record group

RH—Rivers and Harbors Files, Records of the Office of the Chief of Engineers, 1923-1942, RG 77, National Archives

RW—Rufus Woods

SD—Seattle District Records, U.S. Army Corps of Engineers, RG 77, Federal Records Center, Seattle

SDOACE—Seattle District Office, U.S. Army Corps of Engineers

SLD—Seattle Lighting Department Records, University of Washington Library

UW—University of Washington Library, Seattle

Waller Papers—Papers of O.L. Waller, Washington State University

*WDW—Wenatchee Daily World*

Warren Woods Letters—Letters in the possession of Bob Woods, Wenatchee

Woods Diary—Diary of Rufus Woods, *Wenatchee World,* Wenatchee

Woods Papers—Papers of Rufus Woods, *Wenatchee World*, Wenatchee

*WR—Wenatchee Republic*

WSU—Washington State University Library, Pullman

## Notes for Introduction

1. *WDW,* July 2, 1943; May 21; June 27, 1946; Dec. 14, 1948; June 15; Aug. 1, 1949.
2. RW to Richard L. Neuberger, May 9, 1939; to Richard F. Sullivan, May 21, 1935; Fred Berry to RW, Aug. 6, 1941, all Woods Papers; *WDW,* Jan. 5, 6, 1948; Feb. 7, 1949.
3. *WDW,* Dec. 1, 1941; Jan. 1; July 3, 1946; May 4, 1949.
4. *WDW,* Nov. 8, 1941; July 4, 1942; May 4; Dec. 22, 1943; Oct. 29, 1946; June 30, 1949; RW to Co-Workers, Nov. 1944, Woods Papers.
5. RW to Ken Randall, May 15, 1948; to Editor, Yakima Republic, April 12, 1948, Woods Papers; *WDW,* Oct. 29, 1946.
6. *WDW,* Jan. 26, 1948; Nov. 23, 1949; RW to Geo. E. Johnson, Nov. 9, 1944, Woods Papers.
7. *WDW,* May 20, 1943; Feb. 1, 4; May 22; June 19, 1946; Feb. 21, 1948; F. W. Graham to RW, July 24, 1917, Woods Papers.
8. RW to Charles E. Cone, Oct. 22, 1947; to Neuberger, Jan. 11, 1946, Woods Papers.
9. *WDW,* Aug. 5, 1944; Sept. 27, 1946; Jan. 3, 1947; April 25, 1948; April 13, 1949; RW to Frank Sefrit, July 13, 1933; Address to County Commissioners, 1933, both Woods Papers.
10. *WDW,* Jan. 11; Feb. 10; April 1, 1949. The history of the struggle to secure Grand Coulee provides a useful corrective to Donald Worster's "hydraulic West" interpretation. According to Worster, reclamation was, and is, the work of government officials and Eastern corporations intent upon subjecting the West to the control of distant bureaucrats and outside capital. Irrigation destroyed, rather than encouraged, local autonomy through "a new concentration of economic, social, and political power,"

through the creation of "Leviathan in the desert." The Worster theory assumes a certain degree of validity with respect to the outcome of the Grand Coulee fight, although that outcome was more the product of uncoordinated developments than of malevolent design. See Donald Worster, *Rivers of Empire: Water, Aridity, and the Growth of the American West* (New York: Pantheon Books, 1985) and "New West, True West: Interpreting the Region's History," *Western Historical Quarterly*, 18(1987), 151-156.

11. *WDW*, Feb. 13, 1946.
12. RW to Hugh R. Fraser, April 2, 1934; to Sullivan, May 21, 1935; to Mr. and Mrs. Walt Horan, April 23, 1945, Woods Papers; *WDW*, Feb. 4, 1946; Feb. 27, 1947; July 19, 1949.

## Notes for Prologue

1. Paul Kane, *Wanderings of an Artist among the Indians of North America* (Toronto: The Radisson Society of Canada, 1925), 202, 205, 208-209.
2. Bates McKee, *Cascadia: The Geologic Evolution of the Pacific Northwest* (New York: McGraw Hill Book Company, 1972), 271, 283-287.
3. Kane, *Wanderings of an Artist*, 209-210.
4. *Ibid.*, 210-211; Thomas W. Symons, "Report of an Examination of the Upper Columbia River," Senate Ex. Doc. No. 186, 47th Cong., 1st sess., 32. For detailed accounts of river travel ignoring Grand Coulee, see William Denison Lyman, *The Columbia River* (New York: G.P. Putnam's Sons, 1918), 308-309; M. J. Lorraine, *The Columbia Unveiled* (Los Angeles: The Times-Mirror Press, 1924), 268-282.

## Notes for Chapter One

1. *WDW*, March 2, 1932.
2. James C. Olson, *History of Nebraska* (Lincoln: University of Nebraska Press, 1955), 161, 167, 170-172, 177-180.
3. Lebbeus's father, Jacob Woods, was a member of the first American generation of the Woods family. Mary's grandfather was born in Germany and came to the United States in 1801 at the age of 25. Except where otherwise noted, details on the background and Nebraska experiences of the Woods clan are taken from Willa Woods Hiltner and Kathryn Woods Haley, eds., *The Woods Family: Colonial Times to 1979* (Wenatchee: The Wenatchee World, 1979).
4. RW to Emma Crane, Oct. 8, 1948, Woods Papers; *WDW*, May 18, 1922; Dec. 6, 1941; Aug. 30, 1943; Jan. 11, 1947; Willa Woods Hiltner and Kathryn Woods Haley, eds., *The Greenslit Family* (Wenatchee: The Wenatchee World, 1981), 156, 167.
5. *WDW*, Dec. 4, 1923; March 18, 1930; March 2, 1932; Dec. 28, 1938; RW to James E. Lawrence, Dec. 20, 1948, Woods Papers.
6. *WDW*, March 12, 1932; Dec. 7, 1936.
7. *WDW*, Oct. 24; Dec. 27, 1933; March 2, 5, 1932; Aug. 27, 1943.
8. RW to E. Johnson, June 2, 1947, Woods Papers; *WDW*, Jan. 1, 1924; June 22, 1931; Aug. 25, 1943; Olson, *History of Nebraska*, 12-13, 216.
9. Roscoe Pound, in later years dean of the Harvard law school, was a classmate. Woods Diary, Oct. 2, 1910; *WDW*, Jan. 1, 1924; RW to Alfaretta Baker, May 15, 1939; Commencement Address at Grand Coulee, May 28, 1945, both Woods Papers.
10. Woods Diary, Oct. 2, 1910; *WDW*, Oct. 5, 1909; March 8, 1932; July 8, 1938; Feb. 6, 1946; RW to Crane, Oct. 8, 1948, Woods Papers.

11. Robert W. Cherny, *Populism, Progressivism, and the Transformation of Nebraska Politics, 1885-1915* (Lincoln: University of Nebraska Press, 1981), 13-26, 71-73, 161-165; Eva Greenslit Anderson, "Background of Willa Cather's Novels" (M.A. thesis, University of Washington, 1926), 50-51.
12. *WDW*, Nov. 23, 1908; July 10, 1946; RW to Frank Yama, Dec. 5, 1944, Woods Papers.
13. Woods Diary, Oct. 2, 1910; *WDW*, March 1, 5, 10, 1932; Aug. 15, 1934.
14. *WDW*, Aug. 4, 1923; March 7, 1932; July 9, 1937; Dec. 7, 1938; May 20, 1946.
15. The upper Yukon River, including Dawson and the Klondike goldfields, was Canadian territory. *WDW*, March 8, 9, 11, 1932; Aug. 15, 1934; Bruce Mitchell, *The Story of Rufus Woods and the Development of Central Washington* (Wenatchee: The Wenatchee World, 1965), 3.
16. *WDW*, Oct. 4, 1909; March 8, 9, 11, 1932; Aug. 16, 1934; Sept. 28, 1936; Dec. 27, 1939.
17. The brothers spent much of their time at Vashon College digging potatoes in fields belonging to the institution's president. Woods Diary, Oct. 2, 1910; *WDW*, March 8, 10, 12, 1932.
18. *WDW*, Aug. 5, 1909; Jan. 10, 1941.
19. Mitchell, *Story of Rufus Woods*, 3; Woods Diary, Oct. 2, 1910; *WDW*, Jan. 31, 1910; Feb. 23, 1912; March 8, 1932; Aug. 22, 1935.
20. Mitchell, *Story of Rufus Woods*, 3; *WDW*, March 7, 1907; March 1, 10, 11, 1932; Oct. 3, 1943; RW to Mr. and Mrs. Arthur M. Storch, Jan. 21, 1949; to Corwin Shank, March 10, 1949, Woods Papers.

## Notes for Chapter Two

1. July 31, 1908.
2. RW to Mr. and Mrs. Storch, Jan. 21, 1949, Woods Papers. For the reports on Rock Island Rapids, see W. A. Jones to Thomas L. Casey, Oct. 15, 1888; Feb. 15, 1890; J.C. Ensign to Thomas Handbury, Dec. 24, 1889; Handbury to Casey, Dec. 31, 1889, all in *ARCE*, 1890, 3065-3069, 3071; *ARCE*, 1891, 3224-3225.
3. *WDW*, March 18, 1932; July 3, 1935; RW to D.A. Raymond, Oct. 28, 1948, Woods Papers. Also see John Gellatly, *A History of Wenatchee: The Apple Capital of the World* (Wenatchee: Wenatchee Bindery & Printing Co., 1962), 33.
4. Ensign to Handbury, Dec. 24, 1889, in *ARCE*, 1890, 3068-3069; Randall V. Mills, *Stern-Wheelers Up Columbia: A Century of Steamboating in the Oregon Country* (Palo Alto, Cal.: Pacific Books, 1947), 91. On the settlement of the Big Bend, see D. W. Meinig, *The Great Columbia Plain: A Historical Geography, 1805-1910* (Seattle: University of Washington Press, 1968), 334-340. Railroad construction is treated in Robert C. Nesbit, *"He Built Seattle": A Biography of Judge Thomas Burke* (Seattle: University of Washington Press, 1961), chpt. 6. There is a good summary in Bruce Mitchell, *By River, Trail and Rail: A Brief History of the First Century of Transportation in North Central Washington, 1811 to 1911* (Wenatchee: The Wenatchee World, 1968), 21-22.
5. Symons, "Report of an Examination," 53; Gellatly, *History of Wenatchee*, 18-20; *WDW*, June 16, 1933; Dec. 2, 1938; Nesbit, *"He Built Seattle,"* 141; Mitchell, *Story of Rufus Woods*, 3, and *By River, Trail and Rail*, 21-23; Theo. N. Haller to Thomas Burke, April 10, 1891; Wm. P. Watson to Burke, April 5; May 9, 23, 27, 28, 1892; Morgan Carkeek to Burke, May 30; July 6, 1892; Don C. Corbett to Burke, June 10, 1892; A. L. Moore to Burke, July 12, 1892; Arthur Gunn to Burke, Nov. 30, 1901, all Burke Papers.

6. Mills, *Stern-Wheelers Up Columbia*, 91-92; Meinig, *Great Columbia Plain*, 373-374; Mitchell, *By River, Trail and Rail*, 25-26; *WDW*, March 19, 1932; Aug. 8, 1938; Aug. 18, 1939; Sept. 8, 1943.

7. Gellatly, *History of Wenatchee*, 31-34; *WDW*, March 25, 1908; Feb. 20, 1940; Feb. 15, 1943; Otis W. Freeman, "Apple Industry of the Wenatchee Area," *Economic Geography*, 10(1934), 160-162; G.H. Miller and S.M. Thomson, *The Cost of Producing Apples in the Wenatchee Valley, Washington*, USDA Bulletin No. 446 (Washington, D.C.: Government Printing Office, 1917), 4.

8. W. H. Willis to Burke, Sept. 7, 1894; Gunn to Burke, April 7, 1902; Sept. 14, 1903, all Burke Papers; Bruce Mitchell, *Flowing Wealth: The Story of Water Resource Development in North Central Washington, 1870-1950* (Wenatchee: The Wenatchee World, 1967), 9-10; Gellatly, *History of Wenatchee*, 41-52; Freeman, "Apple Industry," 162-163; John Fahey, *Inland Empire: Unfolding Years, 1879-1929* (Seattle: University of Washington Press, 1986), 96-97; *Wenatchee Advance*, May 31, 1902.

9. The Wenatchee District statistical area includes the valley proper and satellite fruit regions along the upper Columbia and the Okanogan River. Miller and Thomson, *Cost of Producing Apples*, 5-6, 8, 34; Freeman, "Apple Industry," 160-161, 167; *WDW*, July 25, 1939; Dec. 22, 1942; Harold H. Maynard, *Marketing Northwestern Apples* (New York: The Ronald Press Company, 1923), 2, 4-5, 9. Of the 2,200 Chelan County farms in operation during the 1920s, slightly over 1,900 were apple orchards.

10. *WDW*, Feb. 3, 1922; March 18, 26, 29; April 14, 1932; Sept. 11, 1935; Feb. 1, 1938; Mitchell, *Flowing Wealth*, 12-13.

11. After selling the *Advance*, Frank Reeves became Wenatchee's leading lawyer. Belle Reeves served for years in the state legislature and then as Washington's secretary of state. *WDW*, Jan. 5, 1906; Aug. 12, 1932; Feb. 1, 1941; Feb. 15; July 3, 1943; Aug. 15, 1944; March 3, 1947; Jan. 3, 1948; Mitchell, *Story of Rufus Woods*, 3; Gellatly, *History of Wenatchee*, 108; RW to Mr. and Mrs. Storch, Jan. 21, 1949, Woods Papers.

12. RW to Edwin Shannon, Nov. 12, 1947; to Mr. and Mrs. Storch, Jan. 21, 1949; to Jack Jett, Nov. 27, 1944, Woods Papers; *WDW*, March 14, 22, 30; April 25, 1932; Nov. 8, 1939; May 6, 1940; Feb. 1, 1941; Jan. 9, 1943; Nov. 13, 1944; March 3, 1947.

13. *WR*, Feb. 2, 9, 16, 23; March 9; April 6; Oct. 26, 1905.

14. Chelan and Kittitas counties shared a single senatorial seat. *WR*, Feb. 16, 23; March 2, 1905; *WDW*, March 14, 1932.

15. The first issue of the *Daily World* appeared on July 3, 1905. *WDW*, March 1, 15; April 2, 1932; July 3, 1935; July 5, 1938; July 3, 1943; Gellatly, *History of Wenatchee*, 109; Charles C. Kerr, *The World of the World: From Frontier to Community, 1905-1980* (Wenatchee: The Wenatchee World, 1980), 20-21.

16. *WDW*, March 14, 1932; Woods Diary, Oct. 2, 1910; RW to C. L. Adams, Jan. 20, 1913, Woods Papers.

17. Romine to JOS, Dec. 23, 1931, O'Sullivan Papers.

18. *WDW*, Nov. 1; Dec. 18, 19, 22, 27, 1905; Jan. 6, 9, 12; Feb. 3, March 13, 15; April 13, 1906; March 30, 1932; March 3, 1947; *WR*, Feb. 9, 1905; Feb. 15, 1906; Gellatly, *History of Wenatchee*, 177. See also Norman H. Clark, *The Dry Years: Prohibition and Social Change in Washington* (Seattle: University of Washington Press, rev. ed., 1988, 1965), 34, 59.

19. *WR*, Feb. 16, 1905; *WDW*, March 30; April 21, 1932; Oct. 7; Nov. 4, 1935; Jan. 28; May 20, 1943; July 6, 1946; Jan. 15, 1948; Gellatly, *History of Wenatchee*, 177-178; Mitchell, *By River, Trail and Rail*, 28-29.

20. RW to T.F. Lewis, June 29, 1909; to W.E. Boston, Sept. 19, 1908; to Clyde C. Green, July 15, 1909; to James Everington, Sr., March 12; April 2; May 24; July 17; Sept. 21; Dec. 6, 1909; Sept. 15, 1910; to Kate Greenslit, July 6, 1912, Woods Papers.

21. On one occasion, Rufus stumbled into a camp of horse thieves who mistook him, with near fatal consequences, for a prowling federal marshal. *WDW*, March 19; April 7, 1932; Aug. 8, 1938; Aug. 19, 1939; March 18, 1943; Meinig, *Great Columbia Plain*, 372-373; Fahey, *Inland Empire*, 102.
22. *WDW*, April 7, 1932; Aug. 19, 1939; March 18, 1943; RW to W.D. Nichols, Feb. ? 1906 (two letters); Nichols to RW, Feb. 15; April 17, 1906, all Woods Papers.
23. *WDW*, Dec. 8, 10, 1906; July 3, 1920; Dec. 21, 1946; Gellatly, *History of Wenatchee*, 109.
24. The transaction was announced to the public as an outright sale. *WDW*, Feb. 27; March 1, 1907; Sept. 6, 1933; Feb. 6, 1940; Dec. 21, 1946; March 3, 1947; Woods Diary, Oct. 2, 1910; Mitchell, *Story of Rufus Woods*, 3.
25. *WDW*, March 1, 1907; July 3, 1935; Aug. 28, 1944; March 3, 1947; RW to Warren W. Woods, April 14, 1908, Warren Woods Letters.
26. The World Advance company continued, for several years, to publish the weekly *Advance*. RW to Frank M. Dallam, March 20; Dec. 21, 1908, Woods Papers; to W. Woods, April 14, 1908, Warren Woods Letters; *WDW*, July 9, 1907; March 15, 21, 1932; Sept. 6, 1933; March 3, 1947.
27. *WDW*, March 15, 1932; July 3, 1935; Feb. 6, 1940; July 3, 1945; Nov. 1, 1946; Woods Diary, Oct. 23, 1910.
28. *WDW*, Nov. 20; Dec. 8, 1908; Jan. 8, 1909; July 3, 1920; March 1, 1932; March 3, 1947; RW to Dallam, Dec. 30, 1908, Woods Papers.
29. Dallam first suggested that he take over as publisher, with Rufus moving to Puget Sound. Warren was the son of Uncle Isaac Woods, whose letters home from Washington state were an important factor in Rufus and Ralph visiting the Pacific Northwest in 1900. RW to W. Woods, April 1, 14, 23; May 1, 1908, Warren Woods Letters; to Dallam, Dec. 21, 1908; ? 1910; Ralph Woods to RW, July 13, 1908; Dallam to RW, Dec. 27, 1908, all Woods Papers; *WDW*, July 15, 1932.
30. Rufus Woods speech of Dec. 20, 1913 on "The Newspaper—Is Its Influence Waning?" and RW to Co-Workers, Nov. 3, 1944, both Woods Papers; *WDW*, Sept. 3, 1908; Sept. 17, 1910. On the early twentieth century Seattle newspaper situation, see Richard C. Berner, *Seattle, 1900-1920: From Boomtown, Urban Turbulence, to Restoration* (Seattle: Charles Press, 1991), 6.
31. *WDW*, June 15; Oct. 17; Dec. 20, 1907; Jan. 16; June 26; July 4, 1908; Oct. 5, 8, 23; Nov. 10, 1909; RW to Charles S. Albert, March 14, 1946, Woods Papers.
32. *WDW*, Jan. 15; March 25, 26; May 25, 1908.
33. Under the local option law, the manufacture, importation, and consumption of alcohol remained legal in "dry" jurisdictions. Clark, *Dry Years*, 90-91; *WDW*, Aug. 16, 20, 25; Sept. 1; Oct. 29, 1909; Aug. 11; Oct. 31; Nov. 4, 7, 9, 1910; Sept. 6, 1912.
34. *WDW*, March 30; April 12, 18, 25; May 9, 15; June 12, 26; Dec. 14, 1907; April 5, 20, 1908; April 19; May 26; June 10, 1909.
35. *WDW*, April 19; Sept. 7, 1907; May 2; July 3, 1908; Jan. 15; Feb. 20; Sept. 15, 1909; March 12, 1910; Mitchell, *Flowing Wealth*, 14.
36. *WDW*, June 5; Aug. 14, 1907; April 22; Nov. 20, 1908; March 11; June 26; July 13; Aug. 26; Sept. 8; Oct. 5, 1909.
37. RW to T. Lewis, July 6, 14, 1909 and undated fragment of 1909 letter; to R. M. Lewis, undated fragment of 1909 letter; to Green, July 15, 1909; to Everington, Dec. 6, 1909, Woods Papers; *WDW*, Oct. 13; Nov. 20, 27, 1908; April 19; July 7-9; Sept. 8; Oct. 21; Nov. 1, 3, 13, 1909; Oct. 9, 1910; Mitchell, *Flowing Wealth*, 14.
38. Agreement of March 11, 1909; RW to T. Lewis, April 11; June 5; July 1, 14; Sept. 8, 1909, all Woods Papers; *WDW*, Nov. 20, 1908; Oct. 16, 1909.

39. See chapter three for the political matters involved in the postmastership fight. RW to T. Lewis, April 11; June 5, 16, 17; Sept. 8, ?, 1909; to Everington, Feb. 5, 1910, Woods Papers; *WDW*, Oct. 16, 23, 1909.

40. *WDW*, Feb. 5; Aug. 10; Sept. 7; Nov. 14, 1910; March 3, 1947; RW to W. Woods, April 23, 1908, Warren Woods Letters; to Dallam, undated 1910 letter, Woods Papers; Woods Diary, Oct. 23, 1910; Mitchell, *Story of Rufus Woods*, 4.

41. *WDW*, April 11; July 25, 1907; June 18; Sept. 29; Nov. 30, 1908; Feb. 19; June 2; July 14, 1909; Jan. 21, 1910.

42. *WDW*, Feb. 5, 1908; July 14; Dec. 11, 1908; Jan. 27; May 18, 24; Oct. 14, 15, 26, 1909; Jan. 15, 20; Aug. 12, 1910; Wenatchee Commercial Club to John Millis, June 1, 1905; J.M. Clapp to F.A. Pope, Nov. 1, 1905; Hiram M. Chittenden to A.A. Mackenzie, June 12, 1907; March 31, 1908; Charles W. Kutz to Chief of Engineers, June 9, 1909, all SD; Miles Poindexter to U.S. Board of Engineers for Rivers and Harbors, July 25, 1911, Poindexter Papers; Mitchell, *By River, Trail and Rail*, 27.

43. *WDW*, Nov. 21, 1908; March 9; May 24; June 8, 30; Aug. 17; Sept. 14, 21, 22; Nov. 8, 29; Dec. 17, 1909; Jan. 19; July 28; Oct. 21; Dec. 15, 1910; Fahey, *Inland Empire*, 150-154; Meinig, *Great Columbia Plain*, 476-479; Mitchell, *By River, Trail and Rail*, 29.

44. *WDW*, April 13, 1907; Nov. 6, 1908; March 23, 1909; Jan. 25, 27; May 27; Oct. 13, 1910; Aug. 13, 1912; Maynard, *Marketing Northwestern Apples*, 5-6.

45. *WDW*, Aug. 11, 1909; Aug. 19, 1935; Feb. 17, 1938; Nov. 13, 1943. On the Yakima Project, see Calvin B. Coulter, "The Victory of National Irrigation in the Yakima Valley, 1902-1906," *PNQ*, 42(1951), 99-122. For the development of irrigation in the West and the genesis of the Reclamation Act, see Donald J. Pisani, *To Reclaim a Divided West: Water, Law, and Public Policy, 1848-1902* (Albuquerque: University of New Mexico Press, 1992).

46. A. J. Ternent to Sec. of Interior, Oct. 27, 1911; S. O. Jayne to Poindexter, Nov. 13, 1911, both Poindexter Papers; RW to O.G.F. Markhus, Dec. 13, 1937; to William Bohrnsen, Aug. 12, 1941; to S.G. Shaw, March 23, 1949; to C.T. Conover, July 5, 1949; David R. McGinnis to Emil Miller, March 4, 1943, all Woods Papers; *WDW*, April 8, 1932; Feb. 18; June 29, 1938; Aug. 19, 1939; Oct. 2, 1941; July 27, 1944; Mitchell, *Flowing Wealth*, 23.

47. Jayne to Poindexter, Nov. 13, 1911; Ternent to Sec. of Interior, Oct. 27, 1911; to Poindexter, Aug. 2, 1912; O.A. Kuck to Poindexter, April 6, 1912; Poindexter to RW, July 21, 1911, all Poindexter Papers; Wesley L. Jones to Chas. E. Myers, Jan. 29, 1919, Jones Papers; *WDW*, Jan. 10; March 8, 19; Dec. 2, 1910; April 12, 1943; Mitchell, *Flowing Wealth*, 23.

48. *WDW*, Jan. 10, 1910; March 5, 1912; F.H. Newell to Poindexter, April 25, 1913; William M. Clapp to Poindexter, Feb. 23, 1916; Poindexter to Ternent, April 18, 1913, all Poindexter Papers; to RW, March 13, 1912; RW Toast at Quincy Banquet, March 4, 1912; Jones to RW, March 15, 1912, all Woods Papers; to H. M. Thatcher, Jan. 10, 1918; to J.R. Omeora, Feb. 24, 1917; Thatcher to Jones, Jan. 4, 1918, all Jones Papers; Mitchell, *Flowing Wealth*, 23-24.

49. *WDW*, April 15; May 17; Oct. 3, 1907; Feb. 17; June 18; July 23, 1908; May 22; Aug. 6; Dec. 31, 1909; July 21, 1910.

50. *WDW*, Sept. 24, 1907; July 9; Dec. 7, 1908; March 17, 1909; Feb. 11; April 16, 1910; Oct. 11, 1941.

51. Woods Diary, Oct. 2, 1910; RW to Everington, May 24, 1909; to W.H. Greenslit, Oct. 12, 1944, Woods Papers; Hiltner and Haley, eds., *Greenslit Family*, 31-49; *WDW*, Nov. 23, 1946.

52. In the pre-air conditioning era, affluent Wenatchee residents like Gellatly spent the hot weather months on Puget Sound or in Cascades retreats. Woods Diary, Oct. 2, Nov. 11, 1910; *WDW*, July 4, 1947; Hiltner and Haley, eds., *Greenslit Family*, 278-279.

53. *WDW*, Sept. 17, 1907.

## Notes for Chapter Three

1. Aug. 5, 1912.
2. *WDW*, Dec. 25, 26, 1907; June 26; July 2, 8; Nov. 23, 1908.
3. *WDW*, April 18; Sept. 3, 1907; July 17; Aug. 18; Dec. 8, 1908; March 4, 1909; April 19; May 31; Aug. 23, 1910.
4. *WDW*, Aug. 26, 1907; June 12; July 13; Sept. 2; Dec. 11, 13, 1908; Feb. 17; March 13; Sept. 10, 1909; June 8; Aug. 16; Sept. 1, 19; Dec. 1, 1910; Feb. 19, 1913; April 13, 1914; RW to Theodore Roosevelt, Jan. ? 1912, Woods Papers.
5. DeVoto's interpretation, wrote Woods in 1935, "is quite in line with some of the things we have mentioned in the past." Bernard DeVoto, "The West: A Plundered Province," *Harpers' Magazine*, 169(1934), 355-364, and "The West Against Itself," *ibid.*, 194(1947), 1-13; *WDW*, April 2, 29; May 4, 21, 1907; Jan. 30; April 23, 1908; April 12, 1909; July 30; Aug. 12; Oct. 15, 1910; April 24; May 2; Oct. 18; Nov. 6, 1911; June 1, 1912; Aug. 7, 12, 1913; April 4, 1935; Jan. 3, 1947.
6. Miller and Thomson, *Cost of Producing Apples*, 6; *WDW*, May 24; June 8, 28, 30; Aug. 17, 1909; Jan. 23, 24; March 11, 1911; March 7; April 8; Aug. 28, 30; Dec. 31, 1912.
7. The complicated senatorial deal also involved creation of a state railroad commission, an important reform victory. *WDW*, April 2, 21; June 1, 24; July 17, 18; Aug. 21, 1908; May 7, 10, 1910; Feb. 7, 1911; Robert D. Saltvig, "The Progressive Movement in Washington" (Ph.D. diss., University of Washington, 1966), 85-87.
8. *WDW*, March 20, 1907; April 21; June 24; July 17, 1908; Jan. 7, 1909; May 12; June 7; Sept. 20; Oct. 14, 1910; Nov. 9, 1912; Saltvig, "Progressive Movement," 119-120, 126-129, 170-178; Claudius O. Johnson, "The Adoption of the Initiative and Referendum in Washington," *PNQ*, 35(1944), 291-303.
9. *WDW*, July 16, 1908; July 14; Aug. 27, 1909; Aug. 6, 1912. The "underlying principle" is quoted in Robert E. Ficken, *The Forested Land: A History of Lumbering in Western Washington* (Seattle: University of Washington Press, 1987), 125-126.
10. *WDW*, Jan. 22; April 29; Nov. 12, 18; Dec. 2, 1909; Feb. 28; July 15, 18; Aug. 13, 30; Oct. 1, 15, 20; Dec. 2, 1910; July 24; Aug. 6, 1912. Younger and better-educated than the typical Washington conservative, Woods was a perfect fit in background and status to the middle class reform profile devised in later years by historians. See William T. Kerr, Jr., "The Progressives of Washington, 1910-12," *PNQ*, 55(1964), 16-27.
11. *WDW*, June 20; July 30; Sept. 26, 1908.
12. *WDW*, April 4; June 1; July 18, 23; Sept. 2, 1908; April 2, 1932; Dec. 18, 1946; Saltvig, "Progressive Movement," 129-133; Howard W. Allen, *Poindexter of Washington: A Study in Progressive Politics* (Carbondale: Southern Illinois University Press, 1981), 14-15, 23-31.
13. *WDW*, May 20; June 12, 21; July 22, 23; Aug. 30; Sept. 27; Oct. 22; Nov. 2, 15; Dec. 1, 6, 1909; Poindexter to RW, Sept. 23, 1909, Woods Papers.
14. *WDW*, Nov. 15, 1909; April 2, 1932; Poindexter to RW, Sept. 23; Nov. 3, 15, 1909; Rufus R. Wilson to RW, Nov. 15, 1909; March 31, 1910; A. Storch to RW, Sept. 30, 1909; Chas. T. Borg to RW, Oct. 29, 1909; R. F. Holm to Jno. Greb, March 26,

1910, all Woods Papers; Allen, *Poindexter*, 49-50; Saltvig, "Progressive Movement," 149-150, 154.

15. Some Jones supporters, believing Burke to be thoroughly corrupt, ignored their leader's interest and backed Poindexter. *WDW*, July 13, 1910; July 15, 1922; April 2, 1932; W. Gale Matthews to Jones, Aug. 6, 1910; John E. Ballaine to Jones, Sept. 20, 1910, both Jones Papers; Nesbit, *"He Built Seattle,"* 413-414; Allen, *Poindexter*, 49.

16. John A. Gellatly to Jones, Dec. 18, 1909, Jones Papers; Holm to Greb, March 26, 1910, Woods Papers; M. T. Hartson to Jones, Nov. 23, 1909, quoted in Allen, *Poindexter*, 51.

17. *WDW*, May 6, 1908; *WR*, Nov. 25; Dec. 2, 9, 16, 23, 30, 1909; Jan. 6, 13; March 3, 17, 24; April 21; May 19; June 9, 1910.

18. *WR*, Nov. 25, 1909; Jan. 6, 1910; B. Davis to RW, April 30, 1910, Woods Papers; Jones to Gellatly, Dec. 24, 1909; Gellatly to Jones, May 1, 1910, both Jones Papers; Allen, *Poindexter*, 51.

19. Poindexter to RW, Jan. 25, 1912; Wilson to RW, March 31, 1910, both Woods Papers; Allen, Po*indexter*, 49-57; Saltvig, "Progressive Movement," 154-156; *WDW*, May 7; June 15; Aug. 1, 26; Sept. 1, 6, 7, 14, 1910; Woods Diary, Oct. 2, 1910; Nesbit, *"He Built Seattle,"* 414-417. William Kerr, analyzing the Poindexter tally and the vote on other progressive candidates and measures, finds that reform drew support from three regions of the state: cities on Puget Sound, wheat-producing areas in southeastern Washington and, in a grab-bag category, Chelan and other "general agricultural counties." Uninformed as to the apple industry, he misses the salient point that affluence linked the wheat and "general agriculture" sections, accounting for the backing of progressivism in both. See Kerr, "Progressives of Washington," 21-25.

20. Ralph Woods wanted Poindexter to run for president in 1912. Woods Diary, Oct. 2, 1910; *WDW*, Dec. 5, 9, 1910; June 19; Oct. 16, 1911; May 5, 1912; Ralph Woods to Poindexter, April 1, 1912; Poindexter to Ralph Woods, June 27, 1911, both Poindexter Papers; RW to Roosevelt, Jan. ? 1912, Woods Papers.

21. *WDW*, May 16-18, 20, 1912; Keith A. Murray, "The Aberdeen Convention of 1912," *PNQ*, 38(1947), 99-108; Saltvig, "Progressive Movement," 253.

22. *WDW*, May 6, 9; June 3, 17, 24; July 1, 11, 1912.

23. *WDW*, July 3, 5, 8, 15, 25; Aug. 17, 22; Sept. 13, 30; Oct. 17; Nov. 8, 25, 1912; Saltvig, "Progressive Movement," 254-265, 286, 291. On Governor Hay's difficulties, see H.J. Bergman, "The Reluctant Dissenter: Governor Hay of Washington and the Conservation Problem," *PNQ*, 62(1971), 27-33.

24. Nominally a progressive, LaFollette had antagonized Washington Bull Moosers by refusing to follow Roosevelt into the third party. *WR*, Oct. 6, 1910; Oct. 2, 12, 14; Dec. 14, 1911; Sept. 7, 10, 1912; Jan. 16, 18, 23; March 1; April 8, 29, 30; May 5, 10, 1913; RW to Poindexter, April 7, 1913; Ralph Woods to Poindexter, May 7, 1913; to Stanton Warburton, May 8, 1913; Poindexter to RW, May 12, 1913, all Woods Papers; Mitchell, *Story of Rufus Woods*, 4; Saltvig, "Progressive Movement," 295-296.

25. *WR*, April 30, 1913; Mitchell, *Story of Rufus Woods*, 4.

26. RW to Fred Simpich, n.d.; to K. Greenslit, July 6, 1912; ? 1913; Dec. 30, 1914; to W.H. Cowles, July 16, 1913; July 16, 1914; April 26, 1916; Dallam to RW, Feb. 7; July 5; Sept. 21, 1912; to Ralph Woods, Feb. 22; March 9; June 3, 13; July 9; Sept. 13, 1912; Agreement of Nov. 24, 1911, all Woods Papers; *WDW*, Oct. 12, 1935; Mitchell, *Story of Rufus Woods*, 4.

27. *WDW*, May 1, 1913; *WR*, May 2, 10, 1913; RW to W.T. Clark, May 2, 1913, Woods Papers; Mitchell, *Story of Rufus Woods*, 4.

28. Ralph Woods to W.S. Trimble, May 1, 1913(two letters); to RW, May 7, 8, 9, 1913, Woods Papers.

29. RW to Board of Directors, Associated Press, April 2, 1910, *ibid.*; *WDW*, April 30, 1913; Jan. 15, 1914; *WR*, April 30; May 1, 1913; Mitchell, *Story of Rufus Woods*, 4.

30. Three elections were required to authorize the takeover of the canal by the Wenatchee Irrigation District in 1915. *WDW*, April 8; Aug. 6, 1914; Mitchell, *Flowing Wealth*, 11; Gellatly, *History of Wenatchee*, 53.

31. *WDW*, April 21; May 9, 1911; March 22; Sept. 27; Oct. 1; Nov. 20, 1912; April 22, 1913; Mitchell, *Story of Rufus Woods*, 6.

32. *WDW*, July 26, 1910; Nov. 20, 1912; June 11, 1932; RW to Cowles, July 16, 1913; to James E. Moore, ? 1913, Woods Papers; Mitchell, *Story of Rufus Woods*, 4.

33. RW to Moore, ? 1913; to Cowles, July 16, 1913; to L. M. Lewis, Jan. 17, 1917; Circulation Statement, Nov. 1, 1915; Circulation Statistics, 1917, all Woods Papers; *WDW*, Sept. 5, 1911; Nov. 9, 1912; April 25, 1917; Mitchell, *Story of Rufus Woods*, 6.

34. M. Heard to RW, July 23, 1913; RW to Mergenthaler Linotype Company, May 16, 20, 1913; R.L. Lusby to RW, Nov. 14; Dec. 7, 1912, all Woods Papers.

35. "Accept our thanks for your kindly offer in regard to The Republic matter," Rufus wrote the Richmond Company in feigned good humor. W.D. Reynolds to RW, June 10, 11, 18; July 10; Nov. 19, 1913; Lusby to RW, May 28; June 25, 1913; RW to Richmond Paper Company, July ?; Oct. 1, 1913; to Ralph Woods, Nov. 24, 1913, all *ibid.*

36. RW to State Board of Health, July 28, 1913; to George Russell Reed, Oct. 1, 1913; to F.J. Whaley, Dec. ? 1912; to K. Greenslit, Dec. 30, 1914, Woods Papers; Mitchell, *Story of Rufus Woods*, 4; Hiltner and Haley, eds., *Greenslit Family*, 279.

37. RW to Cowles, July 16, 1914, Woods Papers; *WDW*, July 5, 1938.

38. *WDW*, June 11, 1932.

39. Reallocation of House seats following the 1910 census gave eastern Washington a second congressional district. RW to Poindexter, n.d., Poindexter Papers; *WDW*, Nov. 1, 1913; Nov. 18, 1915; Saltvig, "Progressive Movement," 342-345; Allen, *Poindexter*, 117-118. Washington voters approved a statewide prohibition initiative in 1914. The returning prominence of social, as opposed to economic, issues aided the reunification effort. See Clark, *Dry Years*, chapt. 8.

40. *WDW*, Aug. 20, 1914; Nov. 18, 1915; Cowles to RW, Feb. 1; March 8; April 7, 1916; N.W. Durham to RW, Feb. 10, 1916; Albert Johnson to RW, March 15, 1916; Victor Murdock to RW, March 21, 1916; O. H. Woody to RW, Feb. 24, 1916; RW to Cowles, April 26, 1916, all Woods Papers.

41. *WDW*, June 30; Aug. 19, 1914; April 20; June 13; Nov. 4, 1916; Poindexter to RW, Dec. 18, 1913, Woods Papers; June 4, 1914, Poindexter Papers.

42. *WDW*, Oct. 9, 10, 31; Nov. 4, 10, 14, 1916; RW to Poindexter, Oct. 5, 1918, Poindexter Papers; Allen, *Poindexter*, 116-117.

## Notes for Chapter Four

1. *WDW*, Jan. 30, 1918.

2. *WDW*, Jan. 14, 1919; June 8; Oct. 20, 1920.

3. *WDW*, May 19, 1913; Feb. 28; Dec. 10, 1914; Aug. 30, 1915; April 11, 1916.

4. *WDW*, Jan. 27; Sept. 15, 1913; May 2, 5; Aug. 30, 1916; June 11, 1918; March 11, 1920.

5. *WDW*, Sept. 20, 25, 1913; Feb. 5; July 22; Aug. 21; Oct. 10, 1914.

6. *WDW*, Oct. 11, 1911; Nov. 27; Dec. 21, 1912; May 17, 1916; July 8, 25, 1919.

7. Rufus also favored the issuance of state bonds for highway construction. *WDW*, Oct. 11, 1911; Nov. 28, 30, 1916; July 11, 25; Sept. 22, 1919; Nov. 1, 1920.

8. Tied up at Wenatchee, the steamers were destroyed in a 1915 fire. The only scheduled commercial navigation left on the upper Columbia was provided by a small vessel running upstream from the mouth of the Okanogan River to Bridgeport at Foster Creek Rapids. RW to Louis W. Hill, Aug. 17, 1916; Graham to RW, July 24, 1917, both Woods Papers; *WDW*, March 20, 28, 29; April 4, 12; May 17, 25, 26; Aug. 23, 25; Sept. 14, 20, 23; Oct. 2, 6; Nov. 6, 1911; April 22; Sept. 16, 1913; March 13; July 8, 1914; Oct. 28; Nov. 20, 1915; Oct. 21, 1916; March 5, 1918; March 12, 1920; Mitchell, *By River, Trail and Rail*, 27, 30, and *Flowing Wealth*, 13; Mills, *Stern-Wheelers Up Columbia*, 93-94.

9. *WDW*, Sept. 12, 1913; Oct. 27, 28, 1915; Nov. 14, 21; Dec. 7, 1916; Aug. 13, 1919; May 11; June 26; Aug. 9; Oct. 16, 1920; H.M. Chittenden, "A 30-Mile Railway Tunnel Under the Cascade Mountains," pamphlet in Chittenden Misc.; Gordon Dodds, *Hiram Martin Chittenden: His Public Career* (Lexington: The University Press of Kentucky, 1973), 150-152; E. Byron Siems to RW, Nov. 23; Dec. 22, 1916; n.d.; Ralph Budd to Siems, Sept. 18, 1916; RW to L. Hill, Aug. 17, 1916, all Woods Papers.

10. *WDW*, Oct. 21, 1913; July 13, 1916; April 28, 1932; RW to E.C. Leedy, Jan. 20; Nov. 3, 26, 1915; Jan. 26, 1916; to Graham, Nov. ? 1915; C.C. Dill to RW, Dec. 16, 1915; Poindexter to RW, June 22, 1915, all Woods Papers; Mitchell, *Story of Rufus Woods*, 4, 6.

11. *WDW*, July 5, 10, 18, 1916; April 28, 1932; Mitchell, *Story of Rufus Woods*, 6.

12. *WDW*, June 30; Aug. 1, 2, 1916; Mitchell, *Story of Rufus Woods*, 6; Jones to Woods, Dec. 16, 1915, Woods Papers.

13. *WDW*, Dec. 22, 28, 1914.

14. *WDW*, Nov. 8, 1911; Gellatly, *History of Wenatchee*, 127; Miller and Thomson, *Cost of Producing Apples*, 8, 19-23; Maynard, *Marketing Northwestern Apples*, 5-6, 14-16, 87-88; Freeman, "Apple Industry," 164-165; Robert C. Nesbit and Charles M. Gates, "Agriculture in Eastern Washington, 1899-1910," *PNQ*, 37(1946), 290-291.

15. RW to Charles N. Crewdson, July 3, 1912; to Mergenthaler Linotype Company, May 20, 1913, Woods Papers; *WDW*, Feb. 17, 21, 23, 24, 27; July 8, 13; Aug. 20; Sept. 16, 30; Oct. 2, 17, 19; Nov. 23, 26; Dec. 4, 9, 26, 1912; April 7; May 8, 1913. See also Fahey, *Inland Empire*, 113-115.

16. *WDW*, Jan. 25; Feb. 1, 5, 26; March 26; April 8, 30; Aug. 2, 1913.

17. *WDW*, April 30; May 8, 9, 14, 16; June 3, 18; Aug. 2; Sept. 29; Dec. 12, 29, 1913; Fahey, *Inland Empire*, 115-116.

18. *WDW*, Aug. 25; Oct. 14; Nov. 4; Dec. 14, 1915; Aug. 10, 18, 23; Sept. 18, 27; Oct. 18, 27; Nov. 2, 8, 22, 1916; Maynard, *Marketing Northwestern Apples*, 37-39.

19. *WDW*, Aug. 10, 14, 18, 19, 1914.

20. *WDW*, Sept. 16; Oct. 9; Nov. 10, 19, 1915; April 20; Aug. 7, 25, 1916; W.E. Humphrey to RW, Feb. 1, 1916; Poindexter to RW, Feb. 9, 1916, both Woods Papers.

21. *WDW*, April 24; May 1, 14; Aug. 8, 10, 1917.

22. *WDW*, Sept. 16, 1908; May 10, 1912; May 14; July 23, 1917; Speech at Mansfield Flag Raising, May 20, 1917, Woods Papers; Saltvig, "Progressive Movement," 446-448; Allen, *Poindexter*, 172-173.

23. *WDW*, April 17; Dec. 12, 13, 1917; Jan. 5, 7, 8, 14, 15, 1918; RW to J.A. Falconer, Jan. 3, 1918; to M.H. Voorhees, Jan. 15, 1918, Woods Papers.

24. Borg to RW, Jan. 1; Feb. 5, 1918; RW to T.S. Elliott, Jan. 15; Feb. 13, 1918; to Falconer, Jan. 3, 1918; to Elizabeth Woods, Jan. 9, 1918; to Voorhees, Jan. 15, 1918, all Woods Papers.

25. RW to Catherine Helm, Oct. 27, 1918, ibid.; *WDW*, April 17; May 7, 17, 26, 30, 1917; Oct. 12; Nov. 23; Dec. 17, 18, 1918; Feb. 7; July 8, 9, 18, 23; Aug. 20; Sept. 20, 1919; March 10, 1922; Woods Diary, April 11; Nov. 11, 1919.

26. Before entering the service, Frank Dallam sold his remaining *World* shares to Rufus and Ralph. RW to K. Greenslit, Dec. 23, 1918; to N.A. Huse, March 30, 1916; to Ralph Cunningham, Feb. 17, 1919; Data on Country, 1917; American Newspaper Publishers Association Questionnaire, Jan. 15, 1918; Dallam to RW, April 8; May 8, 1917; W. A. Bower to RW, Jan. 22; Nov. 20, 26; Dec. 2, 20, 1918; to World Publishing Company, Feb. 7, 1918, all Woods Papers; *WDW*, April 25, 1917; Woods Diary, Feb. 4, 1917; April 11, 1919; May 17; Aug. 1, 1920.

27. RW to Ethel Woods, Feb. 10, 1918; to Joseph Blethen, Aug. 1, 1917; Cowles to RW, March 28; July 13, 1917, all Woods Papers; *WDW*, Aug. 28; Sept. 26; Oct. 25; Nov. 11, 17, 29; Dec. 2, 1916; April 26, 1917. Also see Saltvig, "Progressive Movement," 412-426.

28. *WDW*, July 13, 1917.

29. Woods agreed with a friend's assessment of Lister as "a physical coward." *WDW*, Aug. 6, 28, 29, 1917; C. Will Shaffer to RW, Aug. 31, 1917, Woods Papers. There is an extensive literature on the strike. See Ficken, *Forested Land*, chapt. 11; Harold M. Hyman, *Soldiers and Spruce: Origins of the Loyal Legion of Loggers and Lumbermen* (Los Angeles: Institute of Industrial Relations, 1963); Robert L. Tyler, *Rebels of the Woods: The I.W.W. in the Pacific Northwest* (Eugene: University of Oregon Books, 1967).

30. *WDW*, Jan. 23, 1919.

31. *WDW*, Aug. 6, 1917; Jan. 26; May 8, 13, 25; Oct. 8, 1918.

32. Republican William LaFollette, eastern Washington's other antiwar congressman, was also defeated in 1918. *WDW*, Jan. 12; June 29; Aug. 22; Sept. 7, 1918; April 2, 1932; Borg to RW, Dec. 11, 1918, Woods Papers; Saltvig, "Progressive Movement," 463-464; Mitchell, *Story of Rufus Woods*, 9.

33. *WDW*, Nov. 12, 1918; Feb. 15, 1919.

34. *WDW*, Jan. 7; March 5, 13, 1919.

35. Chas. H. Leavy to KB, Feb. 18, 1942, Billingsley Papers; *WDW*, May 18; June 12, 1920; Aug. 28, 1939; Jan. 14, 1944; Allen, *Poindexter*, 204-206.

36. *WDW*, Feb. 13; March 15; Aug. 28, 1919; Feb. 9; March 28, 1920.

37. *WDW*, July 15, 1919; Woods Diary, March 3, 1918. On the founding of, and national campaign to discredit, the Nonpartisan League, see H.C. Peterson and Gilbert C. Fite, *Opponents of War, 1917-1918* (Madison: The University of Wisconsin Press, 1957), 64-72, 155-156, 186-193. Wartime farm radicalism in Washington is covered in Hamilton Cravens, "The Emergence of the Farmer-Labor Party in Washington Politics, 1919-20," *PNQ*, 57(1966), 148-157; and Carlos A. Schwantes, "Farmer-Labor Insurgency in Washington State: William Bouck, the Grange and the Washington Progressive Farmers," *PNQ*, 76(1985), 2-11.

38. *WDW*, Aug. 2, 18, 1919.

39. *WDW*, Nov. 29, 1918; Jan. 6, 1920; April 25, 1934; June 30, 1943.

## Notes for Chapter Five

1. March 20, 1922.

2. *WDW*, Nov. 29, 30; Dec. 2-4, 10, 14, 26, 28, 1918; Feb. 11, 1939.

3. A.R. Chase to JOS, May 18, 1931, O'Sullivan Papers; Jayne to C.S. Shuff, July 3, 1911, CBSC; T.B. Southard to Jones, July 30, 1922; Walter E. Leigh to Jones, July 14, 1922, both Jones Papers; E.S. Balch to RW, Nov. 27, 1925, Woods Papers; *WDW*,

May 31; June 9, 1920; Feb. 18, 1948. On the rainmaker Hatfield, see Norris Hundley, Jr., *The Great Thirst: Californians and Water, 1770s-1990s* (Berkeley: University of California Press, 1992), 106-110.

4. E.F. Benson to E.F. Blaine, Sept. 28, 1918; D.C. Henny to O.L. Waller, Sept. 12, 1919, both CBSC; Jones to Thatcher, Jan. 10, 1918; to Durham, Jan. 13, 1919; to Myers, Jan. 29, 1919, Jones Papers; First Assistant Secretary to J.J. Boyle, June 10, 1912, DI07-36.

5. Paul C. Pitzer, "Visions, Plans, and Realities: Irrigation on the Columbia Basin Project" (Ph.D. diss., University of Oregon, 1990), 22-23, 46; Matthews to RW, Nov. 27, 1918, Woods Papers. Pitzer cites Matthews's manuscript account of the 1917 meeting, on file in the Boise regional office of the Columbia Basin Project.

6. *WDW*, Dec. 5, 1934; June 26, 1935; Aug. 23, 1937; Jan. 28, 1938; June 1, 1940; N.N. to RW, March 30, 1923, Woods Papers; JOS to Davis, Dec. 22, 1920, O'Sullivan Papers; Pitzer, "Visions, Plans, and Realities," 23; Bruce Mitchell, "Rufus Woods and Columbia River Development," *PNQ*, 52(1961), 140, and *Flowing Wealth*, 24.

7. The article appeared on page seven in a triumph of haphazard organization over editorial significance. *WDW*, July 18, 1918; June 26, 1935; RW to Wellington Pegg, Dec. 4, 1930; to Dook Stanley, Jan. 8, 1934, Woods Papers; Rufus Woods, *The 23-Years' Battle for Grand Coulee Dam* (Wenatchee: *Wenatchee Daily World*, 1944), 2, 10; Mitchell, *Flowing Wealth*, 24, and "Rufus Woods and Columbia River Development," 140; Pitzer, "Visions, Plans, and Realities," 23.

8. C. W. Duncan to County Commissioners, Nov. 27, 1918, Woods Papers. The report was reprinted in *WDW*, July 29, 1938, and in Woods, *23-Years' Battle for Grand Coulee Dam*, 11. Also see Mitchell, *Flowing Wealth*, 24; Pitzer, "Visions, Plans, and Realities," 22-24. Clapp's original formulation of a dam high enough to empty water directly into the coulee was rejected by all engineers as technically impracticable. Even if feasible, moreover, such a dam would have produced diplomatic complications with Canada.

9. Contemporaries often misspelled the damsite as "Albany Falls." Bruce C. Harding, "Water from Pend Oreille: The Gravity Plan for Irrigating the Columbia Basin," *PNQ*, 45(1954), 52-54; Marvin Chase to Davis, Feb. 10, 1919; Ivan E. Goodner to F.E. Weymouth, Sept. 22, 1919, both CBSC; Pitzer, "Visions, Plans, and Realities," 23-24; Mitchell, *Flowing Wealth*, 24.

10. The Kettle Falls project, if built, would have seriously, perhaps fatally, impinged upon Grand Coulee, forcing construction of a lower dam and increasing the required pump lift. "Hydro Electric Plants . . . Above the Mouth of the Snake River," Sept. 1921, SD; *WDW*, June 26; Aug. 9; Oct. 15, 16, 20, 1920; JOS to RW, Oct. 25; Nov. 17, 1920, Woods Papers; Executive Committee Minutes, May 18; July 20, 1921; July 19, 1922, Washington Water Power Company Records, WSU; "Columbia River and Minor Tributaries," House Document No. 103, 73d Cong., 1st sess., 37-39, 838; H.L. Carpenter, "Power Development and Marketing," *Proceedings of the Pacific Northwest Regional Planning Conference, Dec. 12-14, 1934*, 62.

11. The president of the Wenatchee Chamber of Commerce owned $10,000 worth of Puget Power stock, an important factor in the strong support extended the firm by the organization. *WDW*, June 3, 7, 9, 13; Oct. 29, 31; Nov. 6; Dec. 30, 31, 1919; March 3, 20; April 18, 30; May 5, 14, 23; July 20; Aug. 20; Sept. 3, 1921; Mitchell, *Flowing Wealth*, 29-30; RW to JOS, June 30, 1930, O'Sullivan Papers; McGinnis to Willis T. Batcheller, Sept. 13, 1930, Batcheller Papers; W.E. Southard to RW, June 12, 1929, Woods Papers; J.A. Ford to Jones, June 14, 1921, Jones Papers; Waller to Goodner, Aug. 11, 1921; to Fred Adams, Oct. 4, 1921; to Ross K. Tiffany, May 26, 1926, CBSC.

12. Goodner to Weymouth, Sept. 22, 1919; to Chase, Dec. 26, 1919; Waller to Chase, Aug. 12, 1919; to Tiffany, Dec. 16, 1926, all CBSC; to Elwood Mead, Jan. 15, 27, 1927, Waller Papers; Sept. 2, 1927, BR19-29; Southard to Jones, Sept. 13, 1920, Jones Papers; McGinnis to Thomas L. Walsh, June 7, 1929, Woods Papers.

13. Hydro Electric Plants, Seattle Engineer District and Columbia Basin, March 20, 1922, SD; Durham to Jones, Jan. 31, 1919; C.C. Corbaley to Jones, Jan. 17, 1919, both Jones Papers. There was no technical reason for excluding electricity from the Albeni Falls design. The storage dam eventually built at the site contained three generators. L.H. Hewitt to Division Engineer, Oct. 1, 1947, File 1505-22, Albeni Falls Project, SDOACE; "Columbia River and Tributaries, Northwestern United States," House Document No. 531, 81st Cong., 2d sess., 148-150, 600-602.

14. Waller to Chase, Aug. 12, 1919; Henny to Waller, Sept. 12, 1919; R.F. Walter to Waller, Oct. 9, 1919; Tiffany to Waller, Oct. 29, 1919, all CBSC; Jones to Thatcher, Jan. 10, 1918; to P.C. Lorentzen, Aug. 5, 1922; to T. Southard, Aug. 5, 1922, Jones Papers; William S. Forth, "Wesley L. Jones: A Political Biography" (Ph.D. diss., University of Washington, 1962), 449, 674-675.

15. Spokane *Spokesman-Review*, Jan. 14; Feb. 12, 1919; *WDW*, Feb. 20, 1919; RW to Chase, Oct. 7, 1920; Jan. 14, 1922; to Borg, Nov. 12, 1919; to J.A. DeVos, Feb. 5, 1920; Clapp to RW, Nov. 14, 1920, all Woods Papers; Harding, "Water from Pend Oreille," 53-54.

16. According to James O'Sullivan, the commission budgeted $10,000 of its $100,000 appropriation for a cursory examination of Grand Coulee. Adams to Davis, Oct. 20, 1920, Woods Papers; to Waller, May 10, 1921; Louis F. Hart to Chase, March 4, 1919; Goodner to Otto Wollweber, Jan. 30, 1922; Waller to Adams, May 7, 1921, all CBSC; Henny to Chief of Construction, Aug. 26; Dec. 20, 1919; James Munn to Chief of Construction, Dec. 22, 1919; to Chief Engineer, April 4, 1920, all BR19-29; *WDW*, June 7, 1920; Jan. 8, 9; Feb. 13, 1931; Harding, "Water from Pend Oreille," 54-55; Pitzer, "Visions, Plans, and Realities," 26.

17. *WDW*, May 13, 1919; June 7; Aug. 10, 1920; Forth, "Jones," 673. O'Sullivan's articles were reprinted in Woods, *23-Years' Battle for Grand Coulee Dam*, 14-16. See also George Sundborg, *Hail Columbia: The Thirty-Year Struggle for Grand Coulee Dam* (New York: The Macmillan Company, 1954), 32-36, 39-43.

18. *WDW*, June 7; Dec. 16, 1920.

19. Harding, "Water from Pend Oreille," 55-56; Mitchell, *Flowing Wealth*, 24; Waller to W.V. Story, April 21, 1921, Waller Papers. The full report was published as *The Columbia Basin Project* (Olympia: Frank M. Lamborn, Public Printer, 1920).

20. Davis to Columbia Basin Survey Commission, Oct. 30, 1920, CBSC; Weymouth to Henny, Oct. 30, 1919, BR19-29; JOS to RW, Sept. 26; Nov. 29, 1920, Woods Papers; to Henny, Dec. 14, 1920, O'Sullivan Papers; Mitchell, *Flowing Wealth*, 24, 26; *WDW*, Oct. 2, 1920. For a pro-O'Sullivan version claiming that Davis was accurately, and properly, quoted, see Sundborg, *Hail Columbia*, 44-47.

21. Pumping plan supporters claimed that Davis's abrupt dismissal from government service in June 1923 was engineered by the private utility industry in retaliation for his endorsement of Grand Coulee. Adams to Davis, Oct. 20, 1920, Jones Papers; Dec. 4, 1920; Davis to Chase, Oct. 19, 1920; to Columbia Basin Survey Commission, Oct. 30, 1920, all CBSC; to H.L. Johnson, Oct. 19, 1920, Woods Papers; to JOS, Dec. 17, 28, 1920; Henny to JOS, Dec. 9, 1920; JOS to Henny, Dec. 14, 1920; to Davis, Dec. 23, 1920, all O'Sullivan Papers; to RW, Nov. 29, 1920, Woods Papers; *WDW*, Oct. 2, 1935; March 11, 1948. On the Davis firing, part of an Interior Department effort to impose businesslike methods on the Reclamation Bureau, see Gene M. Gressley, "Arthur Powell Davis, Reclamation, and the West," *Agricultural History*, 42(1968), 241-244.

22. Jones to Columbia Basin Survey Commission, April 30, 1920, CBSC; Davis to Jones, Nov. 1, 1920, Jones Papers; JOS to Henny, Nov. 27, 1920, O'Sullivan Papers; Henny, Munn and C.T. Pease to Chief Engineer, Dec. 13, 1920, DI07-36; Harding, "Water from Pend Oreille," 56.

23. Waller to Poindexter, Jan. 21, 1921; J. Stanley Webster to Waller, Jan. 28, 1921; Davis to Goodner, Dec. 22, 1921; Jan. 12, 1922; to Chase, Jan. 15, 1921, all CBSC; Tiffany to Davis, May 17, 1922, BR19-29.

24. Goodner to Batcheller, July 29, 1921; to Henny, Nov. 25, 1921; to Dan A. Scott, Dec. 9, 1921; Henny to Goodner, July 15, 1921, all CBSC; Batcheller to W.J. Coyle, Nov. 15, 1921, Batcheller Papers.

25. "His employment by the state," wrote Ivan Goodner of Batcheller, "has probably been a very poor investment." Southard to E.F. Banker, May 18, 1933, CBC; Goodner to Scott, Feb. 15, 25, 1922; to Waller, Jan. 30, 1922; Scott to Goodner, Jan. 17, 1922, all CBSC; Henny to Batcheller, Dec. 20, 1921; Jan. 22, 1922; Batcheller to Henny, March 1, 1922, all Batcheller Papers; Mitchell, *Flowing Wealth*, 26.

26. Henny to Batcheller, May 25, 1922, Batcheller Papers; to Chief Engineer, Feb. 15, 1922, BR19-29; Goodner to Scott, Feb. 15, 20, 25, 1922; to Waller, Jan. 30, 1922; to W.M. White, Feb. 15; March 14, 1922, all CBSC.

27. Scott to Adams, Dec. 6, 1921; Chase to Geo. W. Goethals, April 12, 1922; Waller to Wollweber, Jan. 30, 1922, all CBSC; Batcheller to Henny, Dec. 19, 1921; Henny to Chief Engineer, Dec. 12, 1921; March 1, 1922, all BR19-29; to Batcheller, Jan. 22, 1922, Batcheller Papers; Waller to Adams, Jan. 30, 1922, Waller Papers; Jones to Ford, Nov. 2, 1921, Jones Papers; Harding, "Water from Pend Oreille," 56-57. On the general's youthful service on the Columbia, see Walter R. Griffin, "George W. Goethals, Explorer of the Pacific Northwest, 1882-1884," *PNQ*, 62(1971), 129-141.

28. One historian calculates that Goethals spent six days in the state. George W. Goethals, Report on Columbia Basin Irrigation Project, March 30, 1922, copy in Batcheller Papers; Harding, "Water from Pend Oreille," 57; Forth, "Jones," 682-683. The general's public image was so positive that later journalistic accounts credited him with recommending construction of Grand Coulee. See Richard L. Neuberger, "The Biggest Thing on Earth," *Harpers Magazine*, 174(1937), 250, 256.

29. JOS to L.C. Edleston, Sept. 3, 1929, O'Sullivan Papers; *WDW*, April 10, 1922; Dec. 31, 1936; Harding, "Water from Pend Oreille," 57.

30. Referring to Grand Coulee, the pro-gravity *Spokesman-Review* asserted that the Goethals report "disposes of that question." Goodner to Chas. P. Dunn, May 1, 1922, CBSC; *WDW*, April 10, 1922; Henny to Davis, June 7, 1922; to Weymouth, April 10, 1922; Davis to Henny, May 13, 1922, all BR19-29.

31. Report to Federal Power Commission on the Use of the Waters of the Upper Columbia River, June 30, 1922, copy in Batcheller Papers; Henny to Davis, March 2; May 22, 1922; to Chief Engineer, March 1, 11, 1922, BR19-29; W.J. Barden to Chief of Engineers, May 1, 1925, SD. A Bureau of Reclamation report, prepared by Homer J. Gault in 1924, was generally favorable to the gravity plan, but concluded that the scheme was "financially infeasible at the present time." A.J. Wiley, Munn, and J.L. Savage to Chief Engineer, April 6, 1924, BR19-29; Harding, "Water from Pend Oreille," 58-59.

32. Harding, "Water from Pend Oreille," 57-60; Mitchell, *Flowing Wealth*, 27; Pitzer, "Visions, Plans, and Realities," 28-31. The league "was so dominated by private power interests opposed to the creation of a federally owned power plant," writes one historian, "that its good faith was open to some slight doubt." Forth, "Jones," 683.

33. A.S. Goss to Herbert Hoover, May 19, 1927, Herbert Hoover Letters, WSU; *Spokane Spokesman-Review*, May 19, 1922.

34. RW to Sefrit, July 13, 1933, Woods Papers.
35. *WDW*, Jan. 14; Feb. 9, 1922; RW to Sefrit, July 13, 1933, Woods Papers.
36. For useful introductions to the early history of the public power movement in Washington, see William O. Sparks, "J.D. Ross and Seattle City Light, 1917-1932" (M.A. thesis, University of Washington, 1964), 80-83; Mitchell, *Flowing Wealth*, 1819.
37. *WDW*, Jan. 13, 1922; April 10; July 19, 1924.
38. *WDW*, Jan. 2; July 17, 19; Oct. 29, 1924. On the Bone-Reed debate, see Robert E. Ficken, *Lumber and Politics: The Career of Mark E. Reed* (Seattle: University of Washington Press, 1979), 88-91, 98; Sparks, "J.D. Ross," 84-86, 88-93; Douglas R. Pullen, "The Administration of Washington State Governor Louis F. Hart, 1919-1925" (Ph.D. diss., University of Washington, 1974), 311-312, 316, 319-329.
39. *WDW*, Oct. 21, 1924.

## Notes for Chapter Six

1. July 23, 1923.
2. *WDW*, June 28, 1920; Nov. 11, 1921.
3. *WDW*, July 7, 1922; Woods Diary, Feb. 16, 1924; RW to K. Greenslit, Dec. 30, 1914, Woods Papers.
4. RW to Helm, Oct. 7, 1920; Sept. 28, 1921; to Warren Sisty, July 16, 1923; to Winfield Harper, July 7, 1925; Comparative Circulation Table, March 1927; Memorandum, March 5, 1946, all Woods Papers; *WDW*, May 21, 1920; May 26, 1921; July 28, 1922; May 4, 1923; Sept. 23, 1925.
5. Abandoning an earlier policy, Woods now ran a comics page. The *World* did not publish a Sunday edition, leaving the local market to imported copies of the Seattle and Spokane papers. RW to Ralph Woods, April 8, 1922; to Paul Cowles, March 15, 1924; to the Grange, Cashmere, Jan. 22, 1924; to Guy C. George and Pegg, Feb. 14, 1924; Circulation Statistics, 1917; Notes on Newspaper Institute, Feb. 17-18, 1928; C.E. Stohl to RW, June 15, 16, 1921; Trimble to RW, Jan. 14, 1920; Pegg to RW, Feb. 21, 1924; Harry L. Bell to RW, Feb. 11, 1924; R.S. Ludington to RW, Feb. 13, 1924; A.N. MacDonald to Editor, Aug. 20, 1924, all Woods Papers; *WDW*, Jan. 24, 1923; March 10, 11; Nov. 21, 1925; July 24, 1926; Dec. 3, 1927; Dec. 24, 1936.
6. *WDW*, Feb. 5; May 3, 5, 1920.
7. *WDW*, May 24; Dec. 21, 1922; Nov. 26, 1924; Dec. 15, 1928; Nov. 2, 4-7, 1929.
8. *WDW*, Jan. 30; July 28; Aug. 7, 1919; March 28; May 11, 21; Oct. 30, 1920.
9. *WDW*, Aug. 7, 1919; April 2, 1921; Sept. 4, 1922.
10. *WDW*, March 1; Oct. 13, 1921; Oct. 6, 1924.
11. *WDW*, Feb. 29; April 26, 1912; June 10, 1913; Dec. 19, 1919; Feb. 23, 1921; Dec. 11, 1922; Feb. 6; July 9, 1923; Sept. 30, 1924.
12. Poindexter to RW, Oct. 21; Dec. 7, 1918, Woods Papers; Allen, *Poindexter*, 116-117, 216-225; *WDW*, July 4, 1919; March 27; April 26; June 14, 18; July 7, 31; Nov. 3, 1920.
13. *WDW*, April 13; July 15; Nov. 6, 1922; RW to W.H. Paulhamus, Feb. 10, 1922, quoted in Allen, *Poindexter*, 249. On the senator's political difficulties, see *ibid.*, 226-248.
14. Dill to Art Garton, Dec. 11, 1947, DC; *WDW*, Sept. 13, 25; Oct. 18; Nov. 2, 4, 6, 1922.
15. *WDW*, Nov. 8, 9, 1922; Jan. 20, 1923; July 22, 1932; Allen, *Poindexter*, 251-254.
16. *WDW*, April 3, 1920; July 5, 1922.
17. *WDW*, April 3, 1920; July 5, 1922; July 20, 26, 31, 1923; Aug. 30, 1924.
18. *WDW*, March 26, 1923; Aug. 9, 1924; N.N. to RW, March 20, 1923, Woods Papers.

19. *WDW*, July 5, 1922; March 7; Aug. 7, 1923; July 28; Aug. 25, 1926; July 26, 27; Aug. 4, 25, 1927; June 9, 15; Aug. 18, 1928; Jan. 15; Feb. 7, 1929.

20. *WDW*, March 18, 1919; Jan. 4, 15, 1923; Dec. 2, 12, 1925; Mitchell, *Flowing Wealth*, 8.

21. In addition to Chase, the reclamation board was composed of the state treasurer, the state auditor, the state agricultural commissioner, and the president of Washington State College. *WDW*, Dec. 27, 1918; July 29; Nov. 18, 1920; March 13, 1922; Jan. 4; April 14; June 18; Nov. 13; Dec. 11, 17, 1923; May 18; June 9; July 14, 28; Nov. 23; Dec. 5, 1925.

22. The stunted federal Okanogan Project was incorporated in the Methow plan. Horace M. Holmes, et al. to Jones, Dec. 6, 1923; M.B. Howe and RW to Jones, June 4, 1919; Chas. A. Johnson to Jones, Jan. 2, 1919, all Jones Papers; *WDW*, March 18; Aug. 20, 1919; April 1, 1920; Dec. 14, 1921; Feb. 4; Aug. 22; Nov. 22, 1922; Jan. 22, 1923; Jan. 12; Feb. 9; Sept. 8, 1924; Nov. 24, 1926; RW to Borg, Nov. 12, 1919; to DeVos, Feb. 5, 1920; to JOS, Dec. 3, 1920; Jay Morrison to RW, Jan. 21, 1920; DeVos to RW, Jan. 30; Feb. 9, 1920, all Woods Papers; Fahey, *Inland Empire*, 95-96; Mitchell, *Flowing Wealth*, 8.

23. *WDW*, April 28, 29; Nov. 22, 1922; Jan. 22, 1923; Jan. 12; Feb. 9, 1924; Nov. 24, 1926.

24. *WDW*, Nov. 11, 1922; Feb. 20, 1923; June 2, 1928.

25. *WDW*, Dec. 10, 1923; June 2-4, 14, 1924; May 13, 1929.

26. RW to John Larrabee, Dec. 20, 1932, Woods Papers; *WDW*, May 18, 19, 24, 1922; May 20; June 1, 1926.

27. *WDW*, May 16, 22, 1922; May 18, 1926.

28. *WDW*, May 17, 22, 1922; May 17, 1926.

29. *WDW*, July 3; Aug. 3, 10, 1923. On the presidential visit to the Northwest, see Robert E. Ficken, "President Harding Visits Seattle," *PNQ*, 67(1975), 105-114.

30. *WDW*, Jan. 28; Feb. 14, 20, 21; March 7, 11, 1924. Woods unintentionally captured the fundamental emptiness of the Harding era by singling out the Immigration Control Act as the principal achievement. Sponsored by Washington's Albert Johnson, the measure reduced admissions from southern and eastern Europe and prohibited immigration from Japan. For an appreciation of Johnson's "excellent work," see *WDW*, Feb. 6, 1923; April 22, 1924.

31. *WDW*, June 16, 28; July 10, 12; Sept. 24, 1924.

32. *WDW*, July 26, 28; Sept. 10, 19; Oct. 7, 13, 31; Nov. 6, 1924.

33. Charley Brown to RW, Sept. 15, 1924; RW to Cone, Oct. 1, 1948, both Woods Papers; *WDW*, Nov. 20, 21, 1923; May 11, 1925; Sept. 13, 1928; Mark E. Reed to RW, Nov. 21, 1923, Reed Papers; Roland H. Hartley to New York *Graphic*, April 8, 1925, Hartley Papers; Ficken, *Lumber and Politics*, 92-96, 99-101.

34. Hartley to RW, Feb. 20; June 24, 1925, Woods Papers; *WDW*, Jan. 6, 15, 17, 23; Feb. 10, 14, 17, 1925; Ficken, *Lumber and Politics*, 102; Albert F. Gunns, "Roland Hill Hartley and the Politics of Washington State" (Ph.D. diss., University of Washington, 1963), 84-86.

35. Hartley boasted of "doing the right thing" even though "it meant the alienation of a large and powerful group of voters." *WDW*, Feb. 26; March 3; April 3; May 2, 4; July 9, 14; Aug. 10; Oct. 2; Nov. 7, 11, 1925; RW to Hartley, June 20, 1925; Hartley to RW, June 24, 1925, both Woods Papers; to Austin Mires, April 25, 1927; Nov. 21, 1928, Mires Papers; Ficken, *Lumber and Politics*, 103-105; Gunns, "Hartley and the Politics of Washington State," 97-103.

36. RW to J.M. Adams, Dec. 11, 1926, Woods Papers; *WDW*, Nov. 11, 18, 20, 21, 24; Dec. 2, 11, 12, 21, 1925; Ficken, *Lumber and Politics*, 106-107.

37. Ficken, *Lumber and Politics*, 112-116; Gunns, "Hartley and the Politics of Washington State," 125-130; Mark E. Reed. et al., "A Statement by the 'Majority,'" in UW; *WDW*, Dec. 11, 17, 1925; March 13; Nov. 15, 1926.

38. *WDW*, Aug. 24, 1925; Oct. 5, 7, 8; Nov. 26, 1926; Ficken, *Lumber and Politics*, 120-122; Gunns, "Hartley and the Politics of Washington State," 138-139, 142-162, 177-183; Henry Suzzallo to W. Lon Johnson, Nov. 5, 1926, Johnson Papers. The Woods twins disagreed over the Suzzallo affair. "I am very glad that Hartley had the courage to fire him," wrote Ralph. Suzzallo, he claimed, had demanded a salary larger than the one paid the president of Yale, had removed or "buffaloed" the "strong men in the University" and had, during his tenure, done "nothing except tramp around the state and play the political game." Ralph Woods to RW, Oct. 8, 1926, Woods Papers.

39. Bullitt, married into the wealthy Stimson family of Seattle, was busily rebuilding the state Democratic Party. Compounding the sense of disaster, Miles Poindexter was defeated in the Republican senatorial primary. The victor in November, moreover, was Clarence Dill, still-despised by the *World*. *WDW*, Sept. 6; Oct. 21, 27; Dec. 15, 1927; Feb. 1, 25; May 19; Aug. 16, 30; Sept. 5, 10, 12-14, 27, 28; Oct. 8, 30; Nov. 3, 7, 10, 13, 1928; Gellatly to Reed, March 28, 1928; A. Scott Bullitt to Reed, Dec. 3, 1928, both Reed Papers; Reed to Johnson, July 23, 1927, Johnson Papers; Ficken, *Lumber and Politics*, 124-128; Robert L. Cole, "The Democratic Party in Washington State, 1919-1933" (Ph.D. diss., University of Washington, 1972), 181-216.

40. *WDW*, Oct. 2, 1926; Jan. 12; Feb. 3, 13, 22; June 13; July 2; Aug. 6; Oct. 1, 11, 31; Nov. 8, 1928.

41. RW to Neubert, July 13, 1927, Woods Papers.

42. W.G. Hooker to RW, Feb. 5, 18, 19, 26; June 14, 1926, ibid.

43. The building, suitably enlarged, still serves as the home of the *World*. Woods Diary, Aug. 29, 1926; Feb. 13, 1927; Dec. 27, 1930; *WDW*, Dec. 27, 1926; May 5, 1927; Feb. 21, 1928; RW to Helm, March 8, 1927, Woods Papers.

44. The Great Northern project was a smaller version of the tunnel proposed by Hiram Chittenden and still favored by Rufus Woods. Woods Diary, Aug. 29, 1926; *WDW*, Feb. 6; March 3; May 7; Sept. 2; Nov. 17; Dec. 23, 1925; June 9; Aug. 16; Dec. 20, 1926; Sept. 22; Oct. 7; Dec. 12, 20, 1927; Jan. 25; May 1; Oct. 12, 1928; Jan. 11, 1929; Mitchell, *Flowing Wealth*, 13-15, and *By River, Trail and Rail*, 24.

45. *WDW*, Feb. 7; Aug. 26, 1919; Jan. 8; Aug. 23, 1920; April 26, 1924; Jan. 29, 1925; Oct. 2, 1928; March 18, 1929; July 31, 1945; Maynard, *Marketing Northwestern Apples*, 2; Freeman, "Apple Industry," 169.

46. Freeman, "Apple Industry," 168-169.

47. *WDW*, April 1, 1921; Oct. 25, 1922; May 22, 1925; July 20; Aug. 18, 1926; May 21, 23, 24, 1927; April 12, 14; Sept. 8; Dec. 27, 1928; Maynard, *Marketing Northwestern Apples*, 14-15.

48. *WDW*, Sept. 29, 1920; Jan. 12, 1922; Jan. 29; Oct. 30, 31, 1925; April 26; July 22; Aug. 17; Sept. 1, 17, 18; Oct. 2; Nov. 13, 1926; May 20; July 19; Oct. 21; Nov. 9, 18; Dec. 1, 1927; Feb. 11; July 3; Aug. 8, 1928; Maynard, *Marketing Northwestern Apples*, 15, 87-88; Freeman, "Apple Industry," 164-166; Miller and Thomson, *Cost of Producing Apples*, 19-23.

49. Trimble to RW, Oct. 17, 1923, Woods Papers; Maynard, *Marketing Northwestern Apples*, 39-40; *WDW*, March 20, 25; June 21, 1922; Feb. 28; Aug. 17; Oct. 10, 15, 17, 1923; Sept. 14, 1925; Oct. 22, 1926; Jan. 24; March 21; July 19; Aug. 15; Nov. 28; Dec. 19, 1927.

50. Freeman, "Apple Industry," 168; *WDW*, Feb. 21; April 28; Oct. 10, 1928; Feb. 28; March 19; April 8, 12, 1929.

51. *WDW*, Dec. 31, 1928; Feb. 14, 20, 25, 1929.

## Notes for Chapter Seven

1. March 12, 1924.
2. *WDW*, July 23; Aug. 14, 18, 1926; June 28; July 9, 1927; July 24, 1928; April 10; May 23; July 6, 12, 13; Aug. 5, 1929; A. Chase to JOS, May 18, 1931, O'Sullivan Papers; Robert E. Ficken and Charles P. LeWarne, *Washington: A Centennial History* (Seattle: University of Washington Press, 1988), 111. See also Paul C. Pitzer, "The Atmosphere Tasted Like Turnips: The Pacific Northwest Dust Storm of 1931," *PNQ*, 79(1988), 50-55.
3. Southard to Jones, April 23, 1924, Jones Papers; Clapp to JOS, Feb. 9, 1927, O'Sullivan Papers.
4. *WDW*, Aug. 20, 1924; June 10; Sept. 25, 1926; Nov. 10, 1927; Dec. 26, 1928; May 21; Oct. 28, 1929.
5. The gravity plan allowed for diversion of some Pend Oreille water into the Spokane River, enhancing electricity generation by the existing plants of the Washington Water Power Company. RW to M.E. Hay, June 29, 1931, Woods Papers; Roy R. Gill to Jones, April 13, 1926; Mark Woodruff to Jones, July 6, 1929, both Jones Papers.
6. Montana Power Company and Bureau of Reclamation development plans related to Flathead Lake effectively eliminated that body of water from consideration under the gravity plan. Tiffany to Waller, May 28, 1927; Woodruff to Tiffany, Nov. 19, 1926; Waller to Tiffany, Jan. 13, 1927, all CBSC. The dealings between Washington and Idaho are briefly covered in Harding, "Water from Pend Oreille," 59.
7. Gill to Tiffany, June 23; July 6, 16, 22, 1926, CBSC; to Jones, Feb. 14, 1927, Jones Papers.
8. Gill to Tiffany, Sept. 22, 1926; Tiffany to Woodruff, Oct. 25, 30, 1926; to Gill, Oct. 17, 1927; to Waller, Dec. 12, 1927; Woodruff to Tiffany, Nov. 1, 6, 24, 1926; June 14, 1928; Waller to Tiffany, Dec. 12, 1927, all CBSC; Clapp to Jones, Feb. 4, 1927, Jones Papers.
9. Boulder Dam was authorized by Congress in June 1929. *WDW*, July 29; Aug. 18, 20, 1927; Goss to Jones, Dec. 21, 1926; Mead to Jones, Aug. 10, 1928; to Robert R. Butler, May 1, 1929, all Jones Papers.
10. "*One* Democratic congressman from the State of Washington obtained one hundred and seventeen votes," complained Roy Gill of the House vote, "whereas *four* Republican congressmen together secured only fifty-four Republican votes." Jones to Southard, April 19, 1929; to Clapp, Dec. 12, 1927; to Gill, May 18, 1927; Jan. 25; Feb. 26, 1929; Gill to Jones, Feb. 21, 1929, all Jones Papers; Hervey Lindley to Tiffany, Feb. 25, 1929, CBSC; *WDW*, Dec. 12, 1928; Feb. 20, 1929; Harding, "Water from Pend Oreille," 60.
11. RW to Jones, Dec. 11, 1931, Woods Papers; Jones to JOS, Oct. 4, 1930, Jones Papers; *WDW*, July 23, 1924.
12. Jones to Gill, Jan. 25, 1929, Jones Papers; Barden to Chief of Engineers, May 1, 1925, SD; Charles McKinley, *Uncle Sam in the Pacific Northwest: Federal Management of Natural Resources in the Columbia River Valley* (Berkeley: University of California Press, 1952), 66-67; Gill to Tiffany, June 2, 1927, CBSC.
13. Barden to Division Engineer, May 2, 1927; Memorandum of Conference, Dec. 11, 1928; Memorandum to Major Butler, April 18, 1928; Jno. S. Butler to Chief of Engineers, Dec. 26, 1928, all SD; Dec. 14, 1928; Jan. 18; March 5; May 2, 1929; Edgar Jadwin to Dist. Engineer, Feb. 7, 1929; Gustave Lukesh to Chief of Engineers, March 7; May 4, 1929, all RH; Herbert Deakyne to Chief of Engineers, March 20, 1929, NPD.
14. Senator Charles McNary of Oregon, another influential Republican, also pressed the Army for action on the Columbia. Gill to Jones, March 15, 1929; Jones to Gill, Jan.

25; Feb. 26; March 22, 1929, all Jones Papers; to Dwight F. Davis, Jan. 15, 1929; Deakyne to Jones, Jan. 22, 1929; Lindley and Gill to Hoover, April 2, 1929, all RH; Lindley to Waller, Feb. 26, 1929, Waller Papers.

15. Woodruff to Jones, Oct. 30, 1929, Jones Papers; Clapp to Woodruff, July 7, 1927; Bell to Southard, Dec. 26, 1930, both O'Sullivan Papers; JOS to RW, July 31, 1931, Woods Papers.

16. A surviving financial statement shows O'Sullivan receiving $3,225 of the $4,563 disbursed during the year ending October 15, 1932. Batcheller to Clapp, July 20, 1929; to JOS, Sept. 28, 1931; R.C. Wightman to JOS, Dec. 23, 1929; Clapp to JOS, May 15, 1930; RW to JOS, Aug. 22, 1929; June 30, 1930, all O'Sullivan Papers; to Pegg, Dec. 4, 1930; to Southard, Aug. 31, 1931; to L.C. Gilman, n.d.; JOS to RW, June 14, 1929; Aug. 6, 1930; July 31, 1931; to Trustees, Wenatchee Chamber of Commerce, Aug. 25, 1930; Itemized Statement, Nov. 1931-Oct. 15, 1932, all Woods Papers. Batcheller and O'Sullivan thought McGinnis had "used our organization to put over some business deal," presumably the sale of land to one of the private utilities.

17. Goss to JOS, Sept. 16, 1929; JOS to Clapp, July 19, 1929; Batcheller to JOS, Nov. 25, 1929, all O'Sullivan Papers; Jones to Woodruff, Sept. 7, 1927, Jones Papers.

18. Southard to Dill, Jan. 14, 1930, Woods Papers; to Jones, Jan. 24, 1930, Jones Papers; Jones to Southard, April 2, 1929; J.P. Simpson to JOS, April 5, 1930, both O'Sullivan Papers; Butler to M.C. Taylor, April 13, 1931, SD.

19. *WDW*, Nov. 12, 1929; JOS to Clapp, July 19, 1929, O'Sullivan Papers; Southard to Jones, Oct. 12, 1929, Jones Papers. On Butler's Tennessee River service, see Leland R. Johnson, *Engineers on the Twin Rivers: A History of the Nashville District, 1769-1978* (Nashville: U.S. Army Engineer District, 1978), 155, 172.

20. Jones to Clapp, Nov. 18, 1929; to Lytle Brown, Dec. 16, 1929; to Woodruff, June 29, 1929; Woodruff to Jones, June 24, 1929; JOS to Jones, Dec. 12, 1929; Southard to Jones, Aug. 26; Oct. 12, 1929, all Jones Papers; to RW, June 12, 1929; S.H. Hedges to Columbia Basin Executive Committee, Dec. 23, 1931, both Woods Papers; J.D. Ross to JOS, May 2; June 18, 1920, O'Sullivan Papers.

21. *WDW*, Oct. 5, 23, 26, 31; Nov. 1, 6, 15, 1929. For a survey of statewide opinion on the crash, see Ficken and LeWarne, *Washington*, 109-111.

22. *WDW*, Jan. 16, 21; March 4, 18; Aug. 5; Sept. 27; Nov. 26, 1930.

23. *WDW*, Feb. 10; July 2; Aug. 6, 29; Dec. 18, 29, 1930; Jan. 10; Feb. 14, 21; April 27, 30, 1931; Ficken and LeWarne, *Washington*, 111.

24. The projected Priest Rapids Dam, further downstream, was stalled by a complicated and prolonged dispute over water rights. *WDW*, Aug. 13, 1925; Nov. 30; Dec. 6, 7, 31, 1928; March 18; Sept. 20, 1929; Mitchell, "Rufus Woods and Columbia River Development," 141-142, and *Flowing Wealth*, 30.

25. *WDW*, Feb. 6; Aug. 3; Sept. 30; Oct. 17; Dec. 13, 1929; Jan. 10; Oct. 20; Nov. 3, 1930; Batcheller to JOS, March 3, 1930; Southard to JOS, April 1, 1930, both O'Sullivan Papers; Mitchell, "Rufus Woods and Columbia River Development," 142-143, and *Flowing Wealth*, 30-31.

26. *WDW*, Feb. 3; Aug. 26; Sept. 23, 1930; April 8, 1931; Simpson to JOS, April 5, 1930, O'Sullivan Papers. On the construction of Rock Island Dam, see T.B. Parker, "Power Development on the Columbia River," *Scientific American*, 145(1931), 300-302.

27. Butler to Chief of Engineers, Oct. 4, 1930, SD; Batcheller to JOS, Feb. 19; March 3, 19, 1930, O'Sullivan Papers.

28. Emphasis in original. Lukesh to Chief of Engineers, Nov. 25, 1929, RH; to Butler, July 8, 1931; S. Matthew to Dist. Engineer, May 21, 1930, both SD.

29. Lukesh to Chief of Engineers, Nov. 25, 1929; Dec. 22, 1930; Oscar Kuentz to Chief of Engineers, Jan. 26, 1932, all RH; Butler to Division Engineer, Nov. 9, 1929; to

Chief of Engineers, Dec. 26, 1928; to Waller, Dec. 23, 1928; to Division Engineer, Portland, April 27, 1931; Sargent to Butler, July 1, 1930; Memorandum to Major Kuentz, July 22, 1931; Barry Dibble to Butler, Aug. 11, 1930; to Kuentz, Sept. 9, 1930; Hugh L. Cooper to Butler, April 23, 1931; Lukesh to Chief of Engineers, Nov. 8, 1929, all SD; to Division Engineer, Dec. 22, 1930; to Dibble, Dec. 31, 1930; Fred C. Schubert and Sargent to Division Engineer, March 6, 1930; Thomas M. Robins to Chief of Engineers, Oct. 24, 1931, all NPD; "Columbia River and Minor Tributaries," 51, 568-570, 592-594, 607-611.

30. "Columbia River and Minor Tributaries," 569-571, 587-588, 720-726; Butler to Chief of Engineers, Aug. 12, 1930; to Lukesh, July 7, 1931, NPD; to Southard, May 13, 1929, SD.

31. Mead to H.W. Bashore, Dec. 2, 1930, BR30-45; to JOS, Sept. 3, 1930; JOS to Mead, Sept. 18, 1930; RW to JOS, July 21; Oct. 18, all O'Sullivan Papers; to Jones, Aug. 7, 1930, Jones Papers.

32. JOS to RW, Feb. 3, 1930; RW to Butler, Aug. 7, 1930; Batcheller to RW, Aug. 6, 1930, all Woods Papers.

33. *WDW*, Oct. 28, 1929; May 13; June 7; Aug. 4, 12, 23, 26; Dec. 3, 10, 24, 1930. Also see RW to Hay, June 29; July 3, 1931, Woods Papers.

34. This account of the European tour is based upon RW to Folks at Home, April 24, 1930; to Willa Lou Woods, May ? 1930; to Joseph Bagen Basbogen, Aug. 7, 1930; Notes from Russia, May 17, 1930, all Woods Papers; *WDW*, Nov. 28, 1929; May 14; June 26-28; July 3-5, 7, 9, 10, 14, 15, 18, 1930.

35. RW to General D. Potocki, Nov. 18, 1930; Notes from Russia, May 17, 1930, both Woods Papers; *WDW*, June 25, 26, 30; July 2, 5, 26, 1930.

36. Technically, the report appeared as House of Representatives Document 103. Many of the photographs, diagrams and other illustrations were left out of the published version to reduce costs. RW to JOS, April 13, 1931, Woods Papers; "Columbia River and Minor Tributaries," 21, 571.

37. "Columbia River and Minor Tributaries," 592-594, 613, 1017-1033, 1037, 1051-1052. The report, observes one historian, "sounded the death knell of the gravity proposal." Harding, "Water from Pend Oreille," 60.

38. The plan pressed into service 96 percent of the river's normal low water flow and required abandonment of Washington Water Power's proposed Kettle Falls dam. "Columbia River and Minor Tributaries," 53-55, 703. For a summary of work on the lower Columbia by the Portland Army office, see William F. Willingham, *Army Engineers and the Development of Oregon: A History of the Portland District, U.S. Army Corps of Engineers* (Washington, D.C.: Government Printing Office, 1983), 93-95.

39. The published report contained only the Grand Coulee plans. "Columbia River and Minor Tributaries," 56, 59, 570-571, 587-588, 726-755, 762-768. On the evolution of Butler's thinking regarding the "low" and "high" dams, see JOS to Batcheller, April 18, 1931, O'Sullivan Papers.

40. "Columbia River and Minor Tributaries," 34-36, 39, 44-50, 854-880.

41. Better foundation conditions eventually produced a shift from Warrendale to the Bonneville site. Unwilling to antagonize the utility interests, the Army made no clear-cut recommendation on the question of whether government or industry should build the dams. *Ibid.*, 2-3, 11, 50; Brown to Sec. of War, March 29, 1932, SD; to Homer T. Bone, Sept. 26, 1933, RH.

42. *WDW*, Sept. 22; Oct. 9, 1931; McGinnis to RW, Aug. 13, 27; Sept. 9, 1931, Woods Papers; RW to L.C. Gilman, Sept. 23, 1931, O'Sullivan Papers.

43. *WDW*, March 1, 10; June 30; Oct. 1; Dec. 15, 1930; Jan. 1, 1931. For an analysis of the true unemployment situation, see William H. Mullins, *The Depression and the*

*Urban West Coast, 1929-1933: Los Angeles, San Francisco, Seattle and Portland* (Bloomington: Indiana University Press, 1991), 23-24, 56-57.

44. *WDW*, May 1, 5, 8, 11, 1931.

45. *WDW*, May 12; Aug. 14, 22; Sept. 19, 26; Oct. 31; Nov. 18; Dec. 8, 16, 1931; RW to John Maher, April 14, 1932; to JOS, Dec. 18, 1931, Woods Papers.

46. *WDW*, Oct. 6, 28; Dec. 5, 1931; Feb. 26; March 23, 26, 29; April 6, 11, 14, 21-23, 26; May 14; June 9, 16, 21, 27; July 8, 9, 15, 20, 23, 25, 28; Aug. 1; Sept. 9, 1932; Clapp to JOS, Sept. 13, 1932; RW to JOS, Sept. 26, 1932, both O'Sullivan Papers; Oct. 5, 1932, Woods Papers.

47. RW to JOS, April 13, 1931; JOS to RW, Sept. 8, 1932; to Clapp and RW, Jan. 30, 1932, all Woods Papers; Kuentz to Jones, Aug. 11, 1931, RH. On the procedure for handling Corps of Engineers reports, see McKinley, *Uncle Sam in the Pacific Northwest*, 7071.

48. *WDW*, Oct. 5, 1931; Gilman to RW, Sept. 24, 1931; E.H. McPherson to RW, Sept. 29, 1931; Batcheller to Christy Thomas, Sept. 10, 1931; to RW, Dec. 30, 1931; Memo, "Columbia Basin Opposition," Jan. 2, 1932; Matthews to C. Hunter Martin, Aug. 26, 1931; JOS to the People of the Northwest, Sept. 20, 1931, all Woods Papers; to Hedges, Nov. 8, 1931; RW to Gilman, Sept. 23, 1931, both O'Sullivan Papers.

49. As part of these arrangements, Billy Clapp was given the minor position on the state payroll previously held by Mark Woodruff. *WDW*, Oct. 9, 1931; Batcheller to RW, Oct. 7, 20, 24, 27, 1931; RW to Gilman, Sept. 13, 1931; to "The Dam University," Oct. 26, 1931; to Batcheller, Oct. 26, 1931; to Graham, Oct. 26, 1931; to JOS, Nov. 17, 18, 23; Dec. 10, 1931, all Woods Papers; Matthews to JOS, Nov. 24, 1931, O'Sullivan Papers.

50. Reports from D.C., Oct. 1931; Report of RW on His Washington D.C. Trip, Sept. 26, 1931-Oct. 20, 1931; RW to JOS, et al., Oct. 6, 1931, all Woods Papers; to Gilman, Sept. 23, 1931; Batcheller to JOS, Sept. 28, 1931, both O'Sullivan Papers.

51. Brief of Conversation with President Hoover, Oct. 8, 1931; Report on Meeting with the President, Oct. 1931, both Woods Papers; Hebbard to Gill, Nov. 6, 1931, Gill Papers.

52. "Columbia River and Minor Tributaries," 5, 12-13, 1066-1067; Barden to Chief of Engineers, Feb. 23, 1932, NPD; JOS to RW, Dec. 17, 27, 1931; RW to JOS, Dec. 22, 1931, all Woods Papers; Clapp to JOS, Dec. 24, 1931, O'Sullivan Papers; *WDW*, Dec. 29, 1931.

53. JOS to RW, Nov. 24, 26, 1931; to Clapp and RW, Jan. 1, 5, 1932, Woods Papers; Gill to Joseph A. Swalwell, Feb. 14, 1932, O'Sullivan Papers.

54. JOS to RW, Nov. 26; Dec. 17, 1931; to Clapp and RW, Jan. 10, 1932; Gill to Swalwell, Feb. 8, 1932, all Woods Papers; Nov. 25, 1931; to Adams, Jan. 23, 1932, O'Sullivan Papers.

55. Jones to Southard, Sept. 2, 1929, Jones Papers; May 27, 1929; Batcheller to JOS, Feb. 15, 1932; Southard to JOS, Feb. 25, 1932, all O'Sullivan Papers; JOS to Clapp and RW, Jan. 5, 1932; RW to JOS, Dec. 18, 1931; to Sefrit, Jan. 30, 1932; H. R. Smith to RW, Jan. 22, 1932, all Woods Papers.

56. Jones to Roy Staley, Feb. 16, 1932; to RW, March 1, 1932; Ralph A. Horr to RW, Feb. 20, 1932; JOS Report, March 1, 1932; JOS to RW, March 1, 1932; to RW and Clapp, March 6, 26, 1932, all Woods Papers.

57. JOS to Ray W. Clark, Feb. 6, 1932; to Clapp and RW, Jan. 1, 5, 1932; RW to JOS, Dec. 22, 1931, all ibid.

58. JOS to Clapp and RW, Jan. 1, 5, 10, 1932; to RW, Nov. 24, 25, 1931, *ibid.* Sam Hill should not be confused with James J. Hill's son-in-law of the same name, a leader of the Washington good roads movement and the builder of Maryhill in Klickitat County.

59. JOS to Clapp and RW, Jan. 10, 11, 1932; to *Daily World*, Jan. 11, 1932, *ibid.*
60. JOS to RW, Nov. 25, 28; Dec. 17, 27, 30, 1931; to Clapp, Jan. 20, 1932; to Clapp and RW, Jan. 29, 30; Feb. 1, 1932, *ibid.*
61. JOS to Clapp, Jan. 20, 1932; to Clapp and RW, Jan. 23, 29; Feb. 1, 1932; to *Daily World*, Feb. 1, 1932, *ibid.*; Extracts from Army Board Hearing, Jan. 18, 1932, BR30-45.
62. JOS to Clapp, RW and Batcheller, Feb. 3, 1932; to RW and Clapp, Feb. 6, 1932; to Clark, Feb. 6, 1932; to RW, March 1, 1932; JOS Report, March 1, 1932, all Woods Papers.
63. JOS to RW and Clapp, March 6, 18, 26; April 7, 1932; to Clapp, April 1, 1932, *ibid.*
64. *WDW*, March 30, 1932; JOS Report, May 14, 1932; JOS to RW, April 17; May 7, 1932; to RW and Clapp, April 16, 28; May 5, 11, 17, 1932, all Woods Papers; June 24, 1932; to Butler, May 4, 1932, O'Sullivan Papers.
65. The Senate hearing, reported O'Sullivan, was "perfunctory" and nothing but "an attempt to show a little action." JOS to Southard, June 2, 1932; to Clapp, June 13, 1932; to RW and Clapp, June 12, 22, 24, 1932, O'Sullivan Papers; July 8, 1932, Woods Papers.
66. JOS to RW, June 30, 1932, O'Sullivan Papers; to RW and Clapp, July 8, 1932, Woods Papers.
67. Financial stringency in Spokane forced Roy Gill to pay his own bill at the Shoreham Hotel. Clapp to JOS, June 8; Aug. 23; Sept. 13, 1932; Southard to JOS, Aug. 29, 1932; JOS to Southard, July 28, 1932; to Clapp, Aug. 24, 1932; to RW, Aug. 17, 25, 1932, all O'Sullivan Papers; to Clark, Aug. 30, 1932; to RW and Clapp, April 29, 1932; RW to JOS, Oct. 5, 1932, all Woods Papers.
68. *WDW*, Aug. 25, 1932; JOS to Clapp, Aug. 24, 1932; RW to JOS, Sept. 6, 1932, both O'Sullivan Papers; Oct. 5, 1932, Woods Papers.
69. Address to Chamber of Commerce, Dec. 4, 1931, Woods Papers.

## Notes for Chapter Eight

1. *WDW*, Feb. 17, 1937.
2. Ficken, *Forested Land*, 183; Mullins, *Depression and the Urban West Coast*, 78-79; Murray Morgan, *Skid Road: An Informal Portrait of Seattle* (Seattle: University of Washington Press ed., 1982, 1951), 224-230; Southard to Jones, May 14, 1932; Batcheller to JOS, Feb. 15, 1932, both O'Sullivan Papers; RW to JOS, Oct. 5, 1932, Woods Papers.
3. *WDW*, April 15; Aug. 15, 25; Oct. 24; Nov. 20; Dec. 10, 1931; March 21; Nov. 11, 1932.
4. *WDW*, April 5; May 6, 1930; Feb. 25; March 12; May 5; June 15, 17; July 29, 30; Aug. 8, 12, 22, 28; Sept. 17, 25, 30; Oct. 1, 27; Nov. 21, 24, 1931; Jan. 6, 21; Feb. 20; April 7; July 30; Aug. 17, 26; Sept. 19, 22; Oct. 5, 10, 11, 25, 1932.
5. *WDW*, July 8, 17, 1931; Jan. 18, 25; Feb. 11; June 17, 24; July 18, 23; Aug. 1; Sept. 27, 1932.
6. In a further example of lack of acumen concerning the Democrats, the *World* urged the party to nominate the aged and eccentric Senator J. Hamilton Lewis of Illinois, a one-time Washington congressman. *WDW*, Jan. 30; Feb. 10, 16; June 13; Sept. 27, 1932.
7. *WDW*, March 4, 22; Sept. 15, 16, 1932; Southard to RW, July 26, 1932, Woods Papers; Ficken, *Lumber and Politics*, 201-202.
8. *WDW*, Sept. 23, 1932.

9. *The Public Papers and Addresses of Franklin D. Roosevelt* (New York: Random House, 13 vols., 1938-1950), 1:727-742. The Portland speech, writes one historian, "must be treated as a milestone in the evolution of a national power policy." Philip J. Funigiello, "The Bonneville Power Administration and the New Deal," *Prologue*, 5(1973), 89. Also see Richard Lowitt, *The New Deal and the West* (Bloomington: Indiana University Press, 1984), 5.

10. Rufus's friend Albert Johnson was defeated in his bid for an eleventh term in the House of Representatives. Ficken, *Lumber and Politics*, 203; Cole, "Democratic Party," 292; *WDW*, Nov. 10, 1932.

11. Ratified in 1933, the Twentieth Amendment moved the inauguration date back from March 4 to January 20. Florence Stanley to JOS, Sept. 8, 1932; JOS to Stanley, Sept. 12, 1932; to Batcheller, Sept. 12, 1932, all O'Sullivan Papers; Gill to Joseph Jacobs, Dec. 18, 1932; Address to Business Men of Seattle, Nov. 25, 1932, both Gill Papers.

12. Matthews to RW, Feb. 13, 1932; RW to Southard, Clapp, Matthews and Paul Patrick, Feb. 11, 1932; Southard to RW, July 25, 27, 30, 1932, all Woods Papers; to JOS, March 21; May 4, 8, 15, 19, 24; July 6, 1932; JOS to Southard, July 28, 1932; Clapp to JOS, April 4, 1932, all O'Sullivan Papers.

13. JOS to Clarence D. Martin, Dec. 20, 1932; Martin to Dill, May 8, 1933, both Martin Papers; *WDW*, Nov. 21, 25, 1932; Mitchell, *Story of Rufus Woods*, 20. For a summary appreciation of Martin, see Norman H. Clark, *Washington: A Bicentennial History* (New York: W. W. Norton & Company, Inc., 1976), 157-159.

14. Martin to Ross, Dec. 31, 1932, Martin Papers; Southard to RW, Dec. 26, 29, 1932; Batcheller to RW, Nov. 26, 30; Dec. 16, 24, 1932, all Woods Papers.

15. The promise to Batcheller, if actually made, had been forgotten, for Rufus at this time broached the topic of becoming engineer-in-charge to Hugh Cooper. Batcheller to RW, Nov. 26, 30; Dec. 16, 1932; Southard to RW, Dec. 26, 29, 1932; Manley A. Haynes to RW, Nov. 26; Dec. 28, 1932; RW to Cooper, Dec. 19, 1932; Cooper to RW, Jan. 10, 1933, all Woods Papers.

16. The unsalaried commissioners received a per diem of $10 when on official business. Cooper to RW, Jan. 25, 1933; RW to Cooper, Jan. 20, 1933, both Woods Papers; to JOS, April 6, 1933; n.d.; Johnson to JOS, March 21, 1933; JOS to Smith, Jan. 20, 1933, all O'Sullivan Papers.

17. RW to Martin, March 18, 1933, Woods Papers; JOS to P. O'Sullivan, March 14, 1933; to Leavy, c. Jan. 1, 1933, O'Sullivan Papers; Mitchell, *Story of Rufus Woods*, 21.

18. Rufus had considerable difficulty securing repayment from the state. At his urging, O'Sullivan's salary was increased from $250 to $300 a month. Minutes, March 29; April 5, 20; Sept. 2, 1933, CBC; JOS to Col. Basin Com., April 27, 1933, Woods Papers; to RW, April 10, 1933; RW to JOS, Oct. 5; Nov. 2; Dec. 21, 1936, all O'Sullivan Papers.

19. JOS to Martin, April 16, 1933, Martin Papers; to Smith, Jan. 30, 1933; to Dill, March 27, 1933; to Sam B. Hill, April 19, 1933; Dill to JOS, March 20, 1933; Hill to JOS, April 13, 1933, all O'Sullivan Papers.

20. Minutes, April 5, 1933; Banker to Dill, April 15, 1933, both CBC; JOS to RW, n.d., O'Sullivan Papers.

21. Goss to JOS, April 13, 1933, O'Sullivan Papers; to RW, Oct. 28, 1942, Woods Papers; Ross to Monrad C. Wallgren, April 4, 1933, SLD. Dill was one of several prominent Democrats endorsing Roosevelt for president in 1931, providing important momentum for the New Yorker's campaign. See Lowitt, *New Deal and the West*, 2.

22. Goss to Martin, April 17, 1933, O'Sullivan Papers; Dill to RW, Feb. 22, 1949, Woods Papers; to Martin, April 17, 19, 21, 1933; to JOS, April 19, 1933; Franklin D. Roosevelt to Dill, April 20, 1933, all Martin Papers. Roosevelt's letter to Dill outlining the

points discussed has been published in Edgar B. Nixon, ed., *Franklin D. Roosevelt and Conservation, 1911-1945* (Hyde Park, N.Y.: Roosevelt Library, 2 vols., 1957), 1:158-159.

23. Dill to Martin, April 17, 19, 21, 26, 1933; to JOS, April 19, 1933; Roosevelt to Dill, April 20, 1933, all Martin Papers; Goss to Martin, April 17, 1933; to JOS, April 17, 1933, O'Sullivan Papers; to RW, June 15, 1933; to KB, Feb. 16, 1943, Woods Papers; Minutes, April 20, 1933; Banker to Matthews, May 2, 1933, both CBC.

24. Dill to Martin, April 21; May 6, 16, 20; June 2, 1933, Martin Papers; RW to JOS, Nov. 14, 1933; JOS to RW, Nov. 15, 1933, both O'Sullivan Papers.

25. Ross to W. J. McKeen and Glen Smith, July 8, 10, 1933, SLD; Ralph D. Nichols to Mrs. Scott Bullitt, July 21, 1933; to Marshall Dana, August 16, 1933; Dill to Nichols, June 12, 1933, all NRPB; Southard to Banker, March 19, 1934, CBC; Batcheller to RW, Sept. 8, 1933, Batcheller Papers; RW to JOS, July 26, 1933, Woods Papers.

26. Goss to RW, Oct. 28, 1942; Dill to RW, Feb. 22, 1949, both Woods Papers; to JOS, April 19, 1933; to Martin, May 6, 1933, Martin Papers.

27. *WDW*, Sept. 22, 1927; Feb. 13; March 7; April 24, 1930; Jan. 17, 1931; July 3, 1933; Ralph Woods to Dill, Aug. 9, 1930; RW to Dill, May 27; June 5, 1933, all Woods Papers. Homer Bone, Washington's other senator, was committed to the Seattle City Light Skagit project and took no action, hostile or favorable, respecting Grand Coulee. Bone to R.R. Waterbury, Oct. 23, 1933, NRPB; Ellsworth C. French to Martin, Dec. 5, 1933, Martin Papers.

28. Johnson to Batcheller, Aug. 18, 1933, Batcheller Papers; RW to Banker, et al., Nov. 10, 1933; Banker to Matthews, May 2, 1933; Matthews to Smith, April 28, 1933, all CBC; Batcheller to JOS, April 21, 1933, O'Sullivan Papers.

29. To hold down costs, Governor Martin even considered having O'Sullivan, a self-taught engineer, prepare the construction plans for the dam. Dill to Martin, June 2, 1933, Martin Papers; RW and Smith to JOS, May 24, 1933; RW to JOS, April 28, 1933; Goss to RW, June 20, 1933; Southard to JOS, June 23, 1933, all O'Sullivan Papers; RW to Dill, June 5, 1933; Southard to RW, June 4, 1933; Goss to RW, June 15, 1933; Batcheller to RW; April 22; June 21, 1933, all Woods Papers; to McGinnis, July 12, 1933, Batcheller Papers; to Banker, May 25, 1933; Southard to Banker, May 18, 1933, both CBC.

30. Dill to Martin, April 21; May 13, 1933; Martin to Dill, April 26; May 8, 1933, all Martin Papers.

31. Clapp to Batcheller, Sept. 29, 1933, Batcheller Papers; Southard to JOS, May 22, 1933; JOS to RW, May 6, 1933; to G.A. Sellar, May 22, 1933, all O'Sullivan Papers; to Banker, May 29; June 1, 1933; Banker to JOS, May 30, 1933, all CBC; Martin to Dill, May 8, 21, 23, 1933; Dill to Martin, May 24, 27, 1933, all Martin Papers; to RW, June 10, 1933; Batcheller to RW, June 21, 1933, both Woods Papers.

32. Minutes, April 20; June 21, 1933; JOS to Banker, May 7, 31, 1933, all CBC; to RW and Smith, May 25, 1933; to Louise Lawton, May 11, 16, 25, 1933; to Southard, May 16, 1933; Southard to JOS, June 23; Oct. 24, 25, 1933, all O'Sullivan Papers; Dill to Martin, May 13, 16, 20, 1933, Martin Papers; Batcheller to Hill, July 15, 1933, Batcheller Papers.

33. Dill to Martin, May 6, 12, 13, 16, 27, 1933, Martin Papers; to RW, June 1, 1933, Woods Papers.

34. Lowitt, *New Deal and the West*, 223-225; Donald C. Swain, "The Bureau of Reclamation and the New Deal, 1933-1940," *PNQ*, 61 (1970), 137-146. Like Grand Coulee, the Central Valley Project began as a state enterprise, only to be transformed into a federal undertaking through financial dependence on Washington, D.C. See Hundley, *Great Thirst*, 248-252. PWA funds were also used to complete Boulder Dam. Joseph

E. Stevens, *Hoover Dam: An American Adventure* (Norman: University of Oklahoma Press, 1988), 233.

35. Payment of the first installment due the Bureau under the contract was delayed for a month, as the state was unable to market the $10 million bond issue prior to resolution of a legal challenge. Batcheller to Hill, July 15, 1933, Batcheller Papers; S.O. Harper to Dana, July 6, 1935; J. E. McGovern to Dana, Aug. 1, 1933, both NRPB; RW to McGinnis, July 21, 1933, Woods Papers; *WDW*, July 22, 1933; Dill to Martin, June 6, 9, 1933, Martin Papers; Minutes, June 29, 30; Aug. 21, 1933; JOS to RW, July 26, 1933, all CBC.

36. Dill to Martin, July 25, 26, 1933, Martin Papers; RW to Smith, July 3, 1933; Horace E. Smith to RW, Sept. 17, 1933; Batcheller to RW, Sept. 21, 1933, all Woods Papers; to W.R. Prowell, July 28; Aug. 18, 1933; to Frank Bell, Aug. 23, 1933; to Clapp, Sept. 25, 1933; Prowell to Batcheller, July 21; Aug. 5, 1933; Southard to Batcheller, July 27, 1933, Batcheller Papers; to JOS, Oct. 25, 1933; JOS to RW, Dec. 26, 1933, both O'Sullivan Papers; *WDW*, Aug. 4, 15, 1933.

37. Dill to RW, Sept. 25, 1933, Woods Papers; Minutes, July 16; Sept. 28; Nov. 25; Dec. 19, 1933, CBC; Southard to JOS, June 23; Oct. 15, 1933, O'Sullivan Papers; F.A. Banks to Dana, Nov. 10, 1933, NRPB.

38. These contracts, worth $92,000, were funded out of the state's $377,000 contribution, but were supervised by the Bureau of Reclamation. Minutes, Sept. 1, 2, 1933, CBC; Walter A. Averill, "What The Grand Coulee Dam Means To The Architect and The Builder," *Pacific Builder and Engineer*, 39(Sept. 16, 1933), 3, and "The Site for Grand Coulee Dam," *ibid.*, 39(Oct. 7, 1933), 14.

39. Dill to Martin, Sept. 13, 1933, Martin Papers; Minutes, Sept. 2, 1933, CBC; RW to Fraser, April 19, 1934, Woods Papers.

40. The *World*, failing to grasp the implications for Grand Coulee, had earlier praised Ickes for insisting that PWA money be treated as "a trust . . . to be spent with intelligent economy." T.H. Watkins, *Righteous Pilgrim: The Life and Times of Harold L. Ickes, 1874-1952* (New York: Henry Holt and Company, Inc., 1990), 371-372; *WDW*, Sept. 29; Nov. 23, 1933; Minutes, Oct. 20, 31, 1933, CBC; RW to Martin, Nov. 21, 1933, Woods Papers.

41. JOS to Martin, Oct. 28, 1933, CBC; to RW, Oct. 28, 1933, O'Sullivan Papers; RW to Dill and John E. Bowen, Oct. 26, 1933, Woods Papers; Dill to Martin, Oct. 28, 1933, Martin Papers.

42. Minutes, Oct. 31, 1933, CBC; RW to Batcheller, Nov. 6, 1933, Woods Papers. James T. Patterson rates Clarence Martin a "particularly uncooperative" New Deal era governor, largely because of his opposition to organized labor. Considering the state-federal relationship on Grand Coulee, this assessment needs revision. See "The New Deal and the West," *PHR*, 38(1969), 322, and *The New Deal and the States: Federalism in Transition* (Princeton, N.J.: Princeton University Press, 1969), 155-156. Earl Pomeroy, also overlooking the significance of dam building, concludes that reductions in welfare spending were Martin's "most noteworthy achievements." See *The Pacific Slope: A History of California, Oregon, Washington, Idaho, Utah and Nevada* (Lincoln: University of Nebraska Press ed., 1991, 1965), 244.

43. The "stroke of a pen" comment referred to both the October 1933 contract and to a subsequent Ickes order officially making Grand Coulee a federal project. *WDW*, Feb. 14, 1946; Goss to Henry P. Carstensen, Feb. 24, 1948, Woods Papers; Minutes, Feb. 2, 1934, CBC.

44. Alice L. Batcheller to RW, Feb. 7, 1940; Clapp to RW, Dec. 18, 1933, both Woods Papers; Minutes, Sept. 1, 28; Oct. 20; Dec. 19, 1933; March 8, 1934; Banker to

Southard, Oct. 20, 28, 1933; Southard to Banker, Oct. 23, 1933, all CBC; Batcheller to Prowell, Oct. 2, 1933, Batcheller Papers.

45. Leonard Arrington makes a correlation "between the decline of per capita personal income, 1929 to 1933, and New Deal expenditures." There appears, however, to be a clear linkage between spending on water projects, involving such additional factors as geography and politics, and the ranking of the states. Leonard Arrington, "The New Deal in the West: A Preliminary Statistical Inquiry," *PHR*, 38(1969), 311-316, and "The Sagebrush Resurrection: New Deal Expenditures in the Western States, 1933-1939," *PHR*, 52(1983), 1-16; Worster, *Rivers of Empire*, 269. For a different statistical ranking that makes the same general point about New Deal spending, see Carlos A. Schwantes, *The Pacific Northwest: An Interpretive History* (Lincoln: University of Nebraska Press, 1989), 306.

46. Address to County Commissioners, 1933; RW to Sefrit, July 13, 1933, both Woods Papers.

## Notes for Chapter Nine

1. Jan. 1, 1935.
2. *WDW*, March 1, 1934; Jan. 16, 1936.
3. Rufus turned down an offer by the Scripps newspaper chain of $400,000 in cash for the *World* in early 1930, a decision he may have privately regretted at various hard-pressed times during the Depression. *WDW*, Jan. 17; Feb. 24; May 12; Nov. 16, 1933; March 1, 1934; April 4, 1935; Report, P.N.C.M.A. Convention, April 9-10, 1933; Ralph Woods to RW, Feb. 25, 1930; RW to JOS, Oct. 5, 1932, all Woods Papers; n.d. but c. Feb. 1933; Clark to JOS, March 10, 1933, both O'Sullivan Papers.
4. *WDW*, Nov. 21, 25; Dec. 8, 14, 30, 1932; March 23; June 14, 27; Sept. 6, 1933; April 30; Oct. 22, 1935; RW to Martin, Sept. 9, 1933; July 14, 1934; Sept. 14, 1936, Woods Papers; Oct. 8, 1936; Martin to Dill, May 8, 1933; Jan. 10; July 18, 1934, all Martin Papers.
5. Outside Wenatchee, "several million dollars" were tied up for months in failed North Central Washington banks. *WDW*, Feb. 8; March 6, 16; July 10, 18; Oct. 14, 1933.
6. RW to Sefrit, March 15, 1933; to Werner Rupp, March ? 1933; to Lorene Burks, March ? 1933; to H.G. Kelly, March 15, 1933; to S.A. Perkins, March 15, 1933; Pacific Northwest Newspaper Association to Publishers, March 15, 1933; Kelly to RW, March 14, 28, 1933, all Woods Papers.
7. *WDW*, March 18; April 26; June 7, 28, 1933.
8. *WDW*, March 30; Aug. 2, 1933; June 14, 15, 18, 1935.
9. Two-thirds of the farm units in Chelan County were mortgaged, producing a built-in, good year and bad year, drain on income. *WDW*, Nov. 8, 14, 16, 30; Dec. 2, 3, 13, 1932; Jan. 6, 9; Feb. 25, 1933; Freeman, "Apple Industry," 167-170.
10. Together, Winesaps and Delicious made up nearly 60 percent of the apples shipped from the Wenatchee District. *WDW*, March 9, 17, 22, 29; April 11, 21, 28; May 3; June 15, 20, 1933; Freeman, "Apple Industry," 169.
11. Long-range national trends, if properly exploited, favored the industry. In the previous two decades, the population of the United States had increased by a third, but apple production—thanks to a 46 percent decrease in the orchard tree inventory—declined by a fifth. *WDW*, Feb. 17, 18; May 1, 20, 22; June 2, 5, 16, 17, 1933; Freeman, "Apple Industry," 168-169.
12. Wenatchee Valley growers at one point set up their own code mechanism and insisted that it, rather than the apparatus under negotiation in Spokane, be responsible for the local scene. *WDW*, June 29; July 4, 13, 15, 19, 26, 31; Aug. 2, 7, 31; Oct. 5, 1933.

13. Implementation of the code was delayed when the official documents, dispatched to Washington for AAA approval, were lost in the mail. *WDW*, Oct. 5, 14, 18; Nov. 29; Dec. 4, 9, 13, 27, 1933.

14. *WDW*, Aug. 11; Dec. 27, 1933; Jan. 30; March 6, 1934; Report for November 1932-1933, Woods Papers.

15. *WDW*, Aug. 4, 9; Sept. 22; Oct. 14, 1933; Aug. 31, 1934.

16. Growers, and their defenders, were an unforgiving lot. During the Second World War, the *World* suggested that Tugwell be appointed governor of Guam and dropped by parachute onto that Japanese-occupied American possession. *WDW*, Sept. 28; Nov. 9, 20; Dec. 15, 1933; Jan. 4; March 7; April 19; June 16, 1934.

17. After working as a consultant for the Corps of Engineers, Henny was considered a traitor in the Bureau. *WDW*, July 26; Dec. 5, 1933; Jan. 17; March 16; April 17, 1934; Goss to JOS, March 20, 1934; JOS to Mrs. J.R. Sabichi, March 14, 1934; to Goss, March 24, 25, 1934; to RW, April 11, 1934, all O'Sullivan Papers; Feb. 27; March 13, 18, 24, 26, 1934; to Columbia Basin Commission, March 26, 1934; Butler to JOS, April 3, 1934; Walter G. Ronald to RW, Feb. 15, 1934, all Woods Papers; JOS to Banker, March 23, 1934; RW to Banker, et al., Nov. 10, 1933, both CBC.

18. JOS to Dill, May 31, 1934, CBC; to Columbia Basin Commission, Nov. 18, 1933; to RW, March 13, 1934; to Clark, Aug. 8, 1934, Woods Papers; RW to JOS, March 5, 1934, O'Sullivan Papers.

19. Dill to JOS, Feb. 23, 1934, Woods Papers; Jan. 31; Feb. 14, 1934; JOS to Southard, Oct. 16, 1933, all O'Sullivan Papers; Banker to Ashley E. Holden, Dec. 29, 1934, CBC.

20. *Newsweek*, 4 (July 7, 1934), 7; Ross to Horr, Jan. 25, 1934; to Tiffany, Aug. 4, 1934; to Charles H. Ireland, Aug. 18, 1934, SLD; RW to Ross, Nov. 27; Dec. 6, 1934, Woods Papers; Robins to Chief of Engineers, June 30, 1937, in House Document No. 704, 75th Cong., 3d sess.; March 3, 1934; Report of Technical Advisory Committee, March 24, 1934; Proceedings of Conference on Power Uses, Dec. 14, 1934, all NPD.

21. Proceedings of Conference on Power Uses, Dec. 14, 1934, NPD; RW to Dana, Dec. 20, 1934; Jan. 1, 1935; B.H. Kizer to Dana, Dec. 19, 1934; JOS to Dana, Dec. 18, 1934, all NRPB; Dec. 20, 1934; to Lewis B. Schwellenbach, Dec. 20, 1934; to RW, Dec. 27, 1934, all O'Sullivan Papers; RW to Ronald, Dec. 24, 1934, Woods Papers; *WDW*, Dec. 15, 28, 1934; Lowitt, *New Deal and the West*, 138-139; McKinley, *Uncle Sam in the Pacific Northwest*, 459-461.

22. RW to JOS, Dec. 5, 1934; to JOS and Holden, Jan. 18, 1935; Notes from D.C., Jan. 16, 17, 1935, all Woods Papers; *WDW*, Dec. 31, 1934; Herman C. Voeltz, "Genesis and Development of a Regional Power Agency in the Pacific Northwest, 1933-43," *PNQ*, 53(1962), 65-67; McKinley, *Uncle Sam in the Pacific Northwest*, 543-545.

23. *WDW*, June 22, 23; Nov. 21, 1934; Owen P. White, "Spare that Desert!" *Collier's*, 93 (June 16, 1934), 10*ff*. For additional examples of media criticism, see Walter Davenport, "Power in the Wilderness," *ibid.*, 94 (Sept. 21, 1935), 10*ff*; "A Portfolio of New Deal Construction," *Fortune*, 14 (Nov. 1936), 76, 79; Jim Marshall, "Dam of Doubt," *Collier's*, 99 (June 19, 1937), 19*ff*. Positive coverage came from Neuberger, "Biggest Thing on Earth" and from Stuart Chase, "Great Dam," *Atlantic Monthly*, 162 (1938), 593-599.

24. JOS to Goss, March 24, 1934, O'Sullivan Papers; *WDW*, Jan. 13; April 13, 17; Oct. 5, 1934; May 22, 1935; April 2, 1936. The dam descriptions are from the titles of Neuberger, "Biggest Thing on Earth" and Robert Ormond Case, "The Eighth World Wonder," *Saturday Evening Post*, 208(July 13, 1935), 23*ff*.

25. *WDW*, Jan. 5; July 27, 28; Aug. 30; Oct. 4, 1934; March 25; July 8, 10, 16-18, 22, 31; Aug. 20, 28, 1935; Dec. 22, 1936; Lowitt, *New Deal and the West*, 34-36.

26. Part of the Six Companies group, led by Henry Kaiser, had already obtained the Bonneville Dam contract. JOS to Dill, May 31, 1934, CBC; to RW, June 6, 25, 1934, Woods Papers; June 5, 7, 1934; to Walter, June 4, 1934; Walter to JOS, June 7, 1934, all O'Sullivan Papers. On the Six Companies, see Stevens, *Hoover Dam*, 34-45; Mark S. Foster, *Henry J. Kaiser: Builder in the Modern American West* (Austin: University of Texas Press, 1989), 46-48.

27. O'Sullivan claimed that friends of Dill threatened to have him fired as secretary of the Columbia Basin Commission for exposing the machinations of the Six Companies. JOS to RW, July 7, 1934, Woods Papers; June 6, 1934; to Clark, July 5, 1934, O'Sullivan Papers. Also see Foster, *Kaiser*, 63.

28. Ross to Robert E. Healy, Oct. 10, 1934, SLD; RW to Frank McCann, et al., July 1, 1935; to Ross, Nov. 27; Dec. 6, 1934; Batcheller to RW, July 5, 1935; JOS to RW, July 2, 1935, all Woods Papers; to Hu Blonk, Nov. 3, 1934, O'Sullivan Papers; *WDW*, Oct. 11, 22, 31; Dec. 1, 1934; Richard C. Berner, *Seattle, 1921-1940: From Boom to Bust* (Seattle: Charles Press, 1992), 420-422.

29. Holden to RW, Oct. 22, Nov. 14, 1934; Jan. 16, 27; Feb. 11; March 9, 22, 1935; to Prowell, Dec. 29, 1934; Batcheller to RW, Aug. 20, 28, 1935; Haynes to RW, March 9; April 11, 1935; RW to Batcheller, Aug. 31, 1935; to Ted Little, Oct. 2, 1935; Ho. Smith to RW, July 6, 1935; Little to RW; Sept. 24, 1935; JOS to RW, July 2, 1935, all Woods Papers; Aug. 16, 1935; to Hill, Oct. 23, 1935; Holden to JOS, Dec. 20, 21, 26, 1934; Jan. 28; March 22; April 11, 1935, all O'Sullivan Papers; to Banker, March 15, 1935, CBC; Berner, *Seattle, 1921-1940*, 418-434. Holden eventually exchanged his lobbying chores for a position with the *World*, then served for years as the highly conservative political editor of the *Spokesman-Review*. As owner of the *Tonasket Tribune* in the Okanogan Valley, he published accusations in 1962 that state legislator John Goldmark was a communist, precipitating a nationally famous libel trial. See William L. Dwyer, *The Goldmark Case: An American Libel Trial* (Seattle: University of Washington Press, 1984), 29-30, 34-35.

30. *WDW*, Nov. 5, 1934; R. J. Kugelman to JOS, Oct. 20, 1934; Feb. 23; June 1, 1935, O'Sullivan Papers; Nov. 10, 24, 1934, Woods Papers; Case, "Eighth World Wonder," 34.

31. Kugelman to JOS, Nov. 10, 1934, Woods Papers; Feb. 23, 1935, O'Sullivan Papers; Case, "Eighth World Wonder," 34; James Rorty, "Grand Coulee," *Nation*, 140 (March 20, 1935), 329; Neuberger, "Biggest Thing on Earth," 251; R.F. Bessey to Glavis, Nov. 22, 1933, NRPB; Blonk to RW, n.d., Billingsley Papers.

32. Mead to Harold L. Ickes, Dec. 19, 27, 1934; May 11, 20; June 4, 1935, DI07-36; to Tiffany, Sept. 19, 1934, Woods Papers; to JOS, Oct. 18, 1934, CBC; JOS to RW, Dec. 10, 1934, O'Sullivan Papers. "Present navigation is negligible in the Grand Coulee section," reported the Corps of Engineers, "and future development so improbable that there was no justification for the installation of locks." W.J.B. Memorandum for General Pillsbury, Aug. 15, 1933, RH.

33. Some political observers contended that Dill withdrew out of fear that his involvement in land speculation would otherwise be exposed to public scrutiny. Others, taking a somewhat more kindly view, maintained that he merely intended to become wealthy from the practice of law. Notes from D.C. trip, Feb. 7, 1935; RW to Ronald, Jan. 31, 1935; to N.D. Showalter, March 20, 1935; to Hill, March 9, 1935; to Bell, March 13, 1935, all Woods Papers; to JOS and Holden, Jan. 18, 1935; to JOS, Jan. 13; Feb. 12, 1935; to Holden, Feb. 5, 1935; to Ervin E. King, Feb. 7, 1935; JOS to RW, Oct. 20, 1934; to Holden, April 16, 1935, all O'Sullivan Papers; *WDW*, July 10, 12, 14; Sept. 7, 22; Oct. 29; Nov. 1, 3, 6, 1934; Feb. 12, 1935.

34. To avoid burdening the cash-poor state, Woods paid his own expenses. Southard to JOS, Oct. 28, 1934; RW to JOS and Holden, Jan. 18, 1935; to JOS, Jan. 24; Feb. 12,

1935, all O'Sullivan Papers; Jan. 26, 1935; to Ronald, Jan. 31, 1935, Woods Papers; Banker to Earling, Feb. 25, 1935, CBC; *WDW*, Feb. 11, 1935.

35. JOS to Banker, et al., May 27, 1935, CBC; to Columbia Basin Commission, June 3, 1935; to RW, May 21; June 7, 1935; Hill to JOS, May 23, 1935; to RW, May 14, 1935; RW to Martin, June 21, 1935, all Woods Papers; to JOS, May 16, 1935, O'Sullivan Papers; Pitzer, "Visions, Plans, and Realities," 34-35. For the legal and political issues animating the Parker Dam dispute, see Hundley, *Great Thirst*, 224-228.

36. Hill to RW, May 14, 1935, Woods Papers; JOS to Banker, et al., May 27, 1935; King to JOS, May 29, 1935, both CBC; Banker to JOS, May 31, 1935, O'Sullivan Papers.

37. A City Light source confided to Willis Batcheller that Ross "had been working on Mr. Hopkins from the time he went into office, for the purpose of discrediting the Grand Coulee project." *WDW*, April 5, 1935; Haynes to RW, April 11, 1935; Batcheller to Underwood, May 29, 1935; Hill to JOS, May 23, 1935; Matthews to RW, April 26, 1935; to Averill, May 31, 1935; RW to Martin, June 1, 1935; to O'Sullivan, May 21, 1935; to JOS, June 1, 1935, all Woods Papers; June 4, 1935; JOS to Hill, May 25, 1935, both O'Sullivan Papers; to Banker, et al., May 27, 1935; Clapp to JOS, Aug. 3, 1935, both CBC; Averill to Dana, June 7, 1935, NRPB.

38. RW Report to the Commission, June 20, 1935; CBC; RW to JOS, June 4, 1935, O'Sullivan Papers; to Martin, June 1, 1935, Woods Papers; *WDW*, May 29, 1935.

39. JOS to Banker, et al., May 27, 1935, CBC; to Columbia Basin Commission, May 28, 1935; to RW; July 3, 1935; Samuel B. Hill Statement Re: Crucial Features of Legislative History of Grand Coulee Dam, n.d.; to KB, Oct. 23, 1936, all Woods Papers; to JOS, Aug. 26, 1935, O'Sullivan Papers.

40. O'Sullivan reported a 196-123 vote. The Senate accepted the amendment without recorded opposition. Hill complained in later years that his "connection with the Grand Coulee project has been ignored by historians." Hill to JOS, Aug. 26, 1935, O'Sullivan Papers; to KB, Oct. 23, 1936; Hill Statement, n.d.; JOS to Columbia Basin Commission, Aug. 28, 1935, all Woods Papers; to Dana, April 10, 1936, NRPB.

41. Harper to Dana, July 6, 1935, NRPB; JOS to Columbia Basin Commission, Aug. 28, 1935; Kugelman to JOS, Nov. 30, 1935, both Woods Papers; Aug. 31, 1935, O'Sullivan Papers; *WDW*, Aug. 26, 1935.

42. Sales of liquor-by-the-drink remained illegal in Washington until 1948. *WDW*, March 21, 31; May 19; June 12, 22-24; Aug. 31; Sept. 1; Dec. 12, 21, 1933; Jan. 5, 15, 24, 26; June 27, 1934; Jan. 12; Feb. 28; April 17; July 5; Nov. 13, 1935; Sept. 5, 1936; Clark, *Dry Years*, 241-247.

43. *WDW*, May 26; June 4; July 4, 10, 11, 13, 1934; July 1, 10; Aug. 20, 1935; Jan. 10, 1935; Martin to RW, June 24, 1935, Woods Papers. On the 1935 lumber strike, see Ficken, *Forested Land*, 209-212.

44. *WDW*, Aug. 26, 1933; Oct. 14, 1936; RW to Martin, Oct. 8, 1936, Martin Papers; Cletus Daniel, "Wobblies on the Farm: The IWW in the Yakima Valley," *PNQ*, 65 (1974), 166-175; James G. Newbill, "Farmers and Wobblies in the Yakima Valley, 1933," *PNQ*, 68 (1977), 80-87.

45. After the 1934 election, the Democrats had majorities of 36-9 in the senate and 95-13 in the house. *WDW*, Sept. 11; Oct. 10, 20; Nov. 8; Dec. 22, 28, 1934; Jan. 31; Feb. 6; March 1; April 20; May 1; Aug. 24; Sept. 3, 13; Oct. 29, 1935.

46. *WDW*, Dec. 8, 1934; Feb. 15, 20; March 15, 23; Nov. 27, 1935; March 31; April 20; May 26; July 24; Aug. 14, 29; Oct. 30, 1936; Mary McCarthy, "Circus Politics in Washington State," *Nation*, 143 (Oct. 17, 1936), 442-444. Also see Richard L. Neuberger, *Our Promised Land* (Moscow: University of Idaho Press ed., 1989, 1938), chapt. 11.

47. O'Sullivan offered himself as a worthy candidate for the position. *WDW*, Jan. 27, 30; Feb. 1, 4; March 3, 12, 1936; Hill to KB, Feb. 12, 1936; to RW, March 4, 1936, Woods Papers; to JOS, March 3, 1936; JOS to Hill, Feb. 7, 1936; to Henry M. White, March 21, 1936; to RW, March 9, 1936, all O'Sullivan Papers; Feb. 29, 1936, CBC. Page had been an assistant to Walker Young, the chief government engineer at Boulder Dam. See Stevens, *Hoover Dam*, 254.
48. JOS to G.H. Plummer, Jan. 14, 1937, Woods Papers; RW to JOS, Oct. 17, 1936, O'Sullivan Papers. Also see Pitzer, "Visions, Plans, and Realities," 36-37.
49. JOS to RW, June 8, 1936; to Columbia Basin Commission, June 11, 1936; Hill to RW, Feb. 24, 1936, all Woods Papers; to JOS, Feb. 24; March 3; April 13, 1936, O'Sullivan Papers; Pitzer, "Visions, Plans, and Realities," 37.
50. Banker to Southard, April 4, 1936, CBC; *WDW*, Jan. 31, 1933; July 9, 12; Aug. 23; Sept. 16, 19, 1935.
51. *WDW*, July 9; Sept. 20; Dec. 2, 1935; March 10, 12; April 28, 1936.
52. The visiting American was unaware of the violent purge just beginning within the Communist Party. Coverage of the European trip is based on Woods travel accounts in *WDW*, June 3-5, 8-13, 15-17, 22, 23, 27, 30, 1936.
53. *WDW*, June 17, 1936.
54. Ignoring the confidential nature of Woods's report on the meeting with Landon, O'Sullivan immediately released the details to the press. K.P. Stoffel to RW, April 8, 1936; William Allen White to RW, Sept. 17, 1936; RW to Budd, Nov. 16, 1935; to Hebberd, June 2, 1936, all Woods Papers; to Friends of Grand Coulee Dam, April 1, 1936; JOS to Thos. B. Hill, May 14, 1936, both CBC; to H. White, July 22, 1936, O'Sullivan Papers; *WDW*, June 13, 1936.
55. *WDW*, Jan. 6, 31; March 2, 14; May 20; July 9, 1936.
56. *WDW*, Jan. 4, 7, 21; Feb. 8; April 4, 20; June 8, 10, 26; July 25; Aug. 4, 27; Oct. 13, 23, 27, 1936.
57. KB to JOS, July 23, 1936; JOS to King, Aug. 21, 1936; to RW, Sept. 5, 1936, all O'Sullivan Papers; Aug. 15, 21, 1936, Woods Papers.
58. O'Sullivan would have run himself if Leavy had not entered the race. Details of the primary campaign are from RW to Bell, Aug. 30, 1936; to JOS, Sept. 4, 7, 1936; JOS to RW, Aug. 15, 21, 1936, all Woods Papers; Sept. 1, 8, 10, 1936; to Goss, Sept. 9, 1936; to King, Sept. 9, 1936; to Hill, Sept. 15, 1936, O'Sullivan Papers; *WDW*, Aug. 29, 1936.
59. J.B. Fink, the acting head of the Department of Conservation and Development, received the job on a permanent basis when Martin decided not to reappoint Banker. JOS to Goss, Sept. 12, 1936; to RW, Sept. 8, 9, 10, 1936, O'Sullivan Papers; Sept. 11, 30, 1936; Matthews to Martin, Sept. 11, 1936; to RW, Sept. 25, 1936; RW to JOS, Sept. 7, 12, 1936; to Bell, Sept. 29, 1936, all Woods Papers.
60. *WDW*, Sept. 26; Oct. 17, 21, 22, 26, 1936; J. M. McCauley to Martin, Oct. 8, 1936, Martin Papers.
61. *WDW*, Jan. 1; Sept. 5; Oct. 26, 27, 1936.
62. *WDW*, Nov. 4, 5, 9, 10, 1936; Woods Diary, Dec. 29, 1936.
63. George F. Yantis to Martin F. Smith, June 7, 1935, NRPB; RW to Fraser, April 2, 1934, Woods Papers; *WDW*, April 29, 1935; Sept. 26; Dec. 3, 1936.
64. *WDW*, Sept. 11, 1934; April 6; July 5, 13, 17; Nov. 30; Dec. 25, 1935.
65. *WDW*, Sept. 24, 1934; April 9; July 22; Nov. 19; Dec. 13, 1935.
66. Twenty-one year Subscriber to RW, Dec. 17, 1934, Woods Papers; *WDW*, Sept. 24, 1934; April 6; July 22, 1935.

## Notes for Chapter Ten

1. *WDW*, Oct. 11, 1941.
2. Woods Diary, Jan. 1; Dec. 29, 1936; June 10, 1937; *WDW*, Dec. 7, 1936; Aug. 25, 1937.
3. This account of the Woods circus experience is based on *WDW*, Aug. 20, 25-28, 1937; RW to Otto Greibling, Oct. 5, 1937; to Skinny Dawson, Oct. 6, 1937; to Jess Atkins and Zack Terrell, Oct. 8, 1937, Woods Papers. Also see Mitchell, *Story of Rufus Woods*, 9, 22, 33.
4. *WDW*, March 5, 10, 13, 16, 23, 24, 27; Oct. 26; Nov. 30, 1937; Jan. 21, 29; March 7; April 8, 25, 28; May 20; July 12; Aug. 1, 15; Oct. 29; Nov. 1, 2, 10, 11, 1938; RW to Richard Hippelhauser, Jan. 30, 1940, Woods Papers; George W. Scott, "The New Order of Cincinnatus: Municipal Politics in Seattle During the 1930s," *PNQ*, 64 (1973), 146.
5. In one of its key changes-of-position, the Supreme Court rejected a challenge by the owners of Wenatchee's Cascadian Hotel to the Washington state minimum wage law for women. *WDW*, Feb. 6, 8, 12; May 27; July 10, 19, 31; Aug. 20, 1937.
6. *WDW*, March 15; April 13; May 26; July 2, 17, 26, 29; Oct. 15, 1937; Oct. 23, 1939.
7. *WDW*, June 16, 1937; Feb. 7; Aug. 6, 19, 31, 1938; July 24; Nov. 22; Dec. 19, 22, 1939.
8. *WDW*, July 8; Aug. 19, 24, 1937; Feb. 3; April 5; May 31; Nov. 3, 1938; April 25; May 13, 1939.
9. *WDW*, April 1; Aug. 1; Sept. 3; Oct. 22, 1938; April 28; Nov. 20, 30, 1939.
10. In a mix-up, the legislature failed to pass the bill officially terminating the commission, allowing O'Sullivan to maintain that the agency remained in existence, albeit without an appropriation. *WDW*, Jan. 11, 30; Feb. 17, 1937; Oct. 9, 1939; JOS to RW, Jan. 15; Feb. 13; July 8, 1937, Woods Papers; Nov. 11, 1936; March 11, 1937; to R. A. Seelig, Feb. 2, 1937; to Leavy, Jan. 13, 25; Feb. 2; March 11, 17; April 1, 1937; to Johnson, March 31, 1937; to Janet Wallace, March 3, 1937; to K. O'Sullivan, May 2, 1937; RW to JOS, Oct. 3, 1936; Leavy to JOS, July 24, 1937, all O'Sullivan Papers. Also see Sundborg, *Hail Columbia*, 298-299.
11. During his service with the SEC, Ross remained superintendent of Seattle City Light. *WDW*, Feb. 4, 1937; Leavy to JOS, Dec. 31, 1936, O'Sullivan Papers; Feb. 6, 1937; Clapp to RW, Nov. 11, 1937; JOS to Martin, Jan. 14, 1937; Roosevelt to Bone, Feb. 10, 1937, all Woods Papers.
12. RW to Irvin Jones, April 16, 1937; to Martin, March 31; April 9, 23, 1937; Notes, April 24, 1937; Leavy to RW, Feb. 6, 12, 1937; Roosevelt to Bone, Feb. 10, 1937, all Woods Papers; JOS to John C. Page, Oct. 19, 1936; to RW, Jan. 3, 1937; to Leavy, Jan. 8, 1937; to Seelig, Feb. 15, 1937, O'Sullivan Papers; JOS Report, May 17, 1937, CBC; *WDW*, Feb. 4, 15, 1937.
13. Prior to its demise, the Columbia Basin Commission had prepared an anti-speculation plan limiting owners of watered tracts to eighty acres. Woods credited Bone's sudden interest in Grand Coulee to concern that Governor Martin might run for the Senate in 1938. B.E. Stoutmyer to JOS, April 3, 1937, O'Sullivan Papers; to RW, Nov. 6, 1937; Nathan R. Margold to Bone, March 27, 1937; RW to Editor, *Harpers' Magazine*, Feb. 2, 1937; to Martin, April 10, 1937; Notes, April 8, 1937, all Woods Papers; Bureau of Reclamation Special Memorandum, April 1, 1940, NRPB. Also see Lowitt, *New Deal and the West*, 165-166.
14. RW to I. Jones, March 26; April 5, 7, 16, 1937; to Martin, March 22, 31; April 9, 10, 1937; Notes, April 27, 1937, all Woods Papers; JOS to Wallace, April 16, 1937,

O'Sullivan Papers; to J.B. Fink, April 12, 1937, CBC; *WDW*, May 11, 17; June 2, 1937.

15. RW to Martin, March 22; April 9, 10, 1937; to I. Jones, March 26; April 7, 16, 1937, Woods Papers.

16. RW to Martin, March 22, 1937; to I. Jones, April 5, 1937; Notes, April 12, 1937, all *ibid.*; JOS to Leavy, Jan. 16; April 1, 3, 1937; to Goss, Jan. 20, 1937; to Johnson, March 31, 1937; to Wallace, April 14, 16, 1937, O'Sullivan Papers; to Fink, April 12, 1937, CBC.

17. Congress passed the anti-speculation bill on May 27. Some observers believed that Roosevelt delayed approval of the extra money in an attempt to induce support of his court-packing plan. RW to Martin, April 10, 1937; to I. Jones, April 26, 27, 1937; Notes, April 24, 1937, all Woods Papers; JOS to Fink, April 9, 12, 25, 1937, CBC; April 26, 1937, O'Sullivan Papers; *WDW*, June 28, 1937.

18. RW to Neuberger, May 9; July 13, 1939, Woods Papers; *WDW*, Dec. 5, 1934; Jan. 25, 1935; March 7; Sept. 26, 1936; July 10, 1937.

19. JOS to Clapp, April 27; May 8, 31, 1937; to Wallace, April 30; May 2, 30, 1937; to K. O'Sullivan, May 2, 1937; Wallace to JOS, April 21; May 3; June 2, 1937, all O'Sullivan Papers; RW to JOS, May 10, 1937, Woods Papers; *WDW*, June 11, 1937.

20. *WDW*, June 11, 1937; Clapp to JOS, May 1; June 1, 1937, O'Sullivan Papers. Contemporary journalistic coverage was fairly balanced in the assessment of credit. Richard Neuberger focused on Woods and Billy Clapp, but also mentioned O'Sullivan and Gale Matthews. *Newsweek* gave equal shares of responsibility to Rufus and to O'Sullivan. Stuart Chase, meanwhile, singled out Clapp as the "father" of the dam. Neuberger, "Biggest Thing on Earth," 256-258, and *Our Promised Land*, 79-80; 84; *Newsweek*, 4 (July 7, 1934), 6-7; Chase, "Great Dam," 598. For an account accepting O'Sullivan's point of view, see Sundborg, *Hail Columbia*, 312-319.

21. Innocently attempting to console O'Sullivan, Ralph Woods wrote that "you have done more for the project than any other one man except Rufus." Southard to RW, Oct. 10, 1937, Woods Papers; to JOS, Aug. 6, 1937; Fink to JOS, May 11, 1937; Clapp to JOS, May 19; June 5, 7, 1937; Leavy to JOS, Aug. 2, 7, 1937; Ralph Woods to JOS, Aug. 17, 1937; JOS to K. O'Sullivan, May 2, 1937; to Seelig, July 19, 1937; to Clapp, July 29, 1937; to Leavy, July 29; Aug. 7, 12, 1937, all O'Sullivan Papers; to Ross, March 5, 1938; Ross to Leavy, Feb. 25, 1938, both SLD.

22. RW to Martin, May 12, 1937; to Phil Swing, Sept. 5, 1938, Woods Papers; *WDW*, March 31; Sept. 22; Oct. 30, 1937; Pitzer, "Visions, Plans, and Realities," 38-39. Roosevelt is quoted in Ficken and LeWarne, *Washington*, 109.

23. Details on the contract affair are taken from JOS to Seelig, Oct. 15, 1937; to Clapp, Dec. 20, 22, 1937; Feb. 3, 1938; to Southard, Jan. 8, 1938; to W.W. Hockaday, Dec. 2, 5, 1937; Jan. 19, 1938; Hockaday to JOS, Nov. 28, 1937, all O'Sullivan Papers; *WDW*, Dec. 8, 10, 1937; Woods Diary, Jan. 30, 1938; Foster, *Kaiser*, 63; Pitzer, "Visions, Plans, and Realities," 39.

24. Ross to Dana, Jan. 14, 1936; to Roosevelt, Feb. 10, 1936; to Banker, March 21, 1936; to Bone, Aug. 3, 1937, SLD; *WDW*, June 8; July 24, 1937; RW to Bone, June 26, 1941, Woods Papers. On the creation of the BPA, see McKinley, *Uncle Sam in the Pacific Northwest*, 157-162; Voeltz, "Genesis and Development of a Regional Power Authority," 65-69.

25. Anticipating his BPA appointment, Ross ordered City Light subordinates to "keep anything controversial on Bonneville [and] Coulee out of the Annual report." Leavy to JOS, Aug. 2, 1937, O'Sullivan Papers; *WDW*, June 5; July 14, 15, 24, 1937; Ross to Ickes, Aug. 13, 1936; to McKeen and Smith, April 12, 1937; to Morris L. Cooke,

Nov. 12, 1936; to Roosevelt, Dec. 15, 1937, SLD; May 31, 1938; Roosevelt to Ross, June 3, 1938, both RH. On Ross's career with the BPA, see Funigiello, "Bonneville Power Administration and the New Deal," 89-93.

26. Memo, Interconnection of Coulee and Bonneville Plants, March 18, 1936; J.D. Ross, Grand Coulee-Bonneville Base, May 5, 1937; Ross to Cooke, Nov. 12, 1936; to Bone, June 3, 1937; to C.E. Magnusson, June 16, 1937; to Leavy, Feb. 25, 1938, all SLD; Leavy to JOS, March 1, 1940; to Southard, March 18, 1940, O'Sullivan Papers; Matthews to RW, Jan. 26, 1938, Woods Papers; *WDW*, Aug. 2, 1938; Aug. 17, 1939. On the construction of the transmission network, see Charles E. Carey, "The Bonneville Project," in *Proceedings of the Fifth Pacific Northwest Regional Planning Conference, April 27-29, 1939*, 13; "Columbia River and Tributaries," House Document No. 403, 87th Cong., 2d sess., Vol. II, App. C, Part 1, 4-5; Part 3, 1; McKinley, *Uncle Sam in the Pacific Northwest*, 170-172.

27. The agency reserved a portion of output for sale at the damsite at $14.50 a kilowatt year, a concession of no value to Wenatchee. Smith to Ivan Bloch, April 21, 1937, SLD; RW to Arthur Langlie, Oct. 4, 1944, Woods Papers; *WDW*, Sept. 2, 1940; Kizer to Bone, March 13, 1941, NRPB. BPA rate policies are summarized in Paul J. Raver speech to Seattle Rotary Club, Dec. 4, 1940, Magnuson House Papers. Also see McKinley, *Uncle Sam in the Pacific Northwest*, 167-168; Funigiello, "Bonneville Power Administration and the New Deal," 89-93; Wesley A. Dick, "Visions of Abundance: The Public Power Crusade in the Pacific Northwest in the Era of J.D. Ross and the New Deal" (Ph.D. diss., University of Washington, 1973), 307-314.

28. Grant County possessed three-fourths of the irrigable acreage in North Central Washington, but only 7 percent of the acres actually receiving water. *WDW*, Aug. 6, 1937; May 25, 1938; Jan. 13; March 31; June 14; Oct. 19, 1939; Ed Davis to Bessey, enclosing tabulation of Irrigable and Irrigated Lands in Washington, March 17, 1943, NRPB.

29. *WDW*, Oct. 27, 1938; June 19; Oct. 19, 1939.

30. RW to Leavy, Jan. 22; June 5, 1940; Speech to Realty Board Meeting, Dec. 29, 1938, all Woods Papers; *WDW*, Jan. 20; Feb. 26; Aug. 5, 1937; Jan. 13, 25; March 5, 23; April 9; June 30; July 5; Sept. 5; Nov. 17, 19, 1938; Aug. 9, 1939.

31. JOS to Southard, Jan. 8, 1938, O'Sullivan Papers; Leavy to RW, Jan. 24; Feb. 19; March 4, 1938, Woods Papers.

32. JOS to Leavy, Dec. 29, 1938; Jan. 8, 1940; Leavy to JOS, Dec. 19, 1938; March 18, 1939; Jan. 25; Feb. 16, 1940, all O'Sullivan Papers; to RW, Dec. 18, 1939; Bone to RW, June 3, 1939, both Woods Papers; *WDW*, Feb. 28, 1940.

33. RW to Don Sterling, Nov. 21, 1938; J.H. Miner to RW, Nov. 30, 1938; Clapp to RW, July 21, 1938, all Woods Papers; to JOS, Jan. 23; March 10, 1938; JOS to John W. Haw, Jan. 23, 1939; to C.C. Morrison, Aug. 15, 1939; Haw to JOS, Jan. 27, 1939, all O'Sullivan Papers; *WDW*, March 22; April 3; May 11, 1939; Pitzer, "Visions, Plans, and Realities," 59-61, 71-75, 360-376. Also see Lowitt, *New Deal and the West*, 169-170.

34. RW to Fink, Oct. 30, 1937, CBC; to Southard, Oct. 6, 1937; to Bone, Oct. 30, 1937; to Clapp and Matthews, Nov. 8, 1937; Clapp to RW, July 21, 1938, all Woods Papers; JOS to Leavy, April 10, 1941; to Schwellenbach, Dec. 5, 1938; to KB, June 30, 1939; to E.B. Duncan, Sept. 28, 1939, O'Sullivan Papers; Pitzer, "Visions, Plans, and Realities," 68.

35. JOS to Clapp, Dec. 22, 27, 1937; Feb. 3, 1938; to E.C. Leedy, Aug. 23, 1938; Feb. 21; April 21; July 28, 1939; to Schwellenbach, Dec. 5, 1938; to I.N. McGrath, March 15; July 20, 1939; to Morrison, Dec. 4, 1938; to McPherson, June 16, 1939; to

Leavy, July 10, 19, 1940; to KB, June 30, 1939, O'Sullivan Papers; Frank C. Jackson to RW, June 9, 1939, Woods Papers; *WDW*, Feb. 20; Dec. 8, 11, 13, 1939; Pitzer, "Visions, Plans, and Realities," 65-70.

36. This account of the European tour is based on *WDW*, Dec. 14, 1937; Jan. 11, 18; March 18; April 13, 19, 21, 23, 30; May 7-12, 14, 19-21, 23, 24, 26, 28, 30, 31; June 1, 3, 4, 6, 7, 16, 17, 23, 1938; Woods Diary, May 17, 31, 1938; RW to Swing, Sept. 5, 1938; to Baker, May 15, 1939, Woods Papers.

37. *WDW*, Sept. 13, 21, 26, 28-30; Oct. 3, 27, 28, 31, 1938.

38. *WDW*, Nov. 11, 15, 16, 24, 28; Dec. 17, 1938; March 20, 25, 27; April 6, 7, 1939.

39. Details of the Asian trip are taken from *WDW*, April 14, 15, 17-19, 22, 24, 25, 29; May 2, 3, 10, 15, 16, 19, 20, 25; June 1, 1939; Woods Diary, May 9, 1939; Ralph McGill to RW, April 27, 1939, Woods Papers.

40. *WDW*, July 17; Aug. 24, 26, 1939.

41. The one amusing aspect of the crisis, to the *World*, was the ideological backing-and-filling forced upon the Washington Commonwealth Federation and other pro-Soviet organizations by the Hitler-Stalin Pact. *WDW*, Aug. 29, 30; Sept. 1, 2, 4, 6, 8, 9, 19, 22, 23, 27; Oct. 3, 4, 6, 16, 18; Dec. 2, 1939.

42. *WDW*, Dec. 6, 8, 1939; Jan. 3; June 5; Aug. 2, 1940. On Representative Magnuson's interest in an Alaska-Washington road, see Heath Twichell, *Northwest Epic: The Building of the Alaska Highway* (New York: St. Martin's Press, 1992), 18-20.

43. National Resources Planning Board, *Pacific Northwest Region: Industrial Development* (Washington, D.C.: Government Printing Office, 1942), 19, 21-22, 30; Statement on Industry, May 29, 1943, enclosed in Bessey to Rex Willard, May 31, 1943, NRPB.

44. *WDW*, Sept. 7; Dec. 5, 27, 30, 1939; March 7, 21; April 4; June 3; Aug. 27, 1940; Ickes to Joseph Guffey, Sept. 26, 1941; Statement on Industry, May 29, 1943, both NRPB; Leavy to JOS, July 16, 1940, O'Sullivan Papers. Also see Gerald D. Nash, *World War II and the West: Reshaping the Economy* (Lincoln: University of Nebraska Press, 1990), 94.

45. The *World* preferred to call the reservoir Great Columbia Lake. Northwest Airlines diverted its Seattle-Spokane flights to allow passengers to view the construction site. *WDW*, May 27; June 8; Oct. 21, 1939; March 26; May 13-15; Aug. 3; Dec. 5, 1940.

46. Seelig to KB, Feb. 29, 1940, Billingsley Papers; *WDW*, Feb. 7; Aug. 9; Sept. 5, 13, 15; Oct. 2, 3, 12, 17, 20; Nov. 10, 18, 27; Dec. 12, 13, 29, 30, 1939; Jan. 20; Feb. 8, 12; March 16, 28; April 11; May 8, 30; June 8, 1940.

47. *WDW*, Jan. 7, 11; March 1; April 28, 1939; Jan. 5, 8; March 2, 25; April 15; May 6, 1940; RW to Kelly, June 19, 1940; Robert M. Mount to K.P. Sexton, April 27, 1938; William Knight to Sexton, March 11; Oct. 24, 1940; Notes on Conversation with Mr. Rufus Woods, et al., Dec. 6, 1940; E. Richardson to Sexton, June 27, 1940, all Woods Papers.

48. Ralph Woods to RW, Aug. 9, 1940; to Sexton, Sept. 3, 1941; Notes on Conversation, Dec. 6, 1940; Knight to Sexton, Aug. 9; Oct. 24, 1940; April 19, 23; May 21; Sept. 6, 1941; to RW, Jan. 27, 1941, all Woods Papers; *WDW*, July 30, 1940.

49. RW to Hippelhauser, Jan. 30, 1940, Woods Papers; *WDW*, Sept. 1; Oct. 25; Nov. 7; Dec. 8, 1939; Feb. 13, 16, 17; April 15, 1940.

50. *WDW*, June 26-29; July 1, 1940; RW to Fred Smith, June 18, 1940, Woods Papers.

51. *WDW*, June 29; July 1, 2, 27, 1940.

52. Woods hoped that the selection of McNary as Willkie's running mate would counter regional concern over the future of development work on the Columbia. *WDW*, June 26, 29; July 1, 4, 26, 29, 1940; RW to Charles McNary, July 6, 1940; to Smith, June 18, 1940, Woods Papers.

53. *WDW*, June 21, 24; July 16, 17, 19, 20, 26, 1940.

54. When the University of Washington student newspaper published an editorial opposing the draft, Rufus demanded that the "young squirt" editor be expelled from the institution for disloyalty to the United States. *WDW*, June 10, 21, 24; Aug. 17; Sept. 18; Oct. 8, 22, 1940.

55. *WDW*, Aug. 30; Sept. 4, 12-14, 17-20, 23, 27; Oct. 1, 10, 17, 29, 1940; Leavy to JOS, Oct. 1, 1940; JOS to RW, Sept. 4, 1940, both O'Sullivan Papers; Mitchell, *Story of Rufus Woods*, 22.

56. *WDW*, Sept. 6, 17, 25, 26; Oct. 3-5, 12, 15, 21, 23, 26, 30, 1940.

57. In the confusion, the 1941 *World Almanac* listed Clarence Dill as the governor of Washington. *WDW*, Nov. 2, 6, 7, 9, 11, 19, 23, 29; Dec. 2, 6, 14, 20, 1940; Jan. 9, 15, 16, 21; Feb. 7, 12, 1941; Mitchell, *Story of Rufus Woods*, 22, 35.

58. *WDW*, Jan. 25, 1939.

## Notes for Chapter Eleven

1. July 4, 1944.

2. *WDW*, Jan. 22; March 22, 1941.

3. Kizer to Bone, March 13, 1941, NRPB; KB to Stoffel, July 4, 1943; to Davis, Sept. 24, 1943; to Tom Welborn, Dec. 2, 1943, Billingsley Papers; JOS to Clapp, July 12, 1942, O'Sullivan Papers; RW to Bone, June 26, 1941, Woods Papers; McKinley, *Uncle Sam in the Pacific Northwest*, 168; Lowitt, *New Deal and the West*, 163.

4. Both bills contained a provision allowing the CPA to acquire private power systems, leading some scholars to contend that opposition came solely from the utilities. The BPA became a permanent institution "by default," notes one historian, rather than by specific action of Congress. Kizer to Bone, March 13; June 21, 26; Aug. 21, 1941; to T.S. Hedges, March 22, 1941; to Yantis, March 10; Aug. 20, 1941; to James P. Pope, June 4, 1941; to Charles W. Eliot, July 21, 1941; to Gilbert White, May 12, 1942; Yantis to Kizer, July 30, 1941; Pacific Northwest Regional Planning Commission to Frederick A. Delano, April 23, 1942; Bone to Kizer, June 20, 1942, all NRPB; Knute Hill to JOS, July 2, 1941; Leavy to JOS, July 2, 1941; Seelig to JOS, July 2, 1941; JOS to Seelig, July 12, 1941, all O'Sullivan Papers; RW to Bone, June 26, 1941, Woods Papers; *WDW*, Jan. 18; Aug. 11, 26, 1941; April 25; May 29; June 30, 1942; Voeltz, "Genesis and Development of a Regional Power Agency," 68-76; McKinley, *Uncle Sam in the Pacific Northwest*, 178-180, 545-546; Lowitt, *New Deal and the West*, 170.

5. A kilowatt hour is the power needed to light a 100-watt bulb for an hour. *WDW*, March 4; April 12; July 17; Sept. 19, 22, 1941; Sept. 21, 1944; National Resources Planning Board, *Pacific Northwest Region*, 29; "Columbia River and Tributaries," App. C, Part 6, 3; "Columbia River and Tributaries, Northwestern United States," House Document No. 531, 81st Cong., 2d Sess., 3156; Gerald D. Nash, *The American West Transformed: The Impact of the Second World War* (Bloomington: Indiana University Press, 1985), 29, and *World War II and the West*, 91-101; McKinley, *Uncle Sam in the Pacific Northwest*, 182.

6. *WDW*, July 29; Sept. 30; Oct. 2; Dec. 22, 1941; RW to Paul Piper, Dec. 17, 1945; Piper to RW, Aug. 4; Oct. 1, 8, 1941, all Woods Papers; Bessey to Willard, May 27, 1943, NRPB; Bonneville Power Administration Service Report, Feb. 12, 1942, Magnuson House Papers; C.R. Moore to Division Engineer, Feb. 17, 1942, RH.

7. Stoffel to KB, Jan. 17, 1943; RW to Ickes, Aug. 18, 1941; to Emil Hurja, Aug. 7, 1941, all Woods Papers; *WDW*, Aug. 12; Oct. 9, 1941.

8. Visiting the Culebra Cut, Rufus was disappointed to find the famous Panama Canal excavation "so very small—compared with our diggin's at Grand Coulee." Details of the Latin American trip are from *WDW*, Jan. 11; Feb. 27; April 22, 30; May 5, 7, 14-16, 20, 26, 27; June 4, 5, 7, 14, 19, 21; July 12, 1941.

9. *WDW*, Feb. 11, 24; March 21; May 29; June 28; July 9; Sept. 13, 17, 20, 1941; RW to Hugh Stewart, Oct. 29, 1941, Woods Papers.

10. *WDW*, Oct. 8; Dec. 30, 31, 1941; May 3, 1943; Hill to KB, Oct. 16, 1941; Leavy to KB, Jan. 2, 1942, both Billingsley Papers.

11. *WDW*, Dec. 9-11, 16, 17, 30, 1941; Jan. 12, 15, 27, 28; Feb. 4, 10, 12, 13, 17, 18, 23, 26; March 3, 4, 6, 11, 20; April 4; June 17, 1942. Also see Ficken and LeWarne, *Washington*, 128-129, 132-136.

12. Chelan County experienced an 11 percent population loss. Leavy to RW, Dec. 30, 1941, Billingsley Papers; Statement on Industry, May 31, 1943; Bessey to Willard, May 27, 1943, enclosing Memorandum on Population, May 25, 1943, both NRPB; *Nash, American West Transformed*, 17, 79, and *World War II and the West*, 101; National Resources Planning Board, *Pacific Northwest Region*, 4-5, 19, 29-30; "Columbia River and Tributaries," App. C, Part 5, 23; Part 6, 4; *Employment Trends in Basic Industries, Sept. 1940-Aug. 1946* (Olympia: State Department of Conservation and Development, 1947), 10; "Columbia River and Tributaries, Northwestern United States," 65, 3110, 3154; *WDW*, Feb. 2; Aug. 1; Dec. 31, 1942; March 29; Aug. 31; Nov. 3, 1943.

13. Grand Coulee's capacity was approximately four times that of Bonneville. Bessey to Willard, May 27, 1943, enclosing Memorandum on Hydroelectric Power, May 25, 1943, NRPB; *WDW*, Aug. 6, 1942; Feb. 20; Nov. 23; Dec. 28, 1943; July 26; Sept. 12, 21; Oct. 13; Nov. 29; Dec. 8, 1944; Frederick Simpich, "Wartime in the Pacific Northwest," *National Geographic*, 28 (Oct. 1942), 15-36; KB to Hugh B. Mitchell, May 21, 1946, Mitchell Papers. On the general subject of power's role in war mobilization, see Philip J. Funigiello, "Kilowatts for Defense: The New Deal and the Coming of the Second World War," *Journal of American History*, 56(1969), 604-620.

14. *WDW*, Jan. 9; April 6; July 22; Aug. 21; Oct. 1, 2, 22; Dec. 11, 1942; Jan. 1, 2, 14, 22; Feb. 8, 15; March 1, 31; Sept. 22, 1943; March 22; Dec. 26, 1944; RW to A.L. Ganson, May 3, 1944; to Fred Koch, Nov. 21, 1944, Woods Papers.

15. *WDW*, Aug. 21; Oct. 6, 14, 15, 1942; Jan. 14, 19; March 1, 22; Sept. 21, 22; Oct. 7, 8, 12, 14, 1943; Jan. 26, 1944; KB to Walt Horan, June 7, 1943; to Stoffel, June 14; Oct. 7, 1943; to Horan and Stoffel, Nov. 24, 1943; Stoffel to KB, June 30; Sept. 16; Oct. 4, 1943; Mitchell to KB, Nov. 13, 1943, Billingsley Papers.

16. *WDW*, Jan. 24; Feb. 16, 25; March 17, 31; July 17, 21; Aug. 5; Sept. 18; Oct. 9, 14, 16, 17, 19-21, 29, 30; Nov. 2, 4, 10, 1942.

17. *WDW*, July 14, 15; Aug. 23; Sept. 4, 1943; Sept. 7, 1944; Erasmo Gamboa, "Mexican Migration into Washington State: A History, 1940-1950," *PNQ*, 72(1981), 121-131, and "Braceros in the Pacific Northwest: Laborers on the Domestic Front, 1942-1947," *PHR*, 56(1981), 378-398.

18. RW to Johnson, Oct. 26, 1944; to Koch, Nov. 21, 1944; to Jett, Nov. 27, 1944; to Lyn R. Leonard, Feb. 5, 1945; to Mrs. M. Glaser, Feb. 8, 1945; to W. Greenslit, April 13, 1945; to Bob Woods, Jan. 3; April 11; May 21, 1945; to Roy V. Montgomery, July 16, 1945, Woods Papers; Woods Diary, Oct. 11, 1942; May 11, 27; July 18; Oct. 16; Dec. 16, 1943; Jan. 5, 1944; Jan. 25; June 9, 1945; *WDW*, Jan. 26; Dec. 28, 1942; Sept. 2, 29; Dec. 31, 1943; Oct. 6, 1944.

19. Woods also joined the industry-seeking efforts of the Decentralization League and the Strategic Industries Board. *WDW*, Feb. 16; April 30; May 1; June 19, 1942; RW to Piper, Dec. 17, 1945, Woods Papers; KB to Davis, June 27, 1942; Leavy to KB,

Feb. 18, 1942, both Billingsley Papers; Herbert J. Wild to District Engineer, April 16, 1942, RH.

20. Director of Conservation and Development Ed Davis served as the chairman and seventh member. KB to Davis, June 27, 1942, Billingsley Papers; Matthews to JOS, Aug. 27, 1942; Clapp to JOS, Sept. 5, 1942; Simpson to JOS, Feb. 2, 1943, all O'Sullivan Papers; RW to Ickes, Jan. 1, 1943; to Davis, May 25, 1943, Woods Papers; *WDW*, Jan. 22; Feb. 1, 2; March 4, 6, 11, 16; April 10; May 28, 1943.

21. KB to Davis, April 12, 1943; to Stoffel, July 9, 1943, Billingsley Papers; JOS to Clapp, Feb. 21; April 17, 27; Nov. 15, 1943; to Blonk, April 24, 1943, O'Sullivan Papers; *WDW*, Feb. 27, 1943.

22. *WDW*, Nov. 30; Dec. 5, 29, 1942; Feb. 6, 18; April 16; May 28; June 25; July 5, 1943; RW to Goss, April 15, 1942; to Compton I. White and Reginald S. Dean, Dec. 3, 1942; KB to Stoffel, Oct. 7, 1943, all Woods Papers; to Yantis, May 15, 1943; to Bone, June 7, 1943, Billingsley Papers.

23. *WDW*, June 4; Nov. 30, 1942; April 9; June 24, 25, 1943; RW to Paul Raver, July 21, 1943; KB to J.V. Rogers, May 7, 1942, both Woods Papers; to Bone, June 16, 1942; to Abe Fortas, June 18, 1942; Stoffel to KB, Oct. 19, 1943, all Billingsley Papers.

24. RW to Raver, April 21, 27, 1942; to KB, April 23, 1942; to DeVos, April 10, 1942; KB to RW, April 24; May 7, 11, 1942; to Horan, Sept. 28, 1943; Horan to KB, Jan. 9, 1943; Leavy to RW, June 6, 1942, all Woods Papers; to KB, Aug. 4; Dec. 11, 1941, Billingsley Papers; H.F. Aumack to Rogers, July 16, 1942, NRPB; *WDW*, July 8, 1942; March 25, 27; April 1-3, 22; Sept. 4, 1943.

25. RW to KB, April 25, 1942; to T.A. Love, March 9, 1943; to Raver, March 23, 1944; Notes, May 18, 1944, all Woods Papers; KB to Welborn, Dec. 6, 1943; to Joseph G. Knapp, Feb. 5, 1944; Raver to Rogers, June 15, 1942; Fortas to KB, June 27, 1942, all Billingsley Papers.

26. Northwest Chemurgy was owned by the Grange, by individual farmers, and by a small number of non-farm investors, including Rufus Woods. *WDW*, Nov. 7, 9, 10, 1942; March 5; Sept. 24; Dec. 4, 1943; March 16, 1944; RW to Carstensen, Jan. 13, 1943; to McGinnis, Nov. 16, 1943; to JOS, Oct. 31, 1944; to Johnson, Nov. 9, 1944; to Ralph M. Murphy, Oct. 22, 1945, Woods Papers; to Wil. Woods, Dec. 1, 19, 1943; Jan. 10, 1944; to Walter F. Hiltner, Dec. 27, 1943; Jan. 5, 1944, in Woods Diary, plus entries for Nov. 24, 1942; March 28; April 23; May 27; June 26; Aug. 6; Oct. 16; Nov. 20, 23; Dec. 16, 1943.

27. Stoffel to KB, March 12, 16, 28, 29, 1943, Woods Papers; KB to Horan, March 9, 1943; to Stoffel, March 16, 1943, Billingsley Papers.

28. KB to Horan, March 9, 1943; Blonk to KB, March 29, 1943, both Billingsley Papers; Introductory entry, F. T. Matthias Diary, Corps of Engineers History Office, Fort Belvoir, Va. On the vital importance of electricity to the selection of a site, see War Production Board to Bonneville Power Administration, May 11, 1944; Leslie R. Groves Memorandum for Undersecretary of War, Aug. 11, 1944, both Manhattan Engineer District Records, RG 77, National Archives. Also see Michele Stenehjeim Gerber, *On the Home Front: The Cold War Legacy of the Hanford Nuclear Site* (Lincoln: University of Nebraska Press, 1992), 22-26.

29. *WDW*, March 13, 15; April 3, 26; May 15; Oct. 28; Dec. 13, 1943; Matthias Diary, March 10; April 19, 23, 25, 27; May 3; June 5, 12, 1943; KB to Stoffel, March 16, 1943, Billingsley Papers; Marc Reisner, *Cadillac Desert: The American West and Its Disappearing Water* (New York: Viking, 1986), 170.

30. One Army study took into consideration the impact of a postwar depression, but still determined that a new dam would be needed by 1950. RW to Horan, Aug. 23, 1943; KB to Horan, June 28, 1943, both Woods Papers; Robert A. Lovett to Cordell Hull,

Aug. 23, 1943; H.G. Roby to Wood, July 26, 1945, both Acc. 68A- 1926, OCE1943; Horan to Carstensen, June 3, 1944, Walt Horan Papers, WSU.

31. Lorraine, *Columbia Unveiled*, 282, 284-286; Stewart Holbrook, *The Columbia* (New York: Rinehart & Co., 1956), 362; Conrad P. Hardy to Division Engineer, Aug. 15, 1945; Review of Report on Columbia River in the Vicinity of Foster Creek, App. I, Geology and Soil Mechanisms, Aug. 15, 1945, both File 150522, Upper Columbia Basin, SDOACE; *Columbia River and Tributaries (CR&T) Study, Reach Inventory*, April 1975, 35-36; *WDW*, Nov. 7, 1947, clipping in CBIAC.

32. Low water flow in the Okanogan River limited use of that stream for reclamation purposes. *WDW*, Sept. 18, 1943; Feb. 15; Dec. 2, 1944; RW to Fred Cunningham, Nov. 28, 1944; to Horan, July 3, 1945, Woods Papers; Hardy to Division Engineer, Aug. 15, 1945, File 1505-22, Upper Columbia Basin, SDOACE.

33. KB to Carstensen, Oct. 17, 1945; RW to Horan, July 3, 1945; Horan to RW, Nov. 5, 1945, all Woods Papers; to Robins, Nov. 2, 1945; Robins to Horan, Nov. 15, 1945, both Horan Papers; Bonneville Power Administration Service Report, Feb. 12, 1942, Magnuson House Papers; Hardy to Division Engineer, Aug. 15, 1945, File 1505-22, Upper Columbia Basin, SDOACE; Blonk to KB, c. Nov. 1945, Billingsley Papers.

34. The Corps of Engineers also considered dams on the Snake River and in Oregon's Willamette Valley to be of more pressing importance than Foster Creek. Horan to RW. Nov. 5, 1945; RW to Horan, July 3, 1945, both Woods Papers; KB to Carstensen, Oct. 23; Nov. 1, 1945, Billingsley Papers; to Horan, March 3, 1948, Horan Papers; Warren G. Magnuson to C. Emerson Morgan, Nov. 5, 1945, Magnuson Senate Papers.

35. KB to Horan, Jan. 15, 1943, Billingsley Papers; RW to Horan, Aug. 23, 1943; June 29, 1945; to Welborn, Dec. 18, 1943; to Duncan, July 19, 1944; to E.O. Holland, Dec. 4, 1944, Woods Papers; *WDW*, May 14; June 28; Nov. 29, 1943; Jan. 24; July 20; Sept. 22, 28, 1944.

36. Storage dams generated electricity, but their primary function was the impoundment of water for improved operation at downstream plants. B.E. Torpen memoranda, Storage for Power, Columbia River Basin, Aug. 1945, File 1505-22, Upper Columbia Basin, SDOACE, and Power and Columbia River Storage: Projects in the Region's Potential, Dec. 12, 1951, CBIAC; *WDW*, Sept. 2, 1944.

37. RW to Love, Aug. 26, 1943; Oct. 12, 1944; to Park, July 1, 1943, Woods Papers; *WDW*, May 10, 1943; Aug. 2, 1944; Background on International Columbia River Investigations, n.d., Acc. 68A-1926, OCE1943; Paul J. Raver, "The Challenge to Statesmanship," *PNQ*, 49 (1958), 99; "Columbia River and Tributaries, Northwestern United States," 395; "Columbia River and Tributaries," 1:128.

38. Construction of Libby Dam began only after conclusion of a diplomatic agreement between the United States and Canada in 1961. Background of International Columbia River Investigations, n.d.; Lovett to Hull, Aug. 23, 1943; Robins to Hardy, April 7, 1945; Hardy to Weber, Sept. 19, 1945, all Acc. 68A-1926, OCE 1943; W.O. Silverthorn to L.L. Wise, Jan. 7, 1955, CBIAC; Interim Report on Kootenay River to the International Joint Commission, Nov. 1, 1950; Hewitt to G.L. Beard, enclosing Preliminary Notes, July 1, 1949, both File 1505-22, Libby Project, SDOACE; *WDW*, Aug. 2, 1944; RW to Love, Sept. 26; Oct. 12, 1944; to Langlie, Oct. 3, 1944, Woods Papers.

39. The Pend Oreille River enters the Columbia a half-mile above the international boundary. Park to Chief of Engineers, March 5, 1942, RH; Lovett to Hull, Aug. 23, 1943, Acc. 68A-1926, OCE1943; Thomas L. Symons to Casey, March 21, 1891, in *ARCE, 1891*, 3250-3252; E.H. Wiecking to KB, June 3, 1943, Billingsley Papers; White to RW, May 25; June 9, 1943, Woods Papers.

40. RW to D.L. Marlett, June 8, 1943; to George H. Campbell, June 14, 1943; to A.F. Winkler, June 14, 1943, Woods Papers; *WDW*, May 22; June 3, 5, 7, 8, 12, 19, 21, 1943. On opposition in Idaho and Montana, also see J.P. Alvey to Mitchell, June 13, 1946, Mitchell Papers.

41. *WDW*, June 5, 8, 21, 1943; Horan to RW, n.d., Woods Papers.

42. Statement on Industry, May 29, 1943, NRPB; RW to Leslie Williams, April 19, 1943; JOS to RW, Oct. 30, 1944, both Woods Pa- pers; to Davis, Oct. 16; Nov. 28, 1943; to Marlett, May 26, 1944; Clapp to JOS, Nov. 19, 1943, all O'Sullivan Papers; *WDW*, July 10, 1941; Dec. 16, 1943; Jan. 5, 27; March 2, 28, 1944; July 11, 1945.

43. RW to Williams, April 19, 1943; Horan to KB, Jan. 3, 1944, both Woods Papers; KB to Horan, Jan. 7, 1944, Billingsley Papers; *WDW*, Oct. 6, 13; Nov. 22; Dec. 14, 1943; Jan. 18; Aug. 26, 1944.

44. Although legally separate entities, Alcan and Alcoa were managed, respectively, by the brothers Edward and Arthur Davis. *WDW*, March 24; April 19, 29, 1943; July 14; Sept. 21, 1945; Horan to RW, June 2, 1943; Welborn to RW, June 10, 1943, Woods Papers; Nash, *World War II and the West*, 103-114.

45. RW to Raver, March 23, 1944; to Samuel Husbands, March 23, 1945; Notes, May 18, 1944; Report to Members of the Commission, July 29, 1944, all Woods Papers; KB to Knapp, Feb. 5, 1944; Mitchell to KB, July 10, 1945, both Billingsley Papers; *WDW*, Oct. 24, 28, 1944; Aug. 21, 1945.

46. *WDW*, Dec. 8, 1944; Stoffel to KB, March 11, 1943; RW to McGinnis, Nov. 16, 1943; to Carstensen, Nov. 18, 1943; April 20; May 11; Nov. 2, 1944; to Charles L. Robinson, Nov. 10, 1944, all Woods Papers; to Wil. Woods, Jan. 10; April 12, 1944, in Woods Diary, plus entries for Aug. 5; Oct. 1, 12; Dec. 5, 1944; Jan. 25; March 23; June 9; Sept. 17, 1945; Cone to KB, Dec. 5, 1944, Billingsley Papers; JOS to Clapp, Feb. 21, 1943; to Margaret Thompson, Sept. 16, 1943, O'Sullivan Papers.

47. *WDW*, March 29; Dec. 15, 1943; Nov. 16; Dec. 6, 12, 1944; RW to C.C. Morrison, Jan. 31, 1945; to Frederick Simpich, Dec. 3, 1945; to Banks, Sept. 26, 1944; to Davis, Oct. 2, 1944; to F. Cunningham, Oct. 12, 1944; to JOS, Oct. 25, 31, 1944, Woods Papers; JOS to Garton, Feb. 6, 1945; to Magnuson, March 2, 1945; Magnuson to JOS, Feb. 22, 1945; Horan to JOS, Feb. 27, 1945, all O'Sullivan Papers.

48. Sister Elizabeth died in Nebraska in February, from injuries suffered in a fall down basement stairs. Matters related to Ralph's death are covered in RW to Johnson, Nov. 20, 1945, Woods Papers; to Members of the Family, Jan. 25; Feb. 25, 1944; to Wil. Woods, Feb. 12, 1944; to Oscar Woods, April 10; May 10, 1944; Report to the Family, July 15, 1944; to the Californians, Aug. 5, 1944, all in Woods Diary.

49. RW to JOS, Oct. 31, 1944; to Horan, Nov. 21, 1944; to Koch, Nov. 21, 1944; to H.M. Peet, Dec. 5, 1944; Report on Washington Trip, June 20, 1944, all Woods Papers; JOS to RW, Oct. 30, 1944, O'Sullivan Papers; Horan to KB, March 20, 1945, Billingsley Papers; *WDW*, July 17; Aug. 8; Oct. 12, 28; Nov. 22, 24, 1944; Mitchell, *Flowing Wealth*, 62-63, and *Story of Rufus Woods*, 36-37.

50. A petition drive sponsored by the Washington Water Power Company sent Initiative 12 back to the electorate in the form of Referendum 25. RW to Johnson, Oct. 26, 1944; to JOS, Oct. 31, 1944, Woods Papers; Bone to KB, Jan. 18; Nov. 3, 1944, Billingsley Papers; *WDW*, Aug. 14; Oct. 25, 27, 30; Nov. 3, 6, 1944; Mitchell, *Flowing Wealth*, 62-63, and *Story of Rufus Woods*, 36-37.

51. RW to W. Cole McCreery, Nov. 9, 1944; to Thomas E. Dewey, Sept. 12, 1944, n.d.; to John E. Blair, Sept. 12, 1944; to W. Greenslit, Oct. 12, 1944, Woods Papers; KB to C.G. Davidson, Jan. 29, 1945, Billingsley Papers.

52. *WDW*, June 26, 27, 30; July 3, 12, 13, 15; Aug. 18; Sept. 9, 18, 19, 27, 29; Oct. 3, 14, 20; Nov. 1, 3, 6, 1944; RW to Stoffel, Sept. 12, 1944; to Johnson, Oct. 26, 1944, Woods Papers.

53. Reflecting the sensitive nature of the split within the Republican Party, Woods avoided analysis of the state election in his *World* column. *WDW*, Nov. 14, 30, 1944; RW to Koch, Nov. 21, 1944; to Langlie, Nov. 9, 1944; to Holden, Nov. 9, 1944; to Davis, Nov. 9, 1944; to J.L. Padfield, Nov. 9, 1944; to Horan, Nov. 21, 1944; to Hal Holmes, Nov. 29, 1944; to Blair, Sept. 22, 1944, Woods Papers; Mitchell, *Flowing Wealth*, 62, and *Story of Rufus Woods*, 37.

54. Woods favored the appointment of former Representative Sam Hill to Wallgren's seat, but was happy to accept Mitchell as an alternative. RW to F. Cunningham, Nov. 28, 1944; to B. Woods, Jan. 3, 1945; to Rupp, Jan. 10, 1945; to Berry, Feb. 5, 1945, Woods Papers; JOS to RW, Jan. 17, 1945, O'Sullivan Papers; Magnuson to KB, Dec. 16, 1944; Hill to KB, Nov. 6; Dec. 18, 30, 1944, all Billingsley Papers; *WDW*, Nov. 11; Dec. 5, 6, 11, 14, 1944.

55. KB to Carstensen, Oct. 7, 1945; RW to B. Woods, May 21, 1945, both Woods Papers; Magnuson to KB, n.d., Billingsley Papers.

56. RW to Horan, Nov. 21, 1944; Aug. 30, 1945; to Raver, April 2, 1943; to Langlie, Sept. 20, 1944; to Martin, Nov. 29, 1944; to Holmes, Nov. 29, 1944; to JOS, Nov. 29, 1944, Woods Papers; *WDW*, Dec. 2, 1944.

57. RW to Robert R. McCormick, July 14, 1944; to Langlie, Sept. 20, 1944; to Jones, Nov. 29, 1944, Woods Papers; *WDW*, Nov. 28, 1944.

58. Raver to KB, Nov. 19, 1943, O'Sullivan Papers; RW to Langlie, Oct. 4, 1944; to JOS, Nov. 29, 1944; to Johnson, Nov. 9, 1944, Woods Papers.

## Notes for Chapter Twelve

1. *WDW*, Dec. 19, 1949.

2. Plutonium from Hanford was used in the second, Nagasaki, atomic bomb. *WDW*, July 21, 30; Aug. 6, 8, 11, 1945; March 14; July 5, 1946; Vincent C. Jones, *Manhattan: The Army and the Atomic Bomb*, U.S. Army in World War II, Special Studies(Washington, D.C.: Center of Military History, 1985), 219-223. The *World* reaction, mixing relief with apprehension, was typical of the regional press. See Ficken and LeWarne, *Washington*, 127-128, 140-142.

3. Woods Diary, Aug. 23, 1945; *WDW*, Aug. 11, 15, 1945; John Gunther, *Inside U.S.A.* (New York: Harper & Brothers, 1947), 119.

4. *WDW*, June 26; July 14; Nov. 9, 1942; June 29, 1943; Jan. 14; Sept. 1, 1944; Sept. 29, 1945; July 11; Aug. 28, 1946; April 15; May 2, 1947.

5. Confusing distinguished appearance with genuine ability, Woods reported that Secretary of State Edward Stettinius, head of the U.S. delegation, was "a big enough man for presidential timber." RW to B. Woods, May 21, 1945; to Neuberger, May 16, 1945, Woods Papers; Woods Diary, May 14, 1945.

6. RW to William L. White, Jan. 5, 1945, Woods Papers; *WDW*, March 19; April 13; July 24; Aug. 10; Sept. 17, 1946.

7. *WDW*, March 8, 13, 17, 18; April 10; June 7, 9, 12; July 3, 16, 1947.

8. *WDW*, Feb. 18; Aug. 15, 23; Sept. 21; Oct. 28, 1946; Jan. 9; March 20; April 14, 1947; March 27; Aug. 17; Oct. 13, 1948; Jan. 8, 1949.

9. *WDW*, May 31, 1946; June 11, 1947; Dec. 10, 1948; June 24; Oct. 12; Dec. 1, 1949; RW to B. Woods, May 21, 1945; to Wm. E. Foster, June 17, 1946; to Inland Empire

Pulp & Paper Co., Nov. 18, 1947, Woods Papers; to KB, Feb. 21, 28; March 7, 1950, Billingsley Papers; Woods Diary, Dec. 18, 1948.

10. *WDW*, May 11; July 1, 1946; March 31, 1947; Carstensen to RW, July 26, 1947; to Members of the Executive Committee, Nov. 7, 1947; RW to Warren L. Hersman, March 24, 1947; to A.C. Adams, July 24, 29, 1947; to Goss, Sept. 8, 1947, all Woods Papers; to KB, Jan. 23, 1950, Billingsley Papers; Woods Diary, Nov. 16, 1946; Jan. 25, 1948.

11. *WDW*, June 5, 13, 15; Aug. 21, 27; Sept. 7; Nov. 29, 1946; Jan. 8, 1947; Oct. 12; Dec. 30, 1948; Jan. 3, 1949; RW to Husbands, March 23, 1945; to Garton, June 13, 1946, Woods Papers; Mitchell to KB, July 10, 1945; Horan to KB, April 1, 1948; KB to Carstensen, Nov. 9, 1946; to Horan, May 20; June 27, 1948, all Billingsley Papers; Mitchell, *Story of Rufus Woods*, 27-28.

12. *WDW*, Jan. 21, 1946; Feb. 17, 1948; Jan. 27, 1949; Bone to KB, Nov. 3, 1944, Billingsley Papers.

13. The state of Washington added a half million permanent residents between 1940 and 1946. *WDW*, July 5, 1945; June 14; Aug. 6, 19, 21, 26, 1946; Jan. 20, 22; March 1; Dec. 30, 1948; Jan. 4; April 20; July 30, 1949; Memorandum, Sept. 12, 1947, CBC. On the disposition of the wartime aluminum plants, see Nash, *World War II and the West*, 114-121.

14. Gunther, *Inside U.S.A.*, 132; Magnuson to Charles J. Bartholet, Sept. 20, 1949, Langlie Papers; Horan to Welborn, Nov. 16, 1944; to Norman Mackenzie, Dec. 27, 1944; to KB, April 11, 1945, Horan Papers. The Neuberger quote is from St. Louis *Post-Dispatch*, May 15, 1949, clipping in Jackson House Papers.

15. Introduced in August 1944 by Senator James Murray of Montana, legislation for a Missouri Valley Authority provided the immediate spark for revival of the CVA issue. RW to Davis, Oct. 2, 1944; to Langlie, Oct. 4, 1944; to Holmes, Nov. 29, 1944; to Martin, Nov. 29, 1944; to Magnuson, Jan. 23, 1945; to Rex L. Nicholson, May 21, 1945; to Goss, Sept. 25, 1948, Woods Papers; to JOS, Nov. 29, 1944, O'Sullivan Papers; KB to Horan, Nov. 21, 1944; to Blonk, Jan. 1, 1945; to Davidson, Jan. 29, 1945, Billingsley Papers; *WDW*, Nov. 29, 1944; McKinley, *Uncle Sam in the Pacific Northwest*, 546-547.

16. Rufus had visited the Tennessee Valley before, on his way home from the 1944 national conventions. KB to Garton, Feb. 13, 1945; to Mitchell, March 21, 1945; RW to KB, March 5, 1945, all Billingsley Papers; to Mitchell, March 23; Oct. 9, 1945; to Magnuson, March 23, 1945; to Horan, March 23; June 18; Oct. 22, 1945; to BPA Advisory Board, March 31, 1945; to B. Woods, April 11, 1945; to W. Greenslit, April 13, 1945, Woods Papers; to Langlie, Feb. 1, 1949, Langlie Papers; *WDW*, Oct. 2, 1944.

17. In an attempt to protect regional interests, the measure also created a Columbia Valley Advisory Council, composed of one representative each from Washington, Oregon, Idaho and Montana, plus three at-large Northwest residents. Mitchell subsequently amended the bill to expressly guarantee existing state water laws and rights. RW to Horan, April 11; June 18, 20; Sept. 10, 1945; to Mackenzie, April 16, 1945; to Dill, April 17, 1945; to Mitchell, Sept. 20, 1945; April 7, 1949; to Peet, Sept. 25, 1945; Horan to RW, May 7, 1945, all Woods Papers; to KB, April 11, 1945; Davidson to KB, Jan. 13, 18, 21, 26, 31; Feb. 7, 1945; Magnuson to KB, Feb. 6, 1945; Blonk to KB, Feb. 15, 1945; Mitchell to KB, March 24, 1945, all Billingsley Papers; KB to JOS, Feb. 5, 1945, O'Sullivan Papers; McKinley, *Uncle Sam in the Pacific Northwest*, 550-556.

18. Horan to KB, Nov. 24, 1944; March 20; May 23, 1945, Billingsley Papers; to RW, March 15, 1946; RW to Horan, April 17; June 18, 20, 1945; to JOS, April 19, 1945, all Woods Papers; McKinley, *Uncle Sam in the Pacific Northwest*, 562.

19. William E. Warne to KB, March 26; April 20, 1945; KB to Davidson, Jan. 15, 1945; to Mitchell, March 21, 1945, all Billingsley Papers; *WDW*, Sept. 12, 1945; George F. Jewett to Horan, Feb. 19; March 23, 1945, Horan Papers; Holden to RW, Nov. 26, 1947; RW to JOS, April 19, 1945; to Fred Lardner, April 23, 1945; to Nicholson, May 21, 1945; to Mitchell, June 18, 1945, all Woods Papers. For general coverage of the CVA issue, see Elmo Richardson, *Dams, Parks & Politics: Resource Development and Preservation in the Truman-Eisenhower Era* (Lexington: University of Kentucky Press, 1973), chapt. 1.

20. Authorized in 1943, the 308 Report review was pushed to the forefront only after the opening of the CVA debate in 1945. Colonel Theron Weaver, the officer in charge of the study, allowed testimony critical of the proposed river authority at public hearings, but refused to allow witnesses to speak in its favor. Weber to Ray Bracelin, Aug. 22, 1946, Acc. 68A-1926, OCE1943; "Columbia River and Tributaries, Northwestern United States," 92, 99-100, 336-337; North Pacific Division Public Notice, Nov. 8, 1948, Langlie Papers; Mitchell to Harry S Truman, March 28, 1949; to J. Harden Peterson, June 10, 1949; to Carstensen, Aug. 1, 1949, Mitchell Papers.

21. Washington's Mon Wallgren initially refused to participate, claiming that his state deserved more than one vote on account of the fact that "a high percentage of the hydro-electric development will take place within its boundaries." Wallgren to Theron Weaver, April 24, 1946; Weaver to Wallgren, April 15, 1946, both CBIAC; Memorandum, "The Corps of Engineers '308 Report,'" n.d., Jackson House Papers; Horan to Tom Humphrey, March 21, 1949, Woods Papers; to KB, April 1, 1947; KB to Leland Olds, March 19, 1946, both Billingsley Papers; to Garton, Dec. 12, 1947, DC; McKinley, *Uncle Sam in the Pacific Northwest*, 467-479.

22. RW to Raver, July 9, 1945; to Neuberger, Aug. 30, 1945; to Peet, Sept. 25; Dec. 10, 1945; to Mitchell, Oct. 9, 1945; to David Lilienthal, Oct. 11, 1945, Woods Papers; KB to Carstensen, Jan. 29, 1946, Billingsley Papers.

23. RW to McGinnis, April 17, 1945; to Horan, March 5, 1946; to Bell, Nov. 13, 1946; to Dill, Nov. 20, 1946; to Irvine, Nov. 20, 1945, Woods Papers.

24. Representative Henry M. Jackson, looking ahead to future statewide races, also helped out with Columbia Basin matters. RW to Horan, Jan. 29; Sept. 10, 1945; KB to Carstensen, Oct. 5, 17; Nov. 3, 11, 1945, all *ibid.*; to Henry M. Jackson, Oct. 11, 1948; to Rogers, Sept. 28, 1949, Billingsley Papers; Cone to Garton, Feb. 8, 1947, DC.

25. RW to T. Hill, June 15, 1945; to Warne, June 21, 1946; to Mitchell, July 25, 1946; to Robert W. Sawyer, Nov. 21, 1946; to Art Burgess, Sept. 21, 1948; Warne to RW, July 15; Aug. 13, 1946; KB to Carstensen, Nov. 1, 1945; Feb. 2, 1946, all Woods Papers; to Horan, Dec. 3, 1946; Alvey to KB, July 31, 1947; JOS to KB, Dec. 21, 1947; Blonk to KB, n.d.; Horan to KB, Dec. 29, 1947, all Billingsley Papers; to JOS, May 22, 1945, O'Sullivan Papers; *WDW*, Dec. 16, 1946; May 8, 1947.

26. RW to Berry, Feb. 5, 1945; to Horan, Jan. 23, 26; April 10, 19, 1946; to Holden, Dec. 2, 1947; to Magnuson, Dec. 29, 1947; to Mrs. Walt Horan, Feb. 2, 1948, Woods Papers; to JOS, Jan. 30, 1948, O'Sullivan Papers; Garton to Dill, Jan. 17, 1947, DC; *WDW*, Aug. 31, 1945; Jan. 5, 17; Feb. 14; April 3; Aug. 21; Sept. 21; Nov. 26; Dec. 19, 31, 1946; Jan. 14; March 8, 15; June 4, 1947.

27. RW to Horan, Sept. 10; Oct. 22, 1945; to N.M. Jones, June 13, 1946; to John Cogswell, Aug. 21, 1946; Mitchell to RW, July 6, 1945; Horan to RW, Nov. 5, 1945; KB to Carstensen, Nov. 1, 10, 1945; Michael W. Straus to Horan, Nov. 22, 1947, all Woods Papers; Warne to KB, May 5; July 3, 1945, Billingsley Papers; *WDW*, Aug. 13, 25, 1945; Feb. 22; March 25-27; June 17; July 22, 1946; Pitzer, "Visions, Plans, and Realities," 87.

28. RW to F. Cunningham, Nov. 28, 1944; to Horan, Sept. 10, 1945; KB to Carstensen, Oct. 17, 30, 1945, all Woods Papers; *WDW*, March 5; May 7, 11, 1946; Magnuson to KB, April 17, 1946, Billingsley Papers; Jackson to Magnuson, June 12, 1946, Jackson House Papers; Mitchell, *Flowing Wealth*, 70-71.

29. The Senate briefly deleted Foster Creek from the bill during deliberations on the rivers and harbors measure, citing the project's lack of multipurpose features. F.O. Hagie to RW, Jan. 2, 1947; Robert R. Willard to KB, May 20, 1946; RW to KB, Nov. 22, 1946; Horan to KB, Aug. 2; Dec. 9, 1946, all Woods Papers; Dec. 2, 1946; R.A. Wheeler to KB, Oct. 16, 1946; Alvey to KB, May 13, 1946; KB to Horan, Dec. 16, 17, 1946, all Billingsley Papers; McKinley, *Uncle Sam in the Pacific Northwest*, 98.

30. KB to Horan, Dec. 28, 1946; to Carstensen, Oct. 3, 1946, Billingsley Papers; Feb. 18, 1946; RW to JOS, Aug. 22, 1946, both Woods Papers; *WDW*, July 29, 1946; Jan. 20, 1947.

31. *WDW*, Nov. 6, 12, 21, 25, 1946; RW to Harry P. Cain, Oct. 28; Nov. 15, 1946, Woods Papers.

32. The BPA rate was approximately one-fourth of that then charged by the Washington Water Power Company. *WDW*, Aug. 7, 1945; Jan. 31; Feb. 10, 1948; RW to Bud Alford, Nov. 12, 1947; to Freeman, March 21, 1947; JOS to RW, Jan. 11; Feb. 24, 1947, all Woods Papers; Magnuson to KB, March 29; June 20, 1947, Billingsley Papers.

33. *WDW*, Feb. 12, March 17, 1947; Hagie to RW, Jan. 2, 1947; RW to Horan, April 15, 1947; Magnuson to RW, July 23, 1949, all Woods Papers; to KB, June 20, 1947; JOS to KB, Dec. 21, 24, 1946; KB to Horan, Dec. 13, 1946; Jan. 2, 1947, all Billingsley Papers; McKinley, *Uncle Sam in the Pacific Northwest*, 115, 209-210.

34. Another Republican proposal would have established the Corps of Engineers as marketing agent for new dams on the Columbia, creating a rival to the BPA, and required that all power sales take place at the dam, ending the federal monopoly on transmission. Willard to KB, March 6, 1947; JOS to RW, Jan. 11, 1947; Jan. 26, 27, 1948, all Woods Papers; Magnuson to KB, June 20, 1947, Billingsley Papers; *WDW*, Feb. 12, 1947; Jan. 24; Feb. 6, 1948.

35. RW to JOS, Feb. 8, 1948, O'Sullivan Papers; to E. L. Skeel, Sept. 24, 1947, DC; Oct. 24, 1947; to Freeman, March 21, 1947; to JOS, March 24, 1947; to Edward W. Allen, April 23, 1947; to Carroll Reece, May 21, 1947; to Horan, Nov. 25, 1947; Horan to RW, Dec. 2, 1947; Cone to Burgess, Nov. 25, 1947; Bell to Cain, Dec. 13, 1947, all Woods Papers; KB to Horan, Dec. 4, 1947, Billingsley Papers; *WDW*, March 21, 29; May 10; June 13, 1947; Jan. 16, 19; Feb. 6, 12, 1948.

36. O'Sullivan Report, Feb. 17, 1948; Magnuson to KB, March 29, 1947; Aug. 2, 1948; Horan to KB, Dec. 29, 1947; March 5, 19; July 21, 1948, all Billingsley Papers; to RW, Feb. 28, 1948; to Hebberd, March 5, 1948, Horan Papers; Garton to Horan, Feb. 6, 1948; H. de Schepper to Garton, July 24, 1947, both DC; JOS to RW, Dec. 24, 1947; Cone to Cain, Nov. 21, 1947, both Woods Papers; *WDW*, April 28; June 13, 1947.

37. Wheeler to Magnuson, March 19, 1947, Magnuson Senate Papers; Horan to Wheeler, Feb. 9, 1948; to RW, Feb. 28, 1948; KB to Horan, Feb. 26, 1948, all Horan Papers; to Jackson, Oct. 11, 1948, Jackson House Papers; O'Sullivan Report, Feb. 29, 1948, Billingsley Papers; RW to JOS, Feb. 28, 1948, O'Sullivan Papers.

38. Details on the trip are from RW to Burgess, Sept. 21, 1948, Woods Papers; *WDW*, Aug. 14, 16-18, 23, 25, 26, 31; Sept. 3, 7-10, 17; Oct. 1, 5, 1948.

39. RW to Simpich, Aug. 16, 1948, Woods Papers; Woods Diary, Aug. 13, 1948; Horan to KB, Aug. 1, 1948, Billingsley Papers.

40. RW to Ted Robertson, May 28, 1947, Woods Papers; *WDW*, May 22, 24, 1948.

41. According to one study, the record 1894 flood would have caused $350 million in damages under 1948 conditions of population and development. *WDW*, May 25-28, 31; June 1-5, 7, 9, 11, 1948; Mitchell, *Flowing Wealth*, 71; "Columbia River and Tributaries, Northwestern United States," 79-80. On Vanport, see Willingham, *Army Engineers and the Development of Oregon*, 151-158.

42. *WDW*, May 27, 29, 31; June 1, 2, 5, 8, 9, 11, 12, 14, 17, 1948.

43. *WDW*, June 15; July 19, 20, 1948; Magnuson to Wheeler, Aug. 17, 1948, Magnuson Senate Papers; Chief Joseph Dam Planning Reports, Jan. 1952 and Jan. 1953; E.C. Itschner to Chief of Engineers, Jan. 15, 1953, all File 1505-22, Upper Columbia Basin, SDOACE.

44. *WDW*, May 12; June 21, 1947; Jan. 2, 24; Feb. 21, 23, 28; March 9; July 23, 24, 28, 1948; RW to Howard Rice, March 31, 1948; to Carstensen, April 16, 1948; to Walter H. Judd, April 19, 1948; to Harold E. Stassen, Oct. 4, 1948, Woods Papers.

45. *WDW*, June 16, 18, 24, 25, 30, 1947; Jan. 2; Feb. 23, 26; March 23; July 24; Nov. 2, 1948.

46. *WDW*, Nov. 3-6, 8, 9, 11; Dec. 6, 1948.

47. *WDW*, Dec. 11, 29, 30, 1948; Jan. 4, 17, 27; Feb. 22, 1949; RW to Cone, Dec. 24, 1948, Woods Papers; Mitchell, *Flowing Wealth*, 71-72.

48. Woods wanted to name the dam after the missionary Marcus Whitman. Following the publisher's death in 1950, friends lobbied for the renaming of the structure as Rufus Woods Dam. RW to Rogers, March 1, 21, 1949; KB to Rogers, May 22, 24, 1949, all DC; to Chester Kimm, March 27, 1949; Royce to KB, May 10, 1949, both Woods Papers; July 5, 1950, Billingsley Papers; Horan to Kimm, Dec. 30, 1948; to Bell, Jan. 12, 1949, Horan Papers; James W. Wallace to Mitchell, July 28, 1950, Mitchell Papers; *WDW*, Jan. 15; Feb. 15, 16; March 26, 31; Oct. 11, 13, 1949.

49. KB to Rogers, May 24, 1949, DC; RW to KB, Feb. 21; March 24, 1950, Billingsley Papers; Chief Joseph Dam Planning Reports, Jan. 1952 and Jan. 1953; Itschner to Chief of Engineers, Jan. 15, 1953, all File 1505-22, Upper Columbia Basin, SDOACE; Holbrook, *Columbia*, 363; D. G. Shingler to Sherman Adams, Feb. 16, 1954; Paul L. Patterson to Langlie, March 1, 1954, all Langlie Papers; Jackson to Rowland S. Hughes, March 19, 1956, Magnuson Senate Papers; *WDW*, June 21; Oct. 27, 1949; Mitchell, *Flowing Wealth*, 72.

50. *WDW*, Jan. 11, 3, 25; May 21; July 15; Dec. 17, 1949; Hewitt to Division Engineer, Oct. 1, 1947, File 1505-22, Albeni Falls Project; to Roger B. McWhorter, May 3, 1949, Acc. 68A-1926, OCE1943; to Beard, enclosing preliminary notes, July 1, 1949, File 1505-22, Libby Project, SDOACE; "Columbia River and Tributaries, Northwestern United States," 135-139, 148-150, 459-468, 479-487, 600-602; Herbert G. West to KB, Oct. 19, 1950; Dill to KB, Jan. 11, 1949, both Billingsley Papers; to Wallgren, Dec. 30, 1948, Langlie Papers; RW to Rogers, Sept. 27, 1949, DC.

51. JOS to J. A. Weber, Jan. 10, 1948, Billingsley Papers; *WDW*, April 6, 9, 13, 18, 20, 25; Oct. 13; Nov. 30, 1949; Gerber, *On the Home Front*, 107-110.

52. Cone to KB, Dec. 2, 5, 1944; RW to KB, Feb. 21; March 8, 1950; KB to RW, May 21, 1950; to Irv Hoff, May 21, 1950; Bell to KB, Feb. 24, 1950, all Billingsley Papers; to Louis Larsen, May 31, 1950; Rogers to KB, March 17, 29, 1950; Hubert H. Walter to Rogers, recd. April 5, 1950; Loen L. Bailie to Rogers, April 7, 1950; Frank A. Stewart to JOS, Nov. 10, 1948, all DC; to RW, Oct. 6, 1948; RW to Cone, Oct. 6, 1948; to Stewart, Sept. 2, 1949, all Woods Papers; Horan to Rogers, April 13, 1950, Langlie Papers; *WDW*, Jan. 9, 1950.

53. Hugh Mitchell was elected to the House of Representatives in 1948. Dill to Garton, Dec. 11, 1947; Horan to Rogers, Jan. 27, 1949, both DC; to KB, Dec. 29, 1948; Jan.

31, 1949, Billingsley Papers; to RW, Feb. 5, 1949; to Humphrey, March 21, 1949, Woods Papers; Magnuson to Bartholet, Sept. 20, 1949; to Langlie, June 25, 1949; Norman A. Schut to Langlie, Feb. 1, 8, 1949, all Langlie Papers; Leslie A. Miller, "The Battle That Squanders Billions," *Saturday Evening Post*, May 14, 1949, clipping in Jackson House Papers; *WDW*, May 12; June 22, 1949; McKinley, *Uncle Sam in the Pacific Northwest*, 563, 643-659.

54. RW to Fred Haley, May 11, 1949; to Horan, June 20, 1949; to Raver, April 6, 1950, Woods Papers; KB to Horan, Jan. 5, 1947; Horan to KB, April 1, 1948, both Billingsley Papers; Clapp to Rogers, Feb. 28, 1949, DC; *WDW*, Feb. 26, 28; Dec. 3, 1949. On California's interest in the Columbia, see Hundley, *Great Thirst*, 329.

55. RW to Horan, Jan. 18, 31, 1949; to Magnuson, Feb. 21, 1949; to Mitchell, Dec. 20, 1948; April 7, 1949; to Haley, May 11, 1949; to Anderson, June 7, 1949; to Don Miller, Aug. 7, 1946, Woods Papers; to Langlie, Feb. 1, 1949, Langlie Papers; *WDW*, March 2, 18, 28; April 20, 23; May 12, 16, 17; June 18, 1949.

56. KB to RW, Aug. 6, 1949, Woods Papers; to Horan, March 2, 1945; Jan. 31, 1949; Jan. 22, 1950; to Dill, July 4, 1949; Harold Nelson to KB, Nov. 22, 1940, all Billingsley Papers; McKinley, *Uncle Sam in the Pacific Northwest*, 636-638.

57. KB to Rogers, March 19, 1949, Woods Papers; to Horan, Jan. 31, 1949; Jan. 22, 1950; to Bell, July 4, 1949, Billingsley Papers; Agreement on Principles and Responsibilities, April 11, 1949; Horan to Langlie, May 13, 1949; Straus to Langlie, May 11, 1949, all Langlie Papers; to Julius A. Krug, Jan. 5, 13, 27, 1949; Davidson to Straus, Dec. 22, 1948; Krug to Lewis Pick, March 23, 1949, all Department of the Interior Records, Office of the Secretary, 1937-1953, RG 48, National Archives; to Mitchell, May 25, 1949, Mitchell Papers; Memorandum, "The Corps of Engineers '308 Report,'" n.d.; Press releases, June 17, 20, 1949, all Jackson House Papers; McKinley, *Uncle Sam in the Pacific Northwest*, 638-643.

58. KB to RW, Aug. 6, 1949; to Rogers, Sept. 25, 1949, Woods Papers; Sept. 28, 1949; to Stewart, Sept. 11, 1949; Horan to KB, Nov. 28, 1949, all Billingsley Papers; *WDW*, Aug. 19; Oct. 5; Dec. 15, 1949.

59. Magnuson to RW, March 9, 1950; KB to RW, Jan. 31; Feb. 2, 1950; to Rogers, Jan. 29; Feb. 6; April 24, 1950, all Woods Papers; Schut to KB, March 7, 1950; Rogers to KB, Oct. 14; Nov. 9, 1949; July 7, 1950, all Billingsley Papers; March 29, 1950; Bell to KB, Feb. 10, 1950; Walters to Rogers, recd. April 5, 1950, all DC.

60. Mitchell, *Flowing Wealth*, 60-63; *WDW*, Dec. 16, 1943; March 6, 1946; KB to Miller, Feb. 18, 1943; to Stoffel, Oct. 19, 1943; Raver to KB, Dec. 17, 1945, all Billingsley Papers; RW to Love, Jan. 23, 1945, Woods Papers.

61. RW to Love, Jan. 23, 1945; to Magnuson, Jan. 23, 1945; to Raver, July 9, 1945; to Horan, Sept. 10, 1945, Woods Papers; to KB, May 15, 1948; Guy C. Myers to KB, Oct. 14, 1948; KB to Rogers, Jan. 27, 1949, all Billingsley Papers; *WDW*, July 9; Aug. 16, 1945; Feb. 21; March 6; April 2, 1946; Dec. 28, 1948; March 11; June 20; July 29; Aug. 13, 1949.

62. Millard, who was defeated for reelection in 1948, failed to follow through on a threatened libel suit. Dill to Myers, Aug. 19, 1948, Myers Papers; *WDW*, Sept. 6, 1946; Jan. 14, 15, 18; June 20; Aug. 28-30; Sept. 2, 1947; Feb. 28, 1949; DeWitt C. Rowland to RW, Sept. 12, 1947; Thomas E. Grady to RW, Sept. 23; Oct. 8, 1947, all Woods Papers; Mitchell, *Flowing Wealth*, 64.

63. *WDW*, Feb. 21-23; April 22, 1949; RW to Wm. D. Devin, Feb. 11, 1949, Woods Papers; Mitchell, *Flowing Wealth*, 65.

64. The Chelan County PUD also acquired the Chelan Falls operations of the Washington Water Power Company. *WDW*, Feb. 24, 26; March 5, 8, 10, 11, 1949; RW to

Myers, March 10, 1949; Myers to RW, March 18, 1949, both Myers Papers; Mitchell, *Flowing Wealth*, 65.

65. Woods Diary, April 26; May 5, 1944; Sept. 17, 1945; Aug. 26, 29; Sept. 3, 4, 1947; April 16, 1948; April 5, 1949; RW to KB, Feb. 27, 1950, Billingsley Papers; to L.0. Studley, Feb. 27, 1950, Woods Papers.

66. RW to KB, Feb. 27, 1950, Billingsley Papers; March 2, 1950; to Leon Milot, Feb. 13, 1950; to Studley, Feb. 27, 1950; to Horan, Feb. 27, 1950, Woods Papers.

67. RW to KB, March 2, 1950; to Maggie Waltho, Feb. 21, 1950; to Mr. and Mrs. Horan, Feb. 21, 1950; to Horan, Feb. 27, 1950; to Mr. and Mrs. Storch, April 7, 1950; Goss to RW, March 15, 1950, all Woods Papers; *WDW*, May 4, 11, 12, 1950.

68. RW to Dill, Nov. 20, 1946, Woods Papers; *WDW*, Jan. 28-30; Feb. 1, 1949; May 29; June 6, 1950.

69. *WDW*, May 29; June 6, 1950.

70. *WDW*, June 6, 1950; KB to Karl Shannon, June 28, 1947, Billingsley Papers.

71. RW to Ed Stone, Dec. 23, 1946; to Editor, Yakima *Republic*, April 12, 1948, Woods Papers; *WDW*, March 3, 1948; Nov. 9, 1949; Aug. 3, 1950.

72. *WDW*, July 23, 1946; Oct. 6, 1948; Nov. 2, 1949; RW to Malaga Grange Members, Feb. 17, 1950, Woods Papers.

73. *WDW*, March 26; Dec. 9, 1948; Jan. 28; March 2, 14; April 7, 1949; June 6, 1950.

74. The Ben Franklin project was named after Benton and Franklin counties, rather than Benjamin Franklin. "Columbia River and Tributaries," 1:228, 230-232; Plan of Survey, Ben Franklin Project, April 29, 1960, File 1517-08, Survey Reports, SDOACE.

# A Note on Sources

Tнis воок ıs based, in the main, upon several primary sources. The Rufus Woods Papers, held in the office of the *Wenatchee World*, are a large and somewhat eclectic collection of correspondence and other materials. Additional Woods letters, plus a substantial amount of documentation relating to his interests, are contained in the James O'Sullivan Papers at the Gonzaga University Library in Spokane. The Kirby Billingsley Papers, in Wenatchee's North Central Washington Museum, cover the activities of Woods during the 1940s. The publisher's prolific writings in the *Wenatchee Daily World* during the years between 1907 and 1950 combine political commentary with autobiographical sketches.

Certain other manuscript collections are essential to an understanding of Woods's career. The Thomas Burke Papers, in the University of Washington Library, include the records of the Wenatchee Development Company. Items on Woods's involvement with the Progressive movement may be found in the Miles Poindexter Papers and in the Wesley Jones Papers, both in the University of Washington Library. The Jones Papers also contain materials vital to the history of the Grand Coulee project, particularly the genesis of the 308 Report. The Washington State Archives in Olympia holds the records of the first and second Columbia Basin Commissions. The federal role in Columbia River development was followed, in the preparation of this book, through the records of the U.S. Army Corps of Engineers, divided between the National Archives and the Seattle Federal Records Center, and those of the Bureau of Reclamation, examined in the National Archives. The papers of O.L. Waller and Roy Gill, at the Washington State University Library, cover the activities of two Grand Coulee opponents. The Seattle Lighting Department records held by the University of Washington Library include correspondence and reports of another opponent, J.D. Ross. The Clarence Martin Papers, in the Washington State University Library, contain vital exchanges between the governor and Senator Clarence Dill on Grand Coulee. The Walt Horan Papers, also at WSU, deal with development matters during and after the Second World War.

The absolutely essential secondary source for this subject is Paul C. Pitzer, *Grand Coulee: Harnessing a Dream* (Pullman: Washington State University Press, 1995). Charles McKinley, *Uncle Sam in the Pacific Northwest: Federal Management of Natural Resources in the Columbia River Valley* (Berkeley: University of California Press, 1952) is an older, albeit still very useful, account of government works on the Columbia. Bruce Mitchell's detailed regional histories were of great importance in the writing of this book: *Flowing Wealth: The Story of Water Resource Development in North Central Washington, 1870-1950* (Wenatchee: *The Wenatchee World*, 1967), and *By River, Trail and Rail: A Brief History of the First Century of Transportation in North Central Washington, 1811 to 1911* (Wenatchee: *The Wenatchee World*, 1968). Earlier Woods biographies include Bruce Mitchell, *The Story of Rufus Woods and the Development of Central Washington* (Wenatchee: *The Wenatchee World*, 1965), and Earl Clark, "Rufus Woods: Grand Coulee Promoter," in the Autumn 1979 issue of *Montana: The Magazine of Western History*.

## Books Cited in the Endnotes

Allen, Howard W. *Poindexter of Washington: A Study in Progressive Politics*. Carbondale: Southern Illinois University Press, 1981.

Berner, Richard C. *Seattle, 1900-1920: From Boomtown, Urban Turbulence to Restoration*. Seattle: Charles Press, 1991.

Chasan, Daniel Jack. *The Fall of the House of WPPSS*. Seattle: Sasquatch Publishing, 1985.

Cherny, Robert W. *Populism, Progressivism, and the Transformation of Nebraska Politics, 1885-1915*. Lincoln: University of Nebraska Press, 1981.

Clark, Norman H. *The Dry Years: Prohibition and Social Change in Washington*. Seattle: University of Washington Press, 1965; rev. ed. 1988.

Dodds, Gordon. *Hiram Martin Chittenden: His Public Career*. Lexington: The University Press of Kentucky, 1973.

Fahey, John. *Inland Empire: Unfolding Years, 1879-1929*. Seattle: University of Washington Press, 1986.

Ficken, Robert E. *The Forested Land: A History of Lumbering in Western Washington*. Seattle: University of Washington Press, 1987.

————. *Lumber and Politics: The Career of Mark E. Reed*. Seattle: University of Washington Press, 1979.

Ficken, Robert E. and Charles P. LeWarne. *Washington: A Centennial History*. Seattle: University of Washington Press, 1988.

Foster, Mark S. *Henry J. Kaiser: Builder in the Modern American West*. Austin: University of Texas Press, 1989.

Gellatly, John. *A History of Wenatchee: The Apple Capital of the World*. Wenatchee: Wenatchee Bindery & Printing Co., 1962.

Gerber, Michele Stenehjeim. *On the Home Front: The Cold War Legacy of the Hanford Nuclear Site*. Lincoln: University of Nebraska Press, 1992.

Gunther, John. *Inside U.S.A.* New York: Harper & Brothers, 1947.

Hiltner, Willa Woods and Kathryn Woods Haley, eds. *The Greenslit Family*. Wenatchee: *The Wenatchee World*, 1981.

_____. *The Woods Family: Colonial Times to 1979*. Wenatchee: *The Wenatchee World*, 1979.

Holbrook, Stewart. *The Columbia*. New York: Holt, Rinehart, & Winston, 1956.

Hundley, Norris Jr. *The Great Thirst: Californians and Water, 1770s-1990s*. Berkeley: University of California Press, 1992.

Hyman, Harold M. *Soldiers and Spruce: Origins of the Loyal Legion of Loggers and Lumbermen*. Los Angeles: Institute of Industrial Relations, 1963.

Jones, Vincent C. *Manhattan: The Army and the Atomic Bomb*. Washington, D.C.: Center of Military History, 1985.

Kane, Paul. *Wanderings of an Artist among the Indians of North America*. Toronto: Raddisson, 1925.

Kerr, Charles C. *The World of the World: From Frontier to Community, 1905-1980*. Wenatchee: *The Wenatchee World*, 1980.

Lorraine, M.J. *The Columbia Unveiled*. Los Angeles: The *Times-Mirror* Press, 1924.

Lowitt, Richard. *The New Deal and the West*. Bloomington: Indiana University Press, 1984.

Lyman, William Denison. *The Columbia River*. New York: G.P. Putnam's Sons, 1918.

Maynard, Harold H. *Marketing Northwestern Apples*. New York: The Ronald Press Co., 1923.

McKee, Bates. *Cascadia: The Geologic Evolution of the Pacific Northwest*. New York: McGraw Hill Book Company, 1972.

McKinley, Charles. *Uncle Sam in the Pacific Northwest: Federal Management of Natural Resources in the Columbia River Valley*. Berkeley: University of California Press, 1952.

Meinig, D.W. *The Great Columbia Plain: A Historical Geography, 1805-1910*. Seattle: University of Washington Press, 1968.

Mills, Randall V. *Stern-Wheelers Up Columbia: A Century of Steamboating in the Oregon Country*. Palo Alto: Pacific Books, 1947.

Mitchell, Bruce. *By River, Trail and Rail: A Brief History of the First Century of Transportation in North Central Washington, 1811-1911*. Wenatchee: *The Wenatchee World*, 1968.

_____. *Flowing Wealth: The Story of Water Resource Development in North Central Washington, 1870-1950*. Wenatchee: *The Wenatchee World*, 1967.

_____. *The Story of Rufus Woods and the Development of Central Washington*. Wenatchee: *The Wenatchee World*, 1965.

Nash, Gerald D. *The American West Transformed: The Impact of the Second World War*. Bloomington: Indiana University Press, 1985.

_____. *World War II and the West: Reshaping the Economy*. Lincoln: University of Nebraska Press, 1990.

Nesbit, Robert C. *"He Built Seattle": A Biography of Judge Thomas Burke*. Seattle: University of Washington Press, 1961.

Netboy, Anthony. *Salmon of the Pacific Northwest: Fish vs. Dams*. Portland: Binfords & Mort, 1958.

Neuberger, Richard L. *Our Promised Land*. New York: The Macmillan Company, 1938; Moscow: University of Idaho Press, 1989.

Olson, James C. *History of Nebraska*. Lincoln: University of Nebraska Press, 1955.

Peterson, H.C. and Gilbert C. Fite. *Opponents of War, 1917-1918*. Madison: The University of Wisconsin Press, 1957.

Pisani, Donald J. *To Reclaim a Divided West: Water, Law, and Public Policy, 1848-1902*. Albuquerque: University of New Mexico Press, 1992.

Reisner, Marc. *Cadillac Desert: The American West and Its Disappearing Water*. New York: Viking, 1986.

Richardson, Elmo. *Dams, Parks & Politics: Resource Development & Preservation in the Truman-Eisenhower Era*. Lexington: University of Kentucky Press, 1973.

Sundborg, George. *Hail Columbia: The Thirty-Year Struggle for Grand Coulee Dam*. New York: The Macmillan Co., 1954.

Thompson, S.M. *The Cost of Producing Apples in the Wenatchee Valley, Washington*. Washington, D.C.: Government Printing Office, 1917.

Twichell, Heath. *Northwest Epic: The Building of the Alaska Highway*. New York: St. Martin's Press, 1992.

Tyler, Robert L. *Rebels of the Woods: The I.W.W. in the Pacific Northwest*. Eugene: University of Oregon Books, 1967.

Willingham, William. *Army Engineers and the Development of Oregon: A History of the Portland District, U.S. Army Corps of Engineers*. Washington, D.C.: Government Printing Office, 1983.

Woods, Rufus. *The 23-Years' Battle for Grand Coulee Dam*. Wenatchee: *Wenatchee Daily World*, 1944.

Worster, Donald. *Rivers of Empire: Water, Aridity, and the Growth of the American West*. New York: Pantheon Books, 1985.

## Articles Cited in the Endnotes

Bergman, H. J. "The Reluctant Dissenter: Governor Hay of Washington and the Conservation Problem." *Pacific Northwest Quarterly*, 62 (1971): 27-33.

Cravens, Hamilton. "The Emergence of the Farmer-Labor Party in Washington Politics, 1919-20." *Pacific Northwest Quarterly*, 57 (1966): 148-157.

DeVoto, Bernard. "The West Against Itself." *Harpers' Magazine*, 194 (1947): 1-13.

_____. "The West: A Plundered Province." *Harpers' Magazine*, 169 (1934): 355-364.

Ficken, Robert E. "President Harding Visits Seattle." *Pacific Northwest Quarterly*, 67 (1975): 105-114.

Freeman, Otis W. "Apple Industry of the Wenatchee Area." *Economic Geography*, 10 (1934): 160-162.

Funigiello, Philip J. "Kilowatts for Defense: The New Deal and the Coming of the Second World War." *Journal of American History*, 56 (1969): 604-620.

Gamboa, Erasmo. "Mexican Migration into Washington State: A History, 1940-1950." *Pacific Northwest Quarterly*, 72 (1981): 121-131.

Gressley, Gene M. "Arthur Powell Davis, Reclamation, and the West." *Agricultural History*, 42 (1968): 241-244.

Griffin, Walter R. "George W. Goethals, Explorer of the Pacific Northwest, 1882-1884." *Pacific Northwest Quarterly*, 62 (1971): 129-141.

Harding, Bruce C. "Water from Pend Oreille: The Gravity Plan for Irrigating the Columbia Basin." *Pacific Northwest Quarterly*, 45 (1954): 52-60.

Johnson, Claudius O. "The Adoption of the Initiative and Referendum in Washington." *Pacific Northwest Quarterly*, 35 (1944): 291-303.

Kerr, William T. Jr. "The Progressives of Washington, 1910-12." *Pacific Northwest Quarterly*, 55 (1964): 16-27.

Mitchell, Bruce. "Rufus Woods and Columbia River Development." *Pacific Northwest Quarterly*, 52 (1961): 139-144.

Murray, Keith A. "The Aberdeen Convention of 1912." *Pacific Northwest Quarterly*, 38 (1947): 99-108.

Nesbit, Robert C. and Charles M. Gates. "Agriculture in Eastern Washington, 1899-1910." *Pacific Northwest Quarterly*, 37 (1946): 279-302.

Neuberger, Richard L. "The Biggest Thing on Earth." *Harpers' Magazine*, 174 (1937): 242-258.

Pitzer, Paul C. "The Atmosphere Tasted Like Turnips: The Pacific Northwest Dust Storm of 1931." *Pacific Northwest Quarterly*, 79 (1988): 50-55.

Raver, Paul J. "The Challenge to Statesmanship." *Pacific Northwest Quarterly*, 49 (1958).

Schwantes, Carlos A. "Farmer-Labor Insurgency in Washington State: William Bouck, the Grange and the Washington Progressive Farmers." *Pacific Northwest Quarterly*, 76 (1985): 2-11.

Scott, George W. "The New Order of Cincinnatus: Municipal Politics in Seattle During the 1930s." *Pacific Northwest Quarterly*, 64 (1973): 137-146.

Simpich, Frederick. "Wartime in the Pacific Northwest." *National Geographic*, 28 (Oct. 1942): 421-464.

Worster, Donald. "New West, True West: Interpreting the Region's History." *Western Historical Quarterly*, 18 (1987): 151-156.

# Acknowledgments

A NUMBER OF individuals and institutions were of vital assistance in the completion of this book. The absolutely first-class treatment extended by the staff of the *Wenatchee World* made the considerable time spent researching the Rufus Woods Papers and old newspaper files pleasant. Numerous conversations with Wilfred Woods and Bruce Mitchell helped refine my understanding of Rufus and of the issues associated with his career in journalism. Archivists and librarians at the University of Washington, Washington State University, and Gonzaga University provided highly professional advice in the use of materials in the possession of those institutions. Staff members at the North Central Washington Museum, the Seattle Federal Records Center, and the National Archives extended similar much-appreciated help.

Paul Pitzer supplied me with copies of his 1990 University of Oregon dissertation, "Visions, Plans, and Realities: Irrigation on the Columbia Basin Project," and of the manuscript of *Grand Coulee: Harnessing a Dream*, published by Washington State University Press in 1994. Wilfred Woods, Bruce Mitchell, and Paul Pitzer kindly read the original draft of *Rufus Woods*.

Keith Petersen of the Washington State University Press encouraged the project and did a superb job of editing the final manuscript. Also at the Press I would like to thank Dave Hoyt, Nancy Grunewald, Wes Patterson, and Beth DeWeese.

Portions of the book appeared, in somewhat altered form, as "Grand Coulee Dam, the Columbia River, and the Generation of Modern Washington" in Richard Lowitt, ed., *Politics in the Postwar American West* (Norman: University of Oklahoma Press, 1995); and as "Grand Coulee and Hanford: The Atomic Bomb and the Development of the Columbia River" in John M. Findlay and Bruce Hevly, eds., *The Atomic West* (Seattle: University of Washington Press, forthcoming). The editors and publishers of these volumes are hereby thanked for their kindness and assistance.

Lorraine and Matthew, finally, kept the home fires burning during my frequent absences on excursions east of the Cascades.

# About the Author

**Robert E. Ficken** is the author of numerous books and articles about the Pacific Northwest, including *Washington: A Centennial History* (with Charles LeWarne), *The Forested Land: A History of Lumbering in Western Washington*, and *Lumber and Politics: The Career of Mark E. Reed*. He has won the F.K. Weyerhaeuser Award from the Forest History Society and the Charles M. Gates Memorial Award from the Washington State Historical Society. He lives in Issaquah, Washington.

# Index